Hanafuda Games

Hanami Edition

Jason Johnson & Antonietta Fazio-Johnson

IndianWolf Studios LLC

2017

Hanafuda Games *Hanami* Edition

ISBN: 978-0-9992802-0-1

Hanami Edition: 2017

IndianWolf Studios LLC
Pittsburgh, Pennsylvania 15216
www.IndianWolfStudios.com
jason.johnson@indianwolfstudios.com

Inner Hue Art Studio LLC
Pittsburgh, Pennsylvania 15216
www.InnerHueArtStudio.com
a.johnson@innerhueartstudio.com

Contact IndianWolf Studios LLC at jason.johnson@indianwolfstudios.com
for any inquiries about this book or *Hanami* playing cards.

Contents

SECTION I *Capture Games*

⦾ Beginner　　⦿ Intermediate　　⦿ Expert

SECTION II *Sequence Games*

SECTION III *Luck Games*

SECTION IV *Fusion Games*

Preface

Note from the Authors:

Many years ago, when we were first introduced to hanafuda, the complex history, pipless floral design, and variety of games intrigued us. At that time, hanafuda were not easy to find in the US and coherent English rules were practically nonexistent. Even as hanafuda slowly became more popular on our side of the globe, the rules for hanafuda games remained difficult to find. This inspired us to create the *Hanafuda Games* rulebook and our Fusion deck. We enjoyed playing hanafuda and wanted to make hanafuda more accessible to new players.

Due to the long history and wide geographical range of hanafuda, a plethora of hanafuda games and variations were created over the years. This book contains our translations and interpretations of how to play 37 of these hanafuda games. We created our rulebook with the goal of being consistent and approachable while preserving the core essence of these hanafuda games. We have also included numerous common gameplay variations ('house rules') that we have learned over the years so that players can customize the games to their own taste.

This book was inspired by our love for hanafuda games and our desire to share those games with others. Countless hours have gone into the creation of this rulebook. Just as hanafuda has spread from country to country, city to city, and home to home, bringing with it new changes and house rules, we hope to continue the legacy by bringing it from our table to yours. We hope that our interpretations of these classic games provide you with many hours of entertainment and bring you a little closer to the world of hanafuda.

We also want to say thank you to all of our amazing Kickstarter backers for their support and enthusiasm during the *Hanami* Kickstarter campaign. With your help we were able to bring the *Hanami* playing card series and the *Hanafuda Games* rulebook to print. We can not tell you how excited we are to have so many people tell us they love the art of *Hanami* and are looking forward to learning how to play hanafuda! Your enthusiasm is an inspiration to us!

Thank you,
Jason & Antonietta

✿.*•.˚ (/^^)乂(^^)/.˚ •*✿

Introduction

Why was this book created?

There are many great hanafuda games. Unfortunately, rules for hanafuda games can be difficult to find and interpret.

Our rulebook gathers the rules into a single clearly written source that makes them easily accessible to players.

What does our book contain?

An in-depth collection of 37 great games, including popular games such as Koi-Koi, Go-Stop, and Hachi-Hachi.

Organized into categories by type and difficulty, this step-by-step rulebook includes intuitive scoring samples, visual references, numerous variants, gameplay samples, and quick reference charts.

Where do I start?

If you are new to hanafuda we recommend reading the following:

Chapter 2 *The Deck*. This chapter describes the design of the hanafuda deck and provides a card reference chart detailing the flower, type, value, and name of the individual cards. This is a great chapter for those new to hanafuda to begin familiarizing themselves with the deck.

Chapter 3 *Before You Begin*. This chapter discusses the setup and basic gameplay mechanics of capture games. This chapter is essential to understanding hanafuda capture games.

Chapter 4 & 5 *Simplified Game for Beginners* and *Matching Flowers*. These are two great beginner games to get players started playing hanafuda. Once players become comfortable with these basic games, they can try other hanafuda games which include more complex gameplay and scoring.

Learning a new game can feel daunting at first, but once you get used to the hanafuda deck and learn some basic gameplay the games become much easier to learn.

How is this book organized?

This book is arranged into five Sections: Capture Games, Sequence Games, Luck Games, Fusion Games, and Quick Reference Charts. Within these sections, the games are organized and color-coded by difficulty.

Section I: Capture games are the most popular hanafuda games and a great way to learn the deck. Capture games involve capturing cards from a field and creating special combinations of cards to score points.

Section II: Sequence games involve playing cards from your hand in sequential order with the objective to empty your hand. Sequence games are a great way to learn hanafuda month order.

Section III: Luck games are simple, fast-paced, gambling-oriented games. Many of the games in this section were traditionally played with Kabufuda decks. Many of these games are similar to Blackjack or Baccarat.

Section IV: Fusion games are a collection of Western-inspired games that we reinterpreted and designed for gameplay with a hanafuda deck. These games provide a familiar platform for Western players to become more comfortable with the hanafuda deck.

Section V: Quick Reference Charts are convenient references intended to aid players with scoring and yaku charts. These charts do not detail the rules for gameplay. Players should be familiar with a game before attempting to use its quick reference.

Note on Gambling:

The games in this book are presented in a non-gambling format to make the games more accessible to a wider audience. Instead, the focus is on earning points and winning rounds.

The historical gambling mechanisms in many hanafuda games tend to be relatively complicated and indirect. However, many of the games can be easily modified for gambling.

Here are some common methods:

- Players pay a fixed amount to the winner of each round or game.
- Players pay the winner based on the amount of points earned (e.g. 10 cents per point).
- The tokens in games that require tokens or chips are assigned a monetary value.
- Players make wagers similar to Poker.

The most suitable approach will differ between games.

Hanami Playing Cards.

This book features the art of *Hanami*. The art, cards, yaku charts, and other references contained in this book utilize the art from the *Hanami* deck series. However, neither the *Hanami* Hanafuda or the *Hanami* Fusion decks are required for you to use this book. A standard hanafuda deck can be used in place of the *Hanami* decks.

Chapter 1
What is Hanafuda?

What is hanafuda?

Hanafuda (known in Korea as "Hwatu") are floral themed playing cards that are rich in symbolism and popular in Japan, Korea, and Hawaii.

Japan historically banned gambling and playing cards from the early 1600's until the late 1800's. It was during this period that hanafuda first originated in Japan.[1] Hanafuda likely gained popularity due to their small concealable size, lack of obvious pips, and use of cultural iconography.

Given the popularity, long history, and wide geographical range of hanafuda, there have been many games invented over the years with numerous variations ('house rules').

Fun fact: The popular game company Nintendo was founded in 1889 as a hanafuda manufacturer.[2]

What does 'hanafuda' mean?

Hanafuda is generally translated as 'flower cards'. However, 'hana' is Japanese for both 'flower' and 'nose'.

This double meaning aided gamblers who could silently tap their nose to indicate their desire to purchase cards or find a gambling group without alerting the authorities.[3] It is rumored that this also helped popularize the 'long nosed goblin' version of the tengu as a hanafuda mascot of sorts.

Why are hanafuda so small?

Traditional hanafuda are typically smaller and thicker than Western playing cards.

"The reason why these cards were made so diminutive was so that, under the strict laws against gambling in this Country [Japan], gamblers, when suddenly surprised, might easily hide them in the palms of their hands or force them into some other small space to avoid detection."[4]

---

1   Harris, Blake J. *Console Wars: Sega, Nintendo, and the Battle that Defined a Generation*. EPub ed. : HarperCollins, 2014. Digital File.
2   "Nintendo History." *Nintendo*. Nintendo of Europe. Web. 2016.
3   "Symbols in Hanafuda." *Hanafuda Hawaii*. Hanafuda Hawaii. Web. 2016.
4   Rossetsu Uchiyama. *The Game of "Hana-awase": Japanese Cards*. Japan: Seishi-bunsha, 1892. Digital File.

Chapter 2
The Deck

About the Deck

Hanfuda decks are comprised of 48 flower cards plus optional Jokers.

- Hanafuda have 12 suits.
- Each suit is represented by a month of the year (e.g. June).
- Each month is represented by a flower (e.g. Peony).
- There are four cards in each month.
- There are four types of cards: Brights, Tens, Ribbons, and Chaffs.
- Each month typically contains 2 valuable cards and 2 Chaffs.
- The *Hanami* edition includes 6 Jokers.

Hanafuda traditionally lack pips and indices. Instead, they rely on imagery to convey their value and importance.

Brights

Tens

Poetry Ribbons

Plain Ribbons

Purple Ribbons

Chaffs

Chaffs

Jokers

The Twelve Months and Their Flowers

The following chart illustrates the twelve months and the flowers which represent them.

Each image is labeled with the card type and value for that card. These are the most commonly assigned card values, *however*, individual hanafuda games may use different values.

It is also important to note that the Brights, Tens, and a few other special cards have unique names. These cards are worth noting for their card value, presence in yaku, and other special uses in games.

Note: The Korean version (Hwatu) traditionally orders the Rain Month as December and the Paulownia month as November.

Tip: Each month of the *Hanami* hanafuda decks were designed to form a tetraptych.

FIGURE 2.1a **The Twelve Months and Their Flowers** (*Hanami* Hanafuda)

January Pine			
Bright (20) Crane	Ribbon (5) Poetry Ribbon	Chaff (1)	Chaff (1)

February Plum			
Ten (10) Nightingale Warbler	Ribbon (5) Poetry Ribbon	Chaff (1)	Chaff (1)

March Cherry (Sakura)			
Bright (20) Curtain	Ribbon (5) Poetry Ribbon	Chaff (1)	Chaff (1)

April Wisteria			
Ten (10) Cuckoo	Ribbon (5) Plain Ribbon	Chaff (1)	Chaff (1)

FIGURE 2.1b **The Twelve Months and Their Flowers (*Hanami* Hanafuda)**

**May
Iris**

Ten (10) Bridge	Ribbon (5) Plain Ribbon	Chaff (1)	Chaff (1)

**June
Peony**

Ten (10) Butterfly	Ribbon (5) Purple Ribbon	Chaff (1)	Chaff (1)

**July
Lespedeza
(Bush Clover)**

Ten (10) Boar	Ribbon (5) Plain Ribbon	Chaff (1)	Chaff (1)

**August
Suzuki
Grass
(Moon)**

Bright (20) Moon	Ten (10) Geese	Chaff (1)	Chaff (1)

FIGURE 2.1c **The Twelve Months and Their Flowers** (*Hanami* Hanafuda)

September Chrysanthemum

Ten (10)
Sake

Ribbon (5)
Purple Ribbon

Chaff (1)

Chaff (1)

October Maple

Ten (10)
Deer

Ribbon (5)
Purple Ribbon

Chaff (1)

Chaff (1)

November Willow (Rain)

Bright (20)
Rainman

Ten (10)
Swallow

Ribbon (5)
Plain Ribbon

Chaff (1)
Storm

December Paulownia

Bright (20)
Phoenix

Chaff (1)
Special Paulownia

Chaff (1)

Chaff (1)

Hanami **Fusion Decks**

The *Hanami* Fusion decks were designed to combine standard poker indices and hanafuda images into a multipurpose deck that could be used to play both Eastern and Western games.

Hanami hanafuda indices were added to indicate the flower, month, and type of each card.

These helpful indices make the Fusion deck a great way to learn & teach hanafuda.

Fusion Card Design

- The standard number indices double as month numbers (e.g. Ace = January, 2 = February, 3 = March, and so on).

- The suit indices indicate standard poker suits.

  The Fusion decks are ordered: ♠, ♣, ♥, ♦.

- The *Hanami* flower indices indicate the flower/month.

- The *Hanami* type indices indicate the hanafuda card type (e.g. Bright, Ten, Poetry Ribbon, Purple Ribbon, Plain Ribbon, or Chaff).

Flower Indices

Pine	Iris	Chrysanthemum
Plum	Peony	Maple
Cherry	Lespedeza	Willow / Rain
Wisteria	Suzuki Grass / Moon	Paulownia

Type Indices

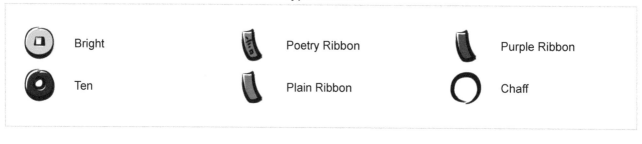

Bright	Poetry Ribbon	Purple Ribbon
Ten	Plain Ribbon	Chaff

FIGURE 2.2a **The Twelve Months and Their Flowers (*Hanami* Fusion)**

**January
Pine**

Bright (20)
Crane

Ribbon (5)
Poetry Ribbon

Chaff (1)

Chaff (1)

**February
Plum**

Ten (10)
Nightingale Warbler

Ribbon (5)
Poetry Ribbon

Chaff (1)

Chaff (1)

**March
Cherry
(Sakura)**

Bright (20)
Curtain

Ribbon (5)
Poetry Ribbon

Chaff (1)

Chaff (1)

**April
Wisteria**

Ten (10)
Cuckoo

Ribbon (5)
Plain Ribbon

Chaff (1)

Chaff (1)

FIGURE 2.2b **The Twelve Months and Their Flowers (*Hanami* Fusion)**

May
Iris

Ten (10)
Bridge

Ribbon (5)
Plain Ribbon

Chaff (1)

Chaff (1)

June
Peony

Ten (10)
Butterfly

Ribbon (5)
Purple Ribbon

Chaff (1)

Chaff (1)

July
Lespedeza
(Bush Clover)

Ten (10)
Boar

Ribbon (5)
Plain Ribbon

Chaff (1)

Chaff (1)

August
Suzuki
Grass
(Moon)

Bright (20)
Moon

Ten (10)
Geese

Chaff (1)

Chaff (1)

FIGURE 2.2c **The Twelve Months and Their Flowers** (*Hanami* Fusion)

September
Chrysan-
themum

Ten (10)
Sake

Ribbon (5)
Purple Ribbon

Chaff (1)

Chaff (1)

October
Maple

Ten (10)
Deer

Ribbon (5)
Purple Ribbon

Chaff (1)

Chaff (1)

November
Willow
(Rain)

Bright (20)
Rainman

Ten (10)
Swallow

Ribbon (5)
Plain Ribbon

Chaff (1)
Storm

December
Paulownia

Bright (20)
Phoenix

Chaff (1)
Special Paulownia

Chaff (1)

Chaff (1)

SECTION I
Capture Games

Chapter 3
Before You Begin

Basic Setup

Determining the First Player

Shuffle the deck.

Each player draws a card from the top of the deck.

The player who drew the earliest month becomes the first player <u>and</u> dealer for the round.

If more than one player tie for the earliest month, then the player with the highest valued card becomes first player.

Cards rank from highest to lowest as follows:
Brights—Tens—Ribbons—Chaffs

If there is still a tie, draw again.

Note: The first player is always the dealer.

Important: The winner of each round becomes the first player of the next round.

Determining the Number of Rounds

Hanafuda games are typically played over a fixed number of rounds.

- 12 rounds (standard game; 'full year')
- 6 rounds (quick game; 'half year')
- 3 rounds (fast game; 'season')

All players should agree on the length of the game before beginning.

Dealing

Each round begins with the current dealer dealing cards to the players and into the field.

The number of cards dealt will vary based on the game and the number of players.

Deal X cards to each player face down.

Deal X cards face up on the table to form the field.

The remaining cards are placed face down to form a draw pile.

Players pick up and view their cards in a "fan" position while keeping them hidden from other players (similar to card games such as Poker or Rummy).

Tip: Deal 1 card to Player A, 1 card to Field, 1 card to Player B. Repeat until the required number of cards have been dealt.

FIGURE 3.1 **Basic Setup**

Checking for Misdeals

A misdeal can be called when any of the following occur:

- If 4 cards of the same month are dealt into the field.
- If a player is dealt 4 sets of 2 (4 pairs). (fig 3.2)
- If a player is dealt 4 of a kind (all of one month).

When a misdeal occurs, all of the cards are returned to the deck and shuffled. The dealer remains the same and the round is dealt again.

Note: While players do not have to claim a misdeal for the cards dealt to their hand, these hands may put the player at a disadvantage.

FIGURE 3.2 **Misdeal**

Checking for Hiki

A hiki occurs when 3 cards of the same month are dealt into the field.

When this occurs these cards are placed into a single stack in the field. (fig 3.3)

The player who plays the remaining card of that month captures the entire stack at once.

FIGURE 3.3 Hiki

Three Phases of Play

Each player's turn occurs in three phases.

A player must perform all three phases during their turn.

After the current player completes their turn, play passes to the next player counterclockwise.

Play continues until all players run out of cards, the deck has been exhausted, and there are no cards left in the field.

Phase One - Matching from Hand

The current player chooses a card from their hand and plays it face up into the field.

This can have one of four results:

- If it matches a card of the same month in the field, then the player places it on top of that card to indicate its capture. (fig 3.4)

- If it matches two cards of the same month in the field, then the player chooses which of the two cards they would like to capture and places it on top of that card to indicate its capture. (fig 3.5)

- If it matches a hiki (set of 3), then the player places it on top of that stack to indicate its capture. (fig 3.6)

- If it does not match any card, then the card is added to the field. (fig 3.7)

Note: If there are no cards remaining in the current players hand, the current player skips Phase One.

FIGURE 3.4 One Match

FIGURE 3.5 Two Match

FIGURE 3.6 Hiki Match

FIGURE 3.7 **No Match**

FIGURE 3.9 **Pair Match**

Phase Two - Matching from Deck

The current player draws a card from the top of the deck and plays it face up into the field.

This card is played in the same way as the card in phase one. <u>However</u>, you can <u>not</u> capture a card that was already captured by the card from phase one.

This can have one of six results:

- If it matches a card of the same month in the field, then the player places it on top of that card to indicate its capture.
- If it matches two cards of the same month in the field, then the player chooses which of the two cards they would like to capture and places it on top of that card to indicate its capture.
- If it matches a hiki (set of 3), then the player places it on top of that stack to indicate its capture.
- If it does not match any card, then the card is added to the field.
- If it matches the pair the player just created in phase one and no other card, then the deck drawn card is added to the field. (fig 3.8)
- If it matches the pair the player just created in phase one and another card in the field, then the player places it on top of the non-paired card. (fig 3.9)

FIGURE 3.8 **Same Match**

Phase Three - Capturing Cards

The current player captures all of the matches that they created in the field during phase one and phase two.

Captured cards are moved into the player's capture area <u>face up</u>.

Note: The player's captured cards must remain visible to all players.

This concludes the current player's turn.

Play passes to the next player.

Play continues in this manner until all players run out of cards, the deck has been exhausted, and there are no cards left in the field.

Note: Players may run out of cards from their hand before the deck is depleted. Players simply ignore phase one and continue play as usual.

Tip: Captured cards should be grouped so that it is easier to determine the status of the game. Depending on the game and player preference they may be grouped by month, yaku, or type (Brights, Tens, etc.)

Ending the Round

The round ends when all players run out of cards, the deck has been exhausted, and there are no cards left in the field.

Players calculate and record their scores for the round.

The winner of the round becomes the dealer of the next round.

Scoring

Scoring varies widely from game to game, however card values and yaku are common scoring metrics in capture games.

Card Values are the point values of the individual cards captured during the round.

Yaku are special combinations of captured cards that are worth points and are often key to winning capture games.

For more detailed scoring instructions, refer to the scoring section of the specific game you are interested in.

Players record the scores for each round.

When the decided number of rounds have been played, players calculate their combined total score for all rounds.

The player with the highest total score is the winner of the game.

Ending the Game

The game ends after the agreed upon number of rounds have been completed.

The winner is the player with the highest total score (i.e. combined total from all rounds).

If there is a tie, then the player who won the most rounds wins.

If there is still a tie, then the players rejoice in their shared victory!

Chapter 4

Simplified Game for Beginners

Difficulty: Absolute Beginner

Players: 2-4

Deck: 48 card flower deck (remove all Jokers)

Rounds: 3, 6, or 12

Objective: Obtain the most points by capturing cards from the field.

Important Notes:
- This hanafuda game is a simplified example game that we created for learning/teaching the basic mechanics present in many hanafuda games. This game is designed to help players become familiar with the basics of card recognition, the three phases of play, matching & capturing, and simplified scoring.

Setup

In a <u>two</u> player game:

Deal 8 cards to each player face down.

Deal 8 cards face up on the table to form the field.

The remaining cards are placed face down to form a draw pile.

In a <u>three</u> player game:

Deal 7 cards to each player face down.

Deal 6 cards face up on the table to form the field.

The remaining cards are placed face down to form a draw pile.

In a <u>four</u> player game:

Deal 5 cards to each player face down.

Deal 8 cards face up on the table to form the field.

The remaining cards are placed face down to form a draw pile.

Check for Misdeals

When a misdeal occurs, all cards are returned to the deck and reshuffled. The dealer remains the same and the round is dealt again.

A misdeal occurs when any of the following occur:

- If 4 cards of the same month are dealt into the field.
- If a player is dealt 4 cards of the same month.
- If a player is dealt 4 sets of 2 (i.e. 4 pairs).

Note: Players do not have to claim a misdeal for the cards dealt to their hand.

Check for Hiki

If 3 cards of the same month are dealt into the field these cards are stacked together to form a hiki. The player who plays the matching card captures all 4 at once.

Playing a Round

Play begins with the first player and continues counter-clockwise.

The current player plays a card from their hand, plays a card from the deck, and then claims the cards that were captured. (See **Three Phases of Play** p. 20).

Play then passes to the next player.

Play continues in this manner until the end of the round.

End of Round

The round ends when all players run out of cards, the deck has been exhausted, and there are no cards left in the field.

The winner of the round becomes the dealer for the next round.

Scoring

Each player's score for the round will be the total value of the cards they captured.

> *Player's Score = Total Value of Player's Captured Cards*

Record the scores for each round.

When the decided number of rounds have been played, players calculate their combined total score for all rounds.

The player with the highest total score is the winner of the game.

Card Values

Brights = 20 pts

Tens = 10 pts

Ribbons = 5 pts

Chaffs = 1 pt

Additional Scoring (Yaku)

Once players become more familiar with this game, simple yaku can be added to the scoring.

Yaku are special combinations that are created from cards captured from the field.

When using the Yaku chart, each player's score for the round will be the total value of the cards they captured plus the value of any yaku they captured.

> *Player's Score = Total Value of Player's Captured Cards + Total Value of Player's Captured Yaku*

Note: Each unique yaku can only be claimed once per round per player. For example, a player who captured 20 Chaffs in a single round can only claim the *Any 10 Chaffs* yaku once.

Players may earn points from each yaku in the following chart.

FIGURE 4.1 Simple Yaku

Earn points from <u>each</u> of the following:

Any 3 Brights = 30 pts

Any 5 Tens = 20 pts

3 Poetry Ribbons = 20 pts

3 Purple Ribbons = 20 pts

4 Plain Ribbons = 20 pts

Any 10 Chaffs = 10 pts

Scoring Examples

Scoring Example

Player A captured 3 Brights, 5 Tens, 3 Plain Ribbons, and 5 Chaffs. (fig 4.2)

Player A's <u>Total Card Value</u> for this round is (3 x 20) + (5 x 10) + (3 x 5) + (5 x 1) = 130 pts.

Player A's <u>Score</u> for the round is 130 pts.

Scoring Example with Yaku

Player A captured 3 Brights, 5 Tens, 3 Plain Ribbons, and 5 Chaffs. (fig 4.2)

Player A's <u>Total Card Value</u> for this round is (3 x 20) + (5 x 10) + (3 x 5) + (5 x 1) = 130 pts.

Player A captured two Yaku: *3 Brights* (30 pts) and *5 Tens* (20 pts).

Player A's <u>Total Yaku Value</u> for this round is (30) + (20) = 50 pts

Player A's <u>Total Score</u> for this round is 130 + 50 = 180 pts.

FIGURE 4.2 Scoring Example

In a single round Player A captured the following:

3 Brights

5 Tens

3 Plain Ribbons

5 Chaffs

Chapter 5
Matching Flowers

Difficulty: Beginner

Players: 2-3

Deck: 48 card flower deck (remove all Jokers)

Rounds: 6 or 12

Objective: Obtain the most points by capturing cards from the field and forming yaku.

Important Notes:
- Matching Flowers is a great game for beginners.

Setup

In a two player game:

Deal 8 cards to each player face down.

Deal 8 cards face up on the table to form the field.

The remaining cards are placed face down to form a draw pile.

In a three player game:

Deal 7 cards to each player face down.

Deal 6 cards face up on the table to form the field.

The remaining cards are placed face down to form a draw pile.

Check for Misdeals

When a misdeal occurs, all cards are returned to the deck and reshuffled. The dealer remains the same and the round is dealt again.

A misdeal occurs when any of the following occur:

- If 4 cards of the same month are dealt into the field.
- If a player is dealt 4 cards of the same month.
- If a player is dealt 4 sets of 2 (i.e. 4 pairs).

Note: Players do not have to claim a misdeal for the cards dealt to their hand.

Check for Hiki

If 3 cards of the same month are dealt into the field these cards are stacked together to form a hiki. The player who plays the matching card captures all 4 at once.

Playing a Round

Play begins with the first player and continues counter-clockwise.

The current player plays a card from their hand, plays a card from the deck, and then claims the cards that were captured. (See **Three Phases of Play** p. 20).

Play then passes to the next player.

Play continues in this manner until the end of the round.

End of Round

The round ends when all players run out of cards, the deck has been exhausted, and there are no cards left in the field.

The winner of the round is the player with the highest score.

The winner of the round becomes the dealer for the next round.

Scoring

Each player's score for the round will be the total value of the cards they captured plus the value of any yaku they captured.

Player's Score = Total Value of Player's Captured Cards + Total Value of Player's Captured Yaku

Record the scores for each round.

When the decided number of rounds have been played, players calculate their combined total score for all rounds.

The player with the highest total score is the winner of the game.

Card Values

Brights = 20 pts
Tens = 10 pts
Ribbons = 5 pts
Chaffs = 1 pt

Yaku

Players can score in each of the following yaku categories. Players total their points from each yaku category.

FIGURE 5.1 **Bright Yaku**

Earn points from <u>one</u> of the following:

5 Brights = 100 pts

4 Dry Brights (excluding Rain) = 60 pts

Spring Semi-Brights = 30 pts

Crane, Moon, Phoenix = 20 pts

FIGURE 5.2 Ribbon Yaku

Earn points from <u>one</u> of the following:

Any 7 Dry Ribbons (excluding Rain) = 40 pts

Any 6 Dry Ribbons (excluding Rain) = 30 pts

Earn points from <u>each</u> of the following:

3 Poetry Ribbons = 40 pts

3 Purple Ribbons = 40 pts

3 Dry Plain Ribbons (excluding Rain) = 20 pts

FIGURE 5.3 Views Yaku

Earn points from <u>one</u> of the following:

The Views = 40 pts

Flower Viewing = 20 pts

Moon Viewing = 20 pts

FIGURE 5.4 Other Yaku

Earn points from <u>each</u> of the following:

Boar, Deer, Butterfly = 20 pts

All 4 Wisteria = 10 pts

All 4 Rain = 10 pts

Scoring Examples

Player A captured 4 Brights, 5 Tens, 3 Ribbons, and 10 Chaffs.

Player A's <u>Total Card Value</u> for this round is
$(4 \times 20) + (5 \times 10) + (3 \times 5) + (10 \times 1) = 155$ pts.

Player A's <u>Total Yaku Value</u> for this round is
$(20) + (20) + (20) + (10) = 70$ pts.

Player A's <u>Total Score</u> for this round is
$(155) + (70) = 225$ pts.

FIGURE 5.6 Scoring Example

In a single round Player A captured the following:

Crane, Moon, Phoenix (20 points)

Boar, Deer, Butterfly (20 points)

3 Dry Plain Ribbons (20 points)

All 4 Wisteria (10 points)

Other Captured Cards

Things to note from the scoring example:

The wisteria ribbon is used in two yaku sets. This is allowed because a player may use the same card to score from more than one yaku category.

Notice that while Player A captured 4 Bright cards, the Rain Bright does not count toward scoring the *4 Dry Bright* yaku because the Rain Bright is considered a "wet" bright and is not included in the *4 Dry Bright* yaku.

The November Willow is considered the Rain month. Therefore, any yaku marked "dry" can not include cards from the Rain month.

Gameplay Variations

Players can choose to include one or more of these variations. Just make sure that everyone agrees.

Game Flow Variations:

Four of a Kind is Not a Misdeal

If all 4 cards of a month are dealt into the field during setup, the dealer automatically captures this set. New cards are dealt onto the field to replace them.

Shorter Rounds

The round ends as soon as all players run out of cards in their hand.

Round Scoring Variations:

Winner Takes All

The winner of a round takes all of the points earned for that round. Totaling both their own and their opponents' score for that round. All other players score 0 points that round.

Low Man Out

If a player manages to score less than 20 points in a single round, then all players score 0 points for that round.

Rain (washes all the points away)

If a player collects all four of the November Rain cards, then their opponents score 0 points for that round.

Game End Scoring Variations:

Counting Rounds Instead of Points

Instead of totaling the points from every round, players total wins. The player who won the most rounds wins the game.

If the players tie, then the player with the highest score wins. If they are still tied, then they rejoice in their shared victory!

First Dealer Tie Breaker

In the case of a tie, the person who was first to deal wins.

Chapter 6

Hana-Awase 1

Difficulty: Beginner

Players: 3-4

Deck: 48 card flower deck (remove all Jokers)

Rounds: 6 or 12

Objective: Obtain the most points by capturing cards from the field and forming yaku.

Setup

In a three player game:

Deal 7 cards to each player face down.

Deal 6 cards face up on the table to form the field.

The remaining cards are placed face down to form a draw pile.

In a four player game:

Deal 5 cards to each player face down.

Deal 8 cards face up on the table to form the field.

The remaining cards are placed face down to form a draw pile.

Check for Misdeals

When a misdeal occurs, all cards are returned to the deck and reshuffled. The dealer remains the same and the round is dealt again.

A misdeal occurs when any of the following occur:

- If 4 cards of the same month are dealt into the field.
- If a player is dealt 4 cards of the same month.

Note: Players do not have to claim a misdeal for the cards dealt to their hand.

Check for Hiki

If 3 cards of the same month are dealt into the field these cards are stacked together to form a hiki. The player who plays the matching card captures all 4 at once.

Playing a Round

Play begins with the first player and continues counter-clockwise.

The current player plays a card from their hand, plays a card from the deck, and then claims the cards that were captured. (See **Three Phases of Play** p. 20.)

Play then passes to the next player.

Play continues in this manner until the end of the round.

End of Round

The round ends when all players run out of cards, the deck has been exhausted, and there are no cards left in the field.

The winner of the round is the player with the highest score.

The winner of the round becomes the dealer for the next round.

Scoring

Each player's score for the round is the total value of their captured cards plus the value of any yaku they captured.

> *Player's Score = Total Value of Player's Captured Cards + Total Value of Player's Captured Yaku*

Record the scores for each round.

When the decided number of rounds have been played, players calculate their combined total score for all rounds.

The player with the highest total score is the winner of the game.

Card Values

Brights = 20 pts

Tens = 10 pts

Ribbons = 5 pts

Chaffs = 1 pt

Yaku

Players can score in each of the following yaku categories. Players total their points from each yaku category.

FIGURE 6.1 Bright Yaku

Earn points from <u>one</u> of the following:

5 Brights = 75 pts

4 Dry Brights (excluding Rain) = 50 pts

Spring Semi-Brights = 35 pts

FIGURE 6.2 Ribbon Yaku

Earn points from <u>each</u> of the following:

Any 7 Dry Ribbons (excluding Rain) = 50 pts

3 Poetry Ribbons = 35 pts

3 Purple Ribbons = 35 pts

FIGURE 6.3 Views Yaku

Earn points from <u>one</u> of the following:

Flower Viewing = 30 pts

Moon Viewing = 20 pts

FIGURE 6.4 Other Yaku

Earn points from the following:

Boar, Deer, Butterfly = 35 pts

Scoring Examples

Player A captured 4 Brights, 5 Tens, 3 Ribbons, and 6 Chaffs.

Player A's <u>Total Card Value</u> for this round is
$(4 \times 20) + (5 \times 10) + (3 \times 5) + (6 \times 1) = 151$ pts.

Player A captured the *Boar, Deer, Butterfly* yaku.

Player A's <u>Total Yaku Value</u> for this round is
$(35) = 35$ pts

Player A's <u>Total Score</u> for this round is
$(151) + (35) = 186$ pts

FIGURE 6.5 Scoring Example

In a single round Player A captured the following:

Boar, Deer, Butterfly (35 points)

Other Captured Cards

Gameplay Variations

Players can choose to include one or more of these variations. Just make sure that everyone agrees.

Game Flow Variations:

Four of a Kind is Not a Misdeal

If all 4 cards of a month are dealt into the field during setup, the dealer automatically captures this set. New cards are dealt onto the field to replace them.

Round Scoring Variations:

Winner Takes All

The winner of a round takes all of the points earned for that round. Totaling both their own and their opponents score for that round.

Dealer Tie Breaker

If there is a tie with a player and the dealer, then the dealer wins.

If the tie is among non-dealers, then the person nearest to the dealer's right wins.

Game End Scoring Variations:

Counting Rounds Instead of Points

Instead of totaling the points from every round, players total wins. The player who won the most rounds wins the game. If the players tie then the player with the highest score wins. If they are still tied, then they rejoice in their shared victory!

First Dealer Tie Breaker

In the case of a tie, the person who was first to deal wins.

Chapter 7

Hana-Awase 2

Difficulty: Beginner

Players: 3

Deck: 48 card flower deck (remove all Jokers)

Rounds: 6 or 12

Objective: Obtain the most points by capturing cards from the field and forming yaku.

Setup

In a <u>three</u> player game:

Deal 7 cards to each player face down.

Deal 6 cards face up on the table to form the field.

The remaining cards are placed face down to form a draw pile.

Check for Misdeals

When a misdeal occurs, all cards are returned to the deck and reshuffled. The dealer remains the same and the round is dealt again.

A misdeal occurs when any of the following occur:

- If 4 cards of the same month are dealt into the field.
- If a player is dealt 4 cards of the same month.

Note: Players do not have to claim a misdeal for the cards dealt to their hand.

Check for Hiki

If 3 cards of the same month are dealt into the field these cards are stacked together to form a hiki. The player who plays the matching card captures all 4 at once.

Playing a Round

Play begins with the first player and continues counter-clockwise.

The current player plays a card from their hand, plays a card from the deck, and then claims the cards that were captured. (See **Three Phases of Play** p. 20.)

Play then passes to the next player.

Play continues in this manner until the end of the round.

End of Round

The round ends when one of the following occurs:

- A player captures a yaku.
- All players run out of cards, the deck has been exhausted, and there are no cards left in the field.

The winner of the round becomes the dealer for the next round.

Scoring

Players first calculate their base score:

Each player's <u>base score</u> is the total value of the player's captured cards minus 88 points.

Base Score = Total Value of Player's Captured Cards - 88 points

If the round ended and <u>no</u> player captured a yaku:

If no player captured a yaku, then each player's base score is their score.

Player's Score = Base Score

The winner of the round is the player with the highest score.

If the round ended and a player captured a yaku:

The player who captured the yaku adds the value of the yaku to their score.

Player's Score = Base Score + Total Value of Player's Captured Yaku

The players who did not capture the yaku subtract the value of the yaku from their score.

Player's Score = Base Score - Total Value of Player's Captured Yaku

The winner of the round is the player who captured a yaku.

Record the scores for each round.

When the decided number of rounds have been played, players calculate their combined total score for all rounds.

The player with the highest total score is the winner of the game.

Card Values

Brights = 20 pts

Tens = 10 pts

Ribbons = 5 pts

Chaffs = 1 pt

Yaku

Players can score in <u>each</u> of the following yaku categories. Players total their points from <u>each</u> yaku category.

FIGURE 7.1 **Bright Yaku**

Earn points from <u>one</u> of the following:

5 Brights = 100 pts

4 Dry Brights (excluding Rain) = 60 pts

FIGURE 7.2 Ribbon Yaku

Earn points from <u>each</u> of the following:

Any 7 Dry Ribbons (excluding Rain) = 60 pts

3 Purple Ribbons = 40 pts

3 Poetry Ribbons = 40 pts

FIGURE 7.3 Chaff Yaku

Earn points from the following:

Any 14 Chaffs = 60 pts

Scoring Example

Player A captured 3 Brights, 3 Ribbons, and 4 Chaffs.

Player A's <u>Total Card Value</u> for this round is
(3 x 20) + (3 x 5) + (4 x 1) = 79 pts.

Player A's <u>Base Score</u> is
(79) - 88 = -9 pts.

Player B captured 1 Bright, 4 Tens, 1 Ribbon, and 2 Chaffs.

Player B's <u>Total Card Value</u> for this round is
(1 x 20) + (4 x 10) + (1 x 5) + (2 x 1) = 67 pts.

Player B's <u>Base Score</u> for this round is
(67) - 88 = -21 pts.

Player C captured 3 Tens, 2 Ribbons, and 5 Chaffs.

Player C's <u>Total Card Value</u> for this round is
(3 x 10) + (2 x 5) + (5 x 1) = 45 pts.

Player C's <u>Base Score</u> for this round is
(45) - 88 = -43 pts.

Player A captured the 3 Poetry Ribbon yaku.

Player A's <u>Total Yaku Value</u> for this round is
(40) = 40 pts.

Player A's <u>Total Score</u> for this round is
(-9) + 40= 31 pts.

Player B's <u>Total Score</u> for this round is
(-21) - (40) = -61 pts.

Player C's <u>Total Score</u> for this round is
(-43) - (40) = -83 pts.

Player A has won this round.

FIGURE 7.4 Scoring Example

	Player A	Player B	Player C
Total Card Value	79	67	45
Minus 88	-88	-88	-88
Total Yaku Value	+40	-40	-40
Total Score	31	-61	-83

FIGURE 7.5 Scoring Example

In a single round Player A captured the following:

3 Poetry Ribbons (40 points)

Other Captured Cards

Gameplay Variations

Players can choose to include one or more of these variations. Just make sure that everyone agrees.

Game Flow Variations:

Bankrupt

Each player starts the game with 200 points. If any player's points are reduced to 0 or less, the game is over. The player with the most points wins.

Round Scoring Variations:

Misery Loves Company

If any player captured 15 points or less then they earn 40 points and all other players lose 40 points. This is in addition to the normal scoring. This is just a bonus.

Worthless Chaff

Chaff cards are worth 0 points.

Chapter 8
Mushi

Difficulty: Beginner

Players: 2

Deck: 40 card flower deck (remove all June Peony, all July Lespedeza, and Joker cards)

Rounds: 6 or 12

Objective: Obtain the most points by capturing cards from the field and forming yaku.

Important Notes:
- The November Rain Storm Chaff is a wild card.

Wild Card

In Mushi, the November Rain Storm Chaff is considered a wild card.

The Storm Chaff can be used to capture <u>any</u> card <u>EXCEPT</u>:
- the other 3 November Rain cards.
- a hiki (set of 3).

Dealt to the Field

If the Storm Chaff was dealt into the field at the start of the round, then the first player to draw a non-November card during their turn <u>must</u> capture it.

Last Card Drawn

If the Storm Chaff is the last card in the deck, it captures all remaining cards in the field (no exceptions).

Leftover Cards

Because of the wild card, most rounds will end with 2 unpaired cards remaining in the field (the last November card and the pair to the card captured by the Storm Chaff).

The player who captured the other two November cards captures the remaining November card.

The other unpaired card is captured by whoever played the Storm Chaff.

Setup

Deal 8 cards to each player face down.
Deal 8 cards face up on the table to form the field.
The remaining cards are placed face down to form a draw pile.

Check for Misdeals

When a misdeal occurs, all cards are returned to the deck and reshuffled. The dealer remains the same and the round is dealt again.

A misdeal occurs when any of the following occur:
- If 4 cards of the same month are dealt into the field.
- If a player is dealt 4 cards of the same month.
- If a player is dealt 4 sets of 2 (i.e. 4 pairs).

Note: Players do not have to claim a misdeal for the cards dealt to their hand.

Check for Hiki

If 3 cards of the same month are dealt into the field these cards are stacked together to form a hiki. The player who plays the matching card captures all 4 at once.

Playing a Round

Play begins with the first player and continues counter-clockwise.

The current player plays a card from their hand, plays a card from the deck, and then claims the cards that were captured. (See **Three Phases of Play** p. 20.)

Play then passes to the next player.

Play continues in this manner until the end of the round.

End of Round

The round ends when all players run out of cards, the deck has been exhausted, and there are no cards left in the field.

The winner of the round is the player with the highest score.

The winner of the round becomes the dealer for the next round.

Scoring

Each player's score for the round will be the total value of the player's captured cards minus 115 points plus the total value of any yaku they captured minus the total value of their opponent's yaku.

Player's Score = (Total Value of Player's Captured Cards - 115) + Total Value of Player's Captured Yaku - Total Value of Opponent's Yaku.

Record the scores for each round.

When the decided number of rounds have been played, players calculate their combined total score for all rounds.

The player with the highest total score is the winner of the game.

Card Values

Brights = 20 pts
Tens = 10 pts
Ribbons = 5 pts
Chaffs = 1 pt

Yaku

Players can score in <u>each</u> of the following yaku categories. Players total their points from <u>each</u> yaku category.

FIGURE 8.1 Yaku

Earn points from <u>each</u> of the following:

5 Brights = 30 pts

Spring Semi-Brights = 25 pts

All 4 Wisteria = 10 pts

All 4 Paulownia = 10 pts

FIGURE 8.2 Scoring Example

In a single round Player A captured the following:

Spring Semi-Brights (25 points)

All 4 Paulownia (10 points)

Other Captured Cards

Scoring Examples

Player A captured 4 Brights, 3 Tens, 3 Ribbons, and 6 Chaffs.

Player A's <u>Total Card Value</u> for this round is
(4 x 20) + (3 x 10) + (3 x 5) + (6 x 1) = 131 pts.

Player A captured the *Spring Semi-Brights* yaku and the *All 4 Paulownia* yaku.

Player A's <u>Total Yaku Value</u> for this round is
(25) + (10) = 35 pts.

Player B captured 1 Bright, 6 Tens, 7 Ribbons, and 18 Chaffs.

Player B's <u>Total Card Value</u> for this round is
(1 x 20) + (4 x 10) + (5 x 5) + (14 x 1) = 99 pts.

Player B captured the *All 4 Wisteria* yaku.

Player B's <u>Total Yaku Value</u> for this round is 10 pts.

Player A's Total Score for this round is
(131 - 115) + (35) - (10) = 41 pts.

Player B's Total Score for this round is
(99 - 115) + (10) - (35) = -41 pts.

Player A has won this round.

Gameplay Variations

Players can choose to include one or more of these variations. Just make sure that everyone agrees.

Game Flow Variations:

Four of a Kind is Not a Misdeal

If all 4 cards of a month are dealt into the field during setup, the dealer automatically captures this set. New cards are dealt onto the field to replace them.

First to 50

The first player to reach 50 points wins.

Round Scoring Variations:

Too Many Brights

The *5 Brights* yaku is not considered a yaku. Therefore, no points are scored for the *5 Brights* yaku.

Game End Scoring Variations:

Counting Rounds Instead of Points

Instead of totaling the points from every round, players total wins. The player who won the most rounds wins the game.

If the players tie then the player with the highest score wins.

Chapter 9

Six Hundred

Difficulty: Beginner

Players: 2-3

Deck: 48 card flower deck (remove all Jokers)

Rounds: Varies

Objective: To be the first player to reach 600 points.

Important Notes:
- The Storm Chaff is a Wild Card. Wild Card rules are unique to this game.
- Card values are unique to this game.

Wild Card

In Six Hundred, the November Rain Storm Chaff is considered a Wild card.

The Wild card can be used to capture <u>any</u> card **except** a hiki (set of 3).

Dealt to the Field

If the Storm Chaff was dealt into the field at the start of the round, then it may be captured by any card.

Leftover Cards

Because of the wild card, most rounds will end with 2 unpaired cards remaining in the field (the last November card and the pair to the card captured by the Storm Chaff). The unpaired cards are left in the field.

Setup

In a <u>two</u> player game:

Deal 8 cards to each player face down.
Deal 8 cards face up on the table to form the field.
The remaining cards are placed face down to form a draw pile.

In a <u>three</u> player game:

Deal 7 cards to each player face down.
Deal 6 cards face up on the table to form the field.
The remaining cards are placed face down to form a draw pile.

Check for Misdeals

When a misdeal occurs, all cards are returned to the deck and reshuffled. The dealer remains the same and the round is dealt again.

A misdeal occurs when any of the following occur:

- If 4 cards of the same month are dealt into the field.
- If a player is dealt 4 cards of the same month.
- If a player is dealt 4 sets of 2 (i.e. 4 pairs).

Note: Players do not have to claim a misdeal for the cards dealt to their hand.

Check for Hiki

If 3 cards of the same month are dealt into the field these cards are stacked together to form a hiki. The player who plays the matching card captures all 4 at once.

Check Hands for Hand Combinations

All players check their individual hands to see if they were dealt any Hand Combinations. (See **Hand Combinations**.)

Hand Combinations are special combinations dealt into the player's hand during Setup.

In order to receive points for a Hand Combination, the player must reveal the cards they are claiming to their opponents.

Each player records any claimed Hand Combinations.

As soon as Hand Combinations are claimed, players hide their hands again.

Playing a Round

Play begins with the first player and continues counter-clockwise.

The current player plays a card from their hand, plays a card from the deck, and then claims the cards that were captured. (See **Three Phases of Play** p. 20).

Play then passes to the next player.

Play continues in this manner until the end of the round.

End of Round

The round ends when all players run out of cards, the deck has been exhausted, and there are no cards left in the field.

The winner of the round is the player with the highest score.

The winner of the round becomes the dealer for the next round.

Scoring

Each player's score for the round will be the total value of the cards they captured plus the value of any yaku they captured plus any Hand Combinations that they claimed.

Player's Score = Total Value of Player's Captured Cards + Total Value of Player's Captured Yaku + Player's Total Hand Combinations

Record the scores for each round.

The game ends when any player's total score is 600 points or higher.

If multiple players have a total score of 600 points or higher, the winner of the game is decided by the following conditions in the following <u>order</u>:

- The player who captured the *4 Dry Brights* yaku wins the game.
- Otherwise, the player who captured the *Any 7 Ribbons* yaku wins the game.
- Otherwise, the player with the highest total score is the winner of the game.

Card Values

Brights = 50
Nightingale Warbler (Feb. Ten) = 50
Tens = 10
Ribbons = 10
Special Paulownia = 10
Chaff = 0

Yaku

Players can score in <u>each</u> of the following yaku categories. Players total their points from <u>each</u> yaku category.

FIGURE 9.1 Bright Yaku

Earn points from <u>each</u> of the following:

4 Dry Brights (excluding Rain) = 600 pts

Crane, Moon, Phoenix = 150 pts

Spring Semi-Brights = 150

FIGURE 9.2a Ribbon Yaku

Earn points from <u>each</u> of the following:

Any 7 Ribbons = 600 pts

FIGURE 9.2b Ribbon Yaku

Earn points from <u>each</u> of the following:

3 Poetry Ribbons = 100 pts

3 Purple Ribbons = 100 pts

3 Dry Plain Ribbons (excluding Rain) = 100 pts

FIGURE 9.3 Views Yaku

Earn points from <u>one</u> of the following:

The Views = 300 pts

Flower Viewing = 100 pts

Moon Viewing = 100 pts

FIGURE 9.4 Other Yaku

Earn points from the following:

Boar, Deer, Butterfly = 300 pts

FIGURE 9.5 Month Yaku

Earn points from <u>each</u> of the following:

All 4 Rain = 200 pts

All 4 Pine = 50 pts

All 4 Plum = 50 pts

All 4 Cherry = 50 pts

All 4 Wisteria = 50 pts

All 4 Suzuki Grass = 50 pts

All 4 Maple = 50 pts

All 4 Paulownia = 50 pts

Hand Combinations:

Players total their points from each Hand Combination category.

Reminder: In order to receive points for a Hand Combination, the player must reveal the cards they are claiming to their opponents.

Note: *3 of a Kind* refers to any 3 cards from the same month.

Note: *All Chaffs* refers to all of the cards dealt to the player's hand. This number will vary based on the number of players.

FIGURE 9.6 Hand Combinations

Earn points from the following:

All Chaffs = 400 pts

Earn points from <u>one</u> of the following:

Any 3 of a Kind = 200 pts

Any 3 of a Kind & Any 3 of a Kind = 400 pts

Scoring Example

Player A had no Hand Combinations.

Player A captured 3 Brights, 4 Tens, 4 Ribbons, and 7 Chaffs.

Player A's Total Card Value for this round is
(3 x 50) + (4 x 10) + (4 x 10) + (7 x 0) = 230 pts.

Player A captured the *Crane, Moon, Phoenix* and the *3 Dry Plain Ribbons* yaku.

Player A's Total Yaku Value for this round is
(150 + 100) = 250 pts.

Player B had no Hand Combinations.

Player B captured 1 Bright, 3 Tens, 4 Ribbons, and 8 Chaffs.

Player B's Total Card Value for this round is
(1 x 50) + (3 x 10) + (4 x 10) + (8 x 0) = 120 pts.

Player B captured the *Flower Viewing* and the *Boar, Deer, Butterfly* the yaku.

Player B's Total Yaku Value for this round is
(100 + 300) = 400 pts.

Player C claimed the *All Chaffs* Hand Combination for 400 pts.

Player C captured 1 Bright, 1 Ten, 1 Ribbon, 7 Chaffs, the Plum Ten and the Special Paulownia.

Player C's Total Card Value for this round is
(1 x 50) + (1 x 10) + (7 x 0) + 50 + 10 = 130 pts.

Player C captured the *All 4 Paulownia* yaku.

Player C's Total Yaku Value for this round is 50 pts.

Player A's total score for this round is
(0) + (230) + (250) = 480 pts.

Player B's total score for this round is
(0) + (120) + (250) = 370 pts.

Player C's total score for this round is
(400) + (130) + (50) = 580 pts.

Player C has won this round.

Gameplay Variations

Players can choose to include one or more of these variations. Just make sure that everyone agrees.

Game Flow Variations:

Shorter Rounds

The round ends as soon as both players run out of cards in their hand.

No Wild

The Storm Chaff is not a Wild card.

Round Scoring Variations:

Sake & Deer Card Values

The Sake card is worth 50 points.
The Deer card is worth 50 points.

Alternate Card Values

The following Card Values replace the standard Card Values:

Brights = 20 pts
Tens = 10 pts
Ribbons = 10 pts
Special Paulownia = 10 pts
Chaffs = 0 pts

Rain Until Sunrise

If a player has a Rain card in their capture area at the end of the round, then all Views yaku that player captured are worth 0 points, <u>unless</u> they also captured the Crane card.

Alternative Yaku Values

3 Poetry Ribbons yaku is worth 150 points.

Spring Semi-Brights yaku is worth 100 points.

Scoring Canceled

If a player's round score is 30 points or less, then all scoring for the round is canceled (including Hand Combinations) <u>unless</u> a player has captured the *4 Dry Brights* yaku.

If the *4 Dry Brights* yaku was captured, then the round is scored as usual.

Note: When calculating whether a player has 30 points or less, the player does not included points received for November Rain and December Paulownia Card Values.

Game End Scoring Variations:

Seven Hundred

The game ends when any player scores 700 points or higher.

The *4 Dry Brights* yaku is worth 700pts.

The *Any 7 Ribbons* yaku is worth 700pts.

All other rules remain the same.

Chapter 10
Hachi-juu Hana

Difficulty: Beginner

Players: 2-3

Deck: 48 card flower deck (remove all Jokers)

Rounds: 6 or 12

Objective: Obtain the most points by capturing cards from the field and forming yaku.

Alternative Names:

- Eighty Flowers

Setup

In a <u>two</u> player game:

Deal 8 cards to each player face down.
Deal 8 cards face up on the table to form the field.
The remaining cards are placed face down to form a draw pile.

In a <u>three</u> player game:

Deal 7 cards to each player face down.
Deal 6 cards face up on the table to form the field.
The remaining cards are placed face down to form a draw pile.

Check for Misdeals

There are no misdeals in Hachi-juu Hana.

If all 4 cards of the same month are dealt into the field at the start of the round, then the dealer automatically captures them.

Check for Hiki

If 3 cards of the same month are dealt into the field these cards are stacked together to form a hiki. The player who plays the matching card captures all 4 at once.

Check Hand for 3 of a Kind

If 3 cards of the same month are dealt into a player's hand, the player may choose to reveal them to their opponents.

If the player succeeds in capturing all 4 cards of the revealed month, then that month's yaku is worth double (i.e 40 pts).

Note: A player may reveal more than one set of 3 cards of the same month.

Playing a Round

Play begins with the first player and continues counter-clockwise.

The current player plays a card from their hand, plays a card from the deck, and then claims the cards that were captured. (See **Three Phases of Play** p. 20).

Play then passes to the next player.

Play continues in this manner until the end of the round.

End of Round

The round ends when all players run out of cards, the deck has been exhausted, and there are no cards left in the field.

The winner of the round is the player with the highest score.

The winner of the round becomes the dealer for the next round.

Scoring

In a two player game:

Each player's score for the round will be the total value of the cards they captured minus 120 points plus the value of any yaku they captured.

> *Player's Score = (Total Value of Player's Captured Cards - 120) + Total Value of Player's Captured Yaku*

The player with the highest score wins the round.

In a three player game:

Each player's score for the round will be the total value of the cards they captured minus 80 points plus the value of any yaku they captured.

> *Player's Score = (Total Value of Player's Captured Cards - 80) + Total Value of Player's Captured Yaku*

The player with the highest score wins the round.

Record the scores for each round.

When the decided number of rounds have been played, players calculate their combined total score for all rounds.

The player with the highest total score is the winner of the game.

Card Values

Brights = 20 pts
Tens = 10 pts
Ribbons = 5 pts
Chaffs = 0 pt

Yaku

Players can score in each of the following yaku categories. Players total their points from each yaku category.

IMPORTANT: When scoring for yaku, November Rain cards may be used as any month. This is for <u>scoring</u> yaku only. Note: The same card may <u>not</u> be used to claim multiple yaku.

For example: If a player captured two April cards and two November cards, they may assign their two November cards as two April cards. By doing so, the player would be able to score points for the *All 4 April* yaku.

FIGURE 10.1 **Month Yaku**

Earn points from <u>each</u> of the following:

All 4 January = 20 pts

All 4 February = 20 pts

All 4 March = 20 pts

All 4 April = 20 pts

All 4 May = 20 pts

All 4 June = 20 pts

All 4 July = 20 pts

All 4 August = 20 pts

All 4 September = 20 pts

All 4 October = 20 pts

All 4 November = 20 pts

All 4 December = 20 pts

Scoring Examples

In a 3 player game:

Player A captured 2 Brights, 3 Tens, 4 Ribbons, and 7 Chaffs.

Player A's Total Card Value for the round is
(2 x 20) + (3 x 10) + (4 x 5) + (7 x 0) = 90 pts.

Player A captured 2 January cards, 4 February cards, 2 May cards, 2 April cards, 2 March cards, and 4 November cards.

Player A chooses to use their 4 November Rain cards to complete the *All 4 January* yaku and the *All 4 March* yaku.

Player A claims the *All 4 January*, the *All 4 February*, and the *All 4 March* yaku.

Player A's Total Yaku Value for this round is
20 + 20 + 20 = 60 pts.

Player A's Total Score for this round is
(90 - 80) + (60) = 70 pts.

Chapter 11
Min-Hwatu

Difficulty: Intermediate

Players: 2-3

Deck: 48 card flower deck (remove all Jokers)

Rounds: 6 or 12

Objective: Obtain the most points by capturing cards from the field and forming yaku.

Important Notes:
- There is an optional variation to the gameplay that includes the use of additional yaku. These yaku are labeled as "optional" in the rules. Players should decide before playing whether these optional yaku should be allowed during scoring.

Setup

Players decide if the *Optional Yaku* will be included in scoring.

In a <u>two</u> player game:

Deal 10 cards to each player face down.
Deal 8 cards face up on the table to form the field.
The remaining cards are placed face down to form a draw pile.

In a <u>three</u> player game:

Deal 7 cards to each player face down.
Deal 6 cards face up on the table to form the field.
The remaining cards are placed face down to form a draw pile.

Check for Misdeals

When a misdeal occurs, all cards are returned to the deck and reshuffled. The dealer remains the same and the round is dealt again.

A misdeal occurs when any of the following occur:

- If 4 cards of the same month are dealt into the field.
- If a player is dealt 4 cards of the same month.
- If a player is dealt 4 sets of 2 (i.e. 4 pairs).

Note: Players do not have to claim a misdeal for the cards dealt to their hand.

Check for Hiki

If 3 cards of the same month are dealt into the field these cards are stacked together to form a hiki. The player who plays the matching card captures all 4 at once.

Playing a Round

Play begins with the first player and continues counter-clockwise.

The current player plays a card from their hand, plays a card from the deck, and then claims the cards that were captured. (See **Three Phases of Play** p. 20.)

Important: There is one <u>exception</u> to the **Three Phases of Play**. If a player draws a card in Phase Two that <u>only</u> matches the pair they just created in Phase One, then the player <u>must</u> leave all three cards in the field as a hiki. The player does not capture any cards this turn.

Play then passes to the next player.

Play continues in this manner until the end of the round.

End of Round

The round ends when all players run out of cards, the deck has been exhausted, and there are no cards left in the field.

The winner of the round is the player with the highest score.

The winner of the round becomes the dealer for the next round.

Scoring

Each player's score for the round will be the total value of the player's captured cards plus the total value of any yaku they captured times the number of <u>opponents</u> minus the total value of each opponent's yaku.

> *Player's Score = Total Value of Player's Captured Cards + (Total Value of Player's Captured Yaku x Number of Opponents) - Total Value of <u>Each</u> Opponent's Yaku*

In other words,

1. Players first determine the total value of their captured cards.
2. Players then determine the total value of their captured yaku (if any).
3. Players then calculate their score using the equation above.

Record the scores for each round.

When the decided number of rounds have been played, players calculate their combined total score for all rounds.

The player with the highest total score is the winner of the game.

Card Values

Brights = 20 pts
Tens = 10 pts
Ribbons = 5 pts
Chaffs = 0 pt

Yaku

Players can score in each of the following yaku categories. Players total their points from <u>each</u> yaku category.

Optional Yaku

In addition to the standard *Yaku* chart, Min-Hwatu has an *Optional Yaku* chart.

The addition of the *Optional Yaku* are an <u>optional</u> variation to gameplay.

Players should decide before playing whether these yaku should be allowed during scoring.

The *Optional Yaku* are scored <u>in addition to</u> the standard Yaku.

When playing with this variation, players can score in each of the following *Yaku* and *Optional Yaku* categories.

Players total their points from each yaku category.

FIGURE 11.1 Yaku

Earn points from <u>each</u> of the following:

3 Poetry Ribbons = 30 pts

3 Purple Ribbons = 30 pts

3 Dry Plain Ribbons (excluding Rain) = 30 pts

All 4 Iris = 20 pts

All 4 Maple = 20 pts

All 4 Rain = 20 pts

FIGURE 11.2 Optional Yaku

Earn points from <u>one</u> of the following:

5 Brights = 200 pts

Spring Semi-Brights = 150 pts

Earn points from <u>one</u> of the following:

The Grand Views = 150 pts

The Views = 100 pts

Earn points from <u>each</u> of the following:

Boar, Deer, Butterfly = 50 pts

Godori = 50 pts

Scoring Examples

Scoring Example for 2 Players

Player A's <u>Total Card Value</u> for this round is 100 pts.

Player A's <u>Total Yaku Value</u> for this round is 30 pts.

Player B's <u>Total Card Value</u> for this round is 140 pts.

Player B's <u>Total Yaku Value</u> for this round is 20 pts.

Player A's <u>Total Score</u> for this round is

$(100) + (30 \times 1) - (20) = 110$ pts.

Player B's <u>Total Score</u> for this round is

$(140) + (20 \times 1) - (30) = 130$ pts.

Player B has won this round.

FIGURE 11.3 Scoring Example for 2 Players

	Player A	Player B
Total Card Value	100	140
Player A's Yaku Value	(30 x 1)	-30
Player B's Yaku Value	-20	(20 x 1)
Total Score	110	130

Scoring Example for 3 Players

Player A's <u>Total Card Value</u> for this round is 80 pts.

Player A's <u>Total Yaku Value</u> for this round is 30 pts.

Player B's <u>Total Card Value</u> for this round is 90 pts.

Player B's <u>Total Yaku Value</u> for this round is 20 pts.

Player C's <u>Total Card Value</u> for this round is 70 pts.

Player C's <u>Total Yaku Value</u> for this round is 50 pts.

Player A's <u>Total Score</u> for this round is

$(80) + (30 \times 2) - (20 + 50) = 70$ pts.

Player B's <u>Total Score</u> for this round is

$(90) + (20 \times 2) - (30 + 50) = 50$ pts.

Player C's <u>Total Score</u> for this round is

$(70) + (50 \times 2) - (30 + 20) = 120$ pts.

Player C has won this round.

FIGURE 11.4 Scoring Example for 3 Players

	Player A	Player B	Player C
Total Card Value	80	90	70
Player A's Yaku Value	(30 x 2)	-30	-30
Player B's Yaku Value	-20	(20 x 2)	-20
Player C's Yaku Value	-50	-50	(50 x 2)
Total Score	70	50	120

Note about scoring: Traditionally, players took the total value of their captured yaku from each of their opponents. This resulted in their opponents each losing that many points and the player gaining the value of their yaku times the number of opponents.

Gameplay Variations

Players can choose to include one or more of these variations. Just make sure that everyone agrees.

Game Flow Variations:

Four of a Kind is Not a Misdeal

If all 4 cards of a month are dealt into the field during setup, the dealer automatically captures this set. New cards are dealt onto the field to replace them.

Round Scoring Variations:

Winner Takes All

The winner of a round takes all of the points earned for that round. Totaling both their own and their opponents score for that round.

Count All Yaku

Players ignore the yaku limitations. Players can score for all of the yaku that they capture in a round.

Only One Yaku

Players can only score for their highest valued captured yaku in a round.

Dealer Tie Breaker

If there is a tie with a player and the dealer, then the dealer wins.

If the tie is among non-dealers, then the person nearest to the dealer's right wins.

Game End Scoring Variations:

Counting Rounds Instead of Points

Instead of totaling the points from every round, players total wins. The player who won the most rounds wins the game. If the players tie then the player with the highest score wins. If they are still tied then they rejoice in their shared victory!

First Dealer Tie Breaker

In the case of a tie, the person who was first to deal wins.

Chapter 12
Koi-Koi

Difficulty: Intermediate

Players: 2

Deck: 48 card flower deck (remove all Jokers)

Rounds: 6 or 12

Objective: Obtain the most points by capturing cards from the field and forming yaku.

Important Notes:
- There is a "Koi-Koi" or "Stop" decision during the capture phase (Phase Three).
- Due to its popularity, Koi-Koi has many gameplay variations.

Calling "Koi-Koi" or "Stop"

Calling "Koi-Koi" or "Stop" occurs after Phase Three of the **Three Phases of Play** (p. 20).

Anytime the active player captures a new yaku or adds to one of their existing yaku, the active player must choose to call "Koi-Koi" or "Stop".

If the active player does not capture or add to a yaku, then play passes to the next player and the game continues as usual.

A player can only call "Koi-Koi" or "Stop" directly after capturing or adding to a yaku on their turn.

Note: Players can only add to their own yaku. Players can not add to yaku made by other players.

Calling Koi-Koi

Calling "Koi-Koi" doubles the points of the next player who calls "Stop" in that round.

When a player calls "Koi-Koi" play passes to the next player and the game continues as usual.

Note: Players can call "Koi-Koi" multiple times, however, the score for the round is only doubled once.

Calling Stop

Calling "Stop" ends the round.

Only the player who called "Stop" can receive points for the round.

If any player previously called "Koi-Koi" that round, then the player who called "Stop" doubles their points.

Tip: While calling "Stop" is a safe approach, it may not lead to a good score. While calling "Koi-Koi" is exciting and may lead to a high score, the opponent can steal your win.

Example 1: Player A captures a yaku and calls "Koi-Koi". Player A captures another yaku and calls "Stop". Player A receives double points and Player B receives 0 points.

Example 2: Player A captures a yaku and calls "Koi-Koi". Player B captures a yaku and calls "Stop". Player B receives double points and Player A receives 0 points.

Example 3: No player calls "Koi-Koi". Player A captures a yaku and calls "Stop". Player A receives points and Player B receives 0 points.

Example 4: Player A captures a yaku and calls "Koi-Koi". The round ends with no player calling "Stop". Player A receives 0 points and Player B receives 0 points.

Example 5: The round ends with no player calling "Stop". Player A receives 0 points and Player B receives 0 points.

Example 6: Player A captures a yaku and calls "Koi-Koi". Player A captures another yaku and calls "Koi-Koi" again. Player A captures another yaku and calls "Stop." Player A receives double points and Player B receives 0 points.

Setup

Deal 8 cards to each player face down.
Deal 8 cards face up on the table to form the field.
The remaining cards are placed face down to form a draw pile.

Check for Misdeals

When a misdeal occurs, all cards are returned to the deck and reshuffled. The dealer remains the same and the round is dealt again.

A misdeal occurs when any of the following occur:

- If 4 cards of the same month are dealt into the field.
- If a player is dealt 4 cards of the same month.
- If a player is dealt 4 sets of 2 (i.e. 4 pairs).

Note: Players do not have to claim a misdeal for the cards dealt to their hand.

Check for Hiki

If 3 cards of the same month are dealt into the field these cards are stacked together to form a hiki. The player who plays the matching card captures all 4 at once.

Playing a Round

Play begins with the first player and continues counter-clockwise.

The current player plays a card from their hand, plays a card from the deck, and then claims the cards that were captured. (See **Three Phases of Play** p. 20.)

If the player captures a yaku or adds to their own existing yaku, then the player must choose to call "Koi-Koi" or "Stop". (See **Calling "Koi-Koi" or "Stop"**.)

If the player did not capture or add to a yaku, then play passes to the next player.

Play continues in this manner until the end of the round.

End of Round

The round ends when one of the following occurs:

- A player calls "Stop".
- All players run out of cards, the deck has been exhausted, and there are no cards left in the field.

The winner of the round becomes the dealer for the next round.

Important: The winner of the round is the player who called "Stop".

If the round ended with no player calling "Stop", then the dealer remains the same.

Scoring

Only the player who called "Stop" receives points.

If <u>neither</u> player called "Stop" before the deck was exhausted, then the round is considered a draw. Both players earn 0 points for that round.

The player's score for the round is equal to the total value of any yaku they captured this round.

> *Player's Score = Total Value of Player's Captured Yaku*

If any player previously called "Koi-Koi" that round, then the player who called "Stop" doubles their points.

> *Player's Score = Total Value of Player's Captured Yaku x 2*

When the decided number of rounds have been played, players calculate their combined total score for all rounds.

The player with the highest total score is the winner of the game.

Yaku

Players can score in <u>each</u> of the following yaku categories. Players total their points from <u>each</u> yaku category.

FIGURE 12.1 **Bright Yaku**

Earn points from <u>one</u> of the following:

5 Brights = 10 pts

4 Dry Brights (excluding Rain) = 8 pts

Any 4 Brights = 7 pts

Any 3 Dry Brights (excluding Rain) = 5 pts

FIGURE 12.2 **Views Yaku**

Earn points from <u>each</u> of the following:

Flower Viewing = 5 pts

Moon Viewing = 5 pts

FIGURE 12.3 **Ribbon Yaku**

Earn points from <u>one</u> of the following:

Any 5 Dry Ribbons (excluding Rain) = 1 pt
+ 1 pt for each additional Ribbon

3 Purple Ribbons = 5 pts + 1 pt for each additional Ribbon

3 Poetry Ribbons = 5 pts + 1 pt for each additional Ribbon

3 Poetry Ribbons & 3 Purple Ribbons = 10 pts
+1 pt for each additional Ribbon

FIGURE 12.4 **Other Yaku**

Earn points from <u>one</u> of the following:

Any 5 Tens = 1 pt + 1 pt for each additional Ten

Boar, Deer Butterfly = 5 pts + 1 pt for each additional Ten

Earn points from the following:

Any 10 Chaffs = 1 pt + 1 pt for each additional Chaff

Scoring Examples

Scoring Example 1

Player A captures *3 Poetry Ribbons* and calls "Stop".

Player A's <u>Total Yaku Value</u> for this round is 5 pts.

Player A's <u>Total Score</u> for this round is 5 pts.

Player B receives 0 pts.

Player A has won this round.

Scoring Example 2

Player A captures *3 Poetry Ribbons* and calls "Koi-Koi".

Player A captures an additional Ribbon and calls "Stop."

Player A's <u>Total Yaku Value</u> for this round is
(5 pts + 1 pt) = 6 pts.

Since "Koi-Koi" was called, Player A's score is doubled.

Player A's <u>Total Score</u> for this round is
(6 pts) x 2 = 12 pts.

Player B receives 0 pts.

Player A has won this round.

Scoring Example 3

Player A captures *3 Poetry Ribbons* and calls "Koi-Koi".

Player B captures *Any 5 Tens* and calls "Stop."

Player B's <u>Total Yaku Value</u> for this round is 1 pt.

Since "Koi-Koi" was called, Player B's score is doubled.

Player B's <u>Total Score</u> for this round is
(1 pt) x 2 = 2 pts.

Player A receives 0 pts.

Player B has won this round.

Scoring Example 4

Player A captures *3 Poetry Ribbons* and calls "Koi-Koi".

Player B captures *Any 5 Tens* and calls "Koi-Koi."

The round ends without any player calling "Stop".

The round is a draw. No players score for this round.

Scoring Example 5

Player A captures *3 Poetry Ribbons* and calls "Koi-Koi".

Player B captures *Any 5 Tens* and calls "Koi-Koi."

Player A captures an additional Ribbon and calls "Stop."

Player A's <u>Total Yaku Value</u> for this round is
(5 pts + 1 pt) = 6 pts.

Since "Koi-Koi" was called, Player A's score is doubled.

Player A's <u>Total Score</u> for this round is
(6 pts) x 2 = 12 pts.

Player B receives 0 pts.

Player A has won this round.

Gameplay Variations

Players can choose to include one or more of these variations. Just make sure that everyone agrees.

Game Flow Variations:

Minimum Points

Players need at least 3 points to be able to call "Stop". Otherwise they automatically call "Koi-Koi".

First to 50

The first player to reach 50 total points wins the game.

Automatic Win

If a player is dealt either 4 pairs or a complete month, the player automatically wins that round. The player receives 6 points.

Shorter Rounds

The round ends as soon as both players run out of cards in their hand.

Four of a Kind is Not a Misdeal

If all 4 cards of a month are dealt into the field during setup, the dealer automatically captures this set. New cards are dealt onto the field to replace them.

Four of a Kind for the Win

If all 4 cards of a month are dealt into the field during setup, the dealer automatically wins that round. The dealer receives 6 points.

Storm is Wild

The Storm is considered a Wild card.

(See **Wild Card** instructions from **Mushi** p. 39)

Brewing Storm

If any August card is dealt into the field during Setup, the Storm is considered a Wild card.

(See **Wild Card** instructions from **Mushi** p. 39)

Steal Points

Players start the game with a given number of points (e.g. 50).

The winner of each round steals the points that they earned that round from their opponent.

Tip: You can use chips or tokens to substitute points.

New Yaku Only

The active player can only call "Koi-Koi" or "Stop" after capturing a new yaku.

Adding to an existing yaku does not give the active player the choice to call "Koi-Koi" or "Stop".

Round Scoring Variations:

Winner Scores All Yaku

The winner of a round scores for all of the yaku that were captured that round. Totaling both their own and their opponent's captured yaku for that round.

Alternative Ribbon Yaku and Other Yaku Charts

This variant replaces the Ribbon Yaku and Other Yaku charts. Note: Bright Yaku and Views Yaku charts remain the same.

- Ribbon Yaku. Earn points from <u>each</u> of the following:

  Any 5 Dry Ribbons (excluding Rain) = 1 pt + 1 pt for each additional Ribbon

  3 Purple Ribbons = 5 pts

  3 Poetry Ribbons = 5 pts

- Other Yaku. Earn points from <u>each</u> of the following:

  Any 5 Tens = 1 pt + 1 pt for each additional Ten

  Boar, Deer, Butterfly = 5 pts

  Any 10 Chaffs = 1 pt + 1 pt for each additional Chaff

Rain & Fog

If a November card (*Rain*) is in the field, then the *Flower Viewing* yaku is worth 0 points.

If a December card (*Fog*) is in the field, then the *Moon Viewing* yaku is worth 0 points.

No Views

Moon Viewing and *Flower Viewing* yaku are <u>not</u> considered yaku.

Views with Friends

A player must capture a Bright, Ribbon, or Other yaku in order to claim a Views yaku.

Bright

If a Bright is dealt onto the field during setup, the score for that round is doubled.

Super Bright

If a Bright is dealt onto the field during setup, then the score for that round is doubled. If their are two Brights, then the score for that round is tripled. If their are three Brights, then the score for that round is quadrupled, and so on.

Koi-Koi! Multiplier

If Koi-Koi has been called once, then the score for the round is doubled. If Koi-Koi has been called twice, then the score for the round is tripled. If Koi-Koi has been called three times, then the score for the round is quadrupled, and so on.

Challenge

When a player calls "Koi-Koi" <u>only</u> the opponent's score is doubled.

Double or Nothing

When a player calls "Koi-Koi" <u>only</u> the player who called "Koi-Koi" has their score doubled.

Lucky 7

If a player's total value of captured yaku for that round is equal to or greater than seven, then their score for that round is doubled. If a player's total value of captured yaku for that round is equal to or greater than seven and any player previously called "Koi-Koi", then the player's score is quadrupled. (Another variation is to triple the score instead of quadrupling it.)

Sake 10 or 1

Sake cup can be counted as either a Ten or a Chaff.

Sake 10 and 1

Sake cup can be counted as both a Ten and a Chaff.

Special Chaffs

The Storm, Special Paulownia, and Sake card each count as 2 Chaffs instead of 1.

Dealers Delight

If no yaku are captured in a round, then the dealer earns 6 points for that round.

Count All Yaku

Players ignore the yaku limitations. Players can score for <u>all</u> of the yaku that they capture in a round.

Only One Yaku

Players can <u>only</u> score for their highest valued captured yaku in a round.

Chapter 13
Oni Koi-Koi

Difficulty: Intermediate

Players: 2

Deck: 48 card flower deck (remove all Jokers)

Rounds: 6 or 12

Objective: Obtain the most points by capturing cards from the field and forming yaku.

Important Notes:
- The Phoenix card is a Wild card. Wild card rules are unique to this game.

Wild Card

In Oni Koi-Koi, the December Phoenix card is a Wild card.

Important: The Wild card can <u>never</u> be used to capture a hiki (set of 3).

Dealt to Player

If the Wild card is dealt to a players hand, it can be used to capture <u>any</u> card.

Important: In order to use the Phoenix as a Wild card, the player must reveal the card to their opponents at the start of the round. Otherwise, it can only be used to match a December card.

Drawn from Deck

If the Wild card was drawn from the deck, then it can be used to capture any non-Chaff card (i.e Bright, Ten, Ribbon).

Dealt to the Field

If the Wild card was dealt into the field, then it can be captured with any non-Chaff card (i.e Bright, Ten, Ribbon).

Last Card Drawn

If the Wild card is the last card in the deck, it captures all remaining cards in the field (no exceptions).

Leftover Cards

Because of the Wild card, most rounds will end with 2 unpaired cards remaining in the field (the last December card and the pair to the card captured by the Wild card).

The player who captured the other two December cards captures the remaining December card.

The other unpaired card is captured by whoever played the Wild.

Calling "Koi-Koi" or "Stop"

Important: Oni Koi-Koi's Calling "Koi-Koi" or "Stop" section is the same as Koi-Koi's. (See **Calling "Koi-Koi" or "Stop"** on page 54 of **Koi-Koi** for unabridged instructions.)

Calling "Koi-Koi" or "Stop" occurs after Phase Three of the **Three Phases of Play** (p. 20).

Anytime the active player <u>captures a new yaku</u> or <u>adds to one of their existing yaku</u>, the active player <u>must</u> choose to call "Koi-Koi" or "Stop".

When a player calls "Koi-Koi", play passes to the next player and the score for the round is doubled for the next player who calls "Stop".

When a player calls "Stop", the round ends. Only the player who called "Stop" receives points for the round.

Setup

Deal 8 cards to each player face down.

Deal 8 cards face up on the table to form the field.

The remaining cards are placed face down to form a draw pile.

Check for Misdeals

When a misdeal occurs, all cards are returned to the deck and reshuffled. The dealer remains the same and the round is dealt again.

A misdeal occurs when any of the following occur:

- If 4 cards of the same month are dealt into the field.
- If a player is dealt 4 cards of the same month.
- If a player is dealt 4 sets of 2 (i.e. 4 pairs).

Note: Players do not have to claim a misdeal for the cards dealt to their hand.

Check for Hiki

If 3 cards of the same month are dealt into the field these cards are stacked together to form a hiki. The player who plays the matching card captures all 4 at once.

Playing a Round

Play begins with the first player and continues counter-clockwise.

The current player plays a card from their hand, plays a card from the deck, and then claims the cards that were captured. (See **Three Phases of Play** p. 20.)

If the player <u>captures a yaku</u> or <u>adds to their own existing yaku</u>, then the player <u>must</u> choose to call "Koi-Koi" or "Stop". (See **Calling "Koi-Koi" or "Stop".**)

If the player did <u>not</u> capture or add to a yaku, then play passes to the next player.

Play continues in this manner until the end of the round.

End of Round

The round ends when one of the following occurs:

- A player calls "Stop".
- All players run out of cards and the deck has been exhausted.

The winner of the round becomes the dealer for the next round.

Important: The winner of the round is the player who called "Stop".

If the round ended with no player calling "Stop", then the dealer remains the same.

Scoring

Only the player who called "Stop" receives points.

If <u>neither</u> player called "Stop" before the deck was exhausted, then the round is considered a draw. Both players earn 0 points for that round.

The player's score for the round is equal to the total value of any yaku they captured this round.

Player's Score = Total Value of Player's Captured Yaku

If any player previously called "Koi-Koi" that round, then the player who called "Stop" doubles their points.

Player's Score = Total Value of Player's Captured Yaku x 2

When the decided number of rounds have been played, players calculate their combined total score for all rounds.

The player with the highest total score is the winner of the game.

Yaku

Players can score in <u>each</u> of the following yaku categories. Players total their points from <u>each</u> yaku category.

FIGURE 13.1 Bright Yaku

Earn points from <u>one</u> of the following:

5 Brights = 15 pts

4 Dry Brights (excluding Rain) = 10 pts

Any 4 Brights = 8 pts

Any 3 Dry Brights (excluding Rain) = 6 pts

FIGURE 13.2 Ribbon Yaku

Earn points from <u>each</u> of the following:

Any 5 Dry Ribbons (excluding Rain) = 1 pt
+ 1 pt for each additional Ribbon

3 Purple Ribbons = 6 pts

3 Poetry Ribbons = 6 pts

FIGURE 13.3 Other Yaku

Earn points from <u>each</u> of the following:

Any 5 Tens = 1 pt + 1 pt for each additional Ten

Any 10 Chaffs = 1 pt + 1 pt for each additional Chaff

Scoring Examples

Scoring Example 1

Player A captures 3 Poetry Ribbons and calls "Stop".

Player A's Total Yaku Value for this round is 6 pts.

Player A's Total Score for this round is 6 pts.

Player B receives 0 pts.

Player A has won this round.

Scoring Example 2

Player A captures 3 Poetry Ribbons and calls "Koi-Koi".

Player A captures Any 5 Dry Ribbons and calls "Stop."

Player A's Total Yaku Value for this round is
(6 pts + 1 pt) = 7 pts.

Since "Koi-Koi" was called, Player A's score is doubled.

Player A's Total Score for this round is
(7 pts) x 2 = 14 pts.

Player B receives 0 pts.

Player A has won this round.

Scoring Example 3

Player A captures 3 Poetry Ribbons and calls "Koi-Koi".

Player B captures Any 5 Tens and calls "Stop."

Player B's Total Yaku Value for this round is 1 pt.

Since "Koi-Koi" was called, Player B's score is doubled.

Player B's Total Score for this round is
(1 pt) x 2 = 2 pts.

Player A receives 0 pts.

Player B has won this round.

Scoring Example 4

Player A captures 3 Poetry Ribbons and calls "Koi-Koi".

Player B captures 5 Tens and calls "Koi-Koi."

The round ends without any player calling "Stop".

The round is a draw.

No players score for this round.

Scoring Example 5

Player A captures 3 Poetry Ribbons and calls "Koi-Koi".

Player B captures 5 Tens and calls "Koi-Koi."

Player A captures Any 5 Dry Ribbons and calls "Stop."

Player A's Total Yaku Value for this round is
(6 pts + 1 pt) = 7 pts.

Since "Koi-Koi" was called, Player A's score is doubled.

Player A's Total Score for this round is
(7 pts) x 2 = 14 pts.

Player B receives 0 pts.

Player A has won this round.

Gameplay Variations

Players can choose to include one or more of these variations. Just make sure that everyone agrees.

Game Flow Variations:

Minimum Points

Players need at least 3 points to be able to call "Stop". Otherwise they automatically call "Koi-Koi".

First to 50

The first player to reach 50 total points wins the game.

Automatic Win

If a player is dealt either 4 pairs or a complete month, the player automatically wins that round. The player receives 6 points.

Shorter Rounds

The round ends as soon as both players run out of cards in their hand.

Four of a Kind is Not a Misdeal

If all 4 cards of a month are dealt into the field during setup, the dealer automatically captures this set. New cards are dealt onto the field to replace them.

Four of a Kind for the Win

If all 4 cards of a month are dealt into the field during setup, the dealer automatically wins that round. The dealer receives 6 points.

Steal Points

Players start the game with a given number of points (e.g. 50).

The winner of each round steals the points that they earned that round from their opponent.

Tip: You can use chips or tokens to substitute points.

Leftovers

Card left in the field at the end of the round remain in the field. They are not given to any player.

Round Scoring Variations:

Winner Scores All Yaku

The winner of a round scores for all of the yaku that were captured that round. Totaling both their own and their opponent's captured yaku for that round.

Bright

If a Bright is dealt onto the field during setup, the score for that round is doubled.

Super Bright

If a Bright is dealt onto the field during setup, then the score for that round is doubled. If their are two Brights, then the score for that round is tripled. If their are three Brights, then the score for that round is quadrupled, and so on.

Koi-Koi! Multiplier

If Koi-Koi has been called once, then the score for the round is doubled. If Koi-Koi has been called twice, then the score for the round is tripled. If Koi-Koi has been called three times, then the score for the round is quadrupled, and so on.

Challenge

When a player calls "Koi-Koi" <u>only</u> the opponent's score is doubled.

Double or Nothing

When a player calls "Koi-Koi" <u>only</u> the player who called "Koi-Koi" has their score doubled.

Lucky 7

If a player's total value of captured yaku for that round is equal to or greater than seven, then their score for that round is doubled. If a player's total value of captured yaku for that round is equal to or greater than seven and any player previously called "Koi-Koi", then the player's score is quadrupled. (Another variation is to triple the score instead of quadrupling it.)

Sake 10 or 1

Sake cup can be counted as either a Ten or a Chaff.

Sake 10 and 1

Sake cup can be counted as both a Ten and a Chaff.

Special Chaffs

The Storm, Special Paulownia, and Sake card each count as 2 Chaffs instead of 1.

Dealers Delight

If no yaku are captured in a round, then the dealer earns 6 points for that round.

Count All Yaku

Players ignore the yaku limitations. Players can score for <u>all</u> of the yaku that they capture in a round.

Only One Yaku

Players can <u>only</u> score for their highest valued captured yaku in a round.

Yaku of the Month

The month corresponding to the current round of the game is considered a yaku worth 4 points.

For example: In round one, *All 4 January* is a valid yaku.

For example: In round two, *All 4 February* is a valid yaku.

For example: In round three, *All 4 March* is a valid yaku.

Chapter 14
Higo-Bana

Difficulty: Intermediate

Players: 2-7 (Best with 2-4)

Deck: 48 card flower deck (remove all Jokers)

Rounds: 6 or 12

Objective: Obtain the most points by capturing cards from the field and forming yaku.

Alternate Names:
- Sakura
- Hawaiian Hanafuda

Important Notes:
- The Storm Chaff is a Wild card. Wild card rules are unique to this game.
- Hiki Rules are unique to this game.
- Card values are unique to this game.
- Team Play. This game can be played with Partners.

Team Play

Higo-Bana can be played with partners.

Teams can be played as 2 vs 2 or 2 vs 2 vs 2 or 3 vs 3.

Partners are seated in alternating order.

FIGURE 14.1 Seating Arrangement for Team Play

Team Size	2 vs 2	2 vs 2 vs 2	3 vs 3
Seating Arrangement	A-B-A-B	A-B-C-A-B-C	A-B-A-B-A-B

When playing in partners, cards that are captured are captured for the team.

Teams place captured cards into a joint capture area.

Players are not allowed to show their partners the cards in their hands.

Hiki

If all 4 cards of the same month are dealt into the field at the start of the round, then the dealer automatically captures them.

If a player sees 4 cards of the same month in any combination (either in hand or in the field) during their turn, that player can announce "Hiki" and capture all 4 cards at once.

Note: The player holding a "hiki" does not have to announce that they are holding a "hiki" unless another player tries to claim one of the cards with the Wild card.

Example 1: Player A has 1 card in their hand that matches 3 in the field. Player A announces "Hiki" and captures the 3 cards in the field in one turn (capturing the full month).

Example 2: Player A has 2 cards in their hand that match 2 in the field. Player A announces "Hiki" and captures the full month.

Example 3: Player A has 3 cards in their hand that match 1 in the field. Player A announces "Hiki" and captures the full month.

Example 4: Player A has 3 card in their hand that matches 1 in the field. Player B tries to capture that card with a Wild card. Player A must announce "Hiki". This stops Player B from capturing that card.

Wild Card

In Higo-Bana, the November Rain Storm Chaff is considered a Wild card.

The Wild card can be used to capture any card EXCEPT

- another player's hiki.

Dealt to the Field

If the Wild card was dealt into the field at the start of the round, a player can capture it with a card of the same month (November Rain).

Drawn from the Deck

If the Wild card is drawn from the deck, it can be used to capture any card in the field or it can be left in the field.

Last Card Drawn

If the Wild card is the last card in the deck, it captures all remaining cards in the field.

Leftover Cards

Because of the Wild card, most rounds will end with 2 unpaired cards remaining in the field (the last November Rain card and the pair to the card captured by the Wild card.)

The player who captured the other two November Rain cards captures the remaining November Rain card.

The other unpaired card is captured by whoever played the Wild card.

Tip: When a card is captured using the Wild card, keep the Wild card paired with the captured card in your capture area.

Setup

In a two player game:

Deal 8 cards to each player face down.

Deal 8 cards face up on the table to form the field.

The remaining cards are placed face down to form a draw pile.

In a three player game:

Deal 7 cards to each player face down.

Deal 6 cards face up on the table to form the field.

The remaining cards are placed face down to form a draw pile.

In a four player game:

Deal 5 cards to each player face down.

Deal 8 cards face up on the table to form the field.

The remaining cards are placed face down to form a draw pile.

In a five player game:

Deal 4 cards to each player face down.

Deal 8 cards face up on the table to form the field.

The remaining cards are placed face down to form a draw pile.

In a six player game:

Deal 3 cards to each player face down.

Deal 12 cards face up on the table to form the field.

The remaining cards are placed face down to form a draw pile.

In a <u>seven</u> player game:

Deal 3 cards to each player face down.

Deal 6 cards face up on the table to form the field.

The remaining cards are placed face down to form a draw pile.

Misdeal & Hiki

There are no misdeals in Higo-Bana.

Check for **Hiki**. If a hiki (i.e. all 4 cards of the same month) is dealt into the field at the start of the round, then the dealer automatically captures them.

Playing a Round

Play begins with the first player and continues counter-clockwise.

The current player plays a card from their hand, plays a card from the deck, and then claims the cards that were captured. (See **Three Phases of Play** p. 20.)

Play then passes to the next player.

Play continues in this manner until the end of the round.

Tip: When a player captures a card worth 0 points they can discard it into a joint discard pile beside the deck.

End of Round

The round ends when all players run out of cards, the deck has been exhausted, and there are no cards left in the field.

The winner of the round is the player with the highest score.

The winner of the round becomes the dealer for the next round.

Scoring

Each player's score for the round will be the total value of the player's captured cards minus 50 points for each yaku that their opponents captured.

> *Player's Score = Total Value of Player's Captured Cards - 50 points for each Yaku captured by each Opponent.*

Record the scores for each round.

When the decided number of rounds have been played, players calculate their combined total score for all rounds.

The player with the highest score is the winner of the game.

Card Values

Brights = 20 pts

Tens = 5 pts

Ribbons = 10 pts

Chaffs = 0 pt

Yaku

Players can score in each of the following yaku categories. Players total their points from each yaku category.

FIGURE 14.2a Yaku

Players may capture <u>each</u> of the following:

Spring Semi-Brights

3 Purple Brights

3 Poetry Brights

3 Dry Plain Ribbons (excluding Rain)

The Views

Boar, Deer, Geese

FIGURE 14.2b Yaku

Players may capture each of the following:

Sake, Deer, Butterfly

Boar, Cuckoo, Bridge

Scoring Examples

Player A's <u>Total Card Value</u> for this round is 90 pts.
Player B's <u>Total Card Value</u> for this round is 75 pts.
Player C's <u>Total Card Value</u> for this round is 80 pts.

Player A captured 0 Yaku.
Player B captured 2 Yaku.
Player C captured 1 Yaku.

Player A's <u>Total Score</u> for this round is
(90) - (50 x 2) - (50 x 1) = -60 pts

Player B's <u>Total Score</u> for this round is
(75) - (50 x 0) - (50 x 1) = 25 pts

Player C's <u>Total Score</u> for this round is
(80) - (50 x 0) - (50 x 2) = -20 pts

Player B has won this round.

FIGURE 14.3 Scoring Example

	Player A	Player B	Player C
Total Card Value	90	75	80
Yaku Penalty	- (50 x 3)	- (50 x 1)	- (50 x 2)
Total Score	-60	25	-20

Additional Scoring Examples

In other words,

Example 1: If a player has 2 yaku, then all other players must deduct 100 points.

Example 2: If there are three players and two players each have 1 yaku, then the two players with yaku must each deduct 50 points and the third player must deduct 100 points.

Example 3: If there are three players and one player has 1 yaku and one player has 2 yaku, then the player with 1 must deduct 100 points, the player with 2 must deduct 50 points, and the player with none must deduct 150 points.

Gameplay Variations

Players can choose to include one or more of these variations. Just make sure that everyone agrees.

Game Flow Variations:

First to X Points

The first player to reach a predetermined number of points wins the game.

Wild Dealt to Field

If the Wild card is dealt into the field at the start of the round, then it is immediately discarded.

Round Scoring Variations:

Rain Man Card Value

The Rain Bright is worth 5 pts.

Special Paulownia Card Value

The Special Paulownia Chaff is worth 10 pts.

100 Lead Final Score

If the winner's score is at least 100 points more than each of their opponent's scores, then the winner's final score is doubled.

50 Lead Final Score

If the winner's score is at least 50 points more than each of their opponent's scores, then the winner's final score is doubled.

100 Lead Card Value

If the winner's Total Card Value is at least 100 points more than each of their opponent's Total Card Values, then the winner's final score is doubled.

50 Lead Card Value

If the winner's Total Card Value is at least 50 points more than each of their opponent's Total Card Values, then the winner's final score is doubled.

Game End Scoring Variations:

Counting Tokens Instead of Points

Each time a player wins a round they receive 1 token.

If the player won the round by more than 50 points, then they receive a total of 2 tokens.

If the player won the round by more than 100 points, then they receive a total of 3 tokens.

Once the set number of rounds have been played, the player with the most tokens wins the game.

Chapter 15
Tensho (Simplified)

Difficulty: Intermediate

Players: 2

Deck: 45 card flower deck (remove Jokers and the 3 December Paulownia Chaffs)

Rounds: Player Determined

Objective: Obtain the most points by capturing cards from the field and forming yaku.

Important Notes:

- This is a simplified version of the game Tensho. The traditional version of Tensho uses a unique month ordering.
- You can find the rules for the traditional version of "Tensho" on page 112.
- There are two sets of yaku in Tensho, but only one may be used per round.

Dealing Method

Traditional games of Tensho use a unique dealing method for setup.

This dealing method is <u>optional</u> as it is not critical to gameplay.

1. Deal 3 cards face down to the field.
2. Deal 3 cards face down in a stack to each corner of the field.
3. Repeat steps 1 and 2.
4. Deal 3 cards face down to the field.
5. Deal 3 cards to the dealer's choice of any two corners of the field.
6. The 6 remaining cards are discarded. They will not be used in the round.
7. The two stacks of 9 on the corners of the field are combined to form the draw pile.
8. The dealer chooses one of the two face down stacks of 6 cards to become their hand.
9. The other player receives the remaining stack of 6 cards as their hand.
10. The 9 face down in the field are turned face up.

Setup

Determine Number of Rounds

Players agree on the number of rounds to play.

Determine Yaku Set

Players agree on the yaku set that will be used for scoring this round.

Note: If the players can not agree on a set then the dealer chooses.

Deal Cards

Deal 6 cards to each player face down.

Deal 9 cards face up on the table to form the field.

Deal 6 cards to a discard. These cards are removed from the round.

The remaining 18 cards are placed face down to form a draw pile.

Check for Misdeals

When a misdeal occurs, all cards are returned to the deck and reshuffled. The dealer remains the same and the round is dealt again.

A misdeal occurs when any of the following occur:

- If 4 cards of the same month are dealt into the field.
- If a player is dealt 4 cards of the same month.

Note: Players do not have to claim a misdeal for the cards dealt to their hand.

Check for Hiki

If 3 cards of the same month are dealt into the field these cards are stacked together to form a hiki. The player who plays the matching card captures all 4 at once.

Playing a Round

Play begins with the first player and continues counter-clockwise.

The current player plays a card from their hand, plays a card from the deck, and then claims the cards that were captured. (See **Three Phases of Play** p. 20.)

Play then passes to the next player.

Play continues in this manner until the end of the round.

December

Since there is only one December Paulownia card in the deck the following rules apply:

- If it is dealt into the field, then no player can capture it.

  The card remains in the field.

- If it is dealt into a player's hand, then that player may automatically capture it.

  The card is placed in that player's capture area.

- If a player draws it from the deck, then that player may automatically capture it.

  The card is placed in that player's capture area.

End of Round

The round ends when one of the following occurs:

- A player captures an automatic win.
- All players run out of cards in their hand.

The winner of the round becomes the dealer for the next round.

Scoring

If a player captured an Automatic Win:

If a player captured a yaku that counts as an Automatic Win, then that player automatically wins the round.

If no player captured an Automatic Win:

If no player captured an <u>Automatic Win</u>, then each player calculates their score.

Each player's score for the round will be the total value of the player's captured yaku.

> *Player's Score = Total Value of Player's Captured Yaku*

The player with the highest <u>Total Yaku Value</u> is the winner of the round.

Resolving Ties

If there is a tie, then the player who captured the <u>most Chaffs</u> wins the round.

If there is still a tie, then each player totals the value of their captured cards.

The player with the highest <u>Total Card Value</u> wins the round.

Determining the Winner of the Game

Record wins for each round.

The player who won the <u>most rounds</u> wins the game.

Card Values

Yaku

Reminder: There are two sets of yaku in Tensho, but only one may be used per round.
Player's may <u>only</u> score from the yaku set that was predetermined during Setup.
Player's total their points from each captured yaku.

FIGURE 15.1 **Yaku (Set One)**

Earn points from <u>each</u> of the following:

Front One Two Three = 100 pts

Back One Two Three = 50 pts

Front One Two Ten = 100 pts

Back One Two Ten = 50 pts

Front Three Four Five = 100 pts

Back Three Four Five = 50 pts

Front Seven Five Three = 100 pts

Back Seven Five Three = 50 pts

Front Seven Eight Nine = 100 pts

Back Seven Eight Nine = 50 pts

Front Ten Nine Six = 100 pts

Back Ten Nine Six = 50 pts

Front Eight Four Eleven = 100 pts

Back Eight Four Eleven = 50 pts

Front Four Six Eleven = 100 pts

Back Four Six Eleven = 50 pts

Front Eight Four Six = 100 pts

Back Eight Four Six = 50 pts

Front Eight Four Six Eleven = 100 pts

Back Eight Four Six Eleven = 50 pts

Front Nine Eleven Three = 100 pts

Back Nine Eleven Three = 50 pts

Front Five Ten Twelve = AUTOMATIC WIN

Back Five Ten Twelve = 50 pts

FIGURE 15.2 Yaku (Set Two)

Earn points from <u>each</u> of the following:

Front One Two Three = 100 pts

Back One Two Three = 50 pts

Front One Two Ten = 100 pts

Back One Two Ten = 50 pts

Front Three Four Five = 100 pts

Back Three Four Five = 50 pts

Front Seven Eight Nine = 100 pts

Back Seven Eight Nine = 50 pts

Front Ten Nine Six = 100 pts

Back Ten Nine Six = 50 pts

Front Nine Eleven Three = 100 pts

Back Nine Eleven Three = 50 pts

Front Ten Seven Eight = 100 pts

Back Ten Seven Eight = 50 pts

Front Eight Nine Ten = 100 pts

Back Eight Nine Ten = 50 pts

Front Seven Eight Nine Ten = 100 pts

Back Seven Eight Nine Ten = 50 pts

Front Five Ten Twelve = 100 pts

Back Five Ten Twelve = AUTOMATIC WIN

One Four Twelve = AUTOMATIC WIN

Scoring Examples

Scoring Example 1
Player A captured no yaku.
Player B captured no yaku.
Player A captured 8 Chaffs.
Player B captured 7 Chaffs.
Player A is the winner of the round.

Scoring Example 2
Player A captured a 100 pt yaku (Front Four Three Five).
Player B captured no yaku.
Player A is the winner of the round.

Scoring Example 3
Player A captured an Automatic Win (One Four Twelve).
Player A is the winner of the round.

Chapter 16

Go-Stop

Difficulty: Expert

Players: 2-7

Deck: 48 card flower deck (plus 1-4 Jokers)

Rounds: Player Determined

Objective: Obtain the most points by capturing cards from the field and forming yaku.

Alternative Names:

- Godori

Important Notes:

- There is a "Go" or "Stop" decision during the capture phase (Phase Three).
- This game includes more advanced play including Bombs, Jokers, and Special Rules.
- It is recommended that tokens (chips, candy, coins, fake money, or whatever you have on hand) or a notepad are used for tracking player points.

Playing with 4-7 Players

While Go-Stop can be played with up to seven players, only three players can participate in any given round.

In order to achieve three players each round, players are given a choice to play or drop out.

This section describes the mechanics for choosing who plays and who drops out.

Note: See **Setup** for instructions on how to play with 2-3 players.

In a 4-6 player game:

Deal 7 cards to each player face down.
Deal 6 cards **face down** to the field.

Important: The cards in the field remain face down until the three players for the round are determined.

In a 7 player game:

Important: There <u>must</u> be at least 1 Joker in the deck.
Each player is dealt 7 cards.
No cards are dealt to the field.

Once the players have been determined and the draw pile has been created, the dealer deals 6 cards face up to create the field.

Determining the Players

The dealer <u>must</u> play.

The choice to play or drop out begins with the player to the right of the dealer and continues counterclockwise.

There <u>must</u> be three players. Therefore,

- as soon as two players (not counting the dealer) choose to play, the remaining players are <u>forced</u> to drop out.
- <u>OR</u>, as soon as enough players drop out, the remaining players are forced to play.

Compensation

When a player is <u>forced</u> to drop out, they may be able to claim compensation.

<u>Only</u> players who are <u>forced</u> to drop out may claim compensation.

Players who drop out <u>voluntarily</u> can **not** claim compensation.

Compensation is collected from each player (other than the dealer) who chose to play.

A player may claim <u>2 points</u> of compensation for <u>each</u> of the following cards in their hand:

- Brights
- Jokers
- Sake
- Storm Chaff
- Special Paulownia Chaff

A player may claim <u>double</u> compensation if they held three cards of the same month in their hand.

When a player claims compensation they <u>must</u> reveal the card(s) that they are claiming compensation for. (Players <u>only</u> reveal the card(s) they are claiming compensation for.)

Note for 4-players: If a player held the Rain Bright and no other Bright, then that player does not receive compensation for the Rain Bright. (This exception only applies in four player games).

Completing Setup

Players who drop out return their hands to the dealer face down.

The dealer shuffles these cards, along with any undealt cards, to create the draw pile.

Play then continues in the same manner as a three player game.

Note: If the round ends with no winner, then the round is redealt to the same three players.

Variant Compensation Rules

When playing with four to seven players the following variations may be applied. Players should decide beforehand which, if any, variations will apply.

Delayed Compensation

Compensation is payed at the <u>end</u> of the round by the <u>losers</u> of the round.

If a round ends with no winner, then the losers of the next round must pay double.

Higher Compensation

Compensation is 3 points instead of 2.

Refresh

When a round ends with no winner, the cards are shuffled and redealt to <u>all</u> players (including those who previously dropped out).

Note: If players are also playing with the *Delayed Compensation* variant, then there would be no compensation payed to players if a round ended with no winner. Nor would compensation be doubled the next round.

Bomb

Bombing the Field

When a player has three cards of the same month in their hand and the remaining fourth card is in the field, the player can choose to play all three of these cards at once. This is called *bombing the field*.

When a player *bombs the field*, that player draws three cards from the deck (instead of one) during Phase Two and matches any appropriate cards in the field. In Phase Three the player captures all of the matches they created in Phase One and Phase Two.

When a player *bombs the field*, that player may run out of cards in their hand before the other players. When this occurs, that player's turn is simply passed. The other players continue play as usual.

For example: During Phase One (Matching from Hand) Player A plays three Peony cards onto the fourth Peony card in the field. During Phase Two (Matching from Deck) Player A draws three consecutive cards from the deck and matches any appropriate cards in the field. An Iris is played onto an Iris, a Plum onto a Plum, and a Cherry, which has no match, is left in the field. In Phase Three (Capturing Cards) Player A captures any matches they made in Phase One and Phase Two. Player A therefor captures four Peony, two Iris, and two Plum cards during their turn.

Variant Bomb Rules

The following are variations to bomb rules. Players should decide beforehand which bomb rules will apply.

Smoke Clears

When a player *bombs the field*, instead of immediately drawing three cards, the player completes their turn by drawing a card from the deck as usual.

Anytime after a bomb is played, the player may choose to pass Phase One (Matching from Hand) of their turn. They may do this up to two times.

Note: That player would still complete Phase Two (Matching from Deck), bringing them back to the correct amount of cards in their hand.

Weak Bomb

A player only draws 2 cards (instead of 3) after *bombing the field*.

Jokers

In Go-Stop, the Jokers are considered bonus cards.

Jokers are worth 1 or 2 or 3 Chaffs. This value is determined during **Setup**. Individual Jokers may be assigned different values.

If a Joker is dealt into the field, the dealer automatically captures it and places it into their capture area.

If a player plays a Joker from their hand, the Joker is placed directly into that player's capture area. That player then draws a card from the deck and plays it as if it were from their hand.

If a player draws a Joker from the deck, the Joker is placed directly into that player's capture area. That player then draws a card from the deck and plays it as usual.

Variant Jokers Rules

The following are variations to Joker rules. Players should decide beforehand which Joker rules will apply.

Special Abilities

Jokers can be assigned special abilities or bonuses.

All Jokers can have the same ability/bonus or each Joker can have a different ability/bonus.

Chaff Magnet

The player who captured the Joker is immediately given a Chaff by each opponent.

Double Points

The player who captured the Joker receives double points if they win the round.

No Bright Penalty

The player who captured the Joker does not have to pay the double penalty for not capturing a Bright.

Deny Losses

The player who captured the Joker does not have to pay third player losses.

Unlucky Joker

When a player makes a match from their hand and then draws a Joker from the deck, the Joker is placed on the match and another card is drawn.

If the drawn card matches the same month (as the previously played card), the Joker is left in the field with the newly created hiki. That player captures no cards.

The next player to match the hiki receives the Joker along with the full month.

Calling "Go" or "Stop"

Calling "Go" or "Stop" occurs at the end of the active player's turn.

The active player <u>must</u> first reach the minimum number of points required to call "Stop" before the active player may choose to call "Go" or "Stop". This number is determined during **Setup**.

If the active player has yet to reach the minimum number of points required to call "Stop", then play automatically passes to the next player and the game continues as usual. (This does not count as calling "Go".)

Once the minimum is reached, anytime the active player <u>captures a new yaku</u> or <u>adds to one of their existing yaku</u>, the active player **must** choose to call "Go" or "Stop".

If the active player does not capture or add to a yaku then play passes to the next player and the game continues as usual.

A player can only call "Go" or "Stop" directly after capturing or adding to a yaku <u>on their turn</u>.

Note: Players can only add to their own yaku. Players can <u>not</u> add to yaku made by other players.

Calling Go

Calling "Go" increases a players potential score by awarding bonus points.

When a player calls "Go" play passes to the next player and the game continues as usual.

Note: Players <u>may</u> call "Go" multiple times. Calling "Go" multiple times further increases a players potential score.

Important: Once a player has called "Go" they do not get the choice to "Go" or "Stop" again until their points are <u>higher</u> than when they last called "Go".

Calling Stop

Calling "Stop" ends the round.

Only the player who called "Stop" can receive points for the round.

Tip: While calling "Stop" may sound like a safe approach, it may not lead to a good score.

Requesting a Draw

When a round ends without a winner it is called a *Draw*.

When a round ends in a *Draw*, the round is redealt to the same three players.

Players may request a *Draw* in games with 3-7 players.

Requesting a Draw

Players can **not** ask for a *Draw* in a <u>two player game</u>.

Only the active player may ask for a *Draw*.

A player can only ask for a *Draw* at the start of their turn.

When a player asks for a *Draw* they must reveal their hand to their opponents.

When a player asks for a *Draw*, the player to the right of that player must choose whether to accept or refuse the request.

- If the player to the right <u>refuses</u>, then the remaining player automatically accepts.
- If the player to the right <u>accepts</u>, then the remaining player may choose to accept or refuse.
  - If <u>both</u> players <u>accept</u>, then the round ends. There is no winner or loser this round. There is no scoring this round. The cards are shuffled and the round is dealt again to the same three players.
- If either player <u>refuses</u>, then the round continues until a player calls "Stop" or the deck is depleted.
  - If the player who refused <u>wins</u> the round, each player pays their own penalty. (See **Scoring**.)
  - If the player who refused <u>loses</u> the round, that player must pay for both losers. The other loser pays nothing. (See **Scoring**.)

Setup

Determine "Stop" minimum:

Players agree on the number of points required to call "Stop".

Some common choices are:

- 3 points for a 3-player game
- 5 points for a 2-player game
- 7 points for a 2-player game

Note: Higher minimums create a more challenging round.

Determine Joker quantity and value:

Players agree on the number of Jokers to include.

Go-Stop is commonly played with 1 or 2 Jokers, however up to 4 can be used.

Players agree on the value of the Jokers. Jokers can be worth 1, 2, or 3 Chaffs.

In a <u>two</u> player game:

Deal 10 cards to each player face down.
Deal 8 cards face up on the table to form the field.
The remaining cards are placed face down to form a draw pile.

In a <u>three</u> player game:

Deal 7 cards to each player face down.
Deal 6 cards face up on the table to form the field.
The remaining cards are placed face down to form a draw pile.

Note: When playing with more than three players see **Playing with 4-7 Players**.

Check for Misdeals

When a misdeal occurs, all of the cards are returned to the deck and shuffled. The dealer remains the same and the round is dealt again.

A misdeal occurs when any of the following occur:

- If 4 cards of the same month are dealt into the field.
- If <u>all</u> players are dealt 4 cards of the same month.

Check Hands

Players check their hands to see if they were dealt 3 or 4 cards of the same month.

- If a player was dealt 3 cards of the same month, they may choose to reveal them to their opponents. If they reveal them, that player will receive double points if they win the round.
- If a player was dealt 2 sets of 3 cards of the same month, they may choose to reveal them to their opponents. If they reveal them, that player will receive quadruple points if they win the round.
- If a player was dealt 4 cards of the same month, they may automatically win the round. They must reveal these cards to their opponents to claim this win. That player receives 5 points from each of their opponents.
- If two players in a 3-player game were each dealt 4 cards of the same month, then both players receive 5 points from the remaining player.

Check Field

Players check the field for hiki (set of 3) and Jokers.

- If 3 cards of the same month are dealt into the field, these cards are stacked together to form a hiki. The player who plays the matching card captures all 4 at once.
- If a Joker is dealt into the field, the dealer automatically captures it and places it in their capture area. Another card is drawn from the deck to replace it in the field.

Playing a Round

Each players turn occurs in four phases.

Play begins with the first player and continues counterclockwise.

Note: The following phases have been modified from the standard **Three Phases of Play**.

Phase One - Matching from Hand

The current player chooses a card from their hand and plays it face up into the field.

This can have one of six results as follows:

- If it matches a card of the same month in the field, the player places it on top of that card to indicate its capture.
- If it matches two cards of the same month in the field, the player chooses which of the two cards they would like to capture and places it on that card to indicate its capture.
- If it matches a hiki (set of 3), the player places it on top of that stack to indicate its capture.*
- If it does not match any card, the card is added to the field.
- If the card is a Joker, the player places it in their capture area. The player then draws a card from the deck and plays it as if it were from their hand.
- If the player has three cards of the same month in their hand and the remaining fourth card is in the field, that player may choose to play all three of these cards at once. This is considered *Bombing the Field*. (See **Bombing the Field**.)

Note: Items marked with an (*) are considered <u>Special Events</u>. (See **Special Events** section of **Phase Three - Capturing Cards**.)

Note: If there are no cards remaining in the current players hand, the current player skips Phase One.

Phase Two - Matching from Deck

The current player draws a card from the top of the deck and plays it face up into the field.

This card is played in the same way as the card in Phase One. <u>However</u>, you can <u>not</u> capture a card that was already captured by the card from phase one.

This can have one of eight results as follows:

- If it matches a card of the same month in the field, the player places it on top of that card to indicate its capture.

- If it matches two cards of the same month in the field, the player chooses which of the two cards they would like to capture and places it on that card to indicate its capture.

- If it does not match any card, the card is added to the field.

- If it matches a hiki (set of 3), the player places it on top of that stack to indicate its capture.*

- If it matches the pair you just created in Phase One and no other card, the deck drawn card is added to the field. This card is stacked on top of the matching pair to create a hiki. The player does <u>not</u> capture these during the capture phase. Instead, these cards are left in the field. The next player to play the matching card captures the stack.*

- If it matches the pair you just created in Phase One and another card in the field, the player places it on top of the non-paired card.*

- If the card is a Joker, the player places it into their capture area. The player then draws another card from the deck and plays it as if it were the deck drawn card.

- If the player played a card to the field in phase one that had no match <u>and</u> the card that the player draws in this phase matches that card, then the player places it on top of that card to indicate its capture.*

Note: Items marked with an (*) are considered <u>Special Events</u>. (See **Special Events** section of **Phase Three - Capturing Cards**.)

Reminder: If the player *bombed the field* in Phase One, then that player draws three cards from the deck instead of one. (See **Bombing the Field**.)

Phase Three - Capturing Cards

The current player captures all of the matches that they created in the field during Phase One and Phase Two and resolves any Special Events.

Captured cards are moved into the players scoring area face up.

Special Events:

Special Events are instances where a player can steal points or Chaffs from their opponents.

There are two categories of Special Events: Steal Chaffs and Steal Points.

Steal Chaffs

The active player receives one Chaff from <u>each</u> opponent (chosen by the opponent) for <u>each</u> of the following Special Events:

- The active player captures a hiki (set of 3).

- The active player empties the field by capturing the final two cards (of different months) in the field. This is <u>not</u> considered a Special Event if it is the final turn of the round.

- The active player plays a card into the field that had no match and then draws a card that matches that card. This is <u>not</u> considered a Special Event if it is the final turn of the round.

- The active player captures all four cards of the same month by using a card from their hand and a card drawn from the deck. This is <u>not</u> considered a Special Event if it is the final turn of the round.

Note: If the opponent does not have any single point Chaffs, then they must surrender a 2 point or 3 point Chaff (e.g. a Joker or a Special Chaff).

Note: If the opponent does not have a Chaff of any kind, then they do not have to give the active player anything.

Steal Points

The active player receives points from each opponent for each of the following Special Events:

- If the active player <u>creates</u> a hiki (set of 3) in their first turn of the round, then the active player immediately takes 3 points from <u>each</u> opponent.

- If a single player <u>creates</u> <u>three</u> hiki (set of 3) in one round, then <u>the round ends</u>. That player <u>immediately</u> takes 5 points from <u>each</u> opponent.

Note: Points that are earned as a result of a Special Event are taken immediately. The player who earned those points keeps those points regardless of whether they win or lose the round. These points are not included in the round scoring.

Phase Four - Check for Captured Yaku

The active player checks their capture area for yaku.

If the active player <u>captured a yaku</u> or <u>added to their own existing yaku</u>, then the active player <u>must</u> choose to call "Go" or "Stop". (See **Calling "Go" or "Stop"**.)

Reminder: The active player can <u>not</u> call "Go" or "Stop" unless they have reached the minimum points allowed to call "Stop".

If the active player did <u>not</u> capture a new yaku or add to their own existing yaku (or if they have yet to reach the minimum), then play automatically passes to the next player and play continues as usual.

End of Round

The round ends when one of the following occurs:

- A player calls "Stop".
- All players run out of cards, the deck has been exhausted, and there are no cards left in the field.
- A player requests a Draw and both opponents accept.

Important: The winner of the round is the player who called "Stop".

The winner of the round becomes the dealer for the next round.

If the round ended in a Draw, then the dealer remains the same and the round is redealt to the same three players.

Scoring

The player who called "Stop" is the winner of the round.

Only the player who called "Stop" receives points.

All other players receive 0 points.

If the round ended and no player called "Stop", then the round is a *Draw*.

All players receive 0 points.

The player's score for the round is equal to the total value of any yaku they captured this round plus any bonus points they received multiplied by any multipliers they earned.

Player's Score = (Total Value of Player's Yaku + Bonus Points) x Any Multipliers

Points that are scored by the winner are taken from each opponent.

Note: The loser's payment to the winner is referred to as a *penalty*.

Bonus Points and Multipliers

The winner may receive additional points and score multipliers in the following situations:

Note: Multipliers are cumulative.

The winner receives additional bonus points for calling "Go":

- If the winner called "Go" once, then they receive 1 bonus point.
- If the winner called "Go" twice, then their score is doubled.
- If the winner called "Go" three times, then their score is tripled.

- If the winner called "Go" more than three times, then their score is multiplied by the number of times that they called "Go".

The winner's score is doubled for each of the following:

- If the winner revealed 3 cards of the same month at the beginning of the round, then their score is doubled.

  Note: If the winner revealed 2 sets of 3 cards of the same month at the beginning of the round, then their score is quadrupled.

- If the winner captured 7 or more Tens, then their score is doubled.
- If the winner *bombed the field*, then their score is doubled.
- If the previous round had no winner, then their score is doubled.

The winner receives additional points from one or more opponents in the following situations:

There are special situations where individual opponents may have to pay extra points.

- If the winner captured a Bright yaku, then any opponent who did not capture at least 1 Bright card must pay double.
- If the winner captured the Chaff yaku, then any opponent who did not capture at least 5 Chaff cards must pay double.

One loser must pay the other loser's penalty to the winner in the following situations:

There are special situations where one loser has to pay the other losers penalty to the winner. In these cases, the other loser pays nothing.

- If one of the losers previous called "Go" and the other loser did not, then the loser who called "Go" must pay the penalty for both losers.
- If a player plays a card from their hand that does not capture anything in the field and another player wins the round by capturing that card on their next immediate turn, then the player who put down that card must pay the other player's penalty in addition to their own. Note: This does not apply if the player offered a *Draw*.
- If a player asks for a Draw and one player both refuses and loses the round. The player who refused must pay the other player's penalty in addition to their own. (See **Requesting a Draw**.)

When the decided number of rounds have been played, players calculate their combined total score for all rounds.

The player with the highest total score is the winner of the game.

Yaku

Players can score in each of the following yaku categories. Players total their points from each yaku category.

FIGURE 16.1 Bright Yaku

Earn points from <u>one</u> of the following:

5 Brights = 15 pts

4 Dry Brights (excluding Rain) = 5 pts

Any 4 Brights (including Rain) = 4 pts

Any 3 Dry Brights (excluding Rain) = 3 pts

Any 3 Brights (including Rain) = 2 pts

FIGURE 16.3 Tens Yaku

Earn points from <u>each</u> of the following:

Godori = 5 pts

Any 5 Tens = 1 pt + 1 pt for each additional Ten

FIGURE 16.2 Ribbon Yaku

Earn points from <u>each</u> of the following:

Any 5 Ribbons = 1 pt + 1 pt for each additional Ribbon

3 Poetry Ribbons = 3 pts

3 Purple Ribbons = 3 pts

3 Dry Plain Ribbons (excluding Rain) = 3 pts

FIGURE 16.3 Chaff Yaku

Earn points from <u>each</u> of the following:

Any 10 Chaffs = 1 pt + 1 pt for each additional Chaff

Important Note: Sake can be counted as <u>either</u> a Ten or as 2 Chaffs.

Important Note: The Storm and Special Paulownia Chaffs each count as 2 Chaffs.

Scoring Examples

Scoring Example 1

In a three player game...

Player A captured 5 points worth of yaku and called "Stop".

Player A's Total Score for the round is 5 pts.

Player A receives 5 points from each opponent.

Therefore, Player A receives a total of 10 points for the round.

Scoring Example 2

In a three player game...

Player A captured 5 points worth of yaku and called "Stop".

Player A had called "Go" once during the round, earning 1 bonus point.

Player A's Total Score for the round is
5 pts + 1 pt = 6 pts.

Player A receives 6 points from each opponent.

Therefore, Player A receives a total of 12 points for the round.

Scoring Example 3

In a three player game...

Player A captured 5 points worth of yaku and called "Stop".

Player A had called "Go" twice during the round, doubling their score.

Player A's Total Score for the round is
5 pts x 2 = 10 pts.

Player A receives 10 points from each opponent.

Therefore, Player A receives a total of 20 points for the round.

Scoring Example 4

In a three player game...

Player A captured 5 points worth of yaku and called "Stop".

Player A had called "Go" once during the round, earning 1 bonus point.

Player A bombed the field during the round, doubling their score.

Player A's Total Score for the round is
(5 pts + 1 pt) x 2 = 12 pts.

Player A receives 12 points from each opponent.

Therefore, Player A receives a total of 24 points for the round.

Scoring Example 5

In a three player game...

Player A captured 5 points worth of yaku and called "Stop".

Player A had called "Go" twice during the round, doubling their score.

Player A bombed the field during the round, doubling their score.

Player A's Total Score for the round is
5 pts x 2 x 2 = 20 pts.

Player A receives 20 points from each opponent.

Therefore, Player A receives a total of 40 points for the round.

Scoring Example 6

In a three player game...

Player A captured 8 points worth of yaku and called "Stop".

Player A had called "Go" three times during the round, tripling their score.

Player A bombed the field during the round, doubling their score.

Player A revealed 3 cards of the same month at the beginning of the round, doubling their score.

Player A's Total Score for the round is
8 pts x 3 x 2 x 2 = 96 pts.

Player A receives 96 points from each opponent.

Therefore, Player A receives a total of 192 points for the round.

Scoring Example 7

In a three player game...

Player A captured 5 points worth of yaku and called "Stop".

Player A's Total Score for the round is 5 pts.

Player B had called "Go" during the round.

Player C never called "Go" during the round.

Player B must pay Player C's penalty.

Player A receives 10 points from Player B and 0 Points from Player C.

Therefore, Player A receives a total of 10 points for the round.

Scoring Example 8

In a three player game...

Player A captured 5 points worth of yaku and called "Stop".

Player A's Total Score for the round is 5 pts.

Player C requested a Draw during the round.

Player B refused the Draw during the round.

Player B must pay Player C's penalty.

Player A receives 10 points from Player B and 0 Points from Player C.

Therefore, Player A receives a total of 10 points for the round.

Scoring Example 9

In a three player game...

Player A captured 5 points worth of yaku (4 Dry Brights) and called "Stop."

Player A's <u>Total Score</u> for the round is 5 pts.

Since Player A's scoring yaku included Brights, any opponent who did not capture at least one Bright card must pay double.

Player B did not capture any Brights, therefore Player B must pay double.

Player C captured one Bright.

Player A receives 10 points from Player B and 5 points from Player C.

Therefore, Player A receives a total of 15 points for the round.

Gameplay Variations

Players can choose to include one or more of these variations. Just make sure that everyone agrees.

Game Flow Variations:

Winning Brights

If a player collects all five Brights, the round immediately ends. The player receives 15 points plus the value of any other yaku that they captured that round. These points are taken from <u>each</u> opponent.

Steal Points

Players start the game with a given number of points.

Tip: You can use chips or tokens to substitute points.

Round Scoring Variations:

Super Sake

The Sake (Chrysanthemum Ten) counts as both a Ten and a Chaff.

Note: This variant replaces the abilities of the Sake cup in the original game.

Super Iris Bridge

The Bridge (Iris Ten) counts as <u>both</u> a Ten <u>and</u> a Chaff.

Note: This variant replaces the abilities of the Sake cup in the original game.

Strong Iris Bridge

The Bridge (Iris Ten) counts as <u>either</u> a Ten <u>or</u> as 2 Chaffs.

Note: This variant replaces the abilities of the Sake cup in the original game.

Triple Hiki

If the active player captures three or more hiki in a round, then the active player takes 2 Chaffs from each opponent.

Hiki Bonus

When the active player captures a hiki in a round, the active player takes 2 Chaffs (instead of 1) from each opponent.

Weak Brights

If the winner captured a Bright <u>yaku</u>, then any opponent who did not capture <u>at least</u> 1 Bright card must pay 2 extra points.

More Chaffs

If the winner captured the Chaff <u>yaku</u>, then any opponent who did not capture <u>at least</u> 7 Chaff cards must pay double.

Higher Stakes

The winner receives additional bonus points for calling "Go":

- If the winner called "Go" once, then they receive 1 bonus point.
- If the winner called "Go" twice, then they receive 2 bonus points.
- If the winner called "Go" three times, then their score is doubled.
- If the winner called "Go" more than three times, then their score is doubled for each time they called "Go" beyond the second.

For example: If a player called "Go" four times their score would be doubled 2 times (i.e. 4x).

For example: If a player called "Go" five times their score would be doubled 3 times (i.e. 8x).

For example: If a player called "Go" six times their score would be doubled 4 times (i.e. 16x).

First Turn Month Capture

If a player captures all four cards of the same month on their first turn of the round, then the player takes 3 points from each opponent.

Weak Rain Man

The Rain Man does not count as a Bright when checking for the Bright double penalty.

Godori

The Godori yaku is worth 3 points instead of 5 points.

Dry Bright not a Yaku

The *Four Dry Brights (excluding rain)* yaku is not a valid yaku.

Responsibility Penalty

Note: This variation replaces the rule in the original game.

If a player plays a card from their hand that does not capture anything in the field and another player wins the round by capturing that card on their next immediate turn, then the player who put down that card must pay the other player's penalty in addition to their own.

The player does **<u>not</u>** have to pay the other loser's penalty if:

- The player offered a *Draw*.
- It was the last card in their hand.
- **Or**, if any card that they played would have had the same result.

Chapter 17
Hachi-Hachi

Difficulty: Expert

Players: 2-7 (Best with 4-6)

Deck: 48 card flower deck (remove Jokers)

Rounds: 12

Objective: Obtain the most points by capturing cards from the field, forming yaku & hand combinations, and completing special achievements.

Alternative Names:

- Eighty-Eight

Important Notes:

- There is a "Continue" or "End" decision.
- This game includes more advanced play including complex scoring.
- It is recommended that tokens (chips, candy, coins, fake money, or whatever you have on hand) or a notepad are used for tracking player points.
- Traditionally players play as many games (12 round sets) as there are players.

Playing with 4-7 Players

While Hachi-Hachi can be played with up to seven players, only three players can participate in any given round.

In order to achieve three players each round, players are given a choice to play or drop out. This section describes the mechanics for choosing who plays and who drops out.

See **Setup** for instructions on how to play with 2-3 players.

In a 4-6 player game:

Deal 7 cards to each player face down.
Deal 6 cards face up on the table to form the field.

In a 7 player game:

Important: 1 Joker must be added to the deck.
Each player is dealt 7 cards.
No cards are dealt to the field.

The player who was dealt the Joker must drop out. This includes the dealer.

If the dealer is dealt the Joker then the dealer must drop out. The person to the right of the dealer becomes the new dealer.

The Joker is discarded and the remaining six cards from that player's hand are placed face up to create the field.

Determining Who Plays

The dealer must play.

The choice to play or drop out begins with the player to the right of the dealer and continues counterclockwise.

There must be three players. Therefore,

- as soon as two players (not counting the dealer) choose to play, the remaining players are forced to drop out.
- OR, as soon as enough players drop out, the remaining players are forced to play.

Pass Penalty

When a player passes they must pay a penalty.

The penalty increases each time a player passes.

- The first player to pass must pay 10 points.
- The second player to pass must pay 15 points.
- The third player to pass must pay 20 points.

The winner of the round receives the points from these penalties as a bonus at the end of the round.

Important: Pass penalties are subject to the Field Multiplier. (See **Determine the Field Multiplier.**)

Compensation

When a player is forced to drop out they may be able to claim compensation for the cards that they were dealt.

Only players who are forced to drop out claim compensation.

Players who drop out voluntarily can **not** claim compensation.

Important: The player who was dealt the Joker can **not** claim compensation.

Compensation is collected from each player (other than the dealer) who chose to play.

A player may claim half the value of any held:

- Hand Combinations (See **Hand Combinations.**)
- Yaku (See **Yaku.**)

A player may claim 3 points of compensation for each of the following cards that were not already compensated for as part of a Hand Combination or Yaku above:

- Bright
- Poetry Ribbon
- Purple Ribbon

When a player claims compensation they must reveal the card(s) that they are claiming compensation for. (Players only reveal the card(s) they are claiming compensation for.)

Important: Compensations are subject to the Field Multiplier. (See **Determine the Field Multiplier.**)

Completing Setup

Players who drop out return their hands to the dealer face down.

The dealer shuffles these cards, along with any undealt cards, to create the draw pile.

Play continues in the same manner as a three player game.

Variants to Determining Players

Drop Out Dealer

Before any cards are dealt for the round, the dealer has the option to drop out.

The player to the right of the dealer becomes the next dealer.

A dealer who chooses to stay is considered a *Blind Stay Dealer*.

A *Blind Stay Dealer* has the opportunity to earn the *Blind Stay* or the *Failed Blind Stay* Special Achievements.

Trade

When the cards are dealt face down to the players, players do not view their hands.

Players may choose to trade their hand <u>once</u>.

Players may <u>only</u> trade for the <u>dealer's hand</u>.

In other words, after a player trades with the dealer, other players can only trade with the person who last traded.

Calling "Continue" or "End"

Calling "Continue" or "End" occurs at the end of the active players turn.

Anytime the active player <u>captures a new yaku</u> or <u>adds to one of their existing yaku</u>, the active player **must** choose to call "Continue" or "End".

If the active player does <u>not</u> capture or add to a yaku, then play passes to the next player and the game continues as usual.

A player can <u>only</u> call "Continue" or "End" directly after capturing or adding to a yaku <u>on their turn</u>.

Note: Players can only add to their own yaku. Players can <u>not</u> add to yaku made by other players.

Calling Continue

Calling "Continue" continues the round and allows players more time to earn a higher score.

When a player calls "Continue", play passes to the next player and the game continues as usual.

Note: A player may call "Continue" multiple times.

Important: Once a player has called "Continue", they do not get the choice to "Continue" or "End" again until their points are <u>higher</u> than when they last called "Continue".

Calling End

Calling "End" ends the round.

Tip: While calling "End" may seem like a safe approach, it may not lead to a good score.

Calling "Cancel"

Cancel

A player that previously chose to "Continue" can chose to "Cancel" if they feel that they are not going to be able to capture another yaku after all.

A player can only call "Cancel" at the start of their turn (before taking any action).

Setup

In a <u>two</u> player game:

Deal 7 cards to each player face down.

Deal 6 cards face up on the table to form the field.

The remaining cards are placed face down to form a draw pile.

Important: Special Achievements do <u>not</u> apply when playing with two players.

In a <u>three</u> player game:

Deal 7 cards to each player face down.

Deal 6 cards face up on the table to form the field.

The remaining cards are placed face down to form a draw pile.

Note: When playing with more than three players see **Playing with 4-7 Players**.

Check for Misdeals

When a misdeal occurs, all of the cards are returned to the deck and reshuffled. The dealer remains the same and the round is dealt again.

A misdeal occurs when 4 cards of the same month are dealt into the field.

Check for Hiki

If 3 cards of the same month are dealt into the field these cards are stacked together to form a hiki. The player who plays the matching card captures all 4 at once.

Determine the Field Multiplier

The cards in the field determine how the points for the round will be calculated.

The field multiplier is determined at the beginning of each round.

There are three possible field multipliers:

1. *"Small Field"* (1x Multiplier)

   If there are <u>no</u> Brights in the field, then 1 point is worth 1 point at the <u>end of the round</u>.

2. *"Large Field"* (2x Multiplier)

   If the Bright from January, March, <u>or</u> August is in the field, then all points are doubled at the <u>end of the round</u>.

3. *"Grand Field"* (4x Multiplier)

   If the Bright from November <u>or</u> December is in the field, then all points are quadrupled at the <u>end of the round</u>.

Important: The field multiplier applies to **all** points earned during the round.

Check Hands for Hand Combinations

All players check their individual hands to see if they were dealt any Hand Combinations. (See **Hand Combinations**.)

Hand Combinations are special combinations dealt into the player's hand during setup.

There are two categories of Hand Combinations: Chaff Combos and Suit Combos.

A player can receive points for <u>one</u> Chaff Combo **and** <u>one</u> Suit Combo.

In order to receive points for a Hand Combination, the player must reveal the cards they are claiming to their opponents in the following way:

- If a player wishes to claim a Chaff Combo, then all Chaffs in their hand must be revealed.
- If a player wishes to claim a Suit Combo, then all cards that are part of that combo must be revealed.

Each player immediately records and scores any claimed Hand Combinations.

Reminder: Hand Combinations are subject to the Field Multiplier. (See **Determine the Field Multiplier**.)

For example: In a Small Field, the *3 of a Kind* Hand Combination is worth 20 points.

For example: In a Large Field, the *3 of a Kind* Hand Combination is worth 40 points.

For example: In a Grand Field, the *3 of a Kind* Hand Combination is worth 80 points.

These points are <u>taken</u> from <u>each</u> opponent participating in the round.

As soon as Hand Combinations are claimed, players hide their hands again.

Playing a Round

Each player's turn occurs in four phases.

Play begins with the first player and continues counterclockwise.

The current player plays a card from their hand, plays a card from the deck, and then claims the cards that were captured. (See **Three Phases of Play** p. 20.)

Phase Four - Check for Captured Yaku

The active player checks their capture area for yaku.

If the active player <u>captured a yaku</u> or <u>added to their own existing yaku</u>, then the active player <u>must</u> choose to call "Continue" or "End". (See **Calling "Continue" or "End"**.)

If the active player did <u>not</u> capture a new yaku or add to their own existing yaku, then play automatically passes to the next player and play continues as usual.

End of Round

The round ends when one of the following occurs:

- A player calls "End".
- A player calls "Cancel".
- All players run out of cards, the deck has been exhausted, and there are no cards left in the field.

Scoring

Players calculate their scores in one of two ways depending on how the round ended.

Reminder: The Field Multiplier applies to all points (Pass Penalties, Compensation, Hand Combinations, Yaku, and Special Achievements).

If the round ended <u>without</u> any player capturing a yaku, then each player calculates their score as follows:

1. First, <u>each</u> player <u>takes</u> the Total Value of their Hand Combinations from each of their active opponents.

2. Next, <u>each</u> player determines their Total Card Value, subtracts 88, and then multiples the result by the Field Multiplier.

   (Player's Total Card Value - 88) x Field Multiplier

3. Then, <u>each</u> player takes the Total Value of their Special Achievements from each of their active opponents.

   Note: Some special achievements cancel all other scoring.

4. Finally, <u>each</u> player combines the results from steps 1-3.

   This is the player's score for the round.

Important: The winner of the round is the player who had the <u>highest Total Card Value</u>.

The winner of the round is the dealer for the next round.

Reminder: The winner of the round claims any **Pass Penalties** that were payed while determining the players for the round.

If the round ended with any player capturing a yaku, then each player calculates their score as follows:

1. First, <u>each</u> player <u>takes</u> the Total Value of their Hand Combinations from <u>each</u> of their active opponents.

2. Next, players score their yaku based on how the round ended:

   - **If a player called "End"**, then that player <u>takes</u> their Total Yaku Value from <u>each</u> of their active opponents.

Only the player who called "End" receives points for their Yaku.

The winner of the round is the player who called "End".

- **If a player called "End" and a single opponent previously called "Continue"**, then the player who called "End" takes double their Total Yaku Value from the player who called "Continue".

  The player who did not call "Continue" or "End" pays nothing.

  Only the player who called "End" receives points for their Yaku.

  The winner of the round is the player who called "End".

- **If a player called "End" and both opponents previously called "Continue"**, then the player who called "End" takes their Total Yaku Value from each active opponent.

  Only the player who called "End" receives points for their Yaku.

  The winner of the round is the player who called "End".

- **If a player called "Cancel"**, then that player takes half the value of their Total Yaku Value from each of their active opponents.

  Only the player who called "Cancel" receives points for their Yaku.

  The winner of the round is the player who called "Cancel".

- **If any player(s) called "Continue" but the deck was exhausted before any player called "End"**, then all players who called "Continue" take half the value of their Total Yaku Value from each of their active opponents.

  The winner of the round is the player who first called "Continue".

3. Then, each player takes the Total Value of their Special Achievements from each of their active opponents.

   Note: Some special achievements cancel all other scoring.

4. Finally, each player combines the results from steps 1-3.

   This is the player's score for the round.

The winner of the round is the dealer for the next round.

Reminder: The winner of the round claims any **Pass Penalties** that were payed while determining the players for the round.

Record the scores for each round.

When the decided number of rounds have been played, players calculate their combined total score for all rounds.

The player with the highest score is the winner of the game.

Card Values

Brights = 20 pts
Tens = 10 pts
Ribbons = 5 pts
Chaffs = 1 pt

Yaku

Players can score in each of the following yaku categories. Players total their points from each yaku category.

Reminder: Yaku values are subject to the round's Field Multiplier.

FIGURE 17.1 Yaku

Earn points from one of the following:

5 Brights = 120 pts

4 Dry Brights (excluding Rain) = 100 pts

Also earn points from each of the following:

3 Poetry Ribbons = 70 pts

3 Purple Ribbons = 70 pts

Any 7 Dry Ribbons (excluding Rain) = 100 pts
+ 10 pts for each additional Ribbon (including Rain)

Hand Combinations

Players may claim <u>one</u> Chaff Combo **and** <u>one</u> Suit Combo.

Players total their points from each Hand Combination category.

Reminder: Hand Combination values are subject to the round's Field Multiplier.

Each player immediately records and scores any claimed Hand Combinations.

These points are taken from each opponent participating in the round.

Reminder: The player must reveal the cards they are claiming. (See **Check Hands for Hand Combinations.**)

IMPORTANT: When scoring for Hand Combinations <u>all</u> of the November Rain Month are considered <u>Chaffs</u>. (This is for Hand Combinations <u>only</u>.)

FIGURE 17.3 Hand Combinations

Chaff Combos

Earn points from <u>one</u> of the following:

Any 2 Ribbons & Any 5 Chaffs = 20 pts

Any 1 Ribbon & Any 6 Chaffs = 30 pts

Any 1 Ten & Any 6 Chaffs = 30 pts

Any 1 Bright & Any 6 Chaffs = 40 pts

Any 7 Chaffs = 40 pts

Suit Combos

Earn points from <u>one</u> of the following:

Any 3 of a Kind = 20 pts

Greater: Any 3 Wisteria = 30 pts

Greater: Any 3 Iris = 30 pts

Greater: Any 3 Lespedeza = 30 pts

Greater: 3 Paulownia Chaffs = 30 pts

Any 4 of a Kind = 60 pts

Any 3 of a Kind & Any 2 Pairs = 70 pts

Any 4 of a Kind & Any 1 Pair = 80 pts

Any 4 of a Kind & Any 3 of a Kind = 200

Any 3 of a Kind & Any 3 of a Kind = 60 pts

Any 3 of a Kind & Any Greater = 70 pts

Any Greater & Any Greater = 80 pts

Any 3 Pairs = 40 pts

Notes:

3 of a Kind refers to 3 cards from the same month.

4 of a Kind refers to 4 cards from the same month.

Pair refers to any 2 cards from the same month.

Special Achievements

Special Achievements are special situations in which a player can earn bonus points.

Special Achievements do <u>not</u> apply when playing with two players.

Points taken for Special Achievements are subject to the Field Multiplier.

Note: The unmodified Total Card Value is the total card value of a player's cards <u>before</u> subtracting eighty-eight and <u>before</u> applying the Field Multiplier.

89 Plus Chaff

If a player claimed any <u>non-bright</u> **Chaff Combo** and had an <u>unmodified</u> Total Card Value of 89 or higher this round, then that player <u>takes</u> 10 points from <u>each</u> of their active opponents.

Note: The non-bright Chaff Combo Hand Combinations are *Any 2 Ribbons & Any 5 Chaffs, Any 1 Ribbons & Any 6 Chaffs, Any 1 Ten & Any 6 Chaffs,* and *Any 7 Chaffs.*

Captured Suit

If a player claimed any **Suit Combo** containing 3 of a Kind <u>and</u> captured all three of those cards, then that player <u>takes</u> 10 points from <u>each</u> of their active opponents.

Note: It is possible to claim this bonus twice if the player revealed two sets of 3 of a Kind when revealing their Hand Combinations.

Note: This Special Achievement does not apply to any Suit Combo containing 4 of a Kind. Therefore, this bonus applies to all Suit Combos **except** *Any 4 of a Kind, Any 4 of a Kind & Any 1 Pair,* and *Any 4 of a Kind & Any 3 of a Kind.*

The following Special Achievements <u>only</u> apply if the round ended <u>without</u> any player capturing a yaku:

88 Hachi-Hachi

If all three players' <u>unmodified</u> Total Card Value for the round are <u>each exactly</u> 88 points, then the dealer <u>takes</u> 100 points from <u>each</u> of their active opponents. The dealer is the winner of the round.

<u>All</u> other scoring for the round is canceled <u>except</u> for Pass Penalties and Compensation.

This means that players do not receive any points for any Hand Combinations, other Special Achievements (including Simple 16), Yaku, or captured cards this round.

168 Plus

If a player's <u>unmodified</u> Total Card Value for the round is 168 or higher, then that player <u>takes</u> 100 points from <u>each</u> of their active opponents plus an additional 10 points for each point over 168. This player is the winner of the round.

Example 1: A player with an unmodified Total Card Value of 168 would take 100 points from each of their active opponents.

Example 2: A player with an unmodified Total Card Value of 170 would take 120 points from each of their active opponents.

<u>All</u> other scoring for the round is canceled <u>except</u> for Pass Penalties and Compensation.

This means that players do not receive any points for any Hand Combinations, other Special Achievements (including Simple 16), Yaku, or captured cards this round.

Simple 16

If a player captures 16 or more Chaffs in a round, then that player takes 120 points from <u>each</u> of their active opponents <u>plus</u> an additional 20 points for <u>each</u> additional Chaff. This player is the winner of the round.

Example 1: A player with 16 Chaffs would take 120 points from each of their active opponents.

Example 2: A player with 18 Chaffs would take 160 points from each of their active opponents.

<u>All</u> other scoring for the round is canceled <u>except</u> for Pass Penalties and Compensation.

This means that players do not receive any points for any Hand Combinations, other Special Achievements, Yaku, or captured cards this round.

The following Special Achievements **only apply if playing with the <u>Drop Out Dealer Variant</u>:**

Blind Stay

In any round where the Blind Stay Dealer's unmodified Total Card Value is 89 points or higher, the Blind Stay Dealer <u>takes</u> 10 points from <u>all</u> players (<u>including</u> those who did not play the round) <u>excluding</u> the 7th player who was forced to drop from drawing the Joker.

Failed Blind Stay

If the round ended with no player capturing a yaku <u>and</u> the Blind Stay Dealer's unmodified Total Card Value is <u>less</u> than 89 points, then the Blind Stay Dealer must <u>pay each</u> of their active opponents 10 points.

The following Special Achievement <u>only</u> applies if playing with the <u>Trade Variant</u>:

Dealer's Hand

If the last player to Trade (i.e. the player with the Dealer's hand) captures an unmodified Total Card Value of 89 points or higher, then that player <u>takes</u> 10 points from <u>all</u> players (including those who did not play the round) <u>excluding</u> the 7th player who was forced to drop from drawing the Joker.

Scoring Examples

Scoring Example 1

A two player game.
A *"Large Field"* (2x Multiplier) was dealt.
No player captured a yaku.

Player A claimed a 40 point Hand Combination (*Any 1 Bright & Any 6 Chaffs*).

Player A multiplies their Hand Combination by the Field Multiplier (40 x 2 = 80 pts).

Player A <u>takes</u> **80** points from Player B.

Player B claimed a 20 point Hand Combination (*Any 3 of a Kind*).

Player B multiplies their Hand Combination by the Field Multiplier (20 x 2 = 40 pts).

Player B <u>takes</u> **40** points from Player A.

Player A's Total Card Value was 141 points.

Player A subtracts 88 from their Total Card Value (141 - 88 = 53 pts).

Player A then multiplies this by the Field Multiplier (53 x 2 = 106 pts).

Player A earns **106** points.

Player B's Total Card Value was 123 points.

Player B subtracts 88 from their Total Card Value (123 - 88 = 35 pts).

Player B then multiplies this by the Field Multiplier (35 x 2 = 70 pts).

Player B earns **70** points.

Player A's <u>Total Score</u> for the round is 80 -40 + 106 = 146 pts.

Player B's <u>Total Score</u> for the round is -80 + 40 + 70 = 30 pts.

Player A is the winner of the round.

FIGURE 17.4 **Scoring Example 1**

Player A	Player B	
+80	-80	Player A's Hand Combination x Field Multiplier
-40	+40	Player B's Hand Combination x Field Multiplier
+106	+70	(Total Card Value - 88) x Field Multiplier
146	30	Total Score

Scoring Example 2

A two player game.
A *"Grand Field"* (4x Multiplier) was dealt.
A yaku was captured this round.

Player A claimed a 30 point Hand Combination (*Greater: Any 3 Wisteria*).

Player A multiplies their Hand Combination by the Field Multiplier (30 x 4 = 120 pts).

Player A takes **120** points from Player B.

Player B claimed no Hand Combinations.

Player B <u>takes</u> **0** points from Player A.

Player B captured a yaku and called "End."

Player B's Yaku was worth 70 points (*3 Poetry Ribbons*).

Player B multiplies their Yaku by the Field Multiplier (70 x 4 = 280 pts).

Player B <u>takes</u> **280** points from Player A.

Player A's <u>Total Score</u> for the round is 120 - 0 - 280 = -160 pts.

Player B's <u>Total Score</u> for the round is -120 + 0 + 280 = 160 pts.

Player B is the winner of the round.

FIGURE 17.5 Scoring Example 2

Player A	Player B	
+120	-120	Player A's Hand Combination x Field Multiplier
0	0	Player B's Hand Combination x Field Multiplier
-280	+280	Yaku x Field Multiplier
-160	160	Total Score

Scoring Example 3

A three player game.
A *"Small Field"* (1x Multiplier) was dealt.
No player captured a yaku.
No Special Achievements were earned.

Player A claimed no Hand Combinations.

Player A takes **0** points from Player B and Player C.

Player B claimed a 20 point Hand Combination (*Any 3 of a Kind*).

Player B multiplies their Hand Combination by the Field Multiplier (20 x 1 = 20 pts).

Player B takes **20** points from Player A and **20** points from Player C.

Player C claimed a 40 point Hand Combination (*Any 7 Chaffs*) and a 40 point Hand Combination (*Any 3 Pairs*).

Player C multiplies their Hand Combinations by the Field Multiplier (80 x 1 = 80 pts).

Player C takes **80** points from Player A and **80** points from Player B.

Player A's Total Card Value was 100 points.

Player A subtracts 88 from their Total Card Value (100 - 88 = 12 pts).

Player A then multiplies this by the Field Multiplier (12 x 1 = 12 pts).

Player A earns **12** points.

Player B's Total Card Value was 90 points.

Player B subtracts 88 from their Total Card Value (90 - 88 = 2 pts).

Player B then multiplies this by the Field Multiplier (2 x 1 = 2 pts).

Player B earns **2** points.

Player C's Total Card Value was 74 points.

Player C subtracts 88 from their Total Card Value (74 - 88 = -14 pts).

Player C then multiplies this by the Field Multiplier (-14 x 1 = -14 pts).

Player C earns **-14** points.

Player A's Total Score for the round is 0 - 20 -80 + 12 = -88 pts.

Player B's Total Score for the round is 0 + 40 - 80 + 2 = -38 pts.

Player C's Total Score for the round is 0 - 20 + 160 -14 = 126 pts.

Player A is the winner of the round.

Reminder: The player with the highest Total Card Value is the winner of the round.

FIGURE 17.6 Scoring Example 3

Player A	Player B	Player C	
0	0	0	Player A's Hand Combination x Field Multiplier
-20	+40	-20	Player B's Hand Combination x Field Multiplier
-80	-80	+160	Player C's Hand Combination x Field Multiplier
+12	+2	-14	(Total Card Value - 88) x Field Multiplier
0	0	0	Special Achievements
-88	-38	126	Total Score

Scoring Example 4

A three player game.
A *"Large Field"* (2x Multiplier) was dealt.
No player captured a yaku.
A Special Achievement was earned.

Player A claimed a 20 point Hand Combination (*Any 3 of a Kind*).

Player A multiplies their Hand Combination by the Field Multiplier (20 x 2 = 40 pts).

Player A takes 40 points from Player B and 40 points from Player C.

Player B claimed a 20 point Hand Combination (*Any 2 Ribbons & 5 Chaffs*).

Player B multiplies their Hand Combination by the Field Multiplier (20 x 2 = 40 pts).

Player B takes **40** points from Player A and **40** points from Player C.

Player C claimed no Hand Combinations.
Player C takes **0** points from Player A and Player B.

Player A's Total Card Value was 88 points.
Player B's Total Card Value was 88 points.
Player C's Total Card Value was 88 points.

Since each player's Total Card Value was 88 points, the Special Achievement 88 *Hachi-Hachi* was earned. According to this Special Achievement, all other scoring for the round is canceled and the dealer receives 100 points. (Note: In a game with more than three players, Pass Penalties and Compensation would be scored as usual.)

Player A multiplies their Special Achievement by the Field Multiplier (100 x 2 = 200 pts).

Player A takes **200** points from Player B and **200** points from Player C.

Player A is the winner of the round.

FIGURE 17.7 **Scoring Example 4**

Player A	Player B	Player C	
+80	-40	-40	Player A's Hand Combination x Field Multiplier
-40	+80	-40	Player B's Hand Combination x Field Multiplier
0	0	0	Player C's Hand Combination x Field Multiplier
0	0	0	(Total Card Value - 88) x Field Multiplier
+400	-200	-200	Special Achievements
400	-200	-200	Total Score

Scoring Example 5

A four player game.
A *"Grand Field"* (4x Multiplier) was dealt.
No player captured a yaku.
A Special Achievements was earned.

When determining players, Player A choses to pass.

Player A must pay a -10 point pass penalty.

Player A multiplies their pass penalty by the Field Multiplier (-10 x 4 = -40 pts).

Player A pays a **-40** point pass penalty.

Player B claimed a 20 point Hand Combination (*Any 3 of a Kind*).

Player B multiplies their Hand Combination by the Field Multiplier (20 x 4 = 80 pts).

Player B takes **80** points from Player C and **80** points from Player D.

Player C claimed a 30 point Hand Combination (*Any 1 Ribbon & Any 6 Chaffs*).

Player C multiplies their Hand Combinations by the Field Multiplier (30 x 4 = 120 pts).

Player C takes **120** points from Player A and **120** points from Player B.

Player D claimed no Hand Combinations.

Player D takes **0** points from Player B and Player C.

Player B's Total Card Value was 98 points.

Player B subtracts 88 from their Total Card Value (98 - 88 = 10 pts).

Player B then multiplies this by the Field Multiplier (10 x 4 = 40 pts).

Player B earns **40** points.

Player C's Total Card Value was 80 points.

Player C subtracts 88 from their Total Card Value (80 - 88 = -8 pts).

Player C then multiplies this by the Field Multiplier (-8 x 4 = -32 pts).

Player C earns **-32** points.

Player D's Total Card Value was 86 points.

Player D subtracts 88 from their Total Card Value (86 - 88 = -2 pts).

Player D then multiplies this by the Field Multiplier (-2 x 4 = -8 pts).

Player D's earns **-8** points.

Player B claims the *Captured Suit* Special Achievement.

Player B receives a bonus 10 points.

Player B multiplies this by the Field Multiplier (10 x 4 = 40 pts)

Player B takes **40** points from Player C and **40** points from Player D.

Player A's Total Score for the round is -40 pts.

Player B's Total Score for the round is 160 - 120 - 0 + 40 + 80 = 160 pts.

Player C's Total Score for the round is -80 + 240 - 0 - 32 - 40 = 88 pts.

Player D's Total Score for the round is -80 - 120 + 0 - 8 - 40 = -248 pts.

Player B is the winner of the round.

The winner of the round claims the pass penalty.

Therefore, Player B receives 40 points, increasing their Total Score to 200 pts.

FIGURE 17.8 **Scoring Example 5**

Player A	Player B	Player C	Player D	
-40				Pass Penalty
	+160	-80	-80	Player B's Hand Combination x Field Multiplier
	-120	+240	-120	Player C's Hand Combination x Field Multiplier
	0	0	0	Player D's Hand Combination x Field Multiplier
	+40	-32	-8	(Total Card Value - 88) x Field Multiplier
	+80	-40	-40	Special Achievements
	+40			Winner Bonus
-40	200	88	-248	Total Score

Scoring Example 6

A four player game.
A *"Large Field"* (2x Multiplier) was dealt.
A yaku was captured this round.
Player A is the dealer.

When determining players, Player B and Player C chose to play.

Player D was forced to drop out.

Player B and Player C must pay compensation to Player D.

Player D was dealt a 40 pt Hand Combination (*Any 3 Pairs*) and an unclaimed Bright (3 pts).

Player D calculates their compensation (40/2 + 3 = 23 pts).

Player D multiplies their compensation by the Field Multiplier (23 x 2 = 46 pts).

Player D is owed 46 points in compensation.

Player D takes **46** pts from Player B and **46** pts from Player C.

Player A claimed a 40 point Hand Combination (*Any 7 Chaffs*).

Player A multiplies their Hand Combinations by the Field Multiplier (40 x 2 = 80 pts).

Player A <u>takes</u> **80** points from Player B <u>and</u> **80** points from Player C.

Player B claimed no Hand Combinations.

Player B <u>takes</u> **0** points from Player A and Player C.

Player C claimed no Hand Combinations.

Player C <u>takes</u> **0** points from Player A and Player B.

Player B captured a yaku and called "End."

Player B's Yaku was worth 100 points (*4 Dry Brights*).

Player B multiplies their Yaku by the Field Multiplier (100 x 2 = 200 pts).

Player B <u>takes</u> **200** pts from Player A <u>and</u> **200** pts from Player C.

Player A's <u>Total Score</u> for the round is 160 - 0 - 0 - 200 = -40 pts.

Player B's <u>Total Score</u> for the round is -46 - 80 + 0 - 0 + 400 = 274 pts.

Player C's <u>Total Score</u> for the round is -46 - 80 - 0 + 0 - 200 = -326 pts.

Player D's <u>Total Score</u> for the round is 92 pts.

Player B is the winner of the round.

FIGURE 17.9 **Scoring Example 6**

Player A	Player B	Player C	Player D	
0	-46	-46	+92	Compensation
+160	-80	-80		Player A's Hand Combination x Field Multiplier
0	0	0		Player B's Hand Combination x Field Multiplier
0	0	0		Player C's Hand Combination x Field Multiplier
-200	+400	-200		Yaku x Field Multiplier
-40	274	-326	92	Total Score

Gameplay Variations

Players can choose to include one or more of these variations. Just make sure that everyone agrees.

Game Flow Variations:

Hidden Field

Cards are dealt to the field face down during setup. The field is not revealed until players are determined.

Open Hand

Cards that were used to claim Hand Combinations remain visible for the round.

Carryover Multiplier

If there are multiple Brights in the field when determining the field size, then the highest multiplier is used for the current round. The next highest multiplier is carried over to the next round.

In any given round the highest available multiplier will always be used.

For example: If the December Bright and the January Bright are dealt into the field, then the current round will be a *"Grand Field"* (4x Multiplier) and the next round will be a *"Large Field"* (2x Multiplier).

Multiple Multiplier

If there are multiple Brights in the field when determining the field size, then the multipliers are combined into a larger multiplier.

For example: If the December Bright and the January Bright are dealt into the field, then the multiplier for the current round will be a 6x Multiplier.

Four & Three

If a player claims the *Any 4 of a Kind & Any 3 of a Kind* Hand Combination, then that player immediately wins the <u>round</u>.

Note: Only Pass Penalties, Compensations, and Hand Combinations are scored that round. The Field Multiplier still applies when calculating scores.

Winning Hand

If a player claims both the *Any 4 of a Kind & Any 3 of a Kind* and the *Any 7 Chaffs* Hand Combinations, then that player immediately wins the <u>round</u>.

That player takes 400 points from <u>each</u> of their opponents (instead of 240).

Note: Only Pass Penalties, Compensations, and Hand Combinations are scored that round. The Field Multiplier still applies when calculating scores.

Round Scoring Variations:

Less Compensation

Compensation for unclaimed Brights, Purple Ribbons, and Poetry Ribbons is 2 points instead of 3 points.

Risk

If a player who called "Continue" fails to call "End" then that player must pay out the value of their yaku to <u>each</u> of their active opponents.

Responsibility Penalty

If a player plays an unmatched card into the field that results in an opponent immediately capturing a yaku on their next turn, then the player who played the unmatched card must pay the yaku penalty of both losers.

Note: This rule <u>only</u> applies to the following yaku: *4 Dry Brights*, *3 Poetry Ribbons*, and *3 Purple Ribbons*.

Note: This penalty does <u>not</u> apply if the player had no choice. (i.e. It was the last card in their hand <u>or</u> if any card that they would have played would have had the same result.)

Worthless Yaku

Players do not receive compensation for held yaku.

Simple 16 Yaku

Simple 16 is not considered a Special Achievement.

Any 16 Chaffs is considered a yaku worth 120 points.

Each of the four November Rain cards may be counted as Chaffs when claiming this yaku.

No Extra Ribbons

The *Any 7 Dry Ribbons* yaku is only worth 100 points. Additional ribbons does not increase the value of this yaku.

Boar, Deer, Butterfly

Boar, Deer, Butterfly is considered a yaku worth 70 points.

Alternate Two Player Game Scoring

This variation modifies scoring for two-player games that end without any player capturing a yaku.

This variation only replaces the second scoring step, all other steps should be completed as usual.

Reminder: The player with the highest Total Card Value is the winner of the round.

2. Next, each player determines their Total Card Value.

   The winner of the round <u>takes</u> the difference in Total Card Values (times the Field Multiplier) from their opponent.

   (Winner's Total Card Value - Opponent's Total Card Value) x Field Multiplier

Game End Scoring Variations:

Campaign

Play as many games (12 rounds) as there are players.

The winner of each game is awarded bonus points equal to 10 times the number of players.

Once all of the games are completed, players calculate their combined total score.

The player with the most points is the winner of the campaign.

Chapter 18
Sudaoshi

Difficulty: Expert

Players: 3

Deck: 48 card flower deck (remove all Jokers)

Rounds: 6 or 12

Objective: Obtain the most points by capturing cards from the field, forming yaku, and forming hand combinations.

Important Notes:
- This game includes more advanced gameplay including complex scoring.
- It is recommended that tokens (chips, candy, coins, fake money, or whatever you have on hand) or a notepad are used for tracking player points.

Setup

Deal 7 cards to each player face down.

Deal 6 cards face up on the table to form the field.

The remaining cards are placed face down to form a draw pile.

Check for Misdeals

When a misdeal occurs, all cards are returned to the deck and reshuffled. The dealer remains the same and the round is dealt again.

A misdeal occurs when 4 cards of the same month are dealt into the field.

Check for Hiki

If 3 cards of the same month are dealt into the field these cards are stacked together to form a hiki. The player who plays the matching card captures all 4 at once.

Assign the Point Burden

Before play begins, each player is assigned a Point Burden for the round as follows:

- The <u>dealer</u> receives a burden of **-100** points.
- The player to the <u>right</u> of the dealer receives a burden of **-110** points.
- The player to the <u>left</u> of the dealer receives a burden of **-120** points.

The *Point Burden* is reassigned <u>each round</u> as follows:

- The player with the <u>highest score</u> for the round becomes the dealer of the next round and receives the **-100** point burden.
- The player with the <u>lowest score</u> for the round receives the **-120** point burden.
- The remaining player receives the -110 point burden.

Each player should record their *Point Burden*.

Fun Fact: The point burden is the total value of all 48 cards in the deck (i.e. 330 points).

Check Hands for Hand Combinations

<u>All</u> players check their individual hands to see if they were dealt any Hand Combinations. (See **Hand Combinations**.)

Hand combinations are special combinations dealt into the player's hand during setup.

There are two categories of Hand Combinations: Chaff Combos and Suit Combos.

A player can receive points for <u>one</u> Chaff Combo **and** <u>one</u> Suit Combo.

In order to receive points for a Hand Combination, the player <u>must</u> reveal the cards they are claiming to their opponents in the following way:

- If a player wishes to claim a Chaff Combo, then all Chaffs in their hand must be revealed.
- If a player wishes to claim a Suit Combo, then all cards that are part of that combo must be revealed.

Each player immediately records and scores any claimed Hand Combinations.

These points are <u>taken</u> from <u>each</u> opponent.

As soon as Hand Combinations are claimed, players hide their hands again.

Playing a Round

Play begins with the first player and continues counter-clockwise.

The current player plays a card from their hand, plays a card from the deck, and then claims the cards that were captured. (See **Three Phases of Play** p. 20.)

Play then passes to the next player.

Play continues in this manner until the end of the round.

End of Round

The round ends when all players run out of cards, the deck has been exhausted, and there are no cards left in the field.

The winner of the round is the player with the highest score.

The winner of the round becomes the dealer for the next round.

The **Point Burden** is reassigned. (See **Setup**.)

Scoring

Each player calculates their score for the round as follows:

1. First, <u>each</u> player <u>takes</u> the Total Value of their Hand Combinations from <u>each</u> of their opponents.
2. Then, <u>each</u> player <u>takes</u> their Total Yaku Value from <u>each</u> of their opponents.

3. Next, <u>each</u> player determines their Total Card Value.

4. Then, <u>each</u> player combines the results from steps 1-3.

5. Finally, <u>each</u> player <u>subtracts</u> their assigned Point Burden.

This is the player's score for the round.

These steps can be simplified and represented by the following set of equations:

FIGURE 18.1 Scoring Equations

Player's Total Hand Combination Value = __ x 2 =			___
First Opponent's Total Hand Combination Value =		-	___
Second Opponent's Total Hand Combination Value =		-	___
Player's Total Yaku Value = __ x 2 =			___
First Opponent's Total Yaku Value =		-	___
Second Opponent's Total Yaku Value =		-	___
Player's Total Card Value =			___
Player's Point Burden =		-	___
Player's Total Score		=	___

Record the scores for each round.

When the decided number of rounds have been played, players calculate their combined total score for all rounds.

The player with highest score is the winner of the game.

Card Values

Curtain = 10 pts
Phoenix = 10 pts
Chaffs = 10 pts
Crane = 5 pts
Moon = 5 pts
Rain Man = 5 pts
Tens = 5 pts
Ribbons = 1 pt

Yaku

There are two yaku categories: Hills and Rain.

<u>Any</u> player can score a yaku in the Hills category.

<u>Only</u> the player with the 120 Point Burden can score from the Rain category.

The players with the 100 and 110 Point Burden can only score <u>one</u> yaku from the Hills category.

The player with the 120 Point Burden can score one yaku from the Hills category <u>and</u> one yaku from the Rain category.

FIGURE 18.2 Hills Yaku

<u>Any</u> player may earn points from <u>one</u> of the following:

Over the Hills (Moon and Geese) = 10 pts

The Hills (All 4 August) = 20 pts

FIGURE 18.3 Rain Yaku

Only the player with the 120 Point Burden may earn points from <u>one</u> of the following:

Under the Rainy Sky (Rain Man and Swallow) = 10 pts

Rainy Sky (All 4 November) = 20 pts

Hand Combinations

Players may claim <u>one</u> Chaff Combo **and** <u>one</u> Suit Combo.

Players total their points from each Hand Combination category.

Each player immediately records and scores any claimed Hand Combinations.

These points are <u>taken</u> from <u>each</u> opponent.

Reminder: The player <u>must</u> reveal the cards they are claiming. (See **Check Hands for Hand Combinations.**)

IMPORTANT: When scoring for Hand Combinations all of the November Rain Month are considered Chaffs. (This is for Hand Combinations <u>only</u>.)

FIGURE 18.4 Hand Combinations

Suit Combos

Earn points from <u>one</u> of the following:

Any 3 of a Kind = 20 pts

Greater: Any 3 Wisteria = 30 pts

Greater: Any 3 Iris = 30 pts

Greater: Any 3 Lespedeza = 30 pts

Greater: 3 Paulownia Chaffs = 30 pts

Any 4 of a Kind = 60 pts

Any 3 of a Kind & Any 2 Pairs = 70 pts

Any 4 of a Kind & Any 1 Pair = 80 pts

Any 4 of a Kind & Any 3 of a Kind = 200 pts

Any 3 of a Kind & Any 3 of a Kind = 60 pts

Any 3 of a Kind & Any Greater = 70 pts

Any Greater & Any Greater = 80 pts

Any 3 Pairs = 40 pts

Notes:

3 of a Kind refers to 3 cards from the same month.

4 of a Kind refers to 4 cards from the same month.

Pair refers to any 2 cards from the same month.

FIGURE 18.5 Hand Combinations

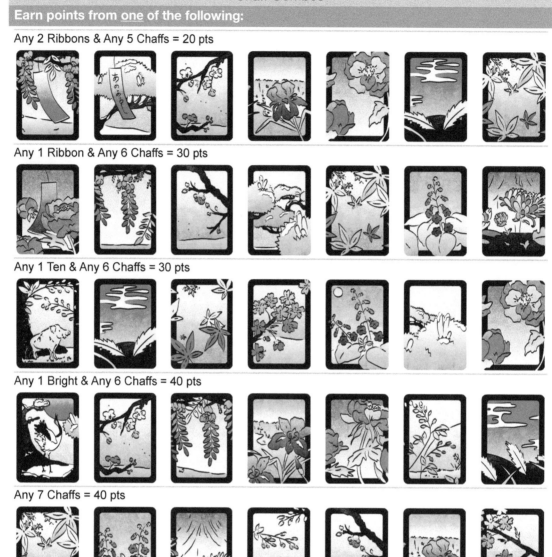

Chaff Combos

Earn points from <u>one</u> of the following:

Any 2 Ribbons & Any 5 Chaffs = 20 pts

Any 1 Ribbon & Any 6 Chaffs = 30 pts

Any 1 Ten & Any 6 Chaffs = 30 pts

Any 1 Bright & Any 6 Chaffs = 40 pts

Any 7 Chaffs = 40 pts

Scoring Examples

Scoring Example

Player A began with a Point Burden of 100.

Player B began with a Point Burden of 110.

Player C began with a Point Burden of 120.

Player A claimed a 20 point Hand Combination (*Any 3 of a Kind*).

Player A <u>takes</u> **20** points from Player B <u>and</u> **20** points from Player C.

Player B claimed no Hand Combinations.

Player B takes **0** points from Player A and Player C.

Player C claimed a 40 point Hand Combination (*Any 7 Chaffs*).

Player C takes **40** points from Player A <u>and</u> **40** points from Player B.

Player A captured no yaku.

Player B captured a yaku worth 10 points (*Over the Hills*).

Player B takes **10** points from Player A <u>and</u> **10** points from Player C.

Player C captured a yaku worth 20 points (*Rainy Sky*).

Player C takes **20** points from Player A <u>and</u> **20** points from Player B.

Player A's <u>Total Card Value</u> was 89 points.
Player B's <u>Total Card Value</u> was 108 points.
Player C's <u>Total Card Value</u> was 133 points.

Player A's Total Score for the round is
(40 - 0 - 40) + (0 - 10 - 20) + 89 - 100 = -41

Player B's Total Score for the round is
(-20 + 0 - 40) + (-0 + 20 - 20) + 108 -110 = -62

Player C's Total Score for the round is
(-20 - 0 + 80) + (-0 - 10 + 40) + 133 -120 = 103

Player C is the winner of the round.

In the following round...
Player A will be assigned the -110 Point Burden.
Player B will be assigned the -120 Point Burden.
Player C will be assigned the -100 Point Burden.

FIGURE 18.6 **Scoring Example**

Player A	Player B	Player C	
-100	-110	-120	Point Burden
+40	-20	-20	Player A's Hand Combination
0	0	0	Player B's Hand Combination
-40	-40	+80	Player C's Hand Combination
0	0	0	Player A's Yaku
-10	+20	-10	Player B's Yaku
-20	-20	+40	Player C's Yaku
+89	+108	+133	Total Card Value
-41	-62	103	Total Score

Gameplay Variations

Players can choose to include one or more of these variations. Just make sure that everyone agrees.

Game End Scoring Variation:

Open Hand

Cards that were used to claim Hand Combinations remain visible for the round.

Game End Scoring Variation:

Counting Rounds instead of Points

Instead of totaling the points from every round, players total wins. The player who won the most rounds wins the game.

If the players tie then the player with the highest score wins. If they are still tied then they rejoice in their shared victory!

Chapter 19
Hachi (Simplified)

Difficulty: Expert

Players: 2

Deck: 48 card flower deck (remove all Jokers)

Rounds: Variable

Objective: Obtain the most points by capturing cards from the field and forming yaku.

Important Notes:

- This is a simplified version of Hachi. The traditional version of Hachi uses a more complex capture mechanic.
- This game uses a unique card capturing mechanic.
- The gameplay is the same as Hachi, however, the capture chart is unique to this version of the game.
- You can find the rules for the traditional version of "Hachi" on page 108.

Capture Chart

Hachi (Simplified) uses unique card capturing mechanics.

Unlike most other Hanafuda games, cards do not capture cards of the same month. Each month can capture the three months that follow that month.

The following is a chart of the months and the months that they can capture:

FIGURE 19.1 **Capture Chart**

Month	Capture
January (1)	Feb (2), Mar (3), April (4)
February (2)	Mar (3), April (4), May (5)
March (3)	April (4), May (5), June (6)
April (4)	May (5), June (6), July (7)
May (5)	June (6), July (7), Aug (8)
June (6)	July (7), Aug (8), Sep (9)
July (7)	Aug (8), Sep (9), Oct (10)
August (8)	Sep (9), Oct (10), Nov (11)
September (9)	Oct (10), Nov (11), Dec (12)
October (10)	Nov (11), Dec (12), Jan (1)
November (11)	Dec (12), Jan (1), Feb (2)
December(12)	Jan (1), Feb (2), Mar (3)

Tip: If playing with the Fusion deck, the months can be identified by using the number indices.

Tip: The simplified version of the capture chart alters the game balance. However, the overall gameplay strategy remains the same as the traditional version.

Setup

Deal 7 cards to each player face down.
Deal 6 cards face up on the table to form the field.
The remaining cards are placed face down to form a draw pile.

Check for Misdeals

When a misdeal occurs, all cards are returned to the deck and reshuffled. The dealer remains the same and the round is dealt again.

A misdeal occurs when 4 cards of the same month are dealt into the field.

Check for Hiki

If 3 cards of the same month are dealt into the field these cards are stacked together to form a hiki. The player who plays the matching card captures all 4 at once.

Playing a Round

Play begins with the first player and continues counter-clockwise.

The current player plays a card from their hand, plays a card from the deck, and then claims the cards that were captured. (See **Three Phases of Play** p. 20.)

Play then passes to the next player.

Play continues in this manner until the end of the round.

End of Round

The round ends when all players run out of cards in their hand.

The winner of the round becomes the dealer for the next round.

Scoring

Each player's score for the round will be the total value of the player's captured cards plus the value of any yaku that they captured.

Player's Score = Total Value of Player's Captured Cards + Total Value of Player's Captured Yaku.

The player with the highest score is the winner of the round.

Record the scores for each round.

Determining the Winner of the Game

If a player wins <u>two consecutive</u> rounds by 20 points or more, then that player wins the game.

Card Values

Brights = 10 pts
Tens = 10 pts
Ribbons = 1 pt
Chaffs = 10 pts

Yaku

Players can score for each of the following yaku.
Players total their points from each captured yaku.

Note: The same card may be used to capture more than one yaku.

FIGURE 19.2 **Yaku**

Earn points from <u>each</u> of the following:

Twelve Four Eleven = 10 pts

Poetry Twelve Four Eleven = 20 pts

Five Six Ten = 10 pts

Poetry Five Six Ten = 20 pts

Five Four Six = 10 pts

Poetry Five Four Six = 20 pts

Seven Five Three = 10 pts

Poetry Seven Five Three = 20 pts

Nine Eleven Three = 10 pts

Poetry Nine Eleven Three = 20 pts

Eight Four Eleven = 10 pts

Poetry Eight Four Eleven = 20 pts

Seven Eight Nine = 10 pts

Poetry Seven Eight Nine = 20 pts

One Two Three = 10 pts

Poetry One Two Three = 20 pts

Three Five Six = 10 pts

Poetry Three Five Six = 20 pts

Ten Seven Eight = 10 pts

Poetry Ten Seven Eight = 20 pts

Scoring Example

Scoring Example

Round 1:

Player A's Total Card Value was 153 points.
Player B's Total Card Value was 133 points.

Player A captured no yaku.
Player B captured no yaku.

Player A's <u>Total Score</u> for the round is 153 points.
Player B's <u>Total Score</u> for the round is 133 points.

Player A wins the round.

Round 2:

Player A's Total Card Value was 131 points.
Player B's Total Card Value was 106 points.

Player A captured a yaku worth 20 points (Poetry *One Two Three*).

Player B captured a yaku worth 10 points (*Five Six Ten*) and a yaku worth 10 points (*Three Five Six*).

Player A's <u>Total Score</u> for the round is
131 + 20 = 151 pts.

Player B's <u>Total Score</u> for the round is
106 + 10 + 10 = 126 pts.

Player A wins the round.

Player A won two consecutive rounds with at least a 20 pt difference.

Player A is the winner of the game.

Chapter 20
Hachi

Difficulty: Expert

Players: 2

Deck: 48 card flower deck (remove all Jokers)

Rounds: Variable

Objective: Obtain the most points by capturing cards from the field and forming yaku.

Important Notes:
- This game uses unique card capturing mechanics.

Capture Chart

Hachi uses unique card capturing mechanics.

Unlike most other Hanafuda games, cards do not generally capture cards of the same month.

The following is a chart of the months and the months that they can capture:

FIGURE 20.1 **Capture Chart**

Month	Capture
January (1)	Feb (2), July (7), Dec (12)
February (2)	Jan (1), June (6), Nov (11)
March (3)	May (5), Oct (10)
April (4)	April (4), Sep (9)
May (5)	Mar (3), Aug (8)
June (6)	Feb (2), July (7), Dec (12)
July (7)	Jan (1), June (6), Nov (11)
August (8)	May (5), Oct (10)
September (9)	Apr (4), Sep (9)
October (10)	Mar (3), Aug (8)
November (11)	Feb (2), July (7), Dec (12)
December(12)	Jan (1), June (6), Nov (11)

Note: It may be helpful to remember that the months that the months can capture are five months apart from one another.

Tip: If playing with the Fusion deck, the months can be identified by using the number indices.

Setup

Deal 7 cards to each player face down.
Deal 6 cards face up on the table to form the field.
The remaining cards are placed face down to form a draw pile.

Check for Misdeals

When a misdeal occurs, all cards are returned to the deck and reshuffled. The dealer remains the same and the round is dealt again.

A misdeal occurs when 4 cards of the same month are dealt into the field.

Check for Hiki

If 3 cards of the same month are dealt into the field these cards are stacked together to form a hiki. The player who plays the matching card captures all 4 at once.

Playing a Round

Play begins with the first player and continues counter-clockwise.

The current player plays a card from their hand, plays a card from the deck, and then claims the cards that were captured. (See **Three Phases of Play** p. 20.)

Play then passes to the next player.

Play continues in this manner until the end of the round.

End of Round

The round ends when all players run out of cards in their hand.

The winner of the round becomes the dealer for the next round.

Scoring

Each player's score for the round will be the total value of the player's captured cards plus the value of any yaku that they captured.

Player's Score = Total Value of Player's Captured Cards + Total Value of Player's Captured Yaku.

The player with the highest score is the winner of the round.

Record the scores for each round.

Determining the Winner of the Game

If a player wins two consecutive rounds by 20 points or more, then that player wins the game.

Card Values

Brights = 10 pts
Tens = 10 pts
Ribbons = 1 pt
Chaffs = 10 pts

Yaku

Players can score for each of the following yaku.
Players total their points from each captured yaku.

Note: The same card may be used to capture more than one yaku.

FIGURE 20.2 **Yaku**

Earn points from <u>each</u> of the following:

Twelve Four Eleven = 10 pts

Poetry Twelve Four Eleven = 20 pts

Five Six Ten = 10 pts

Poetry Five Six Ten = 20 pts

Five Four Six = 10 pts

Poetry Five Four Six = 20 pts

Seven Five Three = 10 pts

Poetry Seven Five Three = 20 pts

Nine Eleven Three = 10 pts

Poetry Nine Eleven Three = 20 pts

Eight Four Eleven = 10 pts

Poetry Eight Four Eleven = 20 pts

Seven Eight Nine = 10 pts

Poetry Seven Eight Nine = 20 pts

One Two Three = 10 pts

Poetry One Two Three = 20 pts

Three Five Six = 10 pts

Poetry Three Five Six = 20 pts

Ten Seven Eight = 10 pts

Poetry Ten Seven Eight = 20 pts

Scoring Example

Scoring Example

Round 1:

Player A's Total Card Value was 153 points.
Player B's Total Card Value was 133 points.

Player A captured no yaku.
Player B captured no yaku.

Player A's <u>Total Score</u> for the round is 153 points.
Player B's <u>Total Score</u> for the round is 133 points.

Player A wins the round.

Round 2:

Player A's Total Card Value was 131 points.
Player B's Total Card Value was 106 points.

Player A captured a yaku worth 20 points (Poetry *One Two Three*).

Player B captured a yaku worth 10 points (*Five Six Ten*) and a yaku worth 10 points (*Three Five Six*).

Player A's <u>Total Score</u> for the round is
131 + 20 = 151 pts.

Player B's <u>Total Score</u> for the round is
106 + 10 + 10 = 126 pts.

Player A wins the round.

Player A won two consecutive rounds with at least a 20 pt difference.

Player A is the winner of the game.

Chapter 21
Tensho

Difficulty: Expert

Players: 2

Deck: 45 card flower deck (remove Jokers and the 3 December Paulownia Chaffs)

Rounds: Player Determined

Objective: Obtain the most points by capturing cards from the field and forming yaku.

Important Notes:
- This game uses unique month ordering.
- There are two sets of yaku in Tensho, but only one may be used per round.

Month Order

Tensho uses a unique month ordering.
The following is a chart of the months and the flowers that represent them:

FIGURE 21.1 **Month Order**

Month	Flower					Month	Flower				
January	Pine					July	Lespedeza				
February	**Rain**					August	Moon				
March	Cherry					September	Chrysanthemum				
April	Wisteria					October	Maple				
May	Iris					November	**Peony**				
June	**Paulownia**					December	**Plum**				

Note: The flowers indicated in bold highlight the non-standard month-flower pairings.

Dealing Method

Traditional games of Tensho use a unique dealing method for setup.

This dealing method is <u>optional</u> as it is not critical to gameplay.

1. Deal 3 cards face down to the field.
2. Deal 3 cards face down in a stack to each corner of the field.
3. Repeat steps 1 and 2.
4. Deal 3 cards face down to the field.
5. Deal 3 cards to the dealer's choice of any two corners of the field.
6. The 6 remaining cards are discarded. They will not be used in the round.
7. The two stacks of 9 on the corners of the field are combined to form the draw pile.
8. The dealer chooses one of the two face down stacks of 6 cards to become their hand.
9. The other player receives the remaining stack of 6 cards as their hand.
10. The 9 face down in the field are turned face up.

Setup

Determine Number of Rounds

Players agree on the number of rounds to play.

Determine Yaku Set

Players agree on the yaku set that will be used for scoring this round.

Note: If the players can not agree on a set then the dealer chooses.

Deal Cards

Deal 6 cards to each player face down.

Deal 9 cards face up on the table to form the field.

Deal 6 cards to a discard. These cards are removed from the round.

The remaining 18 cards are placed face down to form a draw pile.

Check for Misdeals

When a misdeal occurs, all cards are returned to the deck and reshuffled. The dealer remains the same and the round is dealt again.

A misdeal occurs when any of the following occur:

- If 4 cards of the same month are dealt into the field.
- If a player is dealt 4 cards of the same month.

Note: Players do not have to claim a misdeal for the cards dealt to their hand.

Check for Hiki

If 3 cards of the same month are dealt into the field these cards are stacked together to form a hiki. The player who plays the matching card captures all 4 at once.

Playing a Round

Play begins with the first player and continues counter-clockwise.

The current player plays a card from their hand, plays a card from the deck, and then claims the cards that were captured. (See **Three Phases of Play** p. 20.)

Play then passes to the next player.

Play continues in this manner until the end of the round.

December

Since there is only one December card in the deck the following rules apply:

- If it is dealt into the field, no player can capture it.

  The card remains in the field.

- If it is dealt into a player's hand, then that player may automatically capture it.

  The card is placed in that player's capture area.

- If a player draws it from the deck, then that player may automatically capture it.

  The card is placed in that player's capture area.

End of Round

The round ends when one of the following occurs:

- A player captures an automatic win.
- All players run out of cards in their hand.

The winner of the round becomes the dealer for the next round.

Scoring

If a player captured an Automatic Win:

If a player captured a yaku that counts as an <u>Automatic Win</u>, then that player automatically wins the round. (See **Yaku**.)

If no player captured an Automatic Win:

If no player captured an Automatic Win, then each player calculates their score.

Each player's score for the round will be the total value of the player's captured yaku.

> *Player's Score = Total Value of Player's Captured Yaku*

The player with the <u>highest Total Yaku Value</u> is the winner of the round.

Resolving Ties

If there is a tie, then the player who captured the <u>most Chaffs</u> wins the round.

If there is still a tie, then each player totals the value of their captured cards.

The player with the <u>highest Total Card Value</u> wins the round.

Determining the Winner of the Game

Record wins for each round.

The player who won the most rounds wins the game.

Card Values

Yaku

Reminder: There are two sets of yaku in Tensho, but only one may be used per round.

Player's may only score from the yaku set that was determined during Setup.

Player's total their points from each captured yaku.

FIGURE 21.2 Yaku (Set One)

Earn points from <u>each</u> of the following:

Front One Two Three = 100 pts

Front Seven Eight Nine = 100 pts

Front Eight Four Twelve = 100 pts

Back One Two Three = 50 pts

Back Seven Eight Nine = 50 pts

Back Eight Four Twelve = 50 pts

Front One Two Ten = 100 pts

Front Ten Nine Twelve = 100 pts

Front Eight Four Eleven Twelve = 100 pts

Back One Two Ten = 50 pts

Back Ten Nine Twelve = 50 pts

Back Eight Four Eleven Twelve = 50 pts

Front Three Four Five = 100 pts

Front Eight Four Eleven = 100 pts

Front Nine Eleven Three = 100 pts

Back Three Four Five = 50 pts

Back Eight Four Eleven = 50 pts

Back Nine Eleven Three = 50 pts

Front Seven Five Three = 100 pts

Front Four Eleven Twelve = 100 pts

Front Five Six Ten = AUTOMATIC WIN

Back Seven Five Three = 50 pts

Back Four Eleven Twelve = 50 pts

Back Five Six Ten = 50 pts

FIGURE 21.3 Yaku (Set Two)

Earn points from <u>each</u> of the following:

Front One Two Three = 100 pts

Back One Two Three = 50 pts

Front One Two Ten = 100 pts

Back One Two Ten = 50 pts

Front Three Four Five = 100 pts

Back Three Four Five = 50 pts

Front Seven Eight Nine = 100 pts

Back Seven Eight Nine = 50 pts

Front Ten Nine Twelve = 100 pts

Back Ten Nine Twelve = 50 pts

Front Nine Eleven Three = 100 pts

Back Nine Eleven Three = 50 pts

Front Ten Seven Eight = 100 pts

Back Ten Seven Eight = 50 pts

Front Eight Nine Ten = 100 pts

Back Eight Nine Ten = 50 pts

Front Seven Eight Nine Ten = 100 pts

Back Seven Eight Nine Ten = 50 pts

Front Five Six Ten = 100 pts

Back Five Six Ten = AUTOMATIC WIN

One Six Four = AUTOMATIC WIN

Scoring Example

Scoring Example 1

Player A captured no yaku.

Player B captured no yaku.

Player A captured 8 Chaffs.

Player B captured 7 Chaffs.

Player A is the winner of the round.

Scoring Example 2

Player A captured a 100 pt yaku (*Front Four Three Five*).

Player B captured no yaku.

Player A is the winner of the round.

Scoring Example 3

Player A captured an Automatic Win (*One Six Four*).

Player A is the winner of the round.

SECTION II
Sequence Games

Chapter 22
Poka

Difficulty: Beginner

Players: 2

Deck: 48 card flower deck (remove Jokers)

Rounds: Variable

Objective: Be the first player to play all of the cards from their hand.

Important Notes:

- This game requires 9 tokens (chips, candy, coins, fake money, or whatever you have on hand) or a notepad for tracking player points.
- Poka is the base game for Sequence games in this section.

Wild Cards

Wild cards can be played as any month.

There are 3 wild cards in Poka:

- Crane (January Bright)
- January Ribbon
- Nightingale Warbler (February Ten)

FIGURE 22.1 Wild Cards

Setup

Place 9 tokens on the table.

Deal 6 cards to each player face down.

The remaining cards are placed face down on the table to form a draw pile.

Turn up the top card of the draw pile and place it in the center of the field.

This card is considered the base card.

Players pick up and view their cards in a "fan" position while keeping them hidden from other players (similar to card games such as Poker or Rummy).

Check Hands for Automatic Wins

Players check their hands to see if they were dealt an Automatic Win.

If a player is dealt an Automatic Win, that player automatically wins the round.

The player is awarded the corresponding bonus as follows:

- All 3 Wild Cards = 2 tokens
- 3 sets of 2 cards of the same month (i.e. 3 pairs) = 2 tokens
- Any 3 January cards = 2 tokens
- 4 cards of the same month (i.e. 4 of a kind) = 5 tokens

Playing a Round

Play begins with the first player and continues counter-clockwise.

A player takes one of three actions during their turn:

- They may choose to play a card onto the base card.
- They may choose to call "Pass" and pass their turn.
- Or, they are forced to call "Pass" and pass their turn.

If the player chooses to play a card:

The player chooses a sequential card from their hand and plays it face up onto the base card.

The player may play as many cards as they can during their turn, <u>however</u>:

- Each card must be played in <u>ascending sequential</u> order.
- Each card must be played down one at a time.
- Only one card from each month can be played per turn.

For example: Player A has an April, April, May, and March card in their hand. The base card is a March. Player A may only play <u>one</u> of their April cards onto the base card. Player A then plays their May card. The next card played must then be a June, followed by a July, and so on.

Note: The sequence loops. (i.e. December is followed by January.)

When the active player can no longer play a sequential card, that player announces the end of their turn and the player's turn ends.

The next player's turn begins.

The next player must continue the sequence from the top card.

If the player <u>chooses</u> to call "Pass":

If the player chooses not to play <u>any</u> cards on their turn then they must call "Pass".

The player's turn ends and play passes to the next player.

The next player must continue the sequence from the top card.

If the player <u>must</u> call "Pass":

If the player can not play <u>any</u> cards on their turn then they must call "Pass".

The player's turn ends and play passes to the next player.

The next player must continue the sequence from the top card.

When both players <u>consecutively</u> call "Pass":

When both players consecutively call "Pass", a new card is turned up from the draw pile.

This card is the new base card.

Play continues from the new base card with the player that first called "Pass".

Note: If the deck becomes depleted before a player runs out of cards in their hand, then the deck is reshuffled and play continues.

Special Rules During Play

January

If the base card is a January and the active player has both a January and a February in their hand, then the player may play both cards.

This special rule <u>only</u> applies to January.

End of Round

The round ends when a player runs out of cards in their hand.

The winner of the round becomes the dealer for the next round.

Scoring

The first player to play all of the cards from their hand is the winner of the round.

The winner of the round takes 1 token from the table.

If a player manages to play all of the cards in their hand on their <u>first</u> turn, then that player receives 2 tokens instead of 1.

The first player to collect 5 tokens wins the game.

Gameplay Example

Player A was dealt March, February, May, May, December, June.

Player B was dealt January Crane (Wild), January, July, September, November, December.

The base card is an April.

Since only one card can be played per month in Poka, Player A plays down one May card.

Player A then plays down their June card.

Player A has no more sequential cards to play, so they end their turn.

The top card is now June.

Player B plays July.

Player B then plays their January Crane (Wild) as August.

Player B then plays down September.

Player B has no more sequential cards, so they end their turn.

The top card in now September.

Player A has no sequential cards to play, so they must call "Pass".

Player B has no sequential cards to play, so they must call "Pass".

A new card is turned up from the deck to create a new base.

The new base card is October.

Player A was the first to pass, so Player A goes first.

Player A has no sequential cards to play, so they must call "Pass".

Player B then plays down their November, followed by their December, and then January.

Player B is out of cards.

Player B is the winner of the round.

Player B takes 1 token from the table.

Gameplay Variations

Players can choose to include one or more of these variations. Just make sure that everyone agrees.

Game End Scoring Variations:

Best of Five

Place 5 tokens on the table during **Setup** instead of 9.

The first player to collect 3 tokens wins the game.

Best of Three

Place 3 tokens on the table during **Setup** instead of 9.

The first player to collect 2 tokens wins the game.

Chapter 23
Hiyoko (Simplified)

Difficulty: Beginner

Players: 2-4 (Best with 2)

Deck: 45 card flower deck (remove Jokers, the Peony Ribbon, and the 2 Peony Chaffs)

Rounds: 5 or less

Objective: Be the first player to play all of the cards from their hand.

Important Notes:
- You can find the rules for the traditional version of "Hiyoko" on page 133.

Wild Cards

In Hiyoko Simplified, Wild Cards are cards that have special abilities.

There are 10 wild cards in Hiyoko Simplified.

There are two types of Wild Cards: Hand Wilds and Base Wilds.

Hand Wilds are cards that have a special ability <u>only</u> if they are <u>played from a player's hand.</u>

Base Wilds are cards that have a special ability <u>only</u> if they are the <u>base card of the stack.</u>

FIGURE 23.1 **Hand Wild Cards**

Wild Card	Special Ability
	Can be used as any month from January to October.
	Can be used as any month from January to October.
	Can be used as any month from February to November.
	Can be used as any month from February to November.
	Can be used as any month from January to December.

FIGURE 23.2 **Base Wild Cards**

Wild Card	Special Ability
	Can be used as January, but only when this card is the base.
	Can be used as January, but only when this card is the base.
	Can be used as January, but only when this card is the base.
	Can be used as January, but only when this card is the base.
	Can be used any month from January to December, but only when this card is the base.

Setup

Deal 6 cards to each player face down.

The remaining cards are placed face down on the table to form a draw pile.

Turn up the top card of the draw pile and place it in the center of the field.

This card is considered the base card.

Players pick up and view their cards in a "fan" position while keeping them hidden from other players (similar to card games such as Poker or Rummy).

Playing a Round

Important: Hiyoko's Playing a Round section is the same as Poka's. (See **Playing a Round** on page 121 of **Poka** for unabridged instructions.)

Play begins with the first player and continues counter-clockwise.

A player takes one of three actions during their turn:

- They may choose to play a card onto the base card.
- They may choose to call "Pass" and pass their turn.
- Or, they are forced to call "Pass" and pass their turn.

Play alternates between the two players until <u>both</u> players <u>consecutively</u> call "Pass".

When both players consecutively call "Pass", a new card is turned up from the draw pile.

This card is the new base card.

Play continues from this base card with the player that first called "Pass".

Note: If the deck becomes depleted before a player runs out of cards in their hand, then the deck is reshuffled and play continues.

Special Rules During Play

January

If the base card is a January and the active player has both a January and a February in their hand, then the player may play both cards.

This special rule <u>only</u> applies to January.

End of Round

The round ends when a player runs out of cards in their hand.

The winner of the round becomes the dealer for the next round.

Scoring

The first player to play all of the cards from their hand is the winner of the round.

The first player to win 3 rounds wins the game.

Gameplay Example

Player A was dealt March Ribbon (Hand Wild), May, May, June, March, February.

Player B was dealt January Crane (Hand Wild), January, July, September, December, November.

The base card is April.

Since only one card can be played per month in Hiyoko, Player A plays down one May card.

Player A then plays down their June card.

Player A has no more sequential cards to play and wants to keep their Wild card, so they end their turn.

The top card is now June.

Player B plays July.

Player B then plays their January Crane (Hand Wild) as August.

Player B then plays down September.

Player B has no more sequential cards, so they end their turn.

The top card is now September.

Player A has no sequential cards to play, so they must call "Pass".

Player B has no sequential cards to play, so they must call "Pass".

A new card is turned up from the deck to create a new base.

The new base card is December Chaff (Base Wild Card).

Player A was the first to pass, so Player A goes first.

Player A decide to treat the base card as a January.

Player A plays February and March.

Player A then plays their March Ribbon (Hand Wild) as April.

Player A plays May.

Player A is out of cards.

Player A wins the round.

Gameplay Variations

Players can choose to include one or more of these variations. Just make sure that everyone agrees.

Game Flow Variations:

Skip June

Since there is only one June card in the deck, June may be skipped when creating sequences.

Chapter 24

Isuri (Simplified)

Difficulty: Beginner

Players: 2-3

Deck: 46 card flower deck (remove Jokers and the 2 Peony Chaffs)

Rounds: 6

Objective: Be the first player to play all of the cards from their hand.

Important Notes:

- This game requires tokens (chips, candy, coins, fake money, or whatever you have on hand) or a notepad for tracking player points.
- You can find the rules for the traditional version of "Isuri" on page 137.

Wild Cards

In Isuri Simplified, Wild Cards are cards that have special abilities.

Note: The wild cards are the same as the wilds in Hiyoko with the addition of another wild.

There are 11 wild cards in Isuri Simplified.

There are two types of Wild Cards: Hand Wilds and Base Wilds.

Hand Wilds are cards that have a special ability only if they are played from a player's hand.

Base Wilds are cards that have a special ability only if they are the base card of the stack.

FIGURE 24.1 **Hand Wild Cards**

Wild Card	Special Ability
	Can be used as any month from January to October.
	Can be used as any month from January to October.
	Can be used as any month from February to November.
	Can be used as any month from February to November.
	Can be used as any month from January to December.

FIGURE 24.2 **Base Wild Cards**

Wild Card	Special Ability
	Can be used as January, but only when this card is the base.
	Can be used as January, but only when this card is the base.
	Can be used as January, but only when this card is the base.
	Can be used as January, but only when this card is the base.
	Can be used as January, but only when this card is the base.
	Can be used any month from January to December, but only when this card is the base.

Setup

Place 1 token on the table.

Deal 6 cards to each player face down.

The remaining cards are placed face down on the table to form a draw pile.

Turn up the top card of the draw pile and place it in the center of the field.

This card is considered the base card.

Players pick up and view their cards in a "fan" position while keeping them hidden from other players (similar to card games such as Poker or Rummy).

Playing a Round

Important: Isuri's Playing a Round section is the same as Poka's with the exception of <u>two modifications</u> identified as 'Important' below. (See **Playing a Round** on page 121 of **Poka** for unabridged instructions.)

Play begins with the first player and continues counter-clockwise.

A player takes one of three actions during their turn:

- They may choose to play a card onto the base card.
- They may choose to call "Pass" and pass their turn.
- Or, they are forced to call "Pass" and pass their turn.

Important: A player may play multiple cards of the same month at one time.

For example: Player A has an April, April, May, and March card in their hand. The base card is a March. Player A plays both of their April cards onto the base card. Player A then plays their May card. The next card played must then be a June, followed by a July, and so on.

Play alternates between the two players until <u>both</u> players <u>consecutively</u> call "Pass".

Important: When both players consecutively call "Pass" a token is placed on the table.

A new card is turned up from the draw pile.

This card is the new base card.

Play continues from this base card with the player that first called "Pass".

Note: If the deck becomes depleted before a player runs out of cards in their hand, then the deck is reshuffled and play continues.

Special Rules During Play

January

If the base card is a January and the active player has both a January and a February in their hand, then the player may play both cards.

This special rule <u>only</u> applies to January.

End of Round

The round ends when a player runs out of cards in their hand.

The winner of the round becomes the dealer for the next round.

Scoring

The first player to play all of the cards from their hand is the winner of the round.

Points are awarded to the winner of each round.

Points that are scored by the winner are <u>taken</u> from the opponent.

Calculating Base Score

Players calculate the Base Score for the round by multiplying the number of tokens on the table by the number of the month of the last card that the winner played to win the round.

For example: If there were 2 tokens on the table and the last card the winner played was March then the Base Score would by 2 x 3 = 6.

Base Score = Total Tokens x Winner's Last Card

Important: When calculating Base Score, January is considered a 10 (instead of a 1).

The winner calculates their Round Score as follows:

- If the winner won by playing three cards of the same month, then the Base Score is tripled.

Round Score = Base Score x 3

- If the winner won by playing four cards of the same month, then the Base Score is quadrupled.

Round Score = Base Score x 4

- If the winner won by playing five cards of the same month, then the Base Score is quintupled.

Round Score = Base Score x 5

- If the winner won by playing six cards of the same month, then the Base Score is sextupled and increased by 10 times the Total Tokens.

Round Score = Base Score x 6 + (Total Tokens x 10)

- If none of the above conditions were met, then the Base Score is the Round Score.

Round Score = Base Score

If the winner won on their first turn of the round, then the Round Score is increased by 10 times the Total Tokens.

Round Score = Round Score + (Total Tokens x 10)

The winner <u>takes</u> their Round Score from their opponent.

Important: Tokens are <u>not</u> removed from the table after each round. Tokens remain on the table until the end of the game.

When 6 rounds have been played, players calculate their combined total score.

The player with the highest score at the end of 6 rounds wins the game.

Gameplay Example

Player A was dealt May, May, March, February, November, June.

Player B was dealt January Crane (Hand Wild), January, July, September, December, November.

The base card is April.

Since multiple cards can be played per month in Isuri, Player A plays down both of their May cards.

Player A then plays down their June card.

Player A has no more sequential cards to play, so they end their turn.

The top card is now June.

Player B plays July.

Player B then plays their January Crane (Hand Wild) as August.

Player B then plays down September.

Player B has no more sequential cards, so they end their turn.

The top card is now September.

Player A has no sequential cards to play, so they must call "Pass".

Player B has no sequential cards to play, so they must call "Pass".

A token is placed on the table.

A new card is turned up from the deck to create a new base.

The new base card is December Chaff (Base Wild Card).

Player A was the first to pass, so Player A goes first.

Player A decide to treat the base card as a January.

Player A plays February and March.

Player A has no more sequential cards to play, so they end their turn.

The top card is now March.

Player B has no sequential cards to play, so they must call "Pass".

Player A has no sequential cards to play, so they must call "Pass".

A token is placed on the table.

A new card is turned up from the deck to create a new base.

The new base card is October.

Player B was the first to pass, so Player B goes first.

Player B plays November, December, January.

Player B is out of cards.

Player B wins the round.

Player B's Base Score is Tokens (2) x January (1) = 2 pts.

Since Player B's last card was January they multiply their base score by 10.

Player B's Round Score is now 20 pts.

Player B takes 20 points from Player A.

Chapter 25
Kage

Difficulty: Beginner

Players: 2

Deck: 48 card flower deck plus 4-6 Jokers

Rounds: 5 or less

Objective: Be the first player to play all of the cards from their hand.

Important Notes:

- A non-traditional sequence game that we created.
- This game is entirely luck based.

Wild Cards

Jokers are considered Wild Cards.

Wild Cards can be played as any month.

A soon as a Joker is played as a month, they are considered that month.

If a player has a Joker in their hand and no other card that can be played, then the player <u>must</u> play the Joker.

If a player draws a Joker, then they <u>must</u> play it immediately.

Setup

Deal 6 cards to each player face down.

The remaining cards are placed face down on the table to form a draw pile.

Turn up the top card of the draw pile and place it in the center of the field.

This card is considered the discard.

Players pick up and view their cards in a "fan" position while keeping them hidden from other players (similar to card games such as Poker or Rummy).

Check Hands for Automatic Wins

Players check their hands to see if they were dealt an Automatic Win.

If a player is dealt an Automatic Win, that player automatically wins the round.

The following hands are considered Automatic Wins:

- 4 or more Wild Cards
- 4 cards of the same month (i.e. 4 of a kind)

Playing a Round

Play begins with the first player and continues counter-clockwise.

Each player's turn occurs in three phases.

Phase One - Check for Playable Cards

The player checks their hand to see if they have any playable cards.

A playable card is any card that can be played in ascending sequential order from the top card of the discard.

Note: Since Jokers are wild, Jokers are always considered a playable card.

For example: If the top card of the discard is a May, then the only playable cards are a June or a Joker.

If the player does <u>not</u> have a playable card then they proceed to Phase Two.

If the player has a playable card then they proceed to Phase Three.

Phase Two - Drawing from Deck

The player only completes this phase if they do <u>not</u> have any playable cards in their hand.

If the player already has a playable card, then this phase is ignored and the player proceeds to Phase Three.

If the player does <u>not</u> have a playable card, then they <u>must</u> draw a card from the draw pile.

The player must continue to draw cards until they draw a playable card.

Phase Three - Playing Cards

The player chooses a playable card from their hand and plays it face up onto the discard.

The player must play as many cards as they can during their turn, however:

- Each card must be played in <u>ascending</u> <u>sequential</u> order.
- Each card must be played down one at a time.
- Only one card from each month can be played at a time.

For example: If the base card is a March then the player has to play an April. (If they have two April cards they may only play one of them.) The player then has to play a May. This is followed by June, then July and so on.

Note: The sequence loops. (i.e. December is followed by January.)

Important: If the player has a playable card then they must play it. This includes Jokers.

When the active player can no longer play a sequential card or Joker, that player announces the end of their turn and the player's turn ends.

The next player's turn begins.

End of Round

The round ends when one of the following occurs:

- A player runs out of cards in their hand.
- Or, the deck is exhausted.

The winner of the round becomes the dealer for the next round.

Scoring

The first player to play all of the cards from their hand is the winner of the round.

If the round ended with the deck becoming depleted, then the player with the least amount of cards in their hand is the winner.

The first player to win 3 rounds wins the game.

Gameplay Example

Player A was dealt a June, February, May, May, April, December.

Player B was dealt a Joker, January, July, September, October, December.

The discard is a March.

Player A plays down their April card.

Player A then plays down one May card.

Player A then plays down their June card.

Player A has no more sequential cards to play so they end their turn.

The top card of the discard is now June.

Player B plays their July card.

Player B then plays their Joker as August.

Player B then plays down September and then October.

Player B has no more sequential cards so they end their turn.

The top card in of the discard in now October.

Player A has no sequential cards to play. Player A must draw until they draw a playable card.

Player A draws an April.

Since Player A still has no playable card they must draw again.

Player A draws a March and then a Joker.

Player A must play the Joker.

Player A then plays their December.

Player A has no more sequential cards to play so they end their turn.

Player B plays their January.

Player B has no more sequential cards to play so they end their turn.

Player A plays their February, then March, then April, and then May.

Player A is out of cards.

Player A is the winner of the round.

Chapter 26
Hiyoko

Difficulty: Intermediate

Players: 2-4 (Best with 2)

Deck: 45 card flower deck (remove Jokers, the 3 December Paulownia Chaffs)

Rounds: 5 or less

Objective: Be the first player to play all of the cards from their hand.

Important Notes:
- This game uses unique month ordering.

Month Order

Hiyoko uses a unique month ordering. This is the same month ordering that Tensho uses.

The following is a chart of the months and the flowers that represent them:

FIGURE 26.1 **Month Order**

Month	Flower		Month	Flower	
January	Pine		July	Lespedeza	
February	**Rain**		August	Moon	
March	Cherry		September	Chrysanthemum	
April	Wisteria		October	Maple	
May	Iris		November	**Peony**	
June	**Paulownia**		December	**Plum**	

Note: The flowers indicated in bold highlight the non-standard month-flower pairings.

Wild Cards

In Hiyoko, Wild Cards are cards that have special abilities.

There are 10 wild cards in Hiyoko.

There are two types of Wild Cards: Hand Wilds and Base Wilds.

Hand Wilds are cards that have a special ability only if they are played from a player's hand.

Base Wilds are cards that have a special ability only if they are the base card of the stack.

FIGURE 26.2 **Hand Wild Cards**

Wild Card	Special Ability
	Can be used as any month from January to October.
	Can be used as any month from January to October.
	Can be used as any month from February to November.
	Can be used as any month from February to November.
	Can be used as any month from January to December.

FIGURE 26.3 **Base Wild Cards**

Wild Card	Special Ability
	Can be used as January, but only when this card is the base.
	Can be used as January, but only when this card is the base.
	Can be used as January, but only when this card is the base.
	Can be used as January, but only when this card is the base.
	Can be used any month from January to December, but only when this card is the base.

Setup

Deal 6 cards to each player face down.

The remaining cards are placed face down on the table to form a draw pile.

Turn up the top card of the draw pile and place it in the center of the field.

This card is considered the base card.

Players pick up and view their cards in a "fan" position while keeping them hidden from other players (similar to card games such as Poker or Rummy).

Playing a Round

Important: Hiyoko's Playing a Round section is the same as Poka's. (See **Playing a Round** on page 121 of **Poka** for unabridged instructions.)

Play begins with the first player and continues counter-clockwise.

A player takes one of three actions during their turn:

- They may choose to play a card onto the base card.
- They may choose to call "Pass" and pass their turn.
- Or, they are forced to call "Pass" and pass their turn.

Play alternates between the two players until both players consecutively call "Pass".

When both players consecutively call "Pass", a new card is turned up from the draw pile.

This card is the new base card.

Play continues from this base card with the player that first called "Pass".

Note: If the deck becomes depleted before a player runs out of cards in their hand, then the deck is reshuffled and play continues.

Special Rules During Play

January

If the base card is a January and the active player has both a January and a February in their hand, then the player may play both cards.

This special rule <u>only</u> applies to January.

End of Round

The round ends when a player runs out of cards in their hand.

The winner of the round becomes the dealer for the next round.

Scoring

The first player to play all of the cards from their hand is the winner of the round.

The first player to win 3 rounds wins the game.

Gameplay Example

Player A was dealt March Ribbon (Hand Wild), May, May, June, March, February.

Player B was dealt January Crane (Hand Wild), January, July, September, December, November.

The base card is April.

Since only one card can be played per month in Hiyoko, Player A plays down one May card.

Player A then plays down their June card.

Player A has no more sequential cards to play and wants to keep their Wild card, so they end their turn.

The top card is now June.

Player B plays July.

Player B then plays their January Crane (Hand Wild) as August.

Player B then plays down September.

Player B has no more sequential cards, so they end their turn.

The top card is now September.

Player A has no sequential cards to play, so they must call "Pass".

Player B has no sequential cards to play, so they must call "Pass".

A new card is turned up from the deck to create a new base.

The new base card is December Chaff (Base Wild Card).

Player A was the first to pass, so Player A goes first.

Player A decide to treat the base card as a January.

Player A plays February and March.

Player A then plays their March Ribbon (Hand Wild) as April.

Player A plays May.

Player A is out of cards.

Player A wins the round.

Gameplay Variations

Players can choose to include one or more of these variations. Just make sure that everyone agrees.

Game Flow Variations:

Skip June

Since there is only one June card in the deck, June may be skipped when creating sequences.

Chapter 27
Isuri

Difficulty: Intermediate

Players: 2-3

Deck: 46 card flower deck (remove Jokers and the 2 of the December Paulownia Chaffs)

Rounds: 6

Objective: Be the first player to play all of the cards from their hand.

Important Notes:
- This game uses unique month ordering.
- This game requires tokens (chips, candy, coins, fake money, or whatever you have on hand) or a notepad for tracking player points.

Month Order

Isuri uses a unique month ordering. This is the same month ordering that Tensho uses.

The following is a chart of the months and the flowers that represent them:

FIGURE 27.1 **Month Order**

Month	Flower		Month	Flower	
January	Pine		July	Lespedeza	
February	**Rain**		August	Moon	
March	Cherry		September	Chrysanthemum	
April	Wisteria		October	Maple	
May	Iris		November	**Peony**	
June	**Paulownia**		December	**Plum**	

Note: The flowers indicated in bold highlight the non-standard month-flower pairings.

Wild Cards

Wild Cards are cards that have special abilities.

Note: The wild cards are the same as the wilds in Hiyoko with the addition of another wild.

There are 11 wild cards in Isuri.

There are two <u>types</u> of Wild Cards: Hand Wilds and Base Wilds.

Hand Wilds are cards that have a special ability <u>only</u> if they are <u>played from a player's hand</u>.

Base Wilds are cards that have a special ability <u>only</u> if they are the <u>base card of the stack</u>.

FIGURE 27.2 **Hand Wild Cards**

Wild Card	Special Ability
	Can be used as any month from January to October.
	Can be used as any month from January to October.
	Can be used as any month from February to November.
	Can be used as any month from February to November.
	Can be used as any month from January to December.

FIGURE 27.3 **Base Wild Cards**

Wild Card	Special Ability
	Can be used as January, but only when this card is the base.
	Can be used as January, but only when this card is the base.
	Can be used as January, but only when this card is the base.
	Can be used as January, but only when this card is the base.
	Can be used as January, but only when this card is the base.
	Can be used any month from January to December, but only when this card is the base.

Setup

Place 1 token on the table.

Deal 6 cards to each player face down.

The remaining cards are placed face down on the table to form a draw pile.

Turn up the top card of the draw pile and place it in the center of the field.

This card is considered the base card.

Players pick up and view their cards in a "fan" position while keeping them hidden from other players (similar to card games such as Poker or Rummy).

Playing a Round

Important: Isuri's Playing a Round section is the same as Poka's with the exception of <u>two modifications</u> identified as '**Important**' below. (See **Playing a Round** on page 121 of **Poka** for unabridged instructions.)

Play begins with the first player and continues counter-clockwise.

A player takes one of three actions during their turn:
- They may choose to play a card onto the base card.
- They may choose to call "Pass" and pass their turn.
- Or, they are forced to call "Pass" and pass their turn.

Important: A player may play multiple cards of the same month at one time.

For example: Player A has an April, April, May, and March card in their hand. The base card is a March. Player A plays both of their April cards onto the base card. Player A then plays their May card. The next card played must then be a June, followed by a July, and so on.

Play alternates between the two players until both players <u>consecutively</u> call "Pass".

Important: When both players consecutively call "Pass" a token is placed on the table.

A new card is turned up from the draw pile.

This card is the new base card.

Play continues from this base card with the player that first called "Pass".

Note: If the deck becomes depleted before a player runs out of cards in their hand, then the deck is reshuffled and play continues.

Special Rules During Play

January

If the base card is a January and the active player has both a January and a February in their hand, then the player may play both cards.

This special rule <u>only</u> applies to January.

End of Round

The round ends when a player runs out of cards in their hand.

The winner of the round becomes the dealer for the next round.

Scoring

The first player to play all of the cards from their hand is the winner of the round.

Points are awarded to the winner of each round.

Points that are scored by the winner are <u>taken</u> from the opponent.

Calculating Base Score

Players calculate the Base Score for the round by multiplying the number of tokens on the table by the number of the month of the last card that the winner played to win the round.

For example: If there were 2 tokens on the table and the last card the winner played was March then the Base Score would by 2 x 3 = 6.

Base Score = Total Tokens x Winner's Last Card

Important: When calculating Base Score, January is considered a 10 (instead of a 1).

The winner calculates their Round Score as follows:

- If the winner won by playing three cards of the same month, then the Base Score is tripled.

Round Score = Base Score x 3

- If the winner won by playing four cards of the same month, then the Base Score is quadrupled.

Round Score = Base Score x 4

- If the winner won by playing five cards of the same month, then the Base Score is quintupled.

Round Score = Base Score x 5

- If the winner won by playing six cards of the same month, then the Base Score is sextupled and increased by 10 times the Total Tokens.

Round Score = Base Score x 6 + (Total Tokens x 10)

- If none of the above conditions were met, then the Base Score is the Round Score.

Round Score = Base Score

If the winner won on their first turn of the round, then the Round Score is increased by 10 times the Total Tokens.

Round Score = Round Score + (Total Tokens x 10)

The winner <u>takes</u> their Round Score from their opponent.

Important: Tokens are <u>not</u> removed from the table after each round. Tokens remain on the table until the end of the game.

When 6 rounds have been played, players calculate their combined total score.

The player with the highest score at the end of 6 rounds wins the game.

Gameplay Example

Player A was dealt May, May, March, February, November, June.

Player B was dealt January Crane (Hand Wild), January, July, September, December, November.

The base card is April.

Since multiple cards can be played per month in Isuri, Player A plays down both of their May cards.

Player A then plays down their June card.

Player A has no more sequential cards to play, so they end their turn.

The top card is now June.

Player B plays July.

Player B then plays their January Crane (Hand Wild) as August.

Player B then plays down September.

Player B has no more sequential cards, so they end their turn.

The top card is now September.

Player A has no sequential cards to play, so they must call "Pass".

Player B has no sequential cards to play, so they must call "Pass".

A token is placed on the table.

A new card is turned up from the deck to create a new base.

The new base card is December Chaff (Base Wild Card).

Player A was the first to pass, so Player A goes first.

Player A decide to treat the base card as a January.

Player A plays February and March.

Player A has no more sequential cards to play, so they end their turn.

The top card is now March.

Player B has no sequential cards to play, so they must call "Pass".

Player A has no sequential cards to play, so they must call "Pass".

A token is placed on the table.

A new card is turned up from the deck to create a new base.

The new base card is October.

Player B was the first to pass, so Player B goes first.

Player B plays November, December, January.

Player B is out of cards.

Player B wins the round.

Player B's Base Score is Tokens (2) x January (1) = 2 pts.

Since Player B's last card was January they multiply their base score by 10.

Player B's Round Score is now 20 pts.

Player B takes 20 points from Player A.

SECTION III
Luck Games

Chapter 28

Sutda (Simplified)

Difficulty: Beginner

Players: 2-10

Deck: 20 select cards of the flower deck. (2 cards from each of the first 10 months. The first card (Bright or Ten) and the last card (4th Chaff) of each of those 10 months).

Rounds: Player Determined

Objective: To be the player with the highest valued hand.

Important Notes:

- Sutda is a very quick and simple game that was traditionally intended for gambling.
- The basic gameplay of Sutda (Simplified) is the same as Sutda, however the deck and Hand Combos have been modified to make the game easier to play.
- You can find the rules for the traditional version of "Sutda" on page 166.

Setup

Players agree on the number of rounds they want to play.

Deal 2 cards to each player face down.

Playing a Round

Players reveal their cards.

End of Round

The player with the highest ranking Hand Combo wins the round.

The winner of the round becomes the dealer for the next round.

Scoring

Only the winner of the round receives points for their hand.

If a player was dealt a Hand Combo:

The winner of the round is the player with the highest <u>ranking</u> Hand Combo.

The winner receives points for their Hand Combo.

Note: Hand Combos are ranked from 1 to 17. 1 being the highest and 17 the lowest.

If no player was dealt a Hand Combo:

If no player was dealt a Hand Combo this round, then each player calculates their Hand Value.

The Hand Value is the last digit of the sum of the months of the two cards they were dealt.

For example: If a player was dealt a June (6) and a July (7), then the value of their hand is 3.

(6 + 7 = 13) Since the 3 is the last digit of the sum, the Hand Value would be 3.

The player with the highest Hand Value is the winner of the round.

The player with the highest Hand Value receives 1 point for the round.

Note: The Hand Value is only used to determine the winner of the round. The Hand Value is not the hand's point value. The player with the highest Hand Value only receives 1 point for the round.

Players record their scores each round.

The player with the highest total score at the end of the predetermined number of rounds is the winner of the game.

Hand Combos

Hand Combos are ranked from 1 to 17 as follows:

FIGURE 28.1 Hand Combos

Ranked from highest (1) to lowest (17):

1 Curtain and Moon = 10 pts

2 October = 5 pts

3 September = 3 pts

4 August = 3 pts

5 July = 3 pts

6 June = 3 pts

7 May = 3 pts

8 April = 3 pts

9 March = 3 pts

10 February = 3 pts

11 January = 3 pts

12 Crane & Feb Chaff = 1 pt

13 Crane & April Chaff = 1 pt

14 Deer & April Chaff = 1pt

15 Deer & Jan Chaff = 1 pt

16 Crane & Aug Chaff = 1 pt

17 Butterfly & April Chaff = 1 pt

Chapter 29
Hiki-Kabu

Difficulty: Beginner

Players: 2-10

Deck: 40 card flower deck (remove Jokers, all November Rain, and all December Paulownia).

Rounds: Player Determined

Objective: To be the player with the highest total hand value.

Important Notes:

- A quick and simple game that was originally intended for gambling and is similar in gameplay to Blackjack and Baccarat.
- This game is traditionally played with a Kabufuda deck.
- This game requires tokens (chips, candy, coins, fake money, or whatever you have on hand) or a notepad for tracking player points.

Setup

Each player is given an equal amount of chips.

The deck is shuffled by the dealer and passed to each player.

Each player may choose to shuffle and/or cut the deck as desired.

The deck is returned to the dealer.

Deal 1 card to each player face up.

Each player must place the appropriate number of chips onto the table (i.e. pot).

The number of chips is determined by the value of the card that was dealt to them.

For example: If a player was dealt a July (7) then they must place 7 chips in the pot.

Playing a Round

Deal 1 card to each player face down.

Each player looks at their cards.

Each player totals their individual hand.

If the total of the player's hand is 10 or higher, then the first digit is ignored.

Example 1: A player with a July (6) and an August (8) would have a hand total of 4.

(6 + 8 = 14) Since the first digit is ignored then their hand total is 4.

Example 2: A player with a March (3) and a July (7) would have a hand total of 0.

(3 + 7 = 10) Since the first digit is ignored then their hand total is 0.

Each player then has the option to draw a third card.

If the player's current hand total is 7 or higher, then that player can <u>not</u> draw a third card.

If the player's current hand total is 3 or lower, then that player <u>must</u> draw a third card.

If the player's current hand total is between 4 and 6, then the player may <u>choose</u> to draw a third card.

Players reveal their cards.

End of Round

The round ends when the players reveal their cards.

Scoring

Each player totals their individual hand.

As previously explained, if the total of the player's hand is 10 or higher, then the first digit is ignored.

The player with the highest total hand wins the round.

The winner of the round is awarded the pot.

If there is a tie, the players who tied split the pot evenly.

If all players tie, then the dealer wins the round and is awarded the pot.

Special Rules During Scoring

Triple Pot

If a player has 3 cards of the same month in their hand, then their hand is automatically considered a 9.

All players must triple the original amount that they added to the *pot*.

Dealer 9 and 1

If the dealer's first card was a 9 and their second card was a 1, then the dealer wins the round and is awarded the *pot*.

This rule is regardless of what the other player's hands were (including a player with the *Triple Pot*).

This rule <u>only</u> applies to the dealer.

Note: If the dealer's first card was a 1 and the second was a 9, then this rule does <u>not</u> apply.

Gameplay Example

In a three player game.

Player A is dealt a January (1).

Player B is dealt a October (10).

Player C is dealt an August (8).

Player A must place 1 chip into the pot.

Player B must place 10 chips into the pot.

Player C must place 8 chips into the pot.

Player A is then dealt a March (2).

Player B is then dealt an August (8).

Player C is then dealt a July (7).

Player A's total hand is 1 + 2 = 3.
Therefore their hand value is 3.

Player B's total hand is 10 + 8 = 18.
Therefore their hand value is 8.

Player C's total hand is 8 + 7 = 15.
Therefore their hand value is 5.

Player A <u>must</u> draw a third card.

Player B can <u>not</u> draw a third card.

Player C may <u>choose</u> to draw a third card.

Player A draws a June (6).

Player C chooses to draw a card. Player C draws a May (5).

Player A's total hand is 1 + 2 + 6 = 9.
Therefore their hand value is 9.

Player B's total hand is 10 + 8 = 18.
Therefore their hand value is 8.

Player C's total hand is 8 + 7 + 5 = 20.
Therefore their hand value is 0.

Player A is the winner of the round.

Player A is awarded the chips that were placed in the pot.

Chapter 30
Oicho-Kabu

Difficulty: Beginner

Players: 2-10

Deck: 40 card flower deck (remove Jokers, all November Rain, and all December Paulownia).

Rounds: Player Determined

Objective: To win bets against the dealer for the highest valued hand.

Important Notes:

- A quick and simple game that was originally intended for gambling and is similar in gameplay to Baccarat.
- This game is traditionally played with a Kabufuda deck.
- This game requires tokens (chips, candy, coins, fake money, or whatever you have on hand) or a notepad for tracking player points.

In Oicho-Kabu players compete against the dealer to win bets.

Setup

Determine Ground Rules

There are a few gameplay decisions that players must agree on <u>before</u> play.

Ties

Players must decide how wins are to be handled in the case of a tie.

In the case of a tie, <u>either</u>

- the dealer wins
- OR all bets on the column returned.

Maximum Bet

Players must decide what the maximum bet for rounds will be.

The maximum bet is the <u>combined total</u> that <u>all</u> players can bet in a given round.

For example: If the maximum bet is 100 and one player bets 40, then the combined total that the other players bet may not be more than a combined total of 60 points.

Example 1: In a 4 player game. The maximum bet is 100. Player A is the dealer. Player B bets 40. Player C bets 10. Player D can then only bet up to 50. (40 + 10 + 50 =100)

Example 2: In a 4 player game. The maximum bet is 100. Player A is the dealer. Player B bets 50. Player C bets 30. Player D can then only bet up to 20. (50 + 30 + 20 =100)

Note: While a single player could bet the full maximum bid, this is considered very rude and is highly discouraged.

Seating

Determine the dealer. (See **Determining the First Player** p. 19.)

The dealer is seated across from the other players.

Players are seated from right to left in the order of their drawn card.

Note: In Oicho-Kabu there is an advantage to sitting to the right of the dealer.

The Deal

The deck is shuffled by the dealer and passed to each player.

Each player may choose to shuffle and/or cut the deck as desired.

The deck is returned to the dealer.

Playing a Round

Step One - Insight

Deal 1 card to each player (including the dealer) face down.

Each player looks at their card and then sets it aside face down.

Important: This card is not directly used during gameplay.

This card is simply to give each player a personal insight about one card that will not be included in the game.

These cards are set aside face down into a discard and removed from play.

Step Two - First Field

Deal 4 cards in a row to the table face up to create the *first field*.

Note: Regardless of the number of players, the *first field* is always 4 cards. (fig 30.1)

FIGURE 30.1 First Field

First Field

Step Three - Bets

Each player (other then the dealer) chooses a card or cards from the *first field* to bet on.

Player betting order occurs from right to left, beginning with the player to the right of the dealer.

- A player may bet on more than one card.
- A player does not have to bet the same amount on individual cards.
- A player must remain within the maximum bet.
- Each bet is placed on the card that was bet on.

Note: More than one player may bet on the same card, however, the bets must be kept separate from one another.

Step Four - Dealer Draw

The dealer draws 1 card to form the *dealer's hand*.

The dealer may choose to draw this card from **one** of the following:

- The top card of the deck.
- The bottom card of the deck.
- The fourth card from the top of the deck.

This card is placed in front of the dealer <u>face down</u>.

Important: The dealer does **not** look at this card.

Step Five - Second Field

Deal 4 cards face down on the table to create a *second field* below the *first field*. (fig 30.2)

FIGURE 30.2 **Second Field**

Each player (other than the dealer) looks at the <u>face down</u> cards in the *second field*.

Important: Players may <u>only</u> look at the face down card in column(s) that they bet on.

Players total the two cards from that column (i.e. the card from the *first field* and the card from the *second field*).

If the total of the two cards is 10 or higher, then the first digit is ignored.

Example 1: A column with a July (6) and an August (8) would have a total of 4.

(6 + 8 = 14) Since the first digit is ignored then the total is 4.

Example 2: A column with a March (3) and a July (7) would have a total of 0.

(3 + 7 = 10) Since the first digit is ignored then the total is 0.

The cards are returned face down to their prior positions in the *second field*.

Step Six - Third Card

Once all players have had an opportunity to view the cards, players have the option to be dealt a third card to one or more of the column(s) that they bet on.

This option is extended to each player, from right to left, beginning with the player to the right of the dealer.

If more than one player bet on the same card, then the first player asked (i.e. the player closest to the right of the dealer) gets to make the decision.

Note: All players who bet on a particular card are affected by the decision for that card.

Two rules apply when deciding whether to have a third card dealt:

- If the current total of the row is 7 or higher, then a third card can <u>not</u> be dealt.
- If the current total of the row is 3 or lower, then a third card <u>must</u> be dealt.

If a player chooses to have a third card dealt, then the dealer places a third card face up into a third field under the card in question from the *second field*. (fig 30.3)

FIGURE 30.3 **Third Field**

Step Seven - Dealer Second Draw

The dealer draws a second face down card to the *dealer's hand*. (fig 30.4)

Note: The dealer may choose where to draw this card from according to the same rules outlined in **Step Four - Dealer Draw**.

The dealer looks at the *dealer's hand*.

The dealer <u>may</u> choose to draw a third face down card to the *dealer's hand*.

FIGURE 30.4 Dealer's Hand

Reveal

All face down cards are revealed. (fig 30.5)

FIGURE 30.5 Reveal

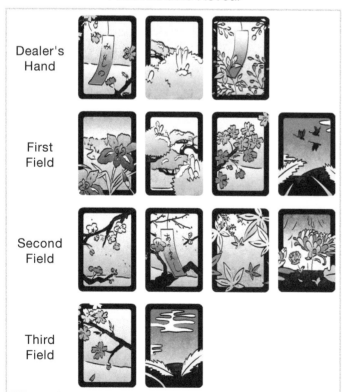

End of Round

The round ends when all cards are revealed.

Scoring

Each column is totaled individually. (fig 30.6)

FIGURE 30.6 Total

As previously explained, if the total is 10 or higher, then the first digit is ignored.

Any player who bet on a column whose total is <u>higher</u> than the *dealer's hand* wins an amount equal to their bet (in addition to having their bet returned).

Any player who bet on a column whose total is <u>less</u> than the *dealer's hand* loses their bet. The dealer takes all bets on that column.

Any column whose total is <u>tied</u> with the dealers hand is handled according to the rules predetermined during **Setup**.

Special Rules During Scoring

Triple

If the cards in the *first field*, *second field*, and *third field* are all of the same month, then any players who bet on that card automatically win. (fig 30.7)

FIGURE 30.7 **Triple**

Any players who bet on that card receive <u>triple</u> the amount of their bet.

Dealer 4 and 1

If the dealer's first card was a 4 and their second card was a 1, then the dealer automatically wins the round and is awarded all bets.

This rule is regardless of what the other totals were (including the special rule *Triple*).

This rule <u>only</u> applies to the dealer.

Note: If the dealer's first card was a 1 and the second was a 4, then this rule does not apply.

Dealer 9 and 1

If the dealer's first card was a 9 and their second card was a 1, then the dealer automatically wins the round and is awarded all bets. (fig 30.8)

FIGURE 30.8 **Dealer 9 and 1**

This rule is regardless of what the other totals were (including the special rule *Triple*).

This rule only applies to the dealer.

Note: If the dealer's first card was a 1 and the second was a 9, then this rule does <u>not</u> apply.

Chapter 31

Kyo-Kabu

Difficulty: Beginner

Players: 2-10

Deck: 40 card flower deck (remove Jokers, all November Rain, and all December Paulownia).

Rounds: Player Determined

Objective: To win bets against the dealer for the highest valued hand.

Important Notes:

- While Kyu-Kabu is traditionally its own distinct game, it is very similar to Oicho-Kabu.
- A quick and simple game that was originally intended for gambling and is similar in gameplay to Baccarat.
- This game is traditionally played with a Kabufuda deck.
- This game requires tokens (chips, candy, coins, fake money, or whatever you have on hand) or a notepad for tracking player points.

In Kyo-Kabu players compete against the dealer to win bets.

Setup

Determine Ground Rules

There are a few gameplay decisions that players must agree on <u>before</u> play.

Ties

Players must decide how wins are to be handled in the case of a tie.

In the case of a tie, <u>either</u>
- the dealer wins
- OR all bets on the column are returned.

Maximum Bet

Players must decide what the maximum bet for rounds will be.

The maximum bet is the <u>combined total</u> that <u>all</u> players can bet in a given round.

For example: If the maximum bet is 100 and one player bets 40, then the combined total that the other players bet may not be more than a combined total of 60 points.

Example 1: In a 4 player game. The maximum bet is 100. Player A is the dealer. Player B bets 40. Player C bets 10. Player D can then only bet up to 50. (40 + 10 + 50 =100)

Example 2: In a 4 player game. The maximum bet is 100. Player A is the dealer. Player B bets 50. Player C bets 30. Player D can then only bet up to 20. (50 + 30 + 20 =100)

Note: While a single player could bet the full maximum bid, this is considered very rude and is highly discouraged.

Seating

Determine the dealer. (See **Determining the First Player** p. 19.)

The dealer is seated across from the other players.

Players are seated from right to left in the order of their drawn card.

Note: In Kyo-Kabu there is an advantage to sitting to the right of the dealer.

The Deal

The deck is shuffled by the dealer and passed to each player.

Each player may choose to shuffle and/or cut the deck as desired.

The deck is returned to the dealer.

Playing a Round

Step One - Insight

Deal 1 card to each player (including the dealer) face down.

Each player looks at their card and then sets it aside face down.

Important: This card is not directly used during gameplay.

This card is simply to give each player a personal insight about one card that will not be included in the game.

These cards are set aside face down into a discard and removed from play.

Step Two - First Field

Deal 4 cards in a row to the table face up to create the *first field*.

Note: Regardless of the number of players, the *first field* is always 4 cards. (fig 31.1)

FIGURE 31.1 First Field

First Field

Step Three - Bets

Each player (other then the dealer) chooses a card from the *first field* to bet on.

Player betting order occurs from right to left, beginning with the player to the right of the dealer.

- A player may <u>only</u> bet on one card.
- A player must remain within the maximum bet.
- Each bet is placed on the card that was bet on.

Note: More than one player may bet on the same card, however, the bets must be kept separate from one another.

Step Four - Dealer Draw

The dealer draws 1 card to form the *dealer's hand*.

The dealer may choose to draw this card from **one** of the following:
- The top card of the deck.
- The bottom card of the deck.
- The fourth card from the top of the deck.

This card is placed in front of the dealer <u>face down</u>.

Important: The dealer does **not** look at this card.

Step Five - Second Field

Deal 4 cards face down on the table to create a *second field* below the *first field*. (fig 31.2)

FIGURE 31.2 Second Field

Each player (other than the dealer) looks at the <u>face down</u> cards in the *second field*.

Important: Players may <u>only</u> look at the face down card in column(s) that they bet on.

Players total the two cards from that column (i.e. the card from the *first field* and the card from the *second field*).

If the total of the two cards is 10 or higher, then the first digit is ignored.

Example 1: A column with a July (6) and an August (8) would have a total of 4.

(6 + 8 = 14) Since the first digit is ignored then the total is 4.

Example 2: A column with a March (3) and a July (7) would have a total of 0.

(3 + 7 = 10) Since the first digit is ignored then the total is 0.

The cards are returned face down to their prior positions in the *second field*.

Step Six - Third Card

Once all players have had an opportunity to view the cards, players have the option to be dealt a third card to one or more of the column(s) that they bet on.

This option is extended to each player, from right to left, beginning with the player to the right of the dealer.

If more than one player bet on the same card, then the first player asked (i.e. the player closest to the right of the dealer) gets to make the decision.

Note: All players who bet on a particular card are affected by the decision for that card.

Two rules apply when deciding whether to have a third card dealt:

- If the current total of the row is 7 or higher, then a third card can <u>not</u> be dealt.
- If the current total of the row is 3 or lower, then a third card <u>must</u> be dealt.

If a player chooses to have a third card dealt, then the dealer places a third card face up into a third field under the card in question from the *second field*. (fig 31.3)

FIGURE 31.3 Third Field

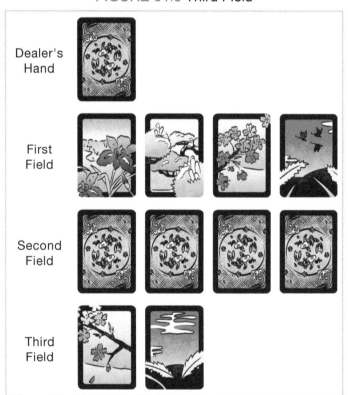

Step Seven - Dealer Second Draw

The dealer draws a second face down card to the *dealer's hand*. (fig 31.4)

Note: The dealer may choose where to draw this card from according to the same rules outlined in **Step Four - Dealer Draw**.

The dealer looks at the *dealer's hand*.

The dealer <u>may</u> choose to draw a third face down card to the *dealer's hand*.

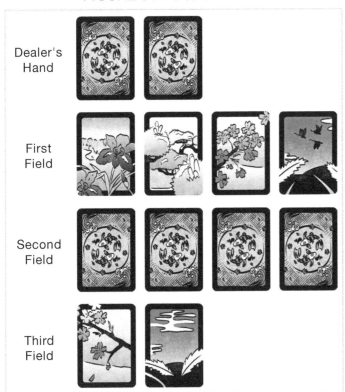

FIGURE 31.4 **Dealer's Hand**

Reveal

All face down cards are revealed. (fig 31.5)

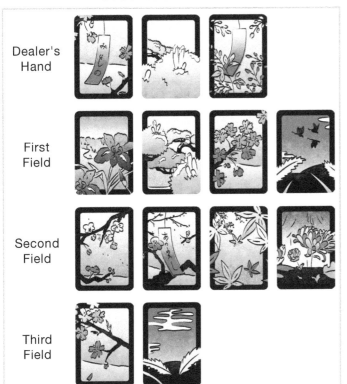

FIGURE 31.5 **Reveal**

End of Round

The round ends when all cards are revealed.

Scoring

Each column is totaled individually. (fig 31.6)

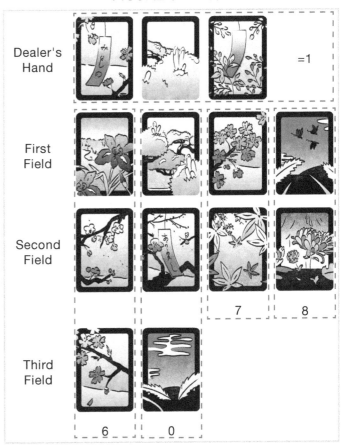

FIGURE 31.6 **Total**

As previously explained, if the total is 10 or higher, then the first digit is ignored.

Any player who bet on a column whose total is <u>higher</u> than the *dealer's hand* wins an amount equal to their bet (in addition to having their bet returned).

Any player who bet on a column whose total is <u>less</u> than the *dealer's hand* loses their bet. The dealer takes all bets on that column.

Any column whose total is <u>tied</u> with the dealers hand is handled according to the rules predetermined during **Setup**.

Special Rules During Scoring

Triple

If the cards in the *first field*, *second field*, and *third field* are all of the same month, then any players who bet on that card automatically win. (fig 31.7)

FIGURE 31.7 **Triple**

Any players who bet on that card receive <u>triple</u> the amount of their bet.

Dealer 9 and 1

If the dealer's first card was a 9 and their second card was a 1, then the dealer automatically wins the round and is awarded all bets. (fig 31.8)

FIGURE 31.8 **Dealer 9 and 1**

This rule is regardless of what the other totals were (including the special rule *Triple*).

This rule only applies to the dealer.

Note: If the dealer's first card was a 1 and the second was a 9, then this rule does <u>not</u> apply.

Chapter 32
Kingo

Difficulty: Beginner

Players: 2-10

Deck: 40 card flower deck (remove Jokers, all November Rain, and all December Paulownia).

Rounds: Player Determined

Objective: To get the closest to 15 without going over.

Important Notes:
- A quick and simple game that was originally intended for gambling and is similar in gameplay to Blackjack.
- This game is traditionally played with a Kabufuda deck.
- This game requires tokens (chips, candy, coins, fake money, or whatever you have on hand) or a notepad for tracking player points.

Setup

Determine Set Bet

Players agree on what the set bet for rounds will be.

This is the set amount that <u>each</u> player (including the dealer) must place in the *pot* per round.

Pot

Each player places the predetermined bet into the pot.

Seating

Determine the dealer. (See **Determining the First Player** p. 19.)

The dealer is seated across from the other players.

Players are seated, from right to left, in the order of their drawn card.

The Deal

The deck is shuffled by the dealer and passed to each player.

Each player may choose to shuffle and/or cut the deck as desired.

The deck is returned to the dealer.

Playing a Round

The dealer deals 1 card to each player (including the dealer) <u>face down</u>.

Each player looks at their card, without revealing it to the other players, and sets it back onto the table in front of them <u>face down</u>.

Each player, beginning with the dealer and continuing from right to left, does the following:

- First, the player draws one card from the deck and places it <u>face up</u> on the table beneath their first card. (fig 32.1)

FIGURE 32.1 Draw

- Then, the player may choose to draw another card <u>or</u> stop.
  - **Important:** The player may only draw another card if their current total is not higher than 15. (fig 32.2)

FIGURE 32.2 Draw Again

- If the player chooses to stop then play passes to the next player.
- The player may continue to draw additional cards (one at a time) until:
  - Their total goes over 15.
  - <u>Or</u>, they choose to stop.

Once a player decides to stop, play passes to the next player who performs the same steps outlined above.

Once all players have decided to stop, all cards are revealed.

End of Round

The round ends when all cards are revealed.

Scoring

Each player's hand is totaled.

If a player's total is 16 or higher, then that player must double their current bet to the *pot*.

The player with a total closest to 15, without going over, is the winner of the round.

The winner of the round is awarded the *pot*.

If there is a tie, then the player's who tied split the *pot* evenly.

If <u>all</u> player's tie, then the dealer is awarded the *pot*.

If <u>all</u> player's totals go over (i.e. are 16 or higher), then the game is considered a draw and a new round is dealt.

Special Rules During Scoring

Triple Fives

If a player's hand consists of exactly three May (5) cards, then all other players must triple their current bet to the pot. (fig 32.3)

FIGURE 32.3 Triple Fives

The player with *Triple Fives* is the winner of the round and is awarded the full *pot*.

Four Five Six

If a player's hand consists of one April (4), one May (5), and one June (6), then all other players must double their current bet to the *pot*. (fig 32.4)

FIGURE 32.4 Four Five Six

The player with *Four Five Six* is the winner of the round and is awarded the full *pot*.

Note: In the rare case that one player collects *Triple Fives* and another player collects *Four Five Six*, then the player with *Triple Fives* wins.

Scoring Example

In a four player game.
The set bet is 10 chips.
Each player places 10 chips in the pot.

Players were dealt the following according to the chart below:

FIGURE 32.5 Player Hands

Player A	Player B	Player C	Player D
15	16	18	14

Player A's hand total is 15, therefore Player A is the winner of the round.

Player B's total was higher than 15, therefore Player B must double their current bet.

Player B increases their current bet in the pot.
(10 x 2 = 20)

Player C's total was higher than 15, therefore Player C must double their current bet.

Player C increases their current bet in the pot.
(10 x 2 = 20)

Since Player A's hand was Triple Fives, Player B, Player C, and Player D must triple their current bets in the pot.

Player B increases their current bet in the pot.
(20 x 3 = 60)

Player C increases their current bet in the pot.
(20 x 3 = 60)

Player D increases their current bet in the pot.
(10 x 3 = 30)

The total pot is now 160.

Player A is awarded the pot of 160.

FIGURE 32.6 **Calculating Pot**

	Player A	Player B	Player C	Player D
Original Set Bet	10	10	10	10
Over 15 Penalty		x2	x2	
Current Bet	10	20	20	10
Triple Five Penalty		x3	x3	x3
Total Bet	10	60	60	30
The total pot is therefore 160.				

Chapter 33

Sota

Difficulty: Intermediate

Players: 2-6

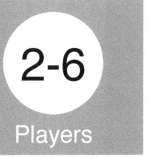

Deck: 20 select cards of the flower deck. (Remove all November, all December, and all Chaffs.)

Rounds: Player Determined

Objective: To be the player with the highest valued hand.

Alternative Names:

- Seotda

Important Notes:

- Sota is a quick game that was traditionally intended for gambling.

Setup

Players agree on the number of rounds they want to play.

Playing a Round

Step One - Deal

Deal 2 cards to each player face down.

Each player looks at their cards while keeping them hidden from the other players.

Step Two - Choose and Reveal

Each player chooses 1 card from their hand to play face-up onto the table.

Step Three - Deal Third Card

Deal 1 card to each player face down.

Each player looks at their cards while keeping them hidden from the other players.

Step Four - Pick Up

Each player picks up their card from the table and returns it to their hand.

Step Five - Discard

Each player discards 1 card from their hand <u>face down</u>.

Step Six - Reveal
Players reveal their cards.

End of Round

The round ends when all players reveal their cards.

Scoring

Only the winner of the round receives points for their hand.

If any player's chosen cards were a Hand Combo:

The winner of the round is the player with the highest ranking Hand Combo.

The winner receives points for their Hand Combo.

Note: Hand Combos are ranked from 1 to 19. 1 being the highest and 19 the lowest.

If no player's chosen cards were a Hand Combo:

Each player calculates their Hand Value.

The Hand Value is the last digit of the sum of the months of their two cards .

For example: If a player had a June (6) and a July (7), then the value of their hand is 3.

(6 + 7 = 13) Since the 3 is the last digit of the sum, the Hand Value would be 3.

The player with the highest Hand Value is the winner of the round.

The player with the highest Hand Value receives 1 point for the round.

Note: The Hand Value is only used to determine the winner of the round. The Hand Value is not the hand's point value. The player with the highest Hand Value only receives 1 point for the round.

Players record their scores each round.

The player with the highest total score at the end of the predetermined number of rounds is the winner of the game.

Special Hand Combinations

Special Hand Combinations are special hand combinations with special abilities.

When a player reveals a Special Hand Combination, special rules will apply based on the combinations revealed that round. See fig 33.2 for Special Hand Combinations.

FIGURE 33.1 Hand Combos

Ranked from highest (1) to lowest (19):

1 Curtain and Moon = 10 pts

2 Crane and Moon = 8 pts

3 Crane and Curtain = 7 pts

4 October = 5 pts

5 September = 3 pts

6 August = 3 pts

7 July = 3 pts

8 June = 3 pts

9 May = 3 pts

10 April = 3 pts

11 March = 3 pts

12 February = 3 pts

13 January = 3 pts

14 Any Jan & Any Feb = 1 pt

15 Any Jan & Any April = 1 pt

16 Any Jan & Any Sep = 1pt

17 Any Jan & Any Oct = 1 pt

18 Any April & Any Oct = 1 pt

19 Any April & Any June = 1 pt

FIGURE 33.2 Special Hand Combinations

Combo	Special Ability	Combo	Special Ability
Any April & Any July 	If the highest revealed Hand Combo was any rank from 4 to 13 (i.e a month combo), then the player with this Special Hand Combo wins the round and earns 3 points. Otherwise, players score as usual.	April Ten & July Ten 	If the highest Hand Combo was rank 2 or 3, then the player with this Special Hand Combo wins the round and earns 5 points. Otherwise, players score as usual.
Any April & Any September 	If the highest Hand Combo was rank 14 or lower, then the round ends in a draw.	April Ten & September Ten 	If the highest Hand Combo was rank 4 or lower, then the round ends in a draw.

Chapter 34

Sutda

Intermediate

Difficulty: Intermediate

Players: 2-10

2-10

Players

Deck: 20 select cards of the flower deck. (2 cards from each of the first 10 months. All cards are Chaffs except for the Curtain and Moon.)

Rounds: Player Determined

L

Luck

Objective: To be the player with the highest valued hand.

Important Notes:
- Sutda is a very quick and simple game that was traditionally intended for gambling.

Setup

Players agree on the number of rounds they want to play.

Deal 2 cards to each player face down.

Playing a Round

Players reveal their cards.

End of Round

The player with the highest ranking Hand Combo wins the round.

The winner of the round becomes the dealer for the next round.

Scoring

Only the winner of the round receives points for their hand.

If a player was dealt a Hand Combo:

The winner of the round is the player with the highest ranking Hand Combo.

The winner receives points for their Hand Combo.

Note: Hand Combos are ranked from 1 to 17. 1 being the highest and 17 the lowest.

If no player was dealt a Hand Combo:

If no player was dealt a Hand Combo this round, then each player calculates their Hand Value.

The Hand Value is the last digit of the sum of the months of the two cards they were dealt.

For example: If a player was dealt a June (6) and a July (7), then the value of their hand is 3.

(6 + 7 = 13) Since the 3 is the last digit of the sum, the Hand Value would be 3.

The player with the highest Hand Value is the winner of the round.

The player with the highest Hand Value receives 1 point for the round.

Note: The Hand Value is only used to determine the winner of the round. The Hand Value is <u>not</u> the hand's point value. The player with the highest Hand Value only receives 1 point for the round.

Players record their scores each round.

The player with the highest total score at the end of the predetermined number of rounds is the winner of the game.

Hand Combos

Hand Combos are ranked from 1 to 17 as follows:

FIGURE 34.1 Hand Combos

Ranked from highest (1) to lowest (17):

1   Curtain and Moon = 10 pts

2   October = 5 pts

3   September = 3 pts

4   August = 3 pts

5   July = 3 pts

6   June = 3 pts

7   May = 3 pts

8   April = 3 pts

9   March = 3 pts

10   February = 3 pts

11   January = 3 pts

12   3rd Jan & 4th Plum = 1 pt

13   3rd Jan & 4th April = 1 pt

14   3rd Oct & 4th April = 1pt

15   3rd Oct & 4th Jan = 1 pt

16   3rd Jan & 4th Aug = 1 pt

17   3rd June & 4th April = 1 pt

SECTION IV
Fusion Games

Chapter 35

Seasons

Beginner

Difficulty: Beginner

Players: 1-4

Players

Deck: 48 card flower deck (plus 4 Jokers)

Rounds: 1

Fusion

Objective: To arrange all 48 flower cards on the table before exposing the 4 Jokers.

Important Notes:

- This game may be helpful to beginners who want to familiarize themselves with a hanafuda deck.
- This game is entirely luck based.

Objective

The object of the game is to arrange each month in the field in ascending order.

For example: January in the first row first column, followed by February in the second row first column, March in the third row first column, April in the fourth row first column, May in the first row second column, June in the second row second column, and so on. (fig 35.1)

FIGURE 35.1 **Objective**

Note: The following rules are for playing with one player. There are gameplay variations for playing with 2-4 players. See **Multiple Players Variation**.

Setup

Deal 48 cards to the table <u>face down</u> in 4 rows of 12 cards each. The remaining 4 cards become the player's hand.

Playing a Round

The player takes the following steps in the following order:

- First, the player chooses 1 card from their hand.
- Next, the player locates the place in the field where that card belongs.
- Then the player picks up that face down card in the field and places it in their hand.
- Then the player then places their card in the field in its place.

The above steps are repeated until one of two things occur:

- All months are revealed in the field in their appropriate places.
- Or, the player holds all 4 Jokers in their hand.

End of Round

The round ends when one of the following occurs:

- All months are revealed in the field in their appropriate places.
- Or, the player holds all 4 Jokers in their hand.

If the player reveals all of the months in the field, then the player <u>wins</u>.

If the player holds the 4 Jokers before all of the months have been revealed in the field, then the player <u>loses</u>.

Multiple Players Variation

There are three gameplay variations for playing with multiple players: Out Variation, Pass Variation, and Cooperative Variation.

Out Variation

In a <u>two</u> player game:

<u>Each</u> player receives 2 cards for their hand.

Players alternate playing a single card into the field.

As soon as a player holds 2 Jokers, they are out.

In a <u>four</u> player game:

<u>Each</u> player receives 1 card for their hand.

Players alternate playing a single card into the field.

As soon as a player holds a Joker, they are out.

Pass Variation

This variation can be played with 2-4 players.

Players pass the 4 card hand to the player to the right of them each time a Joker is drawn.

Cooperative Variation

This variation can be played with 2-4 players.

Players share the 4 card hand.

Players work cooperatively to identify the months and place them in their appropriate places in the field.

Chapter 36

Pyramid

Difficulty: Beginner

Players: 1

Deck: 48 card flower deck (plus 4 Jokers)

Rounds: 1

Objective: To remove all 21 cards from the pyramid by matching cards of the same month.

Overview

Objective

The object of the game is to remove all 21 cards from the pyramid.

This is achieved by matching any two cards of the same month in pairs.

For example: Any January card may pair with any January card. Any February card may pair with any February card. Any March card may pair with any March card, and so on.

Capturing Cards

Any <u>exposed</u> pairs (whether in the pyramid or in pyramid and in the stock) may be captured. (fig 36.1-4)

Captured pairs are removed from the pyramid and/or stock and placed in the discard.

Capturing pairs may expose additional pairs that may then be captured.

Note: Capturing a pair is always optional. Sometimes it may be more strategic to leave a pair in the stock and/or pyramid.

Jokers

Jokers are considered free cards.

Joker cards are discarded without a match.

Therefore, if a player uncovers a Joker in the stock or pyramid, it is automatically placed into the discard.

FIGURE 36.1 Capturable

Draw Pile   Stock

Exposed pair. May be captured.

FIGURE 36.2 Capturable

Exposed pair. May be captured.

FIGURE 36.3 Capturable

Exposed pair. May be captured.

FIGURE 36.4 Blocked

Blocked pair. May **<u>not</u>** be captured.

Setup

Deal 21 cards into a pyramid formation. (fig 36.5)

This is achieved by dealing 1 card in the first row, 2 cards in the second, 3 cards in the third, and so on until there are 6 rows.

Each row should partially overlap the row before it.

The remaining 31 cards are placed face down to form a draw pile.

Turn up 1 card from the draw pile to create a face up stock.

Leave space for a discard.

FIGURE 36.5 **Setup**

Draw Pile   Stock   Discard

Playing a Round

During any given turn, the player may, where applicable, take any of the following actions:

- Match from the pyramid.
- Match from the stock.
- Draw a card.

The player continues taking these actions until the end of the round.

Match from the Pyramid

Capture an exposed pair from the pyramid.

Captured pairs are placed in the discard.

Remember:

- Matches are any two cards of the same month (i.e. pairs).
- Only <u>exposed</u> pairs may be captured. (fig 36.1-4)
- Capturing is optional.

Match from the Stock

If the <u>top</u> card in the stock matches an <u>exposed</u> card in the pyramid, the pair may be captured.

The captured pair is moved to the discard.

Draw a Card

Draw 1 card from the draw pile.

This newly drawn card is placed on the top of the stock (covering the previous card).

Note: Only the <u>top</u> card of the stock can be used. Once a card in the stock is covered it can <u>not</u> be used <u>until</u> it is exposed again.

If the deck becomes exhausted, the round ends. (See **End of Round**.)

End of Round

The round ends when one of the following occur:

- All of the cards are removed from the pyramid.
- Or, the deck has been exhausted.

If the all of the cards are removed from the pyramid, then the player <u>wins</u>.

If the deck becomes exhausted, then the player <u>loses</u>.

Gameplay Variations

The following gameplay variations may be used to increase or decrease the game difficulty.

Multiple variations may be used in a single game.

Variations To Decrease Difficulty:

Jokers Wild

Jokers are considered Wild cards.

Jokers can be used as a match to capture any month.

Three or Less Wins

If 3 or less cards remain in the pyramid, then the player <u>wins</u>.

Reshuffle

The deck may be reshuffled when it is exhausted.

The round ends when one of the following occur:

- All of the cards are removed from the pyramid.
- Or, no more matches can be made (e.g. all remaining matches are blocked).

Free Space

A free space (i.e. reserve) may be used to store any 1 card from the stock or pyramid.

Three Free Spaces

Three free spaces (i.e. reserves) may be used to store any 3 cards from the stock or pyramid.

Variations To Increase Difficulty:

Jokers Match

Jokers must be captured in pairs.

Draw Three

Draw 3 cards instead of 1 for the stock.

The 3 cards should overlap slightly in the stock.

Only the uppermost fully exposed card may be used to make a match.

With this variation, the deck may be reshuffled (up to three times) when it is exhausted.

Larger Pyramid

Deal 7 rows of cards instead of 6 rows to create the pyramid during setup.

Blocked

If a month is blocking its match in the pyramid, the match is considered blocked.

In other words, the example in fig 36.3 would no longer be a legal move. (fig 32.6)

FIGURE 36.6 **Blocked**

Blocked. May **<u>not</u>** be captured.

Chapter 37

Solitaire

Difficulty: Intermediate

Players: 1

Deck: 48 card flower deck (remove all Jokers)

Rounds: 1

Objective: To build up four foundations of ascending months.

Important Notes:
- While this game is categorized as an Intermediate game (and could even be considered Beginner in difficulty), the player needs to be familiar with the months of the hanafuda deck in order to play.

Setup

Deal 21 cards into a row of 6 <u>face-down</u> stacks to create the tableau.

This is done in the following manner:

- Deal 6 adjacent cards in a row.
- Skip the first stack and deal 1 card onto each of the 5 remaining stacks.
- Skip the first two stacks and deal 1 card onto each of the 4 remaining stacks.
- Skip the first three stacks and deal 1 card onto each of the 3 remaining stacks.
- Continue this pattern (skipping the next stack and dealing out 1 card to the remaining stacks) until all 21 cards are dealt into the 6 stacks.

(i.e. The first stack will consist of 1 card, the second adjacent stack will consist of 2 cards, the third will consist of 3 cards, and so on with the last stack consisting of 6 cards.)

The remaining cards are placed face down to form a draw pile.

Turn the top card of each stack in the tableau face up.

Turn up 3 cards from the draw pile to form a stock pile.

Note: The cards in the stock pile should slightly overlap one another so that only the top card (i.e. last drawn card) is fully visible.

Leave space above the tableau for 4 foundations. (fig 37.1)

FIGURE 37.1 **Setup**

Foundations

(1 card) (2 cards) (3 cards) (4 cards) (5 cards) (6 cards)

Tableau

Draw Pile   Stock

Playing a Round

The object of the game is to transfer all of the cards from the tableau and the stock to the four foundations.

During any given turn, the player may, where applicable, take any of the following actions:

- Move a card in the tableau onto one of the following:
  - A foundation. (See **The Foundation**.) (fig 37.2)
  - An exposed card in the tableau. (See **The Tableau**.) (fig 37.3)
  - An empty column in the tableau. (See **Exhausted Stack**.)
- Move a set of cards in the tableau onto one of the following:
  - An exposed card in the tableau. (fig 37.4, fig 37.5)
  - An empty column in the tableau.
- Play a card from the stock onto one of the following:
  - A foundation.
  - An exposed card in the tableau. (fig 37.6)
  - An empty column in the tableau. (fig 37.7)
- Turn up a card from an exposed stack. (See **Exposed Stack**.)
- Draw 3 cards from the draw pile into the stock. (See **The Stock**.)

Note: Cards may only be played onto a card that is fully exposed. (i.e. Cards may not be played into the middle of a column.)

If the draw pile becomes exhausted, the stock is shuffled and 3 new cards are dealt to the stock. The remaining cards are placed face down to create the new draw pile. (See **The Draw Pile**.)

The player continues to build up the four foundations until:

- All of the cards are moved into the four foundations.
- Or, there are no possible moves left.

The Foundation

Each of the four foundations must be built up in <u>ascending</u> order.

Therefore, any card played to a foundation <u>must</u> be one month later in month order than the top card of the foundation.

(i.e. Foundations are built up from January which is followed by February, then March, then April, and so on, with the final card in a foundation being December.)

The base card in each foundation must be a January.

Therefore, as soon as a January becomes available, it is moved to an empty foundation.

A card may be played to a foundation from either:
- the tableau
- or the stock.

Once a card has been placed in a foundation it can not be removed from the foundation.

When all four foundations have been built up from January to December, the player wins the game.

The Stock

Only the last revealed (i.e. top) card of the stock may be used for play.

The top card of the stock may be played on either:
- the tableau.
- or a foundation.

Anytime a card in the stock is used, the newly revealed (i.e. top) card in the stock becomes available for play.

As desired, 3 cards may be drawn from the draw pile and turned over into the stock.

The Draw Pile

If the draw pile becomes exhausted, then the player may do the following:
- shuffle the stock
- and deal 3 new cards to the stock
- and place the remaining cards face down to create the new draw pile.

This may be done as many times as needed or until no further plays are possible.

Note: If there are less than 3 cards remaining in the draw pile, then the player simply deals out the remaining 1 or 2 cards to the stock. The player may play from these cards as usual.

The Tableau

The tableau is used to maneuver cards from the tableau and the stock so that they can eventually be played to the foundations.

The tableau must be built down in descending order.

Therefore, any card played to the tableau must be one month earlier in month than the card beneath it. (e.g. November, October, September and so on.)

Cards may be played to the tableau from:
- the tableau
- or the stock.

Cards from the tableau may be moved within the tableau (from one column to another) as either a single card or as a set of cards.

A set of cards is two or more cards in descending order that are stacked in a column in the tableau.

Anytime a card in the tableau is moved, all cards stacked beneath it (i.e. a set) must move as well.

For example: If the player moves an August onto an exposed September card and a July and June are stacked on the August card, then the August, July, and June cards must all move onto the September card.

Cards from the tableau may be played onto any of the following:
- An exposed card in the tableau.
- An empty column in the tableau.
- A foundation.

Note: Any card played to the tableau should slightly overlap the card that it is played onto.

Exposed Stack

During play, the top face down card of a column (i.e. stack) in the tableau may become exposed (i.e. all face up cards in the column are removed).

Anytime a face down card from a stack in the tableau is exposed, the top card of that stack must immediately be turned up.

Exhausted Stack

During play, a column (i.e. stack) in the tableau may become exhausted (i.e. is emptied).

Anytime a stack in the tableau becomes exhausted, the player may choose to fill the space with one of the following:
- A card from the stock.
- A card from the tableau
- Or, a set of cards from the tableau.

FIGURE 37.2 Tableau to Foundation

FIGURE 37.3 Tableau to Tableau

FIGURE 37.4 Whole Set to Tableau

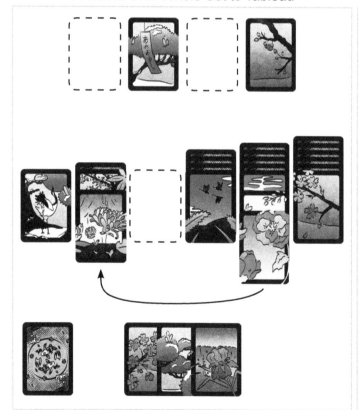

FIGURE 37.5 Part Set to Tableau

FIGURE 37.6 **Stock to Tableau**   FIGURE 37.7 **Stock to Exhausted Stack**

End of Round

The round ends when:

- All of the cards are moved into the four foundations.
- Or, there are no possible moves left.

If the player manages to build up all four foundations from January to December, then the player <u>wins</u>.

Gameplay Variations

The following are gameplay variations that may increase or decrease the game difficulty.

Where applicable, multiple of these variations may be used in a single game.

Variations To Decrease Difficulty:

One Card Stock

Only 1 card is turned over from the draw pile to create the stock instead of 3.

Movable Foundations

Cards may be moved from the foundation to the tableau.

Face Up Stacks

When creating the tableau during setup, all cards in the tableau are dealt face up.

Variations To Increase Difficulty:

Alternating Tableau

When building down cards on the tableau, the cards should alternate based on value.

(e.g. Value-Chaff-Value-Chaff-Value)

Brights, Tens, Ribbons, and the Special Paulownia are considered "Value" cards.

Chaffs and the Rain Ribbon are considered "Chaffs".

Note: If using the Fusion deck, then the player could instead alternate the colors of the suits. (e.g. Black-Red-Black-Red.)

Ordered Foundation

When building up cards to the foundations, the cards should be ordered based on value.

In other words: The first foundation must contain the highest valued card of the month (a Bright or a Ten depending on the month). The second foundation must contain the next valuable card in the month (usually a Ribbon). The third foundation must contain the left Chaff. The fourth foundation must contain the right Chaff.

Example 1: The first foundation would be built up using the 1st card of January, the 1st card of February, the 1st card of March and so on.)

Example 1: The second foundation would be built up using the 2nd card of January, the 2nd card of February, the 2nd card of March and so on.)

Tip: The *Hanami* hanafuda were created so that when the cards in a month are arranged in order of value they create one continuous image.

Larger Tableau

During setup, deal out 7 piles of cards to form the tableau instead of 6.

Jokers

Include 4 Jokers into the deck.

Jokers are considered the 13th month.

Therefore, players build up the foundation from January to Joker and the tableau down Joker to January.

Hidden Stock

During Setup when the 3 cards are turned up from the draw pile to create the stock, only the top card is kept visible.

Exhausted Deck Loss

The game ends when the deck is exhausted.

Note: This variation is commonly combined with the *One Card Stock* variation.

Exhausted Three Times Loss

The game ends when the deck is exhausted three times.

Flipped not Shuffled

Do not shuffle the deck when the stock is exhausted. Instead, the stock is flipped over to create the new draw pile.

Exhausted Stack Restriction

Only a December (or a Joker if playing with the *Jokers* variant) may be moved to fill an empty column.

Unbroken Column

The player may not break up a column by moving only a portion of the cards. The cards must be moved as a unit.

In other words, only full sets (i.e. entire columns) may be moved within the tableau.

Chapter 38

Eight Off

Difficulty: Intermediate

Players: 1

Deck: 48 card flower deck (plus 4 Jokers)

Rounds: 1

Objective: To build up four foundations of ascending months.

Important Notes:
- While this game is categorized as an intermediate game (and could even be considered beginner in difficulty), the player needs to be familiar with the months of the hanafuda deck in order to play.

Setup

Deal 48 cards into a row of 8 face up stacks to create the tableau.

This is done in the following manner:

- Deal 8 adjacent cards in a row.
- Deal another row of 8 cards face up slightly overlapping the previous row.
- Continue this pattern (dealing 8 slightly overlapping cards to the rows) until each of the 8 stacks contain 6 cards each.

The remaining 4 cards are dealt into the top right 4 spaces above the tableau as part of an eight cell reserve.

Leave space above the top left of the tableau for the remaining 4 reserves.

Leave space to the left of the tableau for the 4 foundations. (fig 38.1)

FIGURE 38.1 **Setup**

Reserves

Tableau

Foundations

Playing a Round

The object of the game is to transfer all of the cards from the tableau and reserves to the four foundations.

During any given turn, the player may, where applicable, take any of the following actions:

- Move a card in the tableau onto one of the following:
  - A Foundation. (See **The Foundation**.)
  - An exposed card in the Tableau. (See **The Tableau**.)
  - An empty column in the Tableau. (See **Exhausted Stack**.)
  - An empty cell in the Reserve. (See **The Reserve**.)
- Play a card from the Reserve onto one of the following:
  - A foundation.
  - An exposed card in the tableau.
  - An empty column in the tableau.

Note: A card may only be played onto a card that is fully exposed. (i.e. Cards may not be played into the middle of a column.)

The player continues to build up the four foundations until:

- All of the cards are moved into the four foundations.
- Or, there are no possible moves left.

The Foundation

Each of the four foundations must be built up in <u>ascending</u> order.

Therefore, any card played to a foundation <u>must</u> be one month later in month order than the top card of the foundation.

(i.e. Foundations are built up from January which is followed by February, then March, then April, and so on, with the final card in a foundation being the Joker.)

The base card in each foundation <u>must</u> be a January.

Therefore, as soon as a January becomes available, it is moved to an empty foundation.

A card may be played to a foundation from either:

- the tableau
- or the reserve.

Once a card has been placed in a foundation it <u>may</u> be removed from the foundation.

When all four foundations have been built up from January to Joker, the player wins the game.

The Reserve

There are 8 reserves.

Each reserve may hold 1 card at a time.

A card in the reserve may be played to:

- A foundation.
- An exposed card in the tableau.
- An empty column in the tableau.

The Tableau

The tableau is used to maneuver cards from the tableau and the reserve so that they can eventually be played to the foundations.

The tableau must be built down in <u>descending</u> order.

Therefore, any card played to the tableau <u>must</u> be one month earlier in month than the card beneath it. (e.g. November, October, September and so on.)

A card may be played to the tableau <u>from</u>:

- the tableau
- or the reserve.

Cards from the tableau may only be moved <u>1</u> card at a time. (i.e. Only single cards may move. There are <u>no</u> sets in Eight Off.)

Pro Tip: Technically, a player could move a set of <u>sequential</u> cards <u>if</u> there are sufficient reserves available. The maximum number of sequential cards that a player could move is equal to the number of empty reserves plus 1.

A card from the tableau may be played onto any of the following:

- An exposed card in the tableau.
- An empty column in the tableau.
- A foundation.
- An empty cell in the reserve.

Note: Any card played to the tableau should slightly overlap the card that it is played onto.

Exhausted Stack

During play, a column (i.e. stack) in the tableau may become exhausted (i.e. is emptied).

Anytime a stack in the tableau becomes exhausted, the player may choose to fill the space with one of the following:

- A card from the tableau
- A card from the foundation.
- Or, a card from the reserve.

End of Round

The round ends when:

- All of the cards are moved into the four foundations.
- Or, there are no possible moves left.

If the player manages to build up all four foundations from January to Joker, then the player <u>wins</u>.

Gameplay Variations

The following are gameplay variations that may increase or decrease the game difficulty.

Where applicable, more than one of these variations may be used to vary gameplay.

Variations To Decrease Difficulty:

Eight Open Reserves

The 8 reserves start empty.

During Setup, the 4 cards that would have been dealt to the first four reserves are instead dealt to the first four columns in the tableau.

Variations To Increase Difficulty:

Ordered Tableau

When building down cards on the tableau, the cards should be ordered based on the order of the cards in the month.

Example 1: The 1st card of October, the 1st card of September, the 1st card of August, 1st card of July, and so on.)

Example 2: The 2nd card of October, the 2nd card of September, the 2nd card of August, 2nd card of July, and so on.)

Tip: If the player is using the Fusion deck, simply build the cards based on suit. (e.g. hearts build on to one another, and so on.)

Alternating Tableau

When building down cards on the tableau, the cards should alternate based on value.

(e.g. Value-Chaff-Value-Chaff-Value)

Brights, Tens, Ribbons, and the Special Paulownia are considered "Value" cards.

Chaffs and the Rain Ribbon are considered "Chaffs".

Note: If using the Fusion deck, then the player could instead alternate the colors of the suits. (e.g. Black-Red-Black-Red.)

Ordered Foundation

When building up cards to the foundations, the cards should be ordered based on value.

In other words: The first foundation must contain the highest valued card of the month (a Bright or a Ten depending on the month). The second foundation must contain the next valuable card in the month (usually a Ribbon). The third foundation must contain the left Chaff. The fourth foundation must contain the right Chaff.

Example 1: The first foundation would be built up using the 1st card of January, the 1st card of February, the 1st card of March and so on.)

Example 1: The second foundation would be built up using the 2nd card of January, the 2nd card of February, the 2nd card of March and so on.)

Tip: The *Hanami* hanafuda were created so that when the cards in a month are arranged in order of value they create one continuous image.

Four Reserves

There are only 4 reserves.

During Setup, the 4 cards that would have been dealt to the first four reserves are instead dealt to the first four columns in the tableau.

Joker Reserves

There are only 4 reserves.

During Setup, the 4 cards that would have been dealt to the first four reserves are instead dealt to the first four columns in the tableau.

Jokers are considered an additional 4 reserves.

As the Jokers are revealed they are placed above the tableau to create the remaining four reserves. (For a total of 8 reserves when all Jokers are revealed.)

The Joker reserves are treated the same as the other reserves, the Joker is merely a marker of the acquired reserve. Only one card may be played onto the Joker at a time.

Chapter 39
Hana-Rumi

Difficulty: Intermediate

Players: 2-4

Deck: 48 card flower deck (plus 6 Jokers)

Rounds: Varies

Objective: To be the first player to reach 200 points.

Important Notes:

- Hana-Rumi is a fusion game that we designed to fully incorporate the use of hanafuda with one of our personal favorite childhood card games, Rummy. Although Hana-Rumi draws inspiration from Rummy, this game was designed with the hanafuda deck in mind and will require some familiarity with the hanafuda deck to play.

Jokers

In Hana-Rumi, the four Wet Koi Jokers are considered special Chaffs.

Jokers can be used as a thirteenth month when creating sequential Combinations.

The thirteenth month comes <u>after</u> December and <u>before</u> January.

Note: When playing with the *Hanami* Fusion deck, the Wet Koi Jokers are identified as Kings.

FIGURE 39.1 Wet Koi - Jokers

Wild Cards

In Hana-Rumi, the two Dry Koi Jokers are considered Wild cards.

Wild cards can be used as any card when creating a Combination.

FIGURE 39.2 Dry Koi - Wild Cards

Setup

Deal 7 cards to each player face down.
Deal 1 card face up onto the table to form the discard pile.
The remaining cards are placed face down to form a draw pile.

Players pick up and view their cards in a "fan" position while keeping them hidden from other players (similar to card games such as Poker or Rummy).

Playing a Round

Play begins with the first player and continues clockwise.

Each player's turn consists of three phases.

Phase One - Take from Discard or Draw a Card.

During Phase One, the active player <u>must</u> choose to perform <u>one</u> of two actions:

- Take a card from the discard.
  - The selected card <u>must</u> be used during Phase Two of the player's current turn.
  - The player <u>must</u> take all of the cards overlapping the selected card and add them to their hand. (fig 39.3)
- <u>Or</u>, draw a card from the draw pile and add it to their hand.

FIGURE 39.3 Taking from Discard

Draw Pile   Discard

←Selected Card

If a player takes this card, then they must take all cards after this card.

Phase Two - Form New Combinations or Add to Existing Combinations.

During Phase Two, the active player may choose to <u>form a new Combination</u> from their hand and/or <u>add to a Combination</u> previously played by <u>any</u> player.

A player may form and/or add to multiple Combinations during their turn.

Combinations are sets of three or more cards of the same type, three or more cards of the same month, or a sequence of three or more Chaffs. (See **Combinations**.)

Players do <u>not</u> have to make a Combination during their turn <u>unless</u> they took a card from the discard during Phase One.

If a player took a card from the discard during Phase One, then the player <u>must</u> use that card to form a new Combination <u>or</u> add that card to an existing Combination during this current Phase.

Forming a new Combination:

The active player may choose to play a Combination from their hand face-up into their capture area.

Adding to an existing Combination:

The active player may choose to play a card from their hand that adds to a Combination previously played by any player. This card is played face-up into the active player's capture area.

When adding to an existing Combination, the following restrictions apply:

- Players can not add cards that were replaced by Wild cards.

  For example: If a player previously played three contiguous cards of the same month (Wild-January Ribbon-January Chaff), no player can add the January Crane to that Combination because it was already replaced by the Wild card.

  For example: If a player previously played the Chaff sequence April-Wild-June, no player can add the May Chaff to this sequence because it was already replaced by the Wild card.

- Regardless of who played them, cards that are added to a Combination become part of the Combination. Therefore, players can not add cards that were already added by another player.

  For example: Player A plays a Chaff sequence (April-May-June). On Player B's turn, Player B adds a July Chaff. The next player that chooses to add to that Combination must add an August Chaff or a March Chaff to continue the sequence. They can not add a July Chaff because it was already added to the sequence.

Important Note: Once a card has been used in a Combination, it can not be rearranged, removed, or used in another Combination.

For example: A player who previously played the Chaff sequence May-June-Wild can not rearrange the cards (e.g. Wild-May-June) in the sequence.

For example: A player who previously played the Chaff sequence May-June-Wild can not remove the Wild card in order to allow them to add a July card to the sequence.

For example: A player who played four Bright cards (March-December-January-November) can not remove or reuse the January card to create a contiguous January Combination.

For example: A player who added a Ten to an opponent's Tens Combo can not remove the card or reuse it to create another Combination.

Phase Three - Discard

During Phase Three, the active player must take one card from their hand and add it to the discard pile face up.

Cards added to the discard should overlap partially so that the card beneath it remains identifiable.

If a player discards the last card in their hand, then the round ends. (See **End of Round**).

Important: A player can not end the round by discarding a playable card.

Otherwise, play passes to the next player.

Note: If a player has no cards left in their hand to discard, then play passes to the next player.

Players continue taking turns in this manner until the round ends.

End of Round

The round ends when a player discards the last card from their hand.

This player is the winner of the round.

The winner of the round becomes the dealer for the next round.

Scoring

Each player's score for the round is equal to the total value of the cards in the player's capture area plus the value of any Special Achievements the player completed minus the value of any cards remaining in the player's hand at the end of the round.

Player's Score = Total Value of Player's Captured Cards + Total Value of Player's Special Achievements - Total Value of Cards Remaining in Player's Hand

Record the scores for each round.

Each player calculates their total combined score for all rounds.

The first player to reach 200 points wins the game.

If multiple players reach 200 points, then the player with the highest total score wins the game.

Card Values

Brights = 20 pts
Tens = 10 pts
Ribbons = 5 pts
Chaffs = 1 pt
Wet Koi (Jokers) = 5 pts
Dry Koi (Wilds) = 10 pts

Combinations

Combinations are sets of cards that players play in their capture area during Phase Two.

The are three categories of Combinations that a player may form: Type Combinations, Contiguous Combinations, and Sequential Chaff Combinations.

Type Combinations

Any 3 or more cards of the same <u>type</u> (<u>excluding</u> Chaffs): Brights, Tens, Ribbons, Wet Koi (fig 39.4)

Contiguous Combinations

Any 3 or more <u>contiguous</u> cards of the same month (fig 39.5)

Any month can be used, however all cards <u>must</u> be from the same month.

Important: Cards <u>must</u> be contiguous.

For example: The first three cards of November (i.e Bright, Ten, Ribbon).

For example: The last three cards of November (i.e Ten, Ribbon, Chaff).

Tip: Contiguous cards in *Hanami* create a scene when they are adjacent.

Sequential Chaff Combinations

Any 3 or more <u>sequential</u> Chaffs. (fig 39.6)

Only Chaffs may be used to create a sequence.

Sequential cards are based on month order.

For example: Jan. Chaff, Feb. Chaff, Mar. Chaff

For example: Oct. Chaff, Nov. Chaff, Dec. Chaff

Sequences can wrap.

For example: Dec. Chaff, Wet Koi, Jan. Chaff

For example: Wet Koi, Jan. Chaff, Feb. Chaff

Sequences can <u>not</u> change direction.

For example: Jan. Chaff, Feb. Chaff, Jan. Chaff is <u>not</u> a valid sequence.

FIGURE 39.4 **Type Combinations**

Players may form any of the following:

Any 3 or more Brights

Any 3 or more Tens

Any 3 or more Ribbons

Any 3 or more Wet Koi

FIGURE 39.5 **Contiguous Combinations**

Players may form the following:

Any 3 or more <u>contiguous</u> cards of the same month

FIGURE 39.6 **Sequential Chaff Combinations**

Players may form the following:

Any 3 or more <u>sequential</u> Chaffs

Special Achievements

Special achievements are special situations in which a player can earn bonus points for cards in their capture area.

Note: In order to claim a Special Achievement, all cards required to claim the Special Achievement must be in that player's capture area.

Important: Cards used to claim a Special Achievement may **not** include a Wild Card <u>except</u> for the *Sequence of Five* Special Achievement.

A player can earn multiple Special Achievements in a single round, however, only one Special Achievement can be earned per Combination.

Sequence of Five

If a player forms a Combination of 5 or more <u>sequential</u> Chaffs, that player receives 20 points.

Purple Ribbons

If a player forms a Combination containing 3 Purple Ribbons, that player receives 20 points.

Poetry Ribbons

If a player forms a Combination containing 3 Poetry Ribbons, that player receives 20 points.

Wet Koi

A player may claim points for <u>one</u> of the following:

If a player forms a Combination of 3 Wet Koi, that player receives 20 points.

If a player forms a Combination of 4 Wet Koi, that player receives 40 points.

Complete Month

If a player forms a Combination of a <u>complete</u> month (excluding Wilds), that player receives 40 points.

Scoring Examples

Player A discards their final card and ends the round.

Since Player A discarded their final card, Player A is the winner of the round.

Player A has 3 Tens, 1 Ribbon, and 3 Sequential Chaffs in their capture area.

Player A's <u>Total Card Value</u> for this round is
$(3 \times 10) + (1 \times 5) + (3 \times 1) = 38$ pts.

Player A did not earn any Special Achievements.

Player B has 1 Ten and 4 Ribbons in their capture area.

Player B's <u>Total Card Value</u> for this round is
$(1 \times 10) + (4 \times 5) = 30$ pts.

Player B earned the *3 Purple Ribbons* Special Achievement (20 pts).

Player B had 3 Chaffs remaining in their hand.

Since Player B had cards remaining in their hand, they must deduct the value of these cards from their score.

The total value of the cards remaining in Player B's hand is

$(3 \times 1) = 3$ pts.

Player A's <u>Total Score</u> for the round is
$(38) + (0) - (0) = 38$ pts.

Player B's <u>Total Score</u> for the round is
$(30) + (20) - (3) = 47$ pts.

Player A has won this round.

Chapter 40
Hana-Gin

Difficulty: Intermediate

Players: 2

Deck: 48 card flower deck (plus 6 Jokers)

Rounds: Varies

Objective: To be the first player to reach 100 points.

Important Notes:

- Hana-Gin is a fusion game that we designed to fully incorporate the use of hanafuda with the card game Gin. Although Hana-Gin draws inspiration from Gin, this game was designed with the hanafuda deck in mind and will require some familiarity with the hanafuda deck to play.

Jokers

In Hana-Gin, the four Wet Koi Jokers are considered special Chaffs.

Jokers can be used as a thirteenth month when creating sequential Combinations.

The thirteenth month comes <u>after</u> December and <u>before</u> January.

Note: When playing with the *Hanami* Fusion deck, the Wet Koi Jokers are identified as Kings.

FIGURE 40.1 **Wet Koi - Jokers**

Wild Cards

In Hana-Gin, the two Dry Koi Jokers are considered Wild cards.

Wild cards can be used as any card when creating a Combination.

FIGURE 40.2 **Dry Koi - Wild Cards**

Setup

Deal 9 cards to each player face down.
Deal 1 card face up onto the table to form the discard pile.
The remaining cards are placed face down to form a draw pile.

Players pick up and view their cards in a "fan" position while keeping them hidden from other players (similar to card games such as Poker or Rummy).

Playing a Round

Play begins with the first player and continues clockwise.

Each player's turn consists of three phases.

Phase One - Take from Discard or Draw a Card.

During Phase One, the active player <u>must</u> choose to perform <u>one</u> of two actions:

- Take a card from the discard and add it to their hand.

  The player may <u>only</u> take the topmost card of the discard.

- <u>**Or**</u>, draw a card from the draw pile and add it to their hand.

FIGURE 40.3 Taking from Discard

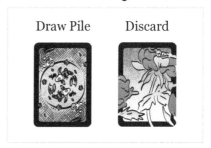

Draw Pile   Discard

Phase Two - Check for Combinations

Combinations are sets of three or more cards of the same type, three or more cards of the same month, or a sequence of three or more Chaffs. (See **Combinations**.)

Important: Each card can only be used in one Combination.

The active player checks their hand for Combinations:

- If the active player can form Combinations that will use at least 7 of the 10 cards in their hand, then they may <u>choose</u> to call "Hana".

  The player discards 1 card.

  The round ends.

- If the active player can form Combinations that will use at least 9 of the 10 cards in their hand, then they may choose to call "Gin".

  The round ends.

- Otherwise, the player proceeds to Phase Three.

Note: Players may choose not to call "Hana" or "Gin", even if they have the Combinations required to do so.

Tip: While calling "Hana" will end the game sooner, it can be risky and typically will not earn a player as many points as calling "Gin".

Phase Three - Discard

During Phase Three, the active player <u>must</u> take <u>one</u> card from their hand and add it to the discard pile face up.

Cards added to the discard should completely cover the cards beneath them.

Play passes to the next player.

Players continue taking turns in this manner until the round ends.

End of Round

The round ends when one of the following occurs:

- A player calls "Hana".
- A player calls "Gin".
- The deck is exhausted.

Both players reveal their hands so that all Combinations and unused cards (i.e. cards not used in a Combination) are visible.

Combinations are placed face-up into the player's capture area.

Unused cards are placed face-up next to the player's capture area.

Scoring

Players calculate their scores in one of two ways depending on how the round ended.

Only the winner of the round receives points for the round.

If a player called "Gin", scoring is calculated as follows:

The player who called "Gin" is the winner of the round.

Only winner of the round receives points for the round.

The winner's score for the round is 20 points plus the value of their opponent's unused cards.

Winner's Score = 20 pts + Total Value of Opponent's Unused Cards

If the winner formed all 10 of their cards into Combinations, then they receive an <u>additional</u> 20 points.

The winner of the round becomes the dealer for the next round.

If a player called "Hana", scoring is calculated as follows:

1. First, the player who did **not** call "Hana" may choose to play their unused cards onto their opponent's Combinations.

   <u>Only</u> the player who did <u>not</u> call Hana may do this.

   For example: Player A may play their unused Ten onto Player B's *Any 3 Tens* Type Combination.

2. Next, <u>each</u> player calculates their Total Unused Card Value by adding the total value of their unused cards.

   For example: If Player A had a January Bright and a November Chaff that were not used in any Combination, they would add 20 + 1. Player A's Total Unused Card Value would therefore be 21 points.

3. Then, players compare their Total Unused Card Values.

   The player with the <u>lowest</u> Total Unused Card Value is the winner of the round.

   If both players have the same Total Unused Card Value, then the player who called "Hana" is the winner of the round.

The winner of the round receives points equal to the Opponent's Total Unused Card Value minus the Winner's Total Unused Card Value.

Winner's Score = Opponent's Total Unused Card Value - Winner's Total Unused Card Value

Only the winner of the round receives points for the round.

If the winner of the round is <u>not</u> the player who called "Hana", then the winner receives an <u>additional</u> 20 points.

The winner of the round becomes the dealer for the next round.

If the deck is exhausted, the round is considered a draw.

No player scores points.

The dealer remains the same.

Record the scores for each round.

Each player calculates their total combined score for all rounds.

The first player to reach 100 points wins the game.

Card Values

Brights = 20 pts
Tens = 10 pts
Ribbons = 5 pts
Chaffs = 1 pt
Wet Koi (Jokers) = 5 pts
Dry Koi (Wilds) = 10 pts

Combinations

Combinations are sets of cards that players play in their capture area during Phase Two.

The are three categories of Combinations that a player may form: Type Combinations, Contiguous Combinations, and Sequential Chaff Combinations.

Type Combinations

Any 3 or more cards of the same <u>type</u> (<u>excluding</u> Chaffs): Brights, Tens, Ribbons, Wet Koi (fig 40.4)

Contiguous Combinations

Any 3 or more <u>contiguous</u> cards of the same month (fig 40.5)

Any month can be used, however all cards <u>must</u> be from the same month.

Important: Cards <u>must</u> be contiguous.

For example: The first three cards of November (i.e Bright, Ten, Ribbon).

For example: The last three cards of November (i.e Ten, Ribbon, Chaff).

Tip: Contiguous cards in *Hanami* create a scene when they are adjacent.

Sequential Chaff Combinations

Any 3 or more <u>sequential</u> Chaffs. (fig 40.6)

Only Chaffs may be used to create a sequence.

Sequential cards are based on month order.

For example: Jan. Chaff, Feb. Chaff, Mar. Chaff

For example: Oct. Chaff, Nov. Chaff, Dec. Chaff

Sequences can wrap.

For example: Dec. Chaff, Wet Koi, Jan. Chaff

For example: Wet Koi, Jan. Chaff, Feb. Chaff

Sequences can <u>not</u> change direction.

For example: Jan. Chaff, Feb. Chaff, Jan. Chaff is <u>not</u> a valid sequence.

FIGURE 40.4 Type Combinations

Players may form any of the following:

Any 3 or more Brights

Any 3 or more Tens

Any 3 or more Ribbons

Any 3 or more Wet Koi

FIGURE 40.5 Contiguous Combinations

Players may form the following:

Any 3 or more <u>contiguous</u> cards of the same month

FIGURE 40.6 Sequential Chaff Combinations

Players may form the following:

Any 3 or more <u>sequential</u> Chaffs

Scoring Examples

Scoring Example 1

Player A ends the round by calling "Hana" and discards a card.

Player A reveals 3 Tens, 4 Sequential Chaffs, an unused Ribbon, and an unused Chaff.

Player A's <u>Total Unused Card Value</u> is
(5 + 1) = 6 pts.

Player B reveals 3 Ribbons, 3 Sequential Chaffs, and 3 unused Chaffs.

Player B adds 1 of their unused Chaffs onto Player A's Sequential Chaffs.

Player B now has 2 unused Chaffs.

Player B's Total <u>Unused Card Value</u> is
(2 x 1) = 2 pts.

Player B's Total Unused Card Value is lower, therefore Player B wins the round.

Player B's <u>Total Score</u> for the round is
(6 - 2) = 4 pts.

Player B receives an additional 20 pts, because Player B was not the player who called "Hana".

Player B's <u>Final Score</u> for the round is 24 pts.

Scoring Example 2

Player A ends the round by calling "Hana" and discards a card.

Player A reveals 4 Tens, 3 Sequential Chaffs, an unused Ribbon, and an unused Chaff.

Player A's <u>Total Unused Card Value</u> is
(5 + 1) = 6 pts.

Player B reveals 3 Ribbons, 4 Sequential Chaffs, and 2 unused Brights.

Player B's Total <u>Unused Card Value</u> is
(2 x 20) = 40 pts.

Player A's Total Unused Card Value is lower, therefore Player A wins the round.

Player A's <u>Total Score</u> for the round is
(40 - 6) = 34 pts.

Scoring Example 3

Player A ends the round by calling "Gin", therefore Player A is the winner of the round.

Player A reveals 5 Tens, 4 Sequential Chaffs, and an unused Ribbon.

Player B reveals 3 Brights, 3 Sequential Chaffs, and 3 unused Chaffs.

Player B's <u>Total Unused Card Value</u> is
(3 x 1) = 3 pts.

Player A's <u>Total Score</u> for the round is
20 + (3) = 23 pts.

Scoring Example 4

Player A ends the round by calling "Gin", therefore Player A is the winner of the round.

Player A reveals 5 Tens, and 5 Sequential Chaffs.

Player B reveals 3 Brights, 3 Sequential Chaffs, and 3 unused Chaffs.

Player B's <u>Total Unused Card Value</u> is
(3 x 1) = 3 pts.

Player A's <u>Total Score</u> for the round is
20 + (3) = 23 pts.

Player A receives an additional 20 pts for using all 10 cards in their hand.

Player A's <u>Final Score</u> for the round is 43 pts.

SECTION V
Quick Reference Charts

Identification Chart : The Twelve Months and Their Flowers

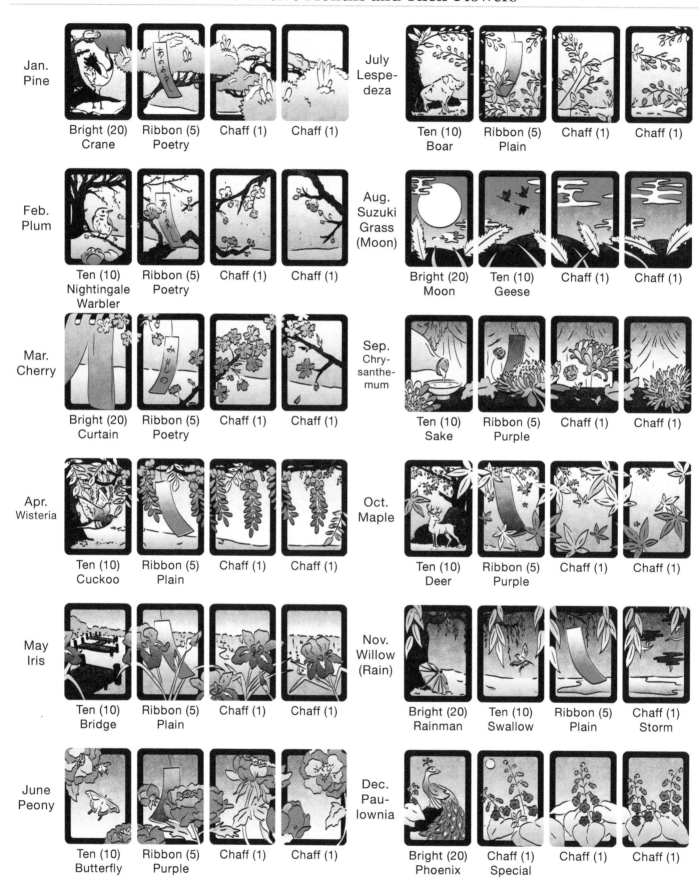

Month				
Jan. Pine	Bright (20) Crane	Ribbon (5) Poetry	Chaff (1)	Chaff (1)
Feb. Plum	Ten (10) Nightingale Warbler	Ribbon (5) Poetry	Chaff (1)	Chaff (1)
Mar. Cherry	Bright (20) Curtain	Ribbon (5) Poetry	Chaff (1)	Chaff (1)
Apr. Wisteria	Ten (10) Cuckoo	Ribbon (5) Plain	Chaff (1)	Chaff (1)
May Iris	Ten (10) Bridge	Ribbon (5) Plain	Chaff (1)	Chaff (1)
June Peony	Ten (10) Butterfly	Ribbon (5) Purple	Chaff (1)	Chaff (1)
July Lespedeza	Ten (10) Boar	Ribbon (5) Plain	Chaff (1)	Chaff (1)
Aug. Suzuki Grass (Moon)	Bright (20) Moon	Ten (10) Geese	Chaff (1)	Chaff (1)
Sep. Chrysanthemum	Ten (10) Sake	Ribbon (5) Purple	Chaff (1)	Chaff (1)
Oct. Maple	Ten (10) Deer	Ribbon (5) Purple	Chaff (1)	Chaff (1)
Nov. Willow (Rain)	Bright (20) Rainman	Ten (10) Swallow	Ribbon (5) Plain	Chaff (1) Storm
Dec. Paulownia	Bright (20) Phoenix	Chaff (1) Special	Chaff (1)	Chaff (1)

Matching Flowers

Source: page 26

Players: 2-3

Deck: 48 card flower deck (remove all Jokers)

Rounds: 6 or 12

Objective: Obtain the most points capturing cards from the field and forming yaku.

# of Players	Dealt to Player	Dealt to Field
2	8	8
3	7	6

Scoring a Round:

Player's Score = Total Value of Player's Captured Cards + Total Value of Player's Captured Yaku

Player with the highest score wins the round.

Card Values:

Brights = 20 pts

Tens = 10 pts

Ribbons = 5 pts

Chaffs = 1 pt

Bright Yaku

Earn points from <u>one</u> of the following:

5 Brights = 100 pts

4 Dry Brights (excluding Rain) = 60 pts

Spring Semi-Brights = 30 pts

Crane, Moon, Phoenix = 20 pts

Other Yaku

Earn points from <u>each</u> of the following:

Boar, Deer, Butterfly = 20 pts

All 4 Wisteria = 10 pts

All 4 Rain = 10 pts

Views Yaku

Earn points from <u>one</u> of the following:

The Views = 40 pts

Flower Viewing = 20 pts

Moon Viewing = 20 pts

Ribbon Yaku

Earn points from <u>one</u> of the following:

Any 7 Dry Ribbons (excluding Rain) = 40 pts

Any 6 Dry Ribbons (excluding Rain) = 30 pts

Earn points from <u>each</u> of the following:

3 Purple Ribbons = 40 pts

3 Poetry Ribbons = 40 pts

3 Dry Plain Ribbons (excluding Rain) = 20 pts

Hana-Awase 1

Source: page 30
Players: 3-4
Deck: 48 card flower deck (remove all Jokers)
Rounds: 6 or 12
Objective: Obtain the most points capturing cards from the field and forming yaku.

# of Players	Dealt to Player	Dealt to Field
3	7	6
4	5	8

Scoring a Round:

Player's Score = Total Value of Player's Captured Cards + Total Value of Player's Captured Yaku

Player with the highest score wins the round.

Card Values:

Brights = 20 pts
Tens = 10 pts
Ribbons = 5 pts
Chaffs = 1 pt

Bright Yaku

Earn points from <u>one</u> of the following:

5 Brights = 75 pts

5 Dry Brights (excluding Rain) = 50 pts

Spring Semi-Brights = 35 pts

Ribbon Yaku

Earn points from <u>each</u> of the following:

Any 7 Dry Ribbons (excluding Rain) = 50 pts

3 Purple Ribbons = 35 pts

3 Poetry Ribbons = 35 pts

Views Yaku

Earn points from <u>one</u> of the following:

Flower Viewing = 30 pts

Moon Viewing = 20 pts

Other Yaku

Earn points from the following:

Boar, Deer, Butterfly = 35 pts

Hana-Awase 2

Source: page 34
Players: 3
Deck: 48 card flower deck (remove all Jokers)
Rounds: 6 or 12
Objective: Obtain the most points capturing cards from the field and forming yaku.

# of Players	Dealt to Player	Dealt to Field
3	7	6

Note: Round ends when a yaku is captured.

Scoring a Round:

Players first calculate their base score:

> *Base Score = Total Value of Player's Captured Cards - 88 points*

If <u>no</u> player captured a yaku:

> *Player's Score = Base Score*

Player with the highest score wins the round.

If a player captured a yaku:

- The player who captured the yaku adds the value of the yaku to their Base Score.

  > *Player's Score = Base Score + Total Value of Player's Captured Yaku*

- The players who did <u>not</u> capture the yaku subtract the value of the yaku from their Base Score.

  > *Player's Score = Base Score - Total Value of Player's Captured Yaku*

Player who captured the yaku wins the round.

Card Values:

Brights = 20 pts
Tens = 10 pts
Ribbons = 5 pts
Chaffs = 1 pt

Bright Yaku

Earn points from <u>one</u> of the following:

5 Brights = 100 pts

4 Dry Brights (excluding Rain) = 60 pts

Ribbon Yaku

Earn points from <u>each</u> of the following:

Any 7 Dry Ribbons (excluding Rain) = 60 pts

3 Purple Ribbons = 40 pts

3 Poetry Ribbons = 40 pts

Chaff Yaku

Earn points from the following:

Any 14 Chaffs = 60 pts

Mushi

Source: page 38

Players: 2

Deck: 40 card flower deck (remove all June Peony, all July Lespedeza, and all Jokers)

Rounds: 6 or 12

Objective: Obtain the most points capturing cards from the field and forming yaku.

# of Players	Dealt to Player	Dealt to Field
2	8	8

Wild Card: Storm Chaff

Scoring a Round:

> *Player's Score = (Total Value of Player's Captured Cards - 115) + Total Value of Player's Captured Yaku - Total Value of Opponent's Yaku.*

Player with the highest score wins the round.

Card Values:

Brights = 20 pts

Tens = 10 pts

Ribbons = 5 pts

Chaffs = 1 pt

Yaku

Earn points from <u>each</u> of the following:

5 Brights = 30 pts

Spring Semi-Brights = 25 pts

All 4 Wisteria = 10 pts

All 4 Paulownia = 10 pts

Six Hundred

Source: page 41
Players: 2-3
Deck: 48 card flower deck (remove all Jokers)
Rounds: Varies
Objective: To be the first player to reach 600 points.

# of Players	Dealt to Player	Dealt to Field
2	8	8
3	7	6

Wild Card: Storm Chaff

Scoring a Round:

Player's Score = Total Value of Player's Captured Cards + Total Value of Player's Captured Yaku + Player's Total Hand Combinations

Game ends when any player's total score is 600 points or higher.

If multiple players have a total score of 600 points or higher, the winner of the game is decided by the following conditions in the following <u>order</u>:

- The player who captured the *4 Dry Brights* yaku wins the game.
- Otherwise, the player who captured the *Any 7 Ribbons* yaku wins the game.
- Otherwise, the player with the highest total score is the winner of the game.

Card Values:
Brights = 50
Nightingale Warbler (Feb. Ten) = 50
Tens = 10
Ribbons = 10
Special Paulownia = 10
Chaff = 0

Bright Yaku

Earn points from <u>each</u> of the following:

4 Dry Brights (excluding Rain) = 600 pts

Crane, Moon, Phoenix = 150 pts

Spring Semi-Brights = 150

Ribbon Yaku

Earn points from <u>each</u> of the following:

Any 7 Ribbons = 600 pts

3 Poetry Ribbons = 100 pts

3 Purple Ribbons = 100 pts

3 Dry Plain Ribbons (excluding Rain) = 100 pts

Views Yaku

Earn points from <u>one</u> of the following:

The Views = 300 pts

Flower Viewing = 100 pts

Moon Viewing = 100 pts

Month Yaku

Earn points from <u>each</u> of the following:

All 4 Rain = 200 pts

All 4 Pine = 50 pts

All 4 Plum = 50 pts

All 4 Cherry = 50 pts

All 4 Wisteria = 50 pts

All 4 Suzuki Grass = 50 pts

All 4 Maple = 50 pts

All 4 Paulownia = 50 pts

Other Yaku

Earn points from the following:

Boar, Deer, Butterfly = 300 pts

Hand Combinations

Earn points from the following:

All Chaffs = 400 pts

Earn points from <u>one</u> of the following:

Any 3 of a Kind = 200 pts

Any 3 of a Kind & Any 3 of a Kind = 400 pts

Hachi-juu Hana

Source: page 46
Players: 2-3
Deck: 48 card flower deck (remove all Jokers)
Rounds: 6 or 12
Objective: Obtain the most points capturing cards from the field and forming yaku.

# of Players	Dealt to Player	Dealt to Field
2	8	8
3	7	6

Note: If a player is dealt 3 of a kind, they may reveal them. If they capture the 4th card, that month's yaku is doubled.

Card Values:
Brights = 20 pts
Tens = 10 pts
Ribbons = 5 pts
Chaffs = 0 pt

Scoring a Round:

In a two player game:

Each player's score for the round will be the total value of the cards they captured minus 120 points plus the value of any yaku they captured.

Player's Score = (Total Value of Player's Captured Cards - 120) + Total Value of Player's Captured Yaku

Player with the highest score wins the round.

In a three player game:

Each player's score for the round will be the total value of the cards they captured minus 80 points plus the value of any yaku they captured.

Player's Score = (Total Value of Player's Captured Cards - 80) + Total Value of Player's Captured Yaku

Player with the highest score wins the round.

Important: When scoring for yaku, November Rain cards may be used as any month.

Month Yaku

Earn points from <u>each</u> of the following:

All 4 January = 20 pts

All 4 February = 20 pts

All 4 March = 20 pts

All 4 April = 20 pts

All 4 May = 20 pts

All 4 June = 20 pts

All 4 July = 20 pts

All 4 August = 20 pts

All 4 September = 20 pts

All 4 October = 20 pts

All 4 November = 20 pts

All 4 December = 20 pts

Min-Hwatu

Source: page 49

Players: 2-3

Deck: 48 card flower deck (remove all Jokers)

Rounds: 6 or 12

Objective: Obtain the most points capturing cards from the field and forming yaku.

# of Players	Dealt to Player	Dealt to Field
2	10	8
3	7	6

Scoring a Round:

Player's Score = Total Value of Player's Captured Cards + (Total Value of Player's Captured Yaku x Number of Opponents) - Total Value of Each Opponent's Yaku

Player with the highest score wins the round.

Card Values:

Brights = 20 pts

Tens = 10 pts

Ribbons = 5 pts

Chaffs = 0 pt

Yaku

Earn points from each of the following:

3 Poetry Ribbons = 30 pts

3 Purple Ribbons = 30 pts

3 Dry Plain Ribbons (excluding Rain) = 30 pts

All 4 Iris = 20 pts

All 4 Maple = 20 pts

All 4 Rain = 20 pts

Optional Yaku

Earn points from one of the following:

5 Brights = 200 pts

Spring Semi-Brights = 150 pts

Earn points from one of the following:

The Grand Views = 150 pts

The Views = 100 pts

Earn points from each of the following:

Boar, Deer, Butterfly = 50 pts

Godori = 50 pts

Koi-Koi

Source: page 53
Players: 2
Deck: 48 card flower deck (remove Jokers)
Rounds: 6 or 12
Objective: Obtain points by capturing cards from the field and forming yaku.

# of Players	Dealt to Player	Dealt to Field
2	8	8

Scoring a Round:

The player who called "Stop" wins the round.

Only the player who called "Stop" scores.

Player's Score = Total Value of Player's Yaku

If <u>any</u> player called "Koi-Koi" the player's score is doubled.

If <u>no</u> player called "Stop" no player earns points.

Bright Yaku

Earn points from <u>one</u> of the following:

5 Brights = 10 pts

4 Dry Brights (excluding Rain) = 8 pts

Any 4 Brights = 7 pts

Any 3 Dry Brights (excluding Rain) = 5 pts

Views Yaku

Earn points from <u>each</u> of the following:

Flower Viewing = 5 pts

Moon Viewing = 5 pts

Ribbon Yaku

Earn points from <u>one</u> of the following:

Any 5 Dry Ribbons (excluding Rain) = 1 pt
+ 1 pt for each additional Ribbon

3 Purple Ribbons = 5 pts + 1 pt for each additional Ribbon

3 Poetry Ribbons = 5 pts + 1 pt for each additional Ribbon

3 Poetry Ribbons & 3 Purple Ribbons = 10 pts
+1 pt for each additional Ribbon

Other Yaku

Earn points from <u>one</u> of the following:

Any 5 Tens = 1 pt + 1 pt for each additional Ten

Boar, Deer Butterfly = 5 pts + 1 pt for each additional Ten

Earn points from the following:

Any 10 Chaffs = 1 pt + 1 pt for each additional Chaff

Oni Koi-Koi

Source: page 59
Players: 2
Deck: 48 card flower deck (remove all Jokers)
Rounds: 6 or 12
Objective: Obtain the most points by capturing cards from the field and forming yaku.

# of Players	Dealt to Player	Dealt to Field
2	8	8

Scoring a Round:

Only the player who called "Stop" receives points.

If <u>neither</u> player called "Stop" before the deck was exhausted, then the round is considered a draw. Both players earn 0 points for that round.

The player's score for the round is equal to the total value of any yaku they captured this round.

Player's Score = Total Value of Player's Captured Yaku

If any player previously called "Koi-Koi" that round, then the player who called "Stop" doubles their points.

Player's Score = Total Value of Player's Captured Yaku x 2

The player with the highest total score is the winner of the game.

Wild Card: Phoenix

The Phoenix must be revealed to be used as a Wild.

The Wild can capture any card when played from hand.

The Wild can not capture Chaffs when drawn from the deck.

The Wild can not be captured by Chaffs when in the field.

Other Yaku

Earn points from <u>each</u> of the following:

Any 5 Tens = 1 pt + 1 pt for each additional Ten

Any 10 Chaffs = 1 pt + 1 pt for each additional Chaff

Bright Yaku

Earn points from <u>one</u> of the following:

5 Brights = 15 pts

4 Dry Brights (excluding Rain) = 10 pts

Any 4 Brights = 8 pts

Any 3 Dry Brights (excluding Rain) = 6 pts

Ribbon Yaku

Earn points from <u>each</u> of the following:

Any 5 Dry Ribbons (excluding Rain) = 1 pt
+ 1 pt for each additional Ribbon

3 Purple Ribbons = 6 pts

3 Poetry Ribbons = 6 pts

Higo-Bana

Source: page 64

Players: 2-7 (Best with 2-4)

Deck: 48 card flower deck (remove all Jokers)

Rounds: 6 or 12

Objective: Obtain the most points capturing cards from the field and forming yaku.

# of Players	Dealt to Player	Dealt to Field
2	8	8
3	7	6
4	5	8
5	4	8
6	3	12
7	3	6

Wild Card: Storm Chaff

Scoring a Round:

Player's Score = Total Value of Player's Captured Cards - 50 points for Each Yaku Captured by Each Opponent

Player with the highest score wins the round.

Card Values:

Brights = 20 pts

Tens = 5 pts

Ribbons = 10 pts

Chaffs = 0 pts

Yaku

Players may capture each of the following:

Spring Semi-Brights

3 Purple Brights

3 Poetry Brights

3 Dry Plain Ribbons (excluding Rain)

The Views

Boar, Deer, Geese

Sake, Deer, Butterfly

Boar, Cuckoo, Bridge

Tensho (Simplified)

Source: page 68

Players: 2

Deck: 45 card flower deck (remove all Jokers and the 3 December Paulownia Chaffs)

Rounds: Player Determined

Objective: Win the most rounds.

# of Players	Dealt to Player	Dealt to Field	Dealt to Discard
2	6	9	6

Scoring a Round:

If a player captured an automatic win, that player wins the round.

If no player captured an automatic win, then the player with the highest Total Yaku Value wins the round.

If there is a tie, then the player with the most Chaffs wins the round.

If there is still a tie, the player with the highest Total Card Value wins the round.

Yaku:

There are two sets of yaku in Tensho, but only one may be used per round.

Card Value

15	5	1	1	7	1	1	1
10	10	1	1	8	1	1	1
3	1	1	1	9	1	1	1
4	1	1	1	10	10	1	1
5	1	1	1	11	1	1	1
10	1	1	1	12			

Yaku (Set One)

Earn points from <u>each</u> of the following:

Front One Two Three = 100 pts

Front Seven Eight Nine = 100 pts

Front Eight Four Six = 100 pts

Back One Two Three = 50 pts

Back Seven Eight Nine = 50 pts

Back Eight Four Six = 50 pts

Front One Two Ten = 100 pts

Front Ten Nine Six = 100 pts

Front Eight Four Six Eleven = 100 pts

Back One Two Ten = 50 pts

Back Ten Nine Six = 50 pts

Back Eight Four Six Eleven = 50 pts

Front Three Four Five = 100 pts

Front Eight Four Eleven = 100 pts

Front Nine Eleven Three = 100 pts

Back Three Four Five = 50 pts

Back Eight Four Eleven = 50 pts

Back Nine Eleven Three = 50 pts

Front Seven Five Three = 100 pts

Front Four Six Eleven = 100 pts

Front Five Ten Twelve = AUTOMATIC WIN

Back Seven Five Three = 50 pts

Back Four Six Eleven = 50 pts

Back Five Ten Twelve = 50 pts

Yaku (Set Two)

Earn points from _each_ of the following:

Front One Two Three = 100 pts

Back Seven Eight Nine = 50 pts

Front Eight Nine Ten = 100 pts

Back One Two Three = 50 pts

Front Ten Nine Six = 100 pts

Back Eight Nine Ten = 50 pts

Front One Two Ten = 100 pts

Back Ten Nine Six = 50 pts

Front Seven Eight Nine Ten = 100 pts

Back One Two Ten = 50 pts

Front Nine Eleven Three = 100 pts

Back Seven Eight Nine Ten = 50 pts

Front Three Four Five = 100 pts

Back Nine Eleven Three = 50 pts

Front Five Ten Twelve = 100 pts

Back Three Four Five = 50 pts

Front Ten Seven Eight = 100 pts

Back Five Ten Twelve = AUTOMATIC WIN

Front Seven Eight Nine = 100 pts

Back Ten Seven Eight = 50 pts

One Four Twelve = AUTOMATIC WIN

Go-Stop

Source: page 73
Players: 2-7
Deck: 48 card flower deck (plus 1-4 Jokers)
Rounds: Player Determined
Objective: Obtain points by capturing cards from the field and forming yaku.

# of Players	Dealt to Player	Dealt to Field
2	10	8
3	7	6

Forced Drop Compensation:
- 2 points per Bright, Joker, Sake, Storm, and/or Special Paulownia in hand.

- If player held 3 cards of the same month, then their compensation is doubled.

Special Events:

Steal Chaffs

The active player receives one Chaff from each opponent for each of the following:
- The active player captures a hiki.

- A player empties the field by capturing the final two cards (of different months) in the field. Does not count on final turn.

- A player plays a card into the field that had no match and then draws that card's match. Does not count on final turn.

- A player captures all four cards of the same month by using a card from their hand and a card drawn from the deck. Does not count on final turn.

Steal Points
- If the active player creates a hiki in their first turn of the round, then the active player immediately takes 3 points from each opponent.

- If a single player creates 3 hiki in one round, then the round ends. That player immediately takes 5 points from each opponent.

Scoring a Round:
The player who called "Stop" is the winner of the round.

Only the player who called "Stop" receives points.

Points that are scored by the winner are taken from each opponent.

> *Player's Score = (Total Value of Player's Yaku + Bonus Points) x Any Multipliers*

Note: Multipliers are cumulative.

Bonus for calling "Go":
- If the winner called "Go" once, they receive 1 bonus point.

- If the winner called "Go" more than once, their score is multiplied by the number of times they called "Go".

Score is doubled for each of the following:
- Winner revealed 3 cards of the same month at the beginning of the round.

Note: If the winner revealed 2 sets of 3 cards of the same month at the beginning of the round, their score is quadrupled.
- Winner captured 7 or more Tens.

- Winner *bombed the field*.

- Previous round had no winner.

Winner receives additional points:
- If winner captured a Bright yaku, then loser(s) with no Bright cards pay double.

- If winner captured the Chaff yaku, then loser(s) with less than 5 Chaff cards pay double.

Loser must pay both loser's penalties if:
- A loser who called "Go" must pay the penalty for a loser who did not call "Go."

- A loser who refused a "Draw" must pay the penalty for a loser who did not refuse.

- If a player plays a card from their hand that does not capture anything in the field and another player wins the round by capturing that card on their next immediate turn, then the player must pay the other loser's penalty in addition to their own. This does not apply if the player offered a *Draw*.

Important Note: Sake can be counted as either a Ten or as 2 Chaffs.
Important Note: The Storm and Special Paulownia Chaffs each count as 2 Chaffs.

Bright Yaku

Earn points from <u>one</u> of the following:

5 Brights = 15 pts

4 Dry Brights (excluding Rain) = 5 pts

Any 4 Brights (including Rain) = 4 pts

Any 3 Dry Brights (excluding Rain) = 3 pts

Any 3 Brights (including Rain) = 2 pts

Tens Yaku

Earn points from <u>each</u> of the following:

Godori = 5 pts

Any 5 Tens = 1 pt + 1 pt for each additional Ten

Ribbon Yaku

Earn points from <u>each</u> of the following:

Any 5 Ribbons = 1 pt + 1 pt for each additional Ribbon

3 Poetry Ribbons = 3 pts

3 Purple Ribbons = 3 pts

3 Dry Plain Ribbons (excluding Rain) = 3 pts

Chaff Yaku

Earn points from <u>each</u> of the following:

Any 10 Chaffs = 1 pt + 1 pt for each additional Chaff

Hachi-Hachi

Source: page 84
Players: 2-7 (Best with 4-6)
Deck: 48 card flower deck (remove Jokers)
Rounds: 12
Objective: Obtain the most points capturing cards, forming yaku & hand combos, and completing special achievements.

# of Players	Dealt to Player	Dealt to Field
2	7	6
3	7	6

Pass Penalty:

First player to pass pays 10 pts.
Second player to pass pays 15 pts.
Third player to pass pays 20 pts.

The winner of the round claims any Pass Penalties that were payed.

Forced Drop Compensation:

- Half the value of held Hand Combos.
- Half the value of held Yaku.
- 3 points per unclaimed Bright, Poetry Ribbon, and/or Purple Ribbon.

Field Multiplier:

No Brights = 1x
Jan. Bright, Mar. Bright, or Aug. Bright = 2x
Nov. Bright or Dec. Bright = 4x

The Field Multiplier applies to Pass Penalties, Compensation, Hand Combinations, Yaku, and Special Achievements.

Card Values:

Brights = 20 pts
Tens = 10 pts
Ribbons = 5 pts
Chaffs = 1 pt

Scoring a Round:

If the round ended <u>without</u> any player capturing a yaku, then each player calculates their scores as follows:

1. First, <u>each</u> player <u>takes</u> the Total Value of their Hand Combinations from <u>each</u> of their active opponents.

2. Next, <u>each</u> player determines their Total Card Value, subtracts 88, and then multiples the result by the Field Multiplier.

   (Player's Total Card Value - 88) x Field Multiplier

3. Then, <u>each</u> player <u>takes</u> the Total Value of their Special Achievements from <u>each</u> of their active opponents.

4. Finally, <u>each</u> player combines the results from steps 1-3.

This is the player's score for the round.

The winner of the round is the player who had the <u>highest</u> Total Card Value.

If the round ended <u>with</u> any player capturing a yaku, then each player calculates their scores as follows:

1. First, <u>each</u> player <u>takes</u> the Total Value of their Hand Combinations from <u>each</u> of their active opponents.

2. Next, players score their yaku based on how the round ended:

   - If a player called "End", then that player <u>takes</u> their Total Yaku Value from <u>each</u> of their active opponents.
     - Only the player who called "End" receives points for their Yaku.
     - The winner of the round is the player who called "End".

   - If a player called "End" <u>and</u> a single opponent previously called "Continue", then the player who called "End" <u>takes</u> <u>double</u> their Total Yaku Value from the player who called "Continue".
     - The player who did not call "Continue" or "End" pays nothing.
     - Only the player who called "End" receives points for their Yaku.
     - The winner of the round is the player who called "End".

   - If a player called "End" <u>and</u> both opponents previously called "Continue", then the player who called "End" <u>takes</u> their Total Yaku Value from <u>each</u> active opponent.
     - Only the player who called "End" receives points for their Yaku.
     - The winner of the round is the player who called "End".

   - If a player called "Cancel", then that player <u>takes</u> <u>half</u> of the value of their Total Yaku Value from <u>each</u> of their active opponents.
     - Only the player who called "Cancel" receives points for their Yaku.
     - The winner of the round is the player who called "Cancel".

   - If any player(s) called "Continue" but the deck was exhausted before any player called "End", then all players who called continue <u>take</u> <u>half</u> the value of their Total Yaku Value from each of their active opponents.
     - The winner of the round is the player who first called "Continue".

3. Then, <u>each</u> player <u>takes</u> the Total Value of their Special Achievements from <u>each</u> of their active opponents.

4. Finally, <u>each</u> player combines the results from steps 1-3.

This is the player's score for the round.

Special Achievements:

Special Achievements do <u>not</u> apply when playing with two players.

89 Plus Chaff

If a player claimed any <u>non-bright</u> Chaff Combo <u>and</u> had an <u>unmodified</u> Total Card Value of 89 or higher this round, then that player <u>takes</u> 10 points from <u>each</u> of their active opponents.

Captured Suit

If a player claimed any Suit Combo containing 3 of a Kind and captured all three of those cards, then that player <u>takes</u> 10 points from <u>each</u> of their active opponents.

Note: It is possible to claim this bonus twice if the player revealed two sets of 3 of a Kind.

Note: This Special Achievement does <u>not</u> apply to any Suit Combo containing 4 of a Kind.

The following Special Achievements <u>only</u> apply if the round ended <u>without</u> any player capturing a yaku:

88 Hachi-Hachi

If all three players' <u>unmodified</u> Total Card Value for the round are <u>each</u> <u>exactly</u> 88 points, then the dealer <u>takes</u> 100 points from <u>each</u> of their active opponents.

Scoring for <u>all</u> Hand Combinations <u>and</u> all other Special Achievements (including Simple 16) this round are canceled.

168 Plus

If a player's <u>unmodified</u> Total Card Value for the round is 168 or higher, then that player <u>takes</u> 100 points from <u>each</u> of their active opponents <u>plus</u> an additional 10 points for <u>each</u> point over 168.

Scoring for <u>all</u> Hand Combinations <u>and</u> all other Special Achievements (including Simple 16) this round are canceled.

Simple 16

If a player captures 16 or more Chaffs in a round, then that player <u>takes</u> 120 points from <u>each</u> of their active opponents <u>plus</u> an additional 20 points for <u>each</u> additional Chaff.

Scoring for <u>all</u> Hand Combinations <u>and</u> all other Special Achievements this round are canceled.

The following Special Achievements <u>only</u> apply if playing with the *Drop Out Dealer* Variant:

Blind Stay

In any round where the *Blind Stay Dealer's* unmodified Total Card Value is 89 points or greater, the Blind Stay Dealer <u>takes</u> 10 points from <u>all</u> players (<u>including</u> those who did not play the round) <u>excluding</u> the 7th player who was forced to drop from drawing the Joker.

Failed Blind Stay

If the round ended with no player capturing a yaku <u>and</u> the *Blind Stay Dealer's* unmodified Total Card Value is less than 89 points, then the *Blind Stay Dealer* must <u>pay</u> <u>each</u> of their active opponents 10 points.

The following Special Achievement <u>only</u> applies if playing with the <u>Trade Variant</u>:

Dealer's Hand

If the last player to Trade (i.e. the player with the Dealer's hand) captures an unmodified Total Card Value of 89 points or greater, that player <u>takes</u> 10 points from <u>all</u> players (including those who did not play the round) <u>excluding</u> the player who was forced to drop from drawing the Joker.

Yaku

Earn points from <u>one</u> of the following:

Five Brights = 120 pts

Four Dry Brights (excluding Rain) = 100 pts

Also earn points from <u>each</u> of the following:

3 Poetry Ribbons = 70 pts

3 Purple Ribbons = 70 pts

Any 7 Dry Ribbons (excluding Rain) = 100 pts
+ 10 pts for each additional Ribbon (including Rain)

Hand Combinations

Suit Combos

Earn points from <u>one</u> of the following:

Any 3 of a Kind = 20 pts

Any 3 of a Kind & Any 2 Pairs = 70 pts

Greater: Any 3 Wisteria = 30 pts

Any 4 of a Kind & Any 1 Pair = 80 pts

Greater: Any 3 Iris = 30 pts

Any 4 of a Kind & Any 3 of a Kind = 200

Greater: Any 3 Lespedeza = 30 pts

Any 3 of a Kind & Any 3 of a Kind = 60 pts

Greater: 3 Paulownia Chaffs = 30 pts

Any 3 of a Kind & Any Greater = 70 pts

Any 4 of a Kind = 60 pts

Any Greater & Any Greater = 80 pts

Any 3 Pairs = 40 pts

Chaff Combos

Earn points from <u>one</u> of the following:

Any 2 Ribbons & Any 5 Chaffs = 20 pts

Any 1 Bright & Any 6 Chaffs = 40 pts

Any 1 Ribbon & Any 6 Chaffs = 30 pts

Any 7 Chaffs = 40 pts

Any 1 Ten & Any 6 Chaffs = 30 pts

When scoring for Hand Combinations all of the November Rain Month are considered Chaffs. (This is for Hand Combinations only.)

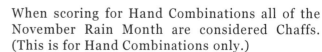

Sudaoshi

Source: page 98
Players: 3
Deck: 48 card flower deck (remove Jokers)
Rounds: 6 or 12
Objective: Obtain the most points capturing cards and forming yaku & hand combinations.

# of Players	Dealt to Player	Dealt to Field
3	7	6

Assigned Point Burden:

Before play begins, each player is assigned a *Point Burden* for the round:

- <u>Dealer</u> receives burden of -100 pts.
- Player to dealer's <u>right</u> receives -110 pts.
- Player to dealer's <u>left</u> receives -120 pts.

The *Point Burden* is reassigned <u>each round</u>:

- <u>Highest</u> scoring player receives -100 pts.
- <u>Lowest</u> scoring player receives -120 pts.
- Remaining player receives -110 pts.

Card Values

Curtain = 10 pts
Phoenix = 10 pts
Chaffs = 10 pts
Crane = 5 pts
Moon = 5 pts
Rain Man = 5 pts
Tens = 5 pts
Ribbons = 1 pt

Yaku:

Players with the 100 and 110 Burden can only score <u>one</u> yaku from the Hills category.

The player with the 120 Burden can score one yaku from the Hills category <u>and</u> one yaku from the Rain category.

Scoring a Round:

Player with the highest score wins the round.

Player's Total Hand Combination Value = ___ x 2 =		___
First Opponent's Total Hand Combination Value =	-	___
Second Opponent's Total Hand Combination Value =	-	___
Player's Total Yaku Value = ___ x 2 =		___
First Opponent's Total Yaku Value =	-	___
Second Opponent's Total Yaku Value =	-	___
Player's Total Card Value =		___
Player's Point Burden =	-	___
Player's Total Score	=	___

Hills Yaku

<u>Any</u> player may earn points from <u>one</u> of the following:

Over the Hills (Moon and Geese) = 10 pts

The Hills (All 4 August) = 20 pts

Rain Yaku

<u>Only</u> the player with the 120 Point Burden may earn points from <u>one</u> of the following:

Under the Rainy Sky (Rain Man and Swallow) = 10 pts

Rainy Sky (All 4 November) = 20 pts

Hand Combinations

Suit Combos

Earn points from <u>one</u> of the following:

Any 3 of a Kind = 20 pts

Greater: Any 3 Wisteria = 30 pts

Greater: Any 3 Iris = 30 pts

Greater: Any 3 Lespedeza = 30 pts

Greater: 3 Paulownia Chaffs = 30 pts

Any 4 of a Kind = 60 pts

Any 3 of a Kind & Any 2 Pairs = 70 pts

Any 4 of a Kind & Any 1 Pair = 80 pts

Any 4 of a Kind & Any 3 of a Kind = 200

Any 3 of a Kind & Any 3 of a Kind = 60 pts

Any 3 of a Kind & Any Greater = 70 pts

Any Greater & Any Greater = 80 pts

Any 3 Pairs = 40 pts

Chaff Combos

Earn points from <u>one</u> of the following:

Any 2 Ribbons & Any 5 Chaffs = 20 pts

Any 1 Bright & Any 6 Chaffs = 40 pts

Any 1 Ribbon & Any 6 Chaffs = 30 pts

Any 7 Chaffs = 40 pts

Any 1 Ten & Any 6 Chaffs = 30 pts

When scoring for Hand Combinations all of the November Rain Month are considered Chaffs. (This is for Hand Combinations only.)

Hachi (Simplified)

Source: page 104
Players: 2
Deck: 48 card flower deck (remove Jokers)
Rounds: Variable
Objective: Win 2 consecutive rounds by 20 points or more.

# of Players	Dealt to Player	Dealt to Field
2	7	6

Scoring a Round:

Player's Score = Total Value of Player's Captured Cards + Total Value of Player's Captured Yaku.

Player with the highest score wins the round.

Card Values:

Brights = 10 pts
Tens = 10 pts
Ribbons = 1 pt
Chaffs = 10 pts

Capture Chart

Month	Capture
January (1)	Feb (2), Mar (3), April (4)
February (2)	Mar (3), April (4), May (5)
March (3)	April (4), May (5), June (6)
April (4)	May (5), June (6), July (7)
May (5)	June (6), July (7), Aug (8)
June (6)	July (7), Aug (8), Sep (9)
July (7)	Aug (8), Sep (9), Oct (10)
August (8)	Sep (9), Oct (10), Nov (11)
September (9)	Oct (10), Nov (11), Dec (12)
October (10)	Nov (11), Dec (12), Jan (1)
November (11)	Dec (12), Jan (1), Feb (2)
December (12)	Jan (1), Feb (2), Mar (3)

Yaku

Earn points from <u>each</u> of the following:

Twelve Four Eleven = 10 pts

Poetry Seven Five Three = 20 pts

One Two Three = 10 pts

Poetry Twelve Four Eleven = 20 pts

Nine Eleven Three = 10 pts

Poetry One Two Three = 20 pts

Five Six Ten = 10 pts

Poetry Nine Eleven Three = 20 pts

Three Five Six = 10 pts

Poetry Five Six Ten = 20 pts

Eight Four Eleven = 10 pts

Poetry Three Five Six = 20 pts

Five Four Six = 10 pts

Poetry Eight Four Eleven = 20 pts

Ten Seven Eight = 10 pts

Poetry Five Four Six = 20 pts

Seven Eight Nine = 10 pts

Poetry Ten Seven Eight = 20 pts

Seven Five Three = 10 pts

Poetry Seven Eight Nine = 20 pts

Hachi

Source: page 108
Players: 2
Deck: 48 card flower deck (remove Jokers)
Rounds: Variable
Objective: Win 2 consecutive rounds by 20 points or more.

# of Players	Dealt to Player	Dealt to Field
2	7	6

Scoring a Round:

Player's Score = Total Value of Player's Captured Cards + Total Value of Player's Captured Yaku.

Player with the highest score wins the round.

Card Values:

Brights = 10 pts
Tens = 10 pts
Ribbons = 1 pt
Chaffs = 10 pts

Capture Chart

Month	Capture
January (1)	Feb (2), July (7), Dec (12)
February (2)	Jan (1), June (6), Nov (11)
March (3)	May (5), Oct (10)
April (4)	April (4), Sep (9)
May (5)	Mar (3), Aug (8)
June (6)	Feb (2), July (7), Dec (12)
July (7)	Jan (1), June (6), Nov (11)
August (8)	May (5), Oct (10)
September (9)	Apr (4), Sep (9)
October (10)	Mar (3), Aug (8)
November (11)	Feb (2), July (7), Dec (12)
December (12)	Jan (1), June (6), Nov (11)

Yaku

Earn points from _each_ of the following:

Twelve Four Eleven = 10 pts

Poetry Seven Five Three = 20 pts

One Two Three = 10 pts

Poetry Twelve Four Eleven = 20 pts

Nine Eleven Three = 10 pts

Poetry One Two Three = 20 pts

Five Six Ten = 10 pts

Poetry Nine Eleven Three = 20 pts

Three Five Six = 10 pts

Poetry Five Six Ten = 20 pts

Eight Four Eleven = 10 pts

Poetry Three Five Six = 20 pts

Five Four Six = 10 pts

Poetry Eight Four Eleven = 20 pts

Ten Seven Eight = 10 pts

Poetry Five Four Six = 20 pts

Seven Eight Nine = 10 pts

Poetry Ten Seven Eight = 20 pts

Seven Five Three = 10 pts

Poetry Seven Eight Nine = 20 pts

Tensho

Source: page 112

Players: 2

Deck: 45 card flower deck (remove all Jokers and the 3 December Paulownia Chaffs)

Rounds: Player Determined

Objective: Win the most rounds.

# of Players	Dealt to Player	Dealt to Field	Dealt to Discard
2	6	9	6

Scoring a Round:

If a player captured an Automatic Win:

That player automatically wins the round.

If <u>no</u> player captured an Automatic Win:

The player with the highest Total Yaku Value is the winner of the round.

Resolving Ties:

If there is a tie, then the player who captured the <u>most Chaffs</u> wins the round.

If there is still a tie, the player with the <u>highest Total Card Value</u> wins the round.

Yaku:

There are two sets of yaku in Tensho, but only <u>one</u> may be used per round.

Card Value

Month	Flower					Month	Flower				
January	Pine					July	Lespedeza				
February	**Rain**					August	Moon				
March	Cherry					September	Chrysanthemum				
April	Wisteria					October	Maple				
May	Iris					November	**Peony**				
June	**Paulownia**					December	**Plum**				

Month Order

Yaku (Set One)

Earn points from <u>each</u> of the following:

Front One Two Three = 100 pts

Front Seven Eight Nine = 100 pts

Front Eight Four Twelve = 100 pts

Back One Two Three = 50 pts

Back Seven Eight Nine = 50 pts

Back Eight Four Twelve = 50 pts

Front One Two Ten = 100 pts

Front Ten Nine Twelve = 100 pts

Front Eight Four Eleven Twelve = 100 pts

Back One Two Ten = 50 pts

Back Ten Nine Twelve = 50 pts

Back Eight Four Eleven Twelve = 50 pts

Front Three Four Five = 100 pts

Front Eight Four Eleven = 100 pts

Front Nine Eleven Three = 100 pts

Back Three Four Five = 50 pts

Back Eight Four Eleven = 50 pts

Back Nine Eleven Three = 50 pts

Front Seven Five Three = 100 pts

Front Four Eleven Twelve = 100 pts

Front Five Six Ten = AUTOMATIC WIN

Back Seven Five Three = 50 pts

Back Four Eleven Twelve = 50 pts

Back Five Six Ten = 50 pts

Yaku (Set Two)

Earn points from <u>each</u> of the following:

Front One Two Three = 100 pts

Front Ten Nine Twelve = 100 pts

Front Seven Eight Nine Ten = 100 pts

Back One Two Three = 50 pts

Back Ten Nine Twelve = 50 pts

Back Seven Eight Nine Ten = 50 pts

Front One Two Ten = 100 pts

Front Nine Eleven Three = 100 pts

Front Five Six Ten = 100 pts

Back One Two Ten = 50 pts

Back Nine Eleven Three = 50 pts

Back Five Six Ten = AUTOMATIC WIN

Front Three Four Five = 100 pts

Front Ten Seven Eight = 100 pts

One Six Four = AUTOMATIC WIN

Back Three Four Five = 50 pts

Back Ten Seven Eight = 50 pts

Front Seven Eight Nine = 100 pts

Front Eight Nine Ten = 100 pts

Back Seven Eight Nine = 50 pts

Back Eight Nine Ten = 50 pts

Poka

Source: page 120
Players: 2
Deck: 48 card flower deck (remove Jokers)
Rounds: Variable
Objective: Be the first player to play all of the cards from their hand.

Setup:

Place 9 tokens on the table.
Deal 6 cards to each player face down.
Turn up 1 card as the base card.

Automatic Wins:

- All 3 Wild Cards = 2 tokens
- 3 pairs = 2 tokens
- Any 3 January cards = 2 tokens
- 4 of a kind = 5 tokens

Wild Cards:

Special Rule:

If the base card is a January and the active player has both a January and a February in their hand, then the player may play both cards.

Scoring a Round:

The first player to play all of the cards from their hand is the winner of the round.

The winner of the round receives 1 token.

If a player manages to play all of the cards in their hand on their first turn, then that player receives 2 tokens instead of 1.

Game End:

The first player to collect 5 tokens wins the game.

Kage

Source: page 130
Players: 2
Deck: 48 card flower deck (plus 4-6 Jokers)
Rounds: 5 or less
Objective: Be the first player to play all of the cards from their hand.

Setup:

Deal 6 cards to each player face down.
Turn up 1 card as the base card.

Reminder: Players are <u>must</u> play as may cards as possible during their turn.

Wild Cards: All Jokers

Automatic Wins:

- 4 or more Wild Cards
- 4 of a Kind

Scoring a Round:

The first player to play all of the cards from their hand is the winner of the round.

Game End:

The first player to win 3 rounds wins the game.

Hiyoko (Simplified)

Source: page 123
Players: 2-4 (Best with 2)
Deck: 45 card flower deck (remove all Jokers, the Peony Ribbon, and the 2 Peony Chaffs.)
Rounds: 5 or less
Objective: Be the first player to play all of the cards from their hand.

Setup:

Deal 6 cards to each player face down.
Turn up 1 card as the base card.

Special Rule:

If the base card is a January and the active player has both a January and a February in their hand, then the player may play both cards.

Scoring:

The first player to play all of the cards from their hand is the winner of the round.

Game End:

The first player to wins 3 rounds wins the game.

Hand Wild Cards

Wild Card	Special Ability
	Can be used as any month from January to October.
	Can be used as any month from January to October.
	Can be used as any month from February to November.
	Can be used as any month from February to November.
	Can be used as any month from January to December.

Base Wild Cards

Wild Card	Special Ability
	Can be used as January, but only when this card is the base.
	Can be used as January, but only when this card is the base.
	Can be used as January, but only when this card is the base.
	Can be used as January, but only when this card is the base.
	Can be used any month from January to December, but only when this card is the base.

Isuri (Simplified)

Source: page 126
Players: 2-3
Deck: 46 card flower deck (remove all Jokers and the 2 Peony Chaffs.)
Rounds: 6
Objective: Be the first player to play all of the cards from their hand.

Setup:

Place 1 token on the table.
Deal 6 cards to each player face down.
Turn up 1 card as the base card.

Special Rule:

If the base card is a January and the active player has both a January and a February in their hand, then the player may play both cards.

Tokens:

When both players consecutively call "Pass" a token is placed on the table. Tokens remain on the table until the end of the game.

Scoring a Round:

The first player to play all of the cards from their hand is the winner of the round.

Points scored by the winner are taken from the loser.

Calculating Base Score:

Base Score = Total Tokens x Winner's Last Card

Reminder: January is a 10 when calculating Base Score.

Calculating Winner's Final Score:

- If the winner won by playing three cards of the same month,

  Round Score = Base Score x 3

- If the winner won by playing four cards of the same month,

  Round Score = Base Score x 4

- If the winner won by playing five cards of the same month,

  Round Score = Base Score x 5

- If the winner won by playing six cards of the same month,

  Round Score = Base Score x 6 + (Total Tokens x 10)

- If none of the above conditions were met, then the Base Score is the Round Score.

  Round Score = Base Score

If the winner won on their first turn of the round, then the Round Score is increased by 10 times the Total Tokens.

  Round Score = Round Score + (Total Tokens x 10)

Hand Wild Cards

Wild Card	Special Ability
	Can be used as any month from January to October.
	Can be used as any month from January to October.
	Can be used as any month from February to November.
	Can be used as any month from February to November.
	Can be used as any month from January to December.

Base Wild Cards

Wild Card	Special Ability
	Can be used as January, but only when this card is the base.
	Can be used as January, but only when this card is the base.
	Can be used as January, but only when this card is the base.
	Can be used as January, but only when this card is the base.
	Can be used as January, but only when this card is the base.
	Can be used any month from January to December, but only when this card is the base.

Hiyoko

Source: page 133
Players: 2-4 (Best with 2)
Deck: 45 card flower deck (remove Jokers and the 3 December Paulownia Chaffs.)
Rounds: 5 or less
Objective: Be the first player to play all of the cards from their hand.

Setup:
Deal 6 cards to each player face down.

Turn up 1 card as the base card.

Special Rule:
If the base card is a January and the active player has both a January and a February in their hand, then the player may play both cards.

Scoring a Round:
The first player to play all of the cards from their hand is the winner of the round.

Game End:
The first player to wins 3 rounds wins the game.

Month Order

Month	Flower		Month	Flower	
January	Pine		July	Lespedeza	
February	**Rain**		August	Moon	
March	Cherry		September	Chrysanthemum	
April	Wisteria		October	Maple	
May	Iris		November	**Peony**	
June	**Paulownia**		December	**Plum**	

Base Wild Cards

Wild Card	Special Ability
	Can be used as January, but only when this card is the base.
	Can be used as January, but only when this card is the base.
	Can be used as January, but only when this card is the base.
	Can be used as January, but only when this card is the base.
	Can be used any month from January to December, but only when this card is the base.

Hand Wild Cards

Wild Card	Special Ability
	Can be used as any month from January to October.
	Can be used as any month from January to October.
	Can be used as any month from February to November.
	Can be used as any month from February to November.
	Can be used as any month from January to December.

Isuri

Source: page 137
Players: 2-3
Deck: 46 card flower deck (remove all Jokers and 2 Paulownia Chaffs.)
Rounds: 6
Objective: Be the first player to play all of the cards from their hand.

Setup:

Place 1 token on the table.

Deal 6 cards to each player face down.

Special Rule:

If the base card is a January and the active player has both a January and a February in their hand, then the player may play both cards.

Tokens:

When both players consecutively call "Pass" a token is placed on the table. Tokens remain on the table until the end of the game.

Scoring a Round:

The first player to play all of the cards from their hand is the winner of the round.

Points scored by the winner are taken from the loser.

Calculating Base Score:

Base Score = Total Tokens x Winner's Last Card

Reminder: January is a 10 when calculating Base Score.

Calculating Winner's Final Score:

- If the winner won by playing three cards of the same month,

  Round Score = Base Score x 3

- If the winner won by playing four cards of the same month,

  Round Score = Base Score x 4

- If the winner won by playing five cards of the same month,

  Round Score = Base Score x 5

- If the winner won by playing six cards of the same month,

  Round Score = Base Score x 6 + (Total Tokens x 10)

- If none of the above conditions were met, then the Base Score is the Round Score.

  Round Score = Base Score

If the winner won on their first turn of the round, then the Round Score is increased by 10 times the Total Tokens.

Round Score = Round Score + (Total Tokens x 10)

Hand Wild Cards

Wild Card	Special Ability
	Can be used as any month from January to October.
	Can be used as any month from January to October.
	Can be used as any month from February to November.
	Can be used as any month from February to November.
	Can be used as any month from January to December.

Base Wild Cards

Wild Card	Special Ability
	Can be used as January, but only when this card is the base.
	Can be used as January, but only when this card is the base.
	Can be used as January, but only when this card is the base.
	Can be used as January, but only when this card is the base.
	Can be used as January, but only when this card is the base.
	Can be used any month from January to December, but only when this card is the base.

Month Order

Month	Flower		Month	Flower	
January	Pine		July	Lespedeza	
February	**Rain**		August	Moon	
March	Cherry		September	Chrysanthemum	
April	Wisteria		October	Maple	
May	Iris		November	**Peony**	
June	**Paulownia**		December	**Plum**	

Sutda (Simplified)

Source: page 143
Players: 2-10
Deck: 20 select cards of the flower deck. (2 cards from each of the first 10 months. The first card (Bright or Ten) and the last card (4th Chaff) of each of those 10 months).
Rounds: Player Determined
Objective: Be the player with the highest valued hand.

Setup:
Deal 2 cards to each player face down.

Scoring a Round:
Only the winner of the round scores for their hand.

If a player was dealt a Hand Combo:
The winner of the round is the player with the highest <u>ranking</u> Hand Combo.

The winner receives points for their Hand Combo.

Note: Hand Combos are ranked from 1 to 17. 1 being the highest and 17 the lowest.

If <u>no</u> player was dealt a Hand Combo:
Each player calculates their Hand Value.
The Hand Value is last digit of the sum of the months of the two cards they were dealt.

The player with the highest Hand Value is the winner of the round.

The player with the highest Hand Value receives 1 point for the round.

Note: The Hand Value is only used to determine the winner of the round. The Hand Value is <u>not</u> the hand's point value. The player with the highest Hand Value only receives 1 point for the round.

Hand Combos

Ranked from highest (1) to lowest (17):

1   Curtain and Moon = 10 pts

2   October = 5 pts

3   September = 3 pts

4   August = 3 pts

5   July = 3 pts

6   June = 3 pts

7   May = 3 pts

8   April = 3 pts

9   March = 3 pts

10   February = 3 pts

11   January = 3 pts

12   Crane & Feb Chaff = 1 pt

13   Crane & April Chaff = 1 pt

14   Deer & April Chaff = 1pt

15   Deer & Jan Chaff = 1 pt

16   Crane & Aug Chaff = 1 pt

17   Butterfly & April Chaff = 1 pt

Sota

Source: page 163
Players: 2-6
Deck: 20 select cards of the flower deck. (Remove all Chaffs, all November, and all December.)
Rounds: Player Determined
Objective: Be the player with the highest valued hand.

Scoring a Round:

Only the winner of the round receives points for their hand.

If any player's chosen cards were a Hand Combo:
The player with highest ranking Hand Combo wins the round.

The winner receives points for their Hand Combo.

Note: Hand Combos are ranked from 1 (highest) to 19 (lowest).

If no player's chosen cards were a Hand Combo:
Each player calculates their Hand Value.
The Hand Value is the last digit of the sum of the months of their two cards.

The player with the highest Hand Value wins the round.

The winner receives 1 point for the round.

Note: Hand Value is only used to determine the round winner. Hand Value is not the hand's point value. The player with the highest Hand Value only receives 1 point for the round.

The player with the highest total score at the end of the predetermined number of rounds is the winner of the game.

Special Hand Combinations	
Combo	**Special Ability**
Any April & Any July	If the highest revealed Hand Combo was any rank from 4 to 13 (i.e a month combo), then the player with this Special Hand Combo wins the round and earns 3 points. Otherwise, players score as usual.
April Ten & July Ten	If the highest Hand Combo was rank 2 or 3, then the player with this Special Hand Combo wins the round and earns 5 points. Otherwise, players score as usual.
Any April & Any September	If the highest Hand Combo was rank 14 or lower, then the round ends in a draw.
April Ten & September Ten	If the highest Hand Combo was rank 4 or lower, then the round ends in a draw.

Hand Combos

Ranked from highest (1) to lowest (19):

1   Curtain and Moon = 10 pts

2   Crane and Moon = 8 pts

3   Crane and Curtain = 7 pts

4   October = 5 pts

5   September = 3 pts

6   August = 3 pts

7   July = 3 pts

8   June = 3 pts

9   May = 3 pts

10   April = 3 pts

11   March = 3 pts

12   February = 3 pts

13   January = 3 pts

14   Any Jan & Any Feb = 1 pt

15   Any Jan & Any April = 1 pt

16   Any Jan & Any Sep = 1pt

17   Any Jan & Any Oct = 1 pt

18   Any April & Any Oct = 1 pt

19   Any April & Any June = 1 pt

Sutda

Source: page 166
Players: 2-10
Deck: 20 select cards of the flower deck. (2 cards from each month <u>excluding</u> November Rain and December Paulownia. All card are Chaffs <u>except</u> for the Curtain and Moon.)
Rounds: Player Determined
Objective: Be the player with the highest valued hand.

Setup:
Deal 2 cards to each player face down.

Scoring a Round:
Only the winner of the round scores for their hand.

If a player was dealt a Hand Combo:
The winner of the round is the player with the highest <u>ranking</u> Hand Combo.

The winner receives points for their Hand Combo.

Note: Hand Combos are ranked from 1 to 17. 1 being the highest and 17 the lowest.

If <u>no</u> player was dealt a Hand Combo:
Each player calculates their Hand Value.

The Hand Value is last digit of the sum of the months of the two cards they were dealt.

The player with the highest Hand Value is the winner of the round.

The player with the highest Hand Value receives 1 point for the round.

Note: The Hand Value is only used to determine the winner of the round. The Hand Value is <u>not</u> the hand's point value. The player with the highest Hand Value only receives 1 point for the round.

Hand Combos

Ranked from highest (1) to lowest (17):

1   Curtain and Moon = 10 pts

2   October = 5 pts

3   September = 3 pts

4   August = 3 pts

5   July = 3 pts

6   June = 3 pts

7   May = 3 pts

8   April = 3 pts

9   March = 3 pts

10   February = 3 pts

11   January = 3 pts

12   3rd Jan & 4th Plum = 1 pt

13   3rd Jan & 4th April = 1 pt

14   3rd Oct & 4th April = 1pt

15   3rd Oct & 4th Jan = 1 pt

16   3rd Jan & 4th Aug = 1 pt

17   3rd June & 4th April = 1 pt

Hana-Rumi

Source: page 187
Players: 2-4
Deck: 48 card flower deck (plus 6 Jokers)
Rounds: Varies
Objective: To be the first player to reach 200 points.

Setup:

Deal 7 cards to each player face down.
Deal 1 card face up onto the table to form the discard pile.

Jokers:

Wild Cards:

Note: A player can <u>not</u> discard a playable card to end the round.

Note: Once a card(s) has been used in a Combination, it can <u>not</u> be rearranged, removed, or used in another Combination.

Scoring a Round:

Player's Score = Total Value of Player's Captured Cards + Total Value of Player's Special Achievements - Total Value of Cards Remaining in Player's Hand

The first player to reach 200 points wins the game.

If multiple players reach 200 points, then the player with the highest total score wins the game.

Card Values:

Brights = 20 pts
Tens = 10 pts
Ribbons = 5 pts
Chaffs = 1 pt
Wet Koi (Jokers) = 5 pts
Dry Koi (Wilds) = 10 pts

Special Achievements:

Note: In order to claim a Special Achievement, all cards required to claim it must be in that player's capture area.

Important: Cards used to claim a Special Achievement may **not** include a Wild Card <u>except</u> for the *Sequence of Five* Special Achievement.

A player can earn multiple Special Achievements per round.
Only one Special Achievement can be earned per Combination.

Sequence of Five

Combination of 5 or more <u>sequential</u> Chaffs = 20 pts.

Purple Ribbons

Combination containing 3 Purple Ribbons = 20 pts.

Poetry Ribbons

Combination containing 3 Poetry Ribbons = 20 pts.

Wet Koi

A player may claim points for <u>one</u> of the following:
Combination of 3 Wet Koi = 20 pts.
Combination of 4 Wet Koi = 40 pts.

Complete Month

Combination of a <u>complete</u> month (excluding Wilds) = 40 pts.

Type Combinations
Players may form any of the following:

<u>Any</u> 3 or more Brights

<u>Any</u> 3 or more Tens

<u>Any</u> 3 or more Ribbons

<u>Any</u> 3 or more Wet Koi

Contiguous Combinations
Players may form the following:

<u>Any</u> 3 or more <u>contiguous</u> cards of the same month

Sequential Chaff Combinations
Players may form the following:

<u>Any</u> 3 or more <u>sequential</u> Chaffs

Hana-Gin

Source: page 192
Players: 2
Deck: 48 card flower deck (plus 6 Jokers)
Rounds: Varies
Objective: To be the first player to reach 100 points.

Setup:
Deal 9 cards to each player face down.
Deal 1 card face up onto the table to form the discard pile.

Jokers:

Wild Cards:

Scoring a Round:
Players calculate scores depending on how the round ended.

If a player called "Gin", scoring is calculated as follows:
The player who called "Gin" is the winner of the round.

Only winner of the round receives points for the round.

> *Winner's Score = 20 pts + Total Value of Opponent's Unused Cards*

If the winner formed all 10 of their cards into Combinations, then they receive an <u>additional</u> 20 points.

The winner of the round becomes the dealer for the next round.

If a player called "Hana", scoring is calculated as follows:

1. First, the player who did **<u>not</u>** call "Hana" may choose to play their unused cards onto their opponent's Combinations.

   <u>Only</u> the player who did <u>not</u> call Hana may do this.

2. Next, <u>each</u> player calculates their Total Unused Card Value by adding the total value of their unused cards.

3. Then, players compare their Total Unused Card Values.

   The player with the <u>lowest</u> Total Unused Card Value is the winner of the round.

   If both players have the same Total Unused Card Value, then the player who called "Hana" is the winner of the round.

   > *Winner's Score = Opponent's Total Unused Card Value - Winner's Total Unused Card Value*

If the winner of the round is <u>not</u> the player who called "Hana", then the winner receives an <u>additional</u> 20 points.

The winner of the round becomes the dealer for the next round.

If the deck is exhausted, the round is considered a draw.
No player scores points.
The dealer remains the same.

The first player to reach 100 points wins the game.

Card Values:
Brights = 20 pts
Tens = 10 pts
Ribbons = 5 pts
Chaffs = 1 pt
Wet Koi (Jokers) = 5 pts
Dry Koi (Wilds) = 10 pts

Type Combinations

Players may form any of the following:

<u>Any</u> 3 or more Brights

<u>Any</u> 3 or more Tens

<u>Any</u> 3 or more Ribbons

<u>Any</u> 3 or more Wet Koi

Contiguous Combinations

Players may form the following:

Any 3 or more <u>contiguous</u> cards of the same month

Sequential Chaff Combinations

Players may form the following:

<u>Any</u> 3 or more <u>sequential</u> Chaffs

CPSIA information can be obtained
at www.ICGtesting.com
Printed in the USA
BVHW02s0427180618
519086BV00024B/82/P

The
SCHOOL
for the
INSANELY
GIFTED

Also by Dan Elish

13
A Novel, with Jason Robert Brown

THE ATTACK OF THE FROZEN WOODCHUCKS

THE WORLDWIDE DESSERT CONTEST

JASON AND THE BASEBALL BEAR

THE GREAT SQUIRREL UPRISING

BORN TOO SHORT
The Confessions of an Eighth-Grade Basket Case

The
SCHOOL
for the
INSANELY
GIFTED

Dan Elish

HARPER

An Imprint of HarperCollins*Publishers*

Library of Congress Cataloging-in-Publication Data
Elish, Dan.
  The School for the Insanely Gifted / Dan Elish. — 1st ed.
    p. cm.
  Summary: Eleven-year-old musical genius Daphna Whispers embarks on a global
journey to find her missing mother, only to uncover a shocking secret about the Blatt
School for the Insanely Gifted where she is a student.
  ISBN 978-0-06-113873-7 (trade bdg.) — ISBN 978-0-06-113874-4 (lib. bdg.)
  [1. Genius—Fiction. 2. Schools—Fiction. 3. Voyages and travels—Fiction.
4. Missing persons—Fiction.]   I. Title.
PZ7.E4257 Sc   2011   2010021962
[Fic]—dc22   CIP
                                                           AC

Typography by Jennifer R. Rozbruch
11 12 13 14 15   CG/RRDB   10 9 8 7 6 5 4 3 2

First Edition

To my insanely terrific wife and kids:
Andrea, Cassie, and John

CONTENTS

1

Daphna Whispers

Like most of the students at the Blatt School for the Insanely Gifted, Daphna Whispers had her share of quirks. Before she sat at the piano to write music, she wolfed three Oreos and drank a glass of cold milk in a single swallow. After that, she cranked the air conditioner—even in the winter—to block out the New York City street noise. Though Daphna no longer sucked her thumb for inspiration, at age eleven and three-quarters she found that her best musical ideas came while she was twirling her hair.

Which was precisely what she was doing one breezy night in late May a few weeks before the end of sixth grade. Hair in hand, she stared down at the slightly yellowed keys of her family's old upright. It was the very same piano she had used to compose all her best pieces—from her first sonata, "The Sad Sandbox," to *Who Needs Thneeds?*, an opera based on Dr. Seuss's *The Lorax*. Now she was working on her first piano rhapsody.

Hearing a rippling arpeggio in her head, Daphna reached for a fountain pen and scribbled a line of notes across the manuscript book before her.

Baa! Baa! Ba, daaah!

Daphna smiled. It felt good to be writing music again. For the past two months, trips to the keyboard had ended in tears—every time she sat down to play, Daphna attacked the keys as if the energy she poured into the notes might bring her mother back. But it never worked. The more furiously Daphna played, the faster the unanswered questions spun through her mind.

Why had her mother flown her single-cockpit World War I B-2 biplane toward Europe?

Baa, da, daaah!

Had she been on assignment as assistant director of the national climate change foundation, or was she pursuing something of her own?

Daa, dee, dee, brrring!

What had she been looking for?

Da, dum!

Why had she crashed into the Atlantic Ocean?

DUM, DAAAAAAAAA . . . CRASH!

Most important, had she survived?

"Let it go, princess. Just let it all go."

That's what Ron said. The building handyman, he had been Daphna's next-door neighbor for as long as she could remember. Now he was her legal guardian. He and his wife, Jazmine, were a caring couple with a loud, lovable three-year-old boy. Best of all, Daphna had convinced them to let her stay across the hall in the one-room apartment she had shared with her mother.

"We're here for you," Jazmine would say. "You know that."

Daphna did know. She enjoyed having a family to call on right across the hall. Most nights, she joined them for dinner, then did her homework at their dining room table. But facts remained facts. Her mother had been missing for two months now—she still didn't have the heart to use the word *dead*—and since her father had died a month before she was born, after drinking a cup of sour yak milk while trekking through western Nepal (or so the story went), Daphna was an orphan. A real-life Oliver Twist.

Daphna wrote another flurry of notes. She gave her hair another good twirl and squinted at the keys, waiting to hear the next phrase in her head. When nothing came, she popped a fourth Oreo into her mouth and closed her eyes. But instead of hearing music, she heard a voice.

"Daph, dude!"

Daphna looked at the grandfather clock that stood by her front door. As she expected, the face of the clock had already disappeared. In its place was a hologram of the face of her friend Harkin Thunkenreiser. Known to classmates by his preferred nickname, the Thunk, Harkin sported long blond hair, which he wore in a thick ponytail. A few months earlier he had rigged Daphna's clock to show his face whenever he spoke into his homemade wristwatch computer.

"I'm running thirty-two seconds behind," Harkin's image said. "Meet you outside the theater."

Just like that, the boy's face disappeared and the face of the clock returned. Daphna drew in a sharp breath. Harkin wasn't the only one who was running late. It was 7:36. As was often the case when Daphna was composing, time had gotten away from her. She had exactly twenty-four minutes to get all the way down to Times Square. True, her friend Cynthia Trustwell had already starred in six Broadway shows, but that didn't mean Daphna could skip the opening night of her seventh.

In a flash, Daphna straightened her music, recapped her fountain pen, then ran to the front hall closet. Her preferred school attire was a pair of jeans, a simple T-shirt (with a picture of a famous composer), and a pair of Velcro sneakers, but tonight she had no choice but to get a little bit fancy. She threw on a red dress, blue leggings, and light green dress shoes. At her bathroom mirror, she brushed out her dark auburn hair, frowned at her nose freckles, and glanced back at the clock. The time was 7:41. Nineteen minutes to get forty blocks downtown to the theater.

Daphna had one more thing she had to do before she could sprint out the door.

She turned to a metal control panel beside the front door. Next to the four silver buttons were these words:

> Living Room
> Kitchen
> Bedroom
> Music Room

Daphna took a final glance around the room, grabbed a piece of music paper off the middle of the floor, then pressed the button next to Living Room. As the hum of the central motor sounded from the ceiling, the piano glided on a track of rollers to the far wall. A small desk and an armchair slid back to the window. With the room cleared, a panel opened on the adjacent wall, and a sofa and love seat moved silently to the center of the room to form an L. Finally, a marble coffee table lowered from the ceiling. In ten seconds, it was done. Music room gone. Living room in place, ready for her return, in case she wanted to watch TV or read a book before bed.

After Harkin had adjusted her old clock to receive his holographic messages, it had taken him only two more days to convert her small studio into a four-room apartment. Yes, there were certainly advantages to going to a school for the insanely gifted.

Taking the steps three at a time, Daphna was soon sprinting through the lobby, where Ron was seeing to his nightly sweep of the entranceway.

"Not so fast," he said. "Isn't it a school night?"

"Yeah," Daphna said. "But a special school night, remember? Cynthia's opening in another show."

Ron rubbed a hand through the girl's hair and forced a smile. "That's right," he said. "But come back right after it's over."

"I won't be late. Promise!"

Daphna ran for the door. A moment later, she was unlocking her scooter from the streetlight in front of her building and pushing herself along 100th Street. At the corner, she stopped for a red light and glanced back in her side-view mirror. Ron was out front, sweeping the last of the day's trash into his dustpan. He waved a final time, then disappeared into the building for the night.

Which was when Daphna noticed a tall man with dark hair and a sharp chin moving quickly up the block. At first she thought nothing of it. But just as she was about to look away, the man stopped outside her apartment building. He peered up and down the block, then trotted up the front steps and looked through the small window on the door. Perhaps he was visiting a neighbor? Or maybe he was just an oddly dressed deliveryman? To Daphna's surprise, instead of ringing the front buzzer, the man took another quick look up and down the block, then scurried off the way he had come.

Daphna considered doubling back to her apartment to make sure everything was all right. But just as she was about to scoot back down the block, she stopped herself. Ever since her mom had gone missing, she had been jumpy. The man was probably just lost. Most likely, he had wandered up the wrong street, then hurried off to find the right address.

With Cynthia's show soon to start, Daphna quickly maneuvered her scooter onto Central Park West and pressed the yellow button on her handlebars. A small motor that was attached to her back wheel roared, and Daphna was soon moving at thirty miles an hour, keeping pace with the cars, buses, and cabs. And the strange man? In the excitement of the coming evening, Daphna forgot all about him. With an eight-o'clock curtain to make, she followed a fast-moving taxi past Columbus Circle and cruised excitedly into the heart of the theater district.

2

The Dancing Doberman

Even after a lifetime of city living, Daphna never ceased to be delighted by Times Square. Looming above the crowds were neon lights and giant billboards advertising some of Broadway's longest-running shows.

CHESTER A. ARTHUR!
America's 21st President:
The man, the myth, the musical!

But staring down at Daphna from the largest billboard of them all—a full forty feet tall—was a photograph of someone who had absolutely nothing to do with show business. Looming high above Times Square was none other than Ignatious Peabody Blatt.

Daphna took in the gargantuan photograph and felt a flush of pride. After all, Ignatious Blatt was the founder of her special school. He was also the undisputed greatest computer wizard of the age. For years, his products had dominated the market.

There was the Blatt-Phone, a cell phone with internet access that could fit in a user's wallet.

There was Blatt-Global, computer software that allowed its user to see satellite pictures of the inside of any home in the world.

There was Peabody-Pitch, a stereo system that

changed music automatically, depending on the user's mood.

Then there was Ignatious's most extraordinary, thrilling invention of all: the Hat-Top computer. A small laptop that attached to a specialized hat, the Hat-Top allowed its user to read emails and write documents while strolling down the street. The day it was released, the lines outside the world's computer stores stretched for blocks.

As a wave of pedestrians crossed the busy street before her, Daphna took another look at the giant billboard. There was no doubt about it: Ignatious Peabody Blatt was as unusual looking as he was brilliant.

His suit was bright turquoise.

His shirt was pink.

His tie was sea green, and his suspenders were orange.

Ignatious's goatee was a smattering of gray and black, but his eyebrows were blondish gold.

His sideburns were red.

His left eyetooth was silver.

Most important of all was the message written in bright purple underneath the enormous picture.

IT'S COMING!

Of course, Daphna and her friends knew precisely what Ignatious meant by those simple words. In fact, *everyone* in the world knew what Ignatious Peabody Blatt meant by those words. He was about to release his latest product. In chat rooms around the globe, an excited public speculated wildly.

"It's the Blatt-Bath! A computer that works in the shower!"

"No, it's a Blatt-Soap! The first computer that does the dishes!"

One reporter had written a front-page story for the *New York Times* claiming that Ignatious was about to release a four-legged laptop that danced hip-hop.

"Hey, girl! Move it along!"

Daphna blinked. While her eyes were lost in the giant billboard, the light had changed. Behind her, the driver of a tour bus was honking. Daphna rolled quickly down Broadway and took a right onto 45th Street. A row of marquees filled the street side by side, bearing the names of more of the season's shows:

> **Meet Me in Duluth, Ruth!**

> *Remembrance of Things Past,*
> THE MUSICAL

THE PENSIVE CHICKEN,
a one-animal show

Before long, Daphna caught a glimpse of the marquee she was looking for: *The Dancing Doberman.* Even from halfway down the block, she could see a row of paparazzi and reporters behind a rope, primed to photograph and interview arriving celebrities. The crowd of opening-night theatergoers, dressed in gowns and suits, moved steadily toward the doors, eagerly clutching tickets. A handful of police officers stood at the curb.

Daphna locked her scooter to a lamppost, then walked into the thick of the crowd. She checked her cell phone. It was eight o'clock sharp. She had made it without a second to spare. Now where was her date?

Exactly thirty-two seconds later, a strange yellow vehicle came rumbling down the street. The front wheels were twice the size of the ones in the rear. A swirl of intertwining pipes rose out of the trunk, then bent forward to make a large figure eight over the top. The contraption seemed to be made out of discarded pieces of yellow scrap metal. The crowd turned from the theater doors to watch as the vehicle glided past the entrance and pulled to a halt just beyond the marquee. Seconds later, the strange car released a stream of blue smoke. The door pushed open, and a short boy with a thick blond ponytail stepped out. He wore a black tuxedo and a pair of white high-tops.

"Harkin!" Daphna called.

"Daph, dude!" the boy said, stepping out onto the street. "My parentals made me finish my engineering work sheet before they let me out."

Daphna wasn't really listening. Her focus was on Harkin's unique mode of transportation. She knew that he had once constructed a working one-man helicopter on his roof, but this vehicle was downright bizarre, even for him.

"What do I call this?" she asked, looking it up and down. "Your Thunkmobile?"

Harkin wagged his head. "That works! I found four or five rusted taxicabs at a garbage dump last weekend and made this heap." He kicked one of the tires. "It'll be cool once I repaint and add a few special features."

"It's cool now," Daphna said. "I was just wondering where you're going to park."

A policeman with an ample potbelly and a thin mustache had the exact same question.

"You are going to have to move this thing," he said, not unkindly. He took a closer look at Harkin. Despite the boy's natural self-confidence, there was no denying that he was no more than twelve. In fact, due to his diminutive stature, he was sometimes mistaken for a boy of eight or nine. Occasionally, his ponytail led some strangers to think he was a girl. "And I don't imagine you have a driver's license?"

"No license required, my man," Harkin said. "Look! This isn't a car at all. It's a go-kart."

The policeman blinked. "A go-kart?"

At that precise moment, Harkin's vehicle seemed to sigh, this time emitting a plume of pink smoke.

"Better watch it," an onlooker said. "That contraption is gonna blow!"

"It's perfectly safe!" Harkin said.

"It's blocking traffic," the policeman said. "Find a place to park it, or I'm going to have to give you a ticket."

Daphna watched Harkin roll up the sleeve of his tuxedo, revealing a small black wristband with a miniature screen and several rows of multicolored buttons. He pressed an orange one, and the car began to whir. Green smoke wafted from under its bottom. Then the car began to shake back and forth wildly.

As the crowd took a fearful step back, the photographers turned their cameras from the entrance of the theater to Harkin's contraption.

"Okay, buddy," the policeman said, waving away the green smoke. "Enough funny business."

Daphna could tell that Harkin wasn't finished—

not yet. He pressed a final button—this one purple. Then it happened: *scwinch!* Just like that, the car scrunched together like an accordion, so quickly photographers weren't even able to get the shot. A second later it rolled sideways, fitting perfectly into a three-foot-wide parking space. The crowd broke into wild applause. Harkin waved to the crowd and bowed.

"Thank you!" he cried.

"Not bad, kid," the policeman said. He winked. "I guess you don't need a license for a go-kart."

An usher stepped out of the theater. "The show's about to start! Anyone with tickets, time to take your seat!"

Harkin looked toward the doors. "I guess that means us. Though a musical about a bunch of dogs is not the Thunk's idea of fun."

Daphna's eyes strayed to a poster outside the front entrance. There were pictures of the cast, each of them dressed as a giant dog.

"What does Cynthia play again?" Harkin went on. "A German shepherd?"

"Nah," Daphna said. "I think a golden retriever."

The two friends joined the crowd pushing for the entrance. Just as they were handing their tickets to one of the ushers, the sound of a siren filled the street. Four police officers on motorcycles cleared the path for a blue stretch limo.

"Whoa," Daphna said. "I wonder who this is?"

Harkin shrugged. "Maybe the pope?"

Daphna didn't know about the pope, but she knew that Broadway openings were often a good place for celebrity sightings. When the limo pulled to a halt, one of the police officers opened the door. As the crowd pushed closer, Daphna stood on tippy-toes to see. A rail-thin woman dressed in an elegant red gown stepped out of the limo, followed by a man in a lime green suit who was as round as his wife was thin.

"It's the mayor!" someone cried.

Indeed it was—Samson Fiorello, the man who had put five more teachers into every public school, replanted Central Park's Great Lawn with palm trees, and built subway cars with coffee bars—one of New York City's most popular leaders in years.

As the crowd cheered, the mayor waved happily, then waddled after his wife toward the entrance.

"Looks like this is the place to be," Daphna said.

Harkin nodded. "Come on. Let's grab our seats."

3

An Antelope and a Flex-Bed

few hours later, Daphna sat in between Cynthia and Harkin in the front seat of the boy's Thunkmobile. The opening of *The Dancing Doberman* had been a triumph. The crowd laughed in all the right places and cheered wildly at the final curtain. Better still, the mayor and his wife gave Cynthia a standing ovation at the end of her first-act solo, "For a Dollar, I'll Holler for a Collar."

"You were great," Daphna told Cynthia. "Really and truly."

Harkin grinned ruefully. "Best musical about dogs I've ever seen."

"Don't listen to him," Daphna said. "You stole the show."

Daphna watched her friend accept the compliment with a satisfied smile. Even out of makeup she looked radiant. As Daphna's mother had always said, "That girl looks glamorous even hanging upside down from a jungle gym." Daphna had to admit it. With long blond hair, poise beyond her years, and a singing voice that the *New York Times* had called "miraculous," Cynthia Trustwell had been a striking presence from the day the two friends had met at the Blatt School playground on the first day of kindergarten. Now, just a month past twelve, Cynthia had the bearing and grace of a true star. Even so, offstage she preferred ripped jeans and oversize cardigan sweaters to fancy dresses. Instead of contact lenses, she wore pink-rimmed glasses.

"Whatever," Cynthia said. She unwrapped a stick of bubble gum and popped it into her mouth. "Harkin's right. It's just a dumb show about a bunch of dumb dogs. Right now, I'm totally focused on my one-woman musical version of *Macbeth*—you know, by Shakespeare? I just wrote an awesome opening number, 'Three Witches in a Pot.' I'd do anything to get it on Broadway. But who's got five million bucks to put on a show?"

"But your songs have got to be better than the junk in *The Dancing Doberman*," Harkin said.

"Don't worry," Cynthia said. "They are."

Daphna smiled. Like many students at the Blatt School, Cynthia had a healthy appreciation of her own abilities.

"So what is this thingamabob that you're driving, anyway?" Cynthia went on to Harkin. "I keep expecting it to either break down or take off to Jupiter. It's really made of a bunch of taxis?"

"And the front seats are from a bus," Harkin said. "That's why it's got such good legroom."

"Have you shown this rig to your parents?" Daphna asked.

"Not yet." Harkin grimaced. "If you can believe it, my dad wants me to come to his lab this Saturday to help him work on some new experiments on the wingspan of a housefly." He honked at a bus and went on. "What could be duller than studying a fly? I was going to spend the weekend finally perfecting Gum-Top!"

"Gum-Top?" Cynthia said. "You're still working on that old thing?"

Harkin nodded. He was just as passionate about his ideas as Cynthia was about hers. "I'm aiming to test it soon. Maybe tomorrow."

"Wait a second," Daphna said. "You mean you've *really* done it?"

The idea was so old that she had forgotten whose idea it had been. Cynthia, the gum chewer, claimed she had thought of it back in first grade. Daphna remembered getting the idea herself a year later one day during recess. Regardless of who was responsible, Daphna had never given it much of a chance. How could a stick of gum be made to work as a minicomputer that allowed its user to see websites in their head as they chewed?

Harkin accelerated past a taxi. "Darn right, I've done it! I just need to make a few minor adjustments."

"Well, lemme be your guinea pig when you test it," Cynthia said. "I'll chew and run searches on rich Broadway producers at the same time."

"Deal."

Harkin took a wide turn and rumbled down 100th Street.

"Thanks for the ride," Daphna said as her friend slowed in front of her building.

Harkin turned to her. "You sure you don't want to come with us to the cast party?"

"Sorry," she said. "Too tired. You guys have fun."

"The mayor is supposed to drop by," Cynthia said. "He promised to do a belly dance."

"Record it for me on your phone." Daphna faked a yawn.

"You don't fool me, kiddo," Cynthia said, blowing another bubble. "You're going to get right back to work on that rhapsody of yours."

Daphna poked Cynthia's bubble with a finger, popping it.

"Maybe," she said.

Daphna gave Cynthia a quick kiss on the cheek, climbed over Harkin, and stumbled onto the sidewalk. After Daphna retrieved her scooter from the contraption's triangular trunk, Harkin called, "Later, Daph, dude!" and peeled out. Daphna chained her scooter to her usual streetlight and trotted up the front steps. The door to Ron's apartment swung open the minute she stepped out of the elevator.

"How was the opening?" he asked.

Daphna shrugged. "If you like singing dogs, it was great." In the background Daphna could hear the distinct sound of his three-year-old son wailing. "Is Little Jack okay?"

"Oh, he's fine," Ron said. "Just had a bad dream."

With that, Jack let out a particularly loud shriek. With a quick "Sweet dreams, princess," Ron disappeared back into his apartment. Daphna pushed open the door to hers. She hung up her coat, then took in the dark room with a sigh. Night was when she missed her mom the most. Daphna longed to tell her about the amazing evening she had just had: the Broadway opening, Harkin's wild new car, seeing the mayor. She longed to feel her mother rub her hands through her thick auburn hair. She even longed to hear her mother call her Miss Sadie P. Snodgrass, the silly pet name she had made up when Daphna was born. "Tell me about school today, Miss Snodgrass," she would say (or "Snods" for short), and Daphna would curl up in her lap and they would talk. Daphna sighed, and a deep sadness washed over her.

Dah, da, da, dum, dum, dee!

Daphna heard the glimmer of a new melody in her head. Time to transform the living room back into a music room and put the finishing touches on her rhapsody. But turning to Harkin's control panel, she stopped short.

Was that a noise?

Daphna knew every sound the old apartment could make. The squeak of the refrigerator. The creak of the closet door. But this particular creak— for that's what it was—sounded different.

Was there a pigeon on the windowsill?

Worse, a mouse in the bathroom?

Daphna drew in a breath and turned slowly to face the empty apartment. The room was still. *Too* still. Was someone hiding behind the sofa? Under the coffee table?

"Relax," she told herself, exhaling. Her heart pounded. "It's okay."

Daphna opened the one window wide and drew in a cleansing breath of warm spring air. The street below was quiet and peaceful. Daphna calmed herself enough to turn back to the apartment when a shadow appeared out of the far closet. Before Daphna could so much as gasp, a tall, dark figure lurched her way but tripped over the coffee table and hit the floor with a loud "Oof!" In the half-light, Daphna saw that the intruder was dressed entirely in black. On his face was a mask that made his eyebrows and ears abnormally large and turned his nose into a snout. Though his face was hidden, Daphna simply knew: it was the same man she had seen lurking outside her building before Cynthia's opening.

"Where is it?" he demanded, rising quickly to his feet.

"Where is what?" Daphna managed.

In a flash, he was across the room, lifting Daphna by the armpits. Up close, the mask was terrifying. It was as though Daphna were being accosted by a giant antelope.

"The Flex-Bed."

At least that's what Daphna thought he said,

because by that point she was too scared to be sure of anything.

"Where'd she keep it? Is it with Billy?"

Billy?

Daphna had never been in a fight in her life, but instinct told her what to do next. As the man lifted her closer to his face—close enough to smell his sour breath through the strange mask—she jerked up her knee and connected with the soft part of his gut. With a loud grunt, the man dropped her to the floor and stumbled backward. Daphna flew across the room and slammed the heel of her palm into the button next to the word Kitchen. The coffee table rose off the floor, and the stove barreled from a far closet toward its place by the grandfather clock. To Daphna's dismay, the man was able to gather his wits enough to dodge it.

"Hah!" he shouted. "Missed!"

But he never saw the refrigerator.

Bam!

Daphna had never been so happy to have needed some air. The intruder somersaulted through the open window and fell two stories onto a parked car. By the time Daphna was at the window herself, he was hobbling down the street.

"Wait!" Daphna called after him. "What's the Flex-Bed? Who's Billy? Who are you?"

The man broke from a pained trot to a half run. A moment later, he was around the corner. Then Daphna heard a frantic knock on her door. She knew who it had to be: Ron. This time he was holding Little Jack, who was wide-awake in his pajamas. Jazmine stood to their side, in her nightgown.

"Are you all right?" she asked.

"We heard the loudest noise," Ron said.

"Big noise!" Jack said. "Like a choo-choo."

Though Daphna briefly considered telling them what had happened, she quickly decided against it.

"No, no," she said. "I'm fine."

Ron looked skeptical. "Really?"

"I just forgot to move a box when I pressed Kitchen. The fridge slammed it out the window."

It took another few minutes, but Daphna finally convinced Ron that she was all right. After a good-night kiss to Little Jack, the family returned to their apartment and Daphna was left alone with her thoughts.

The *Flex-Bed*? What in the world was that? Who was *Billy*?

Daphna considered going to the police, then dismissed the thought. Was there any reason to think she'd be taken seriously if she burst into the local precinct saying that a man dressed as a giant antelope had broken into her home and asked about a Flex-Bed? No, Daphna would be better off investigating the break-in on her own. That didn't mean, however, that she wasn't going to take precautions. At the time he had put in the interchangeable rooms, Harkin had also installed a security system. With a flick of a switch under the windowsill, Daphna's front door automatically triple locked, and retractable bars enclosed the window.

"There we go," Daphna said out loud. "Safe and sound."

She took a final look out the now-barred window. No sign of the strange intruder. She doubted that he would be back—at least not right away. Still, she was too worked up to go to bed. Daphna called Harkin on her cell phone. As the sounds of a wild party filled the room, his face appeared on her grandfather clock.

"Decided to join us?" he called above the sound of a brass band. "The mayor's doing the fox-trot with Cynthia's mom."

Despite everything, Daphna laughed. As she expected, the sound of Harkin's voice made her feel better instantly.

"I'd love to," Daphna said. "But listen up. Something happened."

She spilled the news. Harkin (and then Cynthia, who he had called to the phone) insisted on coming over to keep guard. But Daphna assured them that she was fine.

"A giant antelope?" Harkin said. "Weird."

"And a Flex-Bed?" Cynthia said. "Even weirder."

"You're sure you don't want company?" Harkin asked. "We can start the investigation now. I'll track this antelope down in my Thunkmobile, then run him into the East River."

Daphna knew that it made sense to get right on the intruder's trail, but she was just too exhausted. Instead, she suggested that they continue the discussion the following morning before school, at their usual place—an orange bench that stood by the seesaws in the Blatt School playground.

By the time she hung up, Daphna could barely keep her eyes open. She had flirted with the idea of working on her rhapsody late into the night, but now it was all she could do to change into her pajamas, press the Bedroom button on her control panel, brush her teeth, and crawl into bed. A moment later, she was asleep.

4

Myron Holds His Ground

The next morning, after a quick breakfast with Ron, Jazmine, and Little Jack, Daphna grabbed her book bag and bolted for the door. While most of her classmates commuted to school by bus, car, or subway, Daphna was one of the lucky few who lived in the neighborhood. Down the block, she turned the corner, and moments later, there it stood, nestled between a neighborhood drugstore and an Indian restaurant: the Blatt School for the Insanely Gifted.

The famed school had once been the private residence of Cecil C. Brackerton, one of New York's most prominent millionaires. Though the old home had fallen into disrepair by the time Ignatious had purchased it, he hadn't wasted any time before remodeling it in his own colorful image. He'd had the exterior painted bright yellow and the shutters a vibrant pink. An orange wrought-iron door was installed in front, and the roof was fitted with a giant turquoise dome. The manicured grounds were adorned with beds of violets, lilies, and roses, then enclosed in a fence painted shiny gold. A passerby would not be faulted for thinking the school had been transported to New York from an amusement park.

If only it had a different name. Over the years, Daphna had grown tired of people—sometimes complete strangers—asking her how it felt to be insanely gifted. An old lady had once even stopped her on the street and peered into one of her ears, saying, "Let's see that brilliant mind at work." Why couldn't Ignatious simply have named his school the Blatt Institute? Or at the very least the Blatt School for the *Very* Gifted? But Ignatious wasn't a man to mince words.

"To call the school anything else would be dishonest, wouldn't it?" he had said in an interview a month before the school had opened seven years earlier. "My students have gone through a battery of intensive tests. Every one of them possesses intellectual and creative capabilities that truly are insane!"

Daphna thought back to her first day of kindergarten. How she had clutched her mother's hand in the school yard. How her mom had leaned down to give her a kiss and told her that everything was going to be okay. She had met Harkin, even then in a blond ponytail, while playing with blocks. And Cynthia? After their initial meeting on the playground, she had stood before their class that first day and sung a flawless rendition of "Doe, a deer."

Daphna pushed through the front gate and followed a cobblestone path that veered in and around three separate flower beds, then curved around the back of the building to the playground. Her fellow schoolmates—that year, there were precisely one hundred students in the school, from kindergarten through eighth grade—were killing the final minutes before class playing freeze tag, scaling jungle gyms, and seeing how high they could go on the swings. Daphna cut around a group of kids playing kick the can, heading toward the orange bench near the seesaws and the meeting with her two friends.

It appeared that Cynthia and Harkin had drawn

a crowd. At first, Daphna assumed Cynthia was being mobbed by well-wishers congratulating her on her Broadway opening. Instead, the focus was on a boy wearing bright purple jeans, a lime green polo shirt, and shiny yellow loafers. Perched on his nose was a pair of thick glasses. His hair was slicked back and parted down the middle.

"No, no, no!" he was crying. "It'll be out soon!"

He was Myron Blatt, son of Ignatious Peabody Blatt. It was rumored that Myron had failed the school's rigorous entrance exams and that his father had bent the rules to secure his admission. But whether or not he was truly worthy of the label "insanely gifted," Myron Blatt was still a member in good standing of the seventh grade.

"Very, *very* soon!" he went on.

"When already?" a small boy asked.

He was Daphna's classmate Jean-Claude Broquet, who had moved to the States two years earlier from Paris.

"I don't have exact dates, for crying out loud," Myron said. He had a high voice that cracked when he got excited. "He doesn't tell me everything."

"It's been forever since your dad released the Hat-Top," Jean-Claude went on. "Practically two years!"

"Make that three!" someone cried out.

"Try four!" someone else called.

The crowd surrounding Myron had swelled to include most every child on the playground. Only Thelma Trimm, a thin girl who wore her dirty blond hair in two short pigtails, didn't venture across the playground to see what Myron had to say about his father's new product. Then again, the fact that Thelma preferred to play hopscotch by herself came as no surprise to Daphna. She was so shy that she rarely spoke, and none of the other students knew precisely what her insane gift even was.

"Genius takes time," Myron was now telling the crowd. "And my father *is* a genius."

"Maybe so," Jean-Claude said. "But does he even have a new idea?"

Myron's face turned bright red. "Of course he does!" he cried. "You watch. It'll be great!"

"Where's your dad been?" a girl shouted. "We haven't seen him since the first day of school."

That was Wanda Twiddles. A small girl with dark hair and a pug nose, she was a fifth grader who had been recently contracted by the state of Minnesota to design a new suspension bridge over Lake Superior.

"I know! He skipped town!" This last was spoken by Wilmer Griffith, the largest kid in the eighth grade. All shoulders and muscles, Wilmer more closely resembled a football player than the numbers whiz that he was. "He's in an Eskimo village, working on his new invention. Seal-Top, a computer that juggles a ball on its space bar."

The kids laughed as they often did when Wilmer Griffith said something, whether it was funny or not.

Myron frowned. "My dad is not in hiding. I see him all the time."

"Then why haven't *we* seen him?" a boy asked.

"You must know something about his new product!" Wilmer shouted.

"I know," Jean-Claude Broquet said. "It's a computer that speaks Chinese."

"No, it's the Navel-Top!" Wanda Twiddles cried. "A computer that attaches to your stomach!"

"How about the Ear-Top!"

"Or the Neck-Top!"

"No, the Nose-Top—a computer that has the mouse up the user's nostrils!"

The school yard filled with laughter, and Myron's face burned bright red. Daphna knew it was mean to hold him responsible for his father's actions, but she laughed right along with everyone else.

To his credit, Myron held his ground. Gathering his wits, he stepped onto the first rung of the jungle gym so that he stood a few inches above everyone else.

"My father is Ignatious Peabody Blatt, the greatest computer mind of his age!" he shouted. "Do I need to remind you that the United States government just asked him to donate his brain to the Pentagon when he dies? Or that a strand of his dental floss just sold on eBay for twenty thousand dollars? He'll announce his new product when he's good and ready!"

There was a split second when every student on the playground was absolutely silent. But in the next moment a faint whirring filled the air. A large red shape blocked the morning sun and spread an ever-growing shadow over the yard.

"What's that?" Daphna called.

"It's a blimp!"

"It's an asteroid!"

"It's a flying mastodon!"

"No, no!" Wilmer Griffith said. "It's a giant red helicopter!"

It was true. The helicopter hovered over the playground, sending up a flurry of dust.

By that point Myron was jumping up and down, laughing. "I told you my dad hadn't skipped town! Watch out, world! Here he comes!"

5

The Great Blatt

Everyone knew that Ignatious Peabody Blatt liked to travel by helicopter. Some said he had a fleet of helicopters, one for each day of the week. Some said he even *lived* in his helicopter.

So as the great machine hovered over the playground, Daphna and the rest of the students had no question as to who was on board.

"It's Ignatious, all right," Cynthia said.

"But why is he visiting now?" Harkin wondered.

"It's strange, that's for sure," said Daphna.

Was Ignatious coming to pick up Myron to visit a sick relative? Or to give out a special homework assignment? Or could it be something truly exciting? Was Ignatious going to unveil his new product right then and there?

Quickly, the students cleared a wide landing area at the center of the playground. As the helicopter began its descent to the makeshift helipad, the whir of the rotors became so loud, the students were forced to hold their ears. When the helicopter finally touched down, the pilot cut the engines, and the playground suddenly went still. A third grader made a break for the great red machine, eager to be the first to shake the famous man's hand. But Myron cut him off.

"Be patient," he said.

The back door to the school swung open. Out stepped a tall woman with a regal nose, a prominent Adam's apple, and a penchant for pink high heels. She was Headmistress Elmira Ferguson, the lady in charge of running the school in Blatt's absence.

"All right, children," she called. "Make room for the faculty!"

Daphna, Harkin, and Cynthia moved to the far end to get a better look at the arriving faculty. First out the door of the school was Bobby D'Angelo, an enormously fat science teacher whose jowls sagged almost all the way down to his shoulders. His third-grade elective, Introduction to Black Holes and Other Astral Phenomena, was a school favorite. Next came Horatio Yuri, a squat man no taller than a fire hydrant. Each semester, Mr. Yuri taught a lucky group of fifth graders *War and Peace* in the original Russian. Fast on his heels came Josie Frank. A severe-looking woman who wore riding boots that came all the way up to her upper thighs, her signature class was The Genghis Khan I Love.

Next came Daphna's favorite, Mrs. Zoentrope, her music teacher since kindergarten. An older woman with bright red hair that rose straight up from her head, she waddled into the yard clutching an old musical score. Catching Daphna's eye, she smiled brightly, then followed her colleagues out onto the playground.

One after another they came—thirty teachers in all. Along with traditional subjects such as social studies, math, and history, there were the instructors recruited to teach the more specialized offerings in the Blatt course catalog. The classes in nuclear physics and conversational Swahili. The seminars in Shakespearean humor and bear anatomy. The lectures on medieval cutlery. The list went on and on.

As a hush fell over the playground, a lone

pigeon landed on the helicopter's rotor, took in her surroundings for a moment, then coasted to a window in the neighboring Indian restaurant.

"What's taking him so long?" Daphna whispered to her friends.

Harkin smirked. "Probably brushing his eyebrows."

Daphna giggled. A flurry of whispers circled the playground. Elmira Ferguson took an unsteady step forward on her pink heels to quiet the crowd. As the word *patience* trembled on her lips, the helicopter door burst open.

Students and teachers gasped. As well-groomed as he looked up on a billboard, Ignatious was even more striking in real life. He wore an orange and yellow suit with a lime green tie and purple cowboy boots. His hair, goatee, and blond eyebrows were perfectly combed. His silver tooth sparkled.

"Greetings," he called. "My brilliant students! My wonderful teachers! How good to see you all!"

Cheers filled the playground. Within seconds, those cheers grew into a chant— *"Blatt! Blatt! Blatt!"* Smiling wildly, Ignatious hopped out of the helicopter and waved.

"Did you see his rings?" Daphna whispered to Cynthia.

There was one on each finger.

Her friend nodded. "They say that the one on his pinkie is a Return key with a diamond in the center."

"The ring on his thumb is the world's only emerald cell phone," Harkin said.

Blowing kisses, Ignatious took several strong strides to the far end of the semicircle. From experience in past years, Daphna and her friends knew what was coming next. Though his appearances at the school were rare, Ignatious prided himself on keeping up with each student's accomplishments. Every time he visited, the great man took it upon himself to greet each and every child personally.

"My dear Jean-Claude!" He took the boy's hand in his and shook it hard. "Madame Camus told me you translated the Gettysburg Address into Medieval French. So useful! So insanely gifted! And my, oh my," Ignatious said, moving down the line, "it's Wanda Twiddles. How is work on the suspension bridge coming? What's next? A bridge from New York to Moscow?"

After dispensing with Jean-Claude and Wanda, he continued working his way down the semicircle, patting heads and shaking hands.

"And is that you, Steven?" he asked a serious-looking fourth grader. "I hear you're making remarkable progress on your second novel. Is it really about a blind raccoon who leads a team of sled dogs to the North Pole? And Wilmer!" he went on, shaking the big eighth grader's hand. "Thank goodness someone finally figured it out. Of course, there's only one billion astral miles between the third moon of Jupiter and the ninth planet in the Andromeda galaxy. Genius, my boy. Genius!"

Ignatious moved down the line, passing out compliments to the students and nodding at the teachers, pumping every person's hand like he was their long-lost brother. He even had words for his very own son. "Never forget, Myron," he said, pinching the boy's cheek, "a hearty breakfast enriches the mind. Look what I found on the kitchen table!"

Ignatious reached into his pocket and produced a single bite of what appeared to be a leftover waffle.

"Sorry, Dad," the boy stammered, and dutifully gobbled it up.

As Daphna watched Ignatious move closer and closer, her heartbeat quickened. Though the Great Blatt never had an unkind word to say about anyone, his fame intimidated her. Soon Ignatious was standing in front of Cynthia, holding her hands in his.

"Ms. Trustwell. You've done it again! I just read the review in this morning's *Times*." He reached into his coat pocket, pulled out the paper, and riffled to the correct page. "'Cynthia Trustwell does for dogs what Thomas Jefferson did for freedom.' Exquisite!

Do come by my office later this morning. I want to pick out a night to see it, then have dinner with you and your parents. We must celebrate."

Though she knew that Cynthia would most probably make fun of it later, Daphna could tell that she was pleased. Praise from Ignatious Peabody Blatt always made a person feel special. An offer to share a meal? That was unheard of.

"Of course," Cynthia said.

Ignatious had already turned to Harkin. He was pumping his arm so hard, Daphna worried he might pull it off.

"And Mr. Thunkenreiser," Ignatious said, "your new car sounds ingenious." He chuckled. "Or is it really just a large go-kart? Oh, whatever it is, you must take me for a ride. May I add that your blond ponytail is looking particularly stylish this morning!"

"Thanks," Harkin muttered.

Ignatious moved before Daphna. Up close, the colors on his orange and yellow suit were so vibrant, she practically had to squint. His purple cowboy boots glinted brightly in the early-morning sun.

Daphna swallowed hard, too overwhelmed to speak.

"The composer extraordinaire!" Ignatious cried.

Daphna felt him take her hands in his.

"I'm still so upset about your poor mother," he

said as he shook his head sadly. "Such a kind lady. Such a beautiful soul. I can't tell you how much we admire how you've soldiered on over the past two months." Then he smiled. "Did I tell you how much I love your Piano Sonata no. 3 in C Major? I listen to it daily. I was telling your mother that very thing just before spring break."

"You saw my mother?" Daphne asked. "Before she . . ." She swallowed, unable to bring herself to finish the sentence.

Ignatious didn't miss a beat. "Didn't you know? She dropped by my office to talk about your work."

A breath away from crying, Daphna blinked back her tears.

"Remember, my dear," Ignatious went on, "if there's ever anything you need, you know who to ask."

Such kindness!

"That's so nice of you," Daphna stammered.

Ignatious gave Daphna's hand a short squeeze, then spun around.

"Tell me, have I said hello to all the children?"

Students and teachers looked as one over to the far side of the playground to Thelma Trimm, still engrossed in her private game of hopscotch, pigtails flapping. But if Ignatious was insulted, he didn't show it. On the contrary, he seemed delighted.

"You keep playing hopscotch, Thelma, dear," he called. "Think deep thoughts. That's how I got where I am today, dear friends," he went on, turning back to face the students and faculty. "By being like young Miss Trimm. By marching to my own strange beat and engaging openly with the world and all of its possibilities. In any case, young Thelma can hear what I'm going to say from over there. Now, students, tell me: Who here has heard of *The Cody Meyers Show*?"

Daphna looked at Harkin and Cynthia. Everyone had heard of Cody Meyers, the host of the most-watched talk show in the country.

"Everyone?" Ignatious said. "I'm booked to appear as his guest this Monday afternoon. To spice things up, I proposed to Mr. Meyers that I bring along one of my students. One of my most insanely gifted. In fact, the absolutely *most* insanely gifted student of all!"

For a moment the school yard was dead silent. And then everyone was talking at once—even the teachers. This was incredible news. While the students at the Blatt School were all brilliant, they all had unique talents. Never before had there been an attempt to single out the best!

"The most insanely gifted?" Jean-Claude Broquet blurted out. "But how will you choose?"

Ignatious hopped onto the first rung of the

jungle gym, just as his son had done earlier. The children pushed close. As a delivery truck noisily pulled to the front of the neighboring Indian restaurant, Ignatious milked the drama for everything he was worth, using the shiny diamond in his Return ring to tweak his goatee.

"Correct me if I'm wrong," he said. "Everyone here is working on an end-of-the-year project? Of course you are! This Monday morning there will be an assembly in the school theater. At that time, each student will be given the chance to give a short demonstration of what you've been up to. Wilmer can show us his research on alien life in the Andromeda galaxy. Miss Twiddles can show us her designs for her suspension bridge. When everyone who wants has had a chance to compete, the very best will be declared the lucky winner of the Insanity Cup and come with me to *The Cody Meyers Show* that afternoon to show the country his or her special gift!"

"That's me!" a third-grade girl suddenly screamed. "Who else here speaks ten languages?"

"It's me!" yelled a short boy with wire-frame glasses. "I'm writing a novel in Swahili."

"Who cares about Swahili?" a girl cried. "Mine's in Polish!"

That's all it took for the dam to burst. Though the students at the Blatt School tried to be mutually supportive, it didn't take much to bring out their competitive natures. Wild shouts echoed through the school yard.

"I'm working on a cure for mad cow disease!"

"I've already cured it!"

"I've made a robot with nine arms!"

"My raspberry jam has the protein content of steak!"

"I've cloned a goat!"

"I've cloned a mastodon!"

"I'm creating something so insane, I can't even talk about it!" Harkin shouted, his ponytail swinging wildly back and forth. "But hear this: chewing gum will never be the same!"

Not to be outdone, Cynthia put a foot up on the seesaw. "Friends, Romans, classmates! Welcome to the dawn of a new age in theater! I'm talking about my one-woman *Macbeth*. When I find a producer with a little imagination, it'll be good-bye to dressing up as a golden retriever eight shows a week. I'll finally be recognized for what I am: a true artist!"

As the swirl of voices overlapped and grew in intensity, Daphna listened, equal parts appalled and fascinated. Her fellow classmates were all very smart—brilliant, even. But wasn't she just as good? How many children had written a sonata at age two and a half? Or a full-length opera at age eight?

Daphna wasn't the type to blow her own horn, but was there anything wrong with standing up for what she could do? Not at all.

Daphna drew in a deep breath, ready to give herself the shout-out she deserved. Before she could, a voice rose above the tumult.

"*You think you're all so great?* Well, I'm better than everyone. I've developed a laser that can fix satellites from Earth. I've invented a lip balm that stimulates brain waves. Within the next three years, I plan to travel back in time to witness the big bang."

All eyes turned to the hopscotch court, stunned. Was that Thelma Trimm, jumping up and down, bragging wildly?

"How nice to finally hear her lovely voice," Ignatious said. "Remember, students. Never become so self-involved that you don't appreciate the hidden talents of your classmates." Ignatious stood to full height and gestured grandly to Thelma. "Keep plugging, Thelma. Your inventions sound truly insane."

Thelma turned red briefly, chewed on a pigtail, then went back to her hopscotch. The Great Blatt turned to face the rest of the students.

"Listen, carefully!" he shouted, jumping down to the ground from the jungle gym. "To give you all time to prepare for Monday's little assembly, regular classes are canceled for today. Although I would like nothing more than to spend the day visiting, urgent business beckons. Good luck! Time to get to work. Be insane! Be gifted! And you might take home the first-ever Insanity Cup!"

The Great Blatt walked through the sea of students, shaking hands, slapping backs, and flashing smiles for one and all, until he disappeared into the school building.

6

The Old Manuscript

The moment Ignatious was gone, students pushed and shoved toward the school.

"Make way for the winner!" Wilmer Griffith called, elbowing his way toward the door.

"Out of my way, you big lug," Wanda Twiddles said. Though only in fifth grade and half his height, she had no compunction about elbowing him back. "It's all me!"

"In your dreams," Wilmer said. "No way you're going to make it on *Cody Meyers* with a blueprint of a stupid bridge."

"Better a bridge than a chart of the Andromeda galaxy! Talk about a snooze!"

By that point the large boy and the pug-nosed girl were nose to nose.

"You're out of your mind!"

"Am not!"

"Are too!"

Arguments burst out like brush fires around the school yard. With Mr. D'Angelo and Mr. Yuri standing guard by the door to make sure no one got trampled, Daphna held back with Harkin and Cynthia to avoid the rush.

"I take it you're going to work on Gum-Top?" Daphna asked Harkin.

"*Shhhh!*" Harkin said. "Remember: no one else knows about it. But come by for a test chew at the end of the day."

"I'll warm up my jaws," Cynthia said. "And lucky me. I have to drop by Ignatious's office to pick a date for him to see the show. I mean, if the Great Blatt speaks, we have to obey, right?"

Though Cynthia tried to act blasé, Daphna could see that she was excited. Who wouldn't be?

"Anyway," Cynthia went on, "gotta run. I'm almost done with my closing number, 'Macbeth's Mambo.' It's brilliant."

Cynthia zigzagged and shimmied in and around the crowd toward the entrance.

"That's my cue, Daph, dude," Harkin said. "Catch you later for a test chew."

"I'll be there," Daphna said.

Harkin took advantage of his short but sturdy frame to barrel his way to the door.

As her two friends disappeared inside the building, Daphna heard the opening strain of her rhapsody in her head, a rolled minor-seventh chord followed by a series of arpeggios that climbed higher and higher up the keyboard. It was certainly a stirring first few measures. But maybe there was still room for improvement? Closing her eyes, Daphna heard the music again, but this time she assigned the various piano parts to trumpets, violins, clarinets, and cellos. Orchestrated, the piece was even more vibrant. Daphna opened her eyes, her heart beating wildly.

All her pieces—even her opera—had been written for piano. Was her rhapsody the piece to stretch her musical imagination? If so, could she possibly orchestrate it by Monday? Daphna needed a second opinion and needed it now. That meant Mrs. Zoentrope.

At the door to the school, Mr. D'Angelo and Mr. Yuri were calling for the final stragglers to come inside. Daphna didn't have to be told twice. She sprinted for the door.

Pushing through the orange back entrance, Daphna stood in the school's main lobby. From the science labs in the lower levels came the usual thrum of beeps, clicks, pops, and hisses; from the hallways above came shouts of excited children. Daphna knew of no place on Earth so full of energy as her school. It was as if the building itself pulsed with life, feeding off the wild insanity of the students.

Standing before her, smack in the middle of the lobby, gazing approvingly over his creation, stood a life-size statue of the school's famous founder. Like Ignatious himself, the statue was dressed flamboyantly in a light blue suit, polka-dot bow tie, and orange boots. To its right was the glass display case that housed samples of all of his greatest inventions, from Blatt-Global to the Hat-Top. On the statue's left was a plaque that spelled out the Blatt School creed:

> BE INSANELY GIFTED!
> WORK INSANELY HARD!
> BE INSANELY GOOD!

Daphna had read the words hundreds of times and thought nothing of them. In light of Ignatious's unexpected appearance at the school, she found them newly inspiring. Why not shoot for the moon and orchestrate her rhapsody? It would be a lot to do by Monday, but shouldn't she try?

Of course she should.

Daphna knew exactly what she needed to get first. A short time before her mother had disappeared— two days, in fact—she had come home with a gift wrapped in light lavender paper.

"This is for you, Miss Sadie P. Snodgrass," she had said. "Use it for an extra-special piece."

Inside the wrapping was a notebook of blank music paper. But what a notebook! The pages were a beautiful shade of creamy yellow. The music staves were not printed by a machine but etched by an expert calligrapher. On the front cover was a picture of Mozart at a harpsichord. As her mother had requested, Daphna had tucked it away, waiting to use it for an "extra-special piece."

That moment had arrived.

The large bell situated in the very top of the school's turquoise dome echoed down to the lobby. Daphna galloped up a sweeping circular stairway that led to the upper classrooms, going over the opening phrases of her rhapsody again and again, trying it out with different instruments. Her music carried her up three more floors, down a long hallway, past the main dining hall, then up another, narrower stairway. After that, she ran down another hallway, past a row of classrooms and the student lounge, and finally up another two stairways, these narrower still, until she reached a landing with a red carpet. Before her was a solid oak door: her office. On top of offering state-of-the-art science labs and classrooms, the Blatt School offered every single student—all one hundred of them—his or her own private work space to cultivate his or her own insane gifts.

Daphna barged inside and went straight to her bookshelf. She was so focused on retrieving her manuscript and getting up to Mrs. Zoentrope that she didn't see the dim figure hunched by the console piano that stood against the window—not at first. As her eyes began to adjust to the half-light, she gasped. Her legs suddenly felt like two thin twigs.

Could it be? Had the antelope man followed her to school?

"Who are you?" Her heart pounded. Unlike in her apartment, there was no button to push to send a refrigerator flying across the room. "What do you want?"

Daphna stepped back to the door and steeled herself for another attack. The intruder stood. This was no antelope man! Daphna blinked, more confused than scared. In fact, the dark figure was no taller than she was. As her eyes fully adjusted, Daphna saw the yellow loafers. She gasped again—this time not out of fear but surprise.

"Myron?" she said.

The boy grinned.

"Boy, am I confused." He chuckled. "I was looking for Mr. Yuri's office. He's my adviser. Maybe he's a floor below you. Or maybe above you. I lose track in this building." He wrinkled his brow. "What floor are we on anyway?"

Gathering her wits, Daphna eyed Myron. With all the winding stairways and long hallways, the Blatt School was notorious for being tough to navigate. More than once, Daphna had absentmindedly forgotten what floor she was on. Even so, wouldn't Myron have realized he was in the wrong office right away?

"We're on the eighth floor," Daphna said.

"My bad," Myron said. "Mr. Yuri is on the seventh."

The boy moved to his left to try to leave. But Daphna blocked his path and stared him down. Though she couldn't imagine that Myron had any connection to the antelope man, she was getting tired of snoops.

"How long were you in here?"

"Two seconds tops," Myron said. "Honest. That's how long it took for my eyes to adjust to the dark." Out came another high-pitched giggle. "What do you think? I was trying to steal your music? Everyone knows I can't read a note."

Daphna frowned. Something didn't add up. Then again, Myron had a point. Why in the world would he want her music? Before she could ask him more, the boy pushed past her.

"Later, Daphna," he called, and hurried down the stairwell.

Daphna watched him go. Should she follow behind? Question him further? Daphna considered it but then held her ground. Maybe Myron had been up to something, but that still didn't make him dangerous. Myron Blatt was no antelope man. Besides, she had work to do.

Daphna flicked on the light, dropped to her knees, and riffled through her music. Her special manuscript paper was right where she had left it, in between a book of the Chopin waltzes and the Gershwin preludes. She shoved the notebook into her book bag and headed down the hall to a final staircase, this one the narrowest of all. Taking the steps three at a time, Daphna flew to the top floor of the school and pushed through an oak door. Before her on a large blue door was a sign that read: Music Department.

"Is that you, Daphna?" a bright, fluty voice called. It was Mrs. Zoentrope. "I've been waiting for you, my dear! Come in! Come in!"

7

A Clue in the Music

Each time she set foot inside, Daphna was amazed by her teacher's office. Every available inch of wall space was covered with music. Beethoven sonatas were taped haphazardly next to Schubert études. Debussy's "Claire de lune" was upside down next to Brahms's Rhapsody in G Minor. The entire second movement of Haydn's Symphony no. 75 ran sideways alongside the far wall. In the corner of the office stood a small wood desk, piled almost all the way up to the ceiling with musty manuscripts. In the opposite corner was a dusty baby grand piano.

Daphna stepped over a pile of sheet music. Sitting in a small rocker in the middle of the room, the old teacher brushed a hand through her bright red hair and smiled broadly. There was little doubt that Daphna was her favorite pupil.

"Hello to you, Daphna dear. Do you have something to play for me?"

"It's not completely finished," Daphna said. She took off her book bag and reached for her music. "I still have a page to go."

"Then I'll hear what you have," her teacher said.

Stepping over two more piles of music, Daphna took a seat at the piano. She dutifully spread the music to her rhapsody before her even though she knew the piece by heart. Still, looking down at the piano keys, some yellowed with age, Daphna hesitated. Never before had she written a piece of music with such powerful emotional underpinnings. Every note was an homage to her mother. Every note would remind her of her loss.

"Whenever you're ready," Mrs. Zoentrope said gently.

Daphna looked up to meet her teacher's reassuring gaze.

"I was thinking of orchestrating this," she said.

The teacher nodded and pursed her lips. "Or-chestration? You're more than ready to give it a try. But let's have a listen and see. Go ahead, dear. I'm sure it's lovely."

Daphna looked back at the keys. With her teacher's encouragement, she heard the opening phrase in her head and plunged right in. The first phrase reverberated happily through the small office, as if the great composers whose sheet music was taped to the walls were welcoming Daphna into their company.

Dee, duh, dee, brrring!

Daphna relaxed. Glancing up, she saw that her teacher's eyes had begun to well up. Daphna played with even more passion, attacking the keys when the piece was loud and dramatic but caressing them during the slower, lush sections. In fact, Daphna was so moved by the power of her own composition that she felt tears in her own eyes. As the last chord rang through the office, Daphna reached for a tissue and dabbed her eyes. Mrs. Zoentrope was sitting stone still, totally motionless, staring straight ahead, brown eyes wide and glazed. A thin smile curved on her lips.

"Mrs. Z?" Daphna said.

To her surprise, her teacher didn't move.

"Mrs. Z?" Daphna repeated, this time more sharply. "Are you okay?"

The teacher shook herself gently, as if waking from a dream, then closed her eyes for a moment to collect herself.

"Astonishing." Her thin smile grew into a baffled grin. "I do believe I went into some sort of trance."

"A trance?" Daphna said. "Sorry!"

"No apology necessary, my dear." The teacher wagged her head in wonder, then looked at Daphna, eyes bright. "What a trance it was! I was transported to an extraordinarily lovely state. I feel positively renewed. As though all the bad thoughts and feelings that rattle around my mind have been collected in a paper bag and tossed out the window." The old lady was practically shaking. "Daphna, dear! I've never felt better. Your music has the power to heal!"

"To heal?" the girl stammered.

"Yes, yes," Mrs. Zoentrope said. "Never let anyone tell you that music can't deeply affect the emotions. Your music especially."

Daphna couldn't have been more pleased. But it was all too strange.

"You're really saying it was *my* piece that put you in a trance?"

Mrs. Zoentrope nodded. "What else could it have been, my dear? Has this ever happened before?"

Daphna shook her head. "Not that I know of. . . ." She paused.

"What, my dear?" The teacher smiled. "You're remembering something."

Daphna swallowed hard. "I think it *has* happened before."

Mrs. Zoentrope's red hair seemed to stand at attention, arching even more severely upward.

"It has?" she asked. "Tell me!"

"I don't know. I was so young."

"Remember what you can. Speak. Speak!"

Daphna told the story—or what she remembered of it:

She was three, and she and her mother had been in their small apartment.

Daphna had sat at the piano to play "The Sad Sandbox" for the first time.

By the end of the piece, her mother was staring straight ahead, motionless, her eyes unblinking. Daphna remembered how terrified she had been. Why was her mother suddenly a zombie? Was she alive? Had Daphna killed her?

"Mom?" she had asked. Then again with more force. "MOM!"

To Daphna's immense relief, her mother had smiled, then shaken herself and looked around the room as if waking from a dream.

"Are you all right?" Daphna had asked. "Where did you go?"

Her mother had practically glowed. "To a wonderful

place, darling. It was strange. I knew you were here, calling for me. But your beautiful music touched me so deeply that I couldn't move. My mind cleared completely. Bad thoughts turned to good. What an amazing feeling!"

"That's precisely how I feel," Mrs. Zoentrope said, rising to her feet. "I knew you were calling me, but I couldn't respond. My mind was filled with such lovely thoughts and feelings."

Daphna couldn't believe it.

"And you still think it was my music?"

"Of course it was your music!" Mrs. Zoentrope exclaimed. She smiled, exposing a brilliant flash of white, marred only by a front tooth that was the same light yellow as her piano keys. She laughed, producing a sound like a witch's cackle that might have been frightening had Mrs. Zoentrope not been such a kind woman. "We'll just have to warn the audience at the assembly on Monday to sit down, won't we? We wouldn't want anyone to fall over and hurt themselves."

Daphna was enormously gratified, but she still had one last question. "So you don't think I need to orchestrate it?"

The teacher shook her head. "No, no, no, Daphna." She took Daphna's hand in hers. Mrs. Zoentrope's fingers were long and thin. Daphna could feel the bones under the skin. "Sometimes less is more. You've written a gorgeous piano rhapsody that has the gentle spirit of your mother. Just finish it as it is, and you'll have a masterpiece." Then the teacher laughed, filling the room with another rousing cackle. "If you want to orchestrate something, write a symphony next!"

Daphna's eyes went wide. "A symphony?" she stammered. "You're joking."

"Not at all, my dear!" Mrs. Zoentrope said. "Mozart wrote his first when he was only eight. What's stopping you?"

Daphna let the thought settle in her mind. A symphony? One of music's longest classical forms and greatest challenges, it was the style of piece that her favorite composers—Beethoven, Mozart, and Brahms—had all written so beautifully. But could she really do it? Did she have the talent? Then, like a gift, a melody came to her fully formed.

Baa, baa, dee, dah! Baa, baa, dee, bum!

The perfect opening for a longer piece. Daphna turned to page one of the notebook her mother had given her and reached for a pen.

"I knew it!" Mrs. Zoentrope said. "You have an idea already."

Daphna smiled. "I think I do."

She wrote out the eight notes, then closed the book. As she did, a plain piece of cardboard fell out of the book onto her lap.

"What's that?" Mrs. Zoentrope asked.

Daphna had no idea. At first she assumed it was part of the manuscript book—maybe a flyer advertising the store where her mother had bought it. When she turned the cardboard over for a closer look, Daphna lost her breath.

It wasn't a piece of cardboard. In Daphna's hands was a photograph.

With trembling fingers, Daphna held it close. Two men and a woman, probably in their early twenties, were posing by what appeared to be the entranceway to a school.

"Are you all right?" Mrs. Zoentrope asked. There was an edge of concern in her voice.

"It's my mother."

Daphna traced her mother's face with her fingers. Her blond hair hung loosely down past her shoulders. Her smile was open and inviting. Her mom looked pretty, yes, but that was only part of it. Daphna had never seen her look so relaxed.

"She looks happy," Daphna said. "So do the two men. I wonder what they're laughing at."

It appeared as though whoever had snapped the picture had just cracked a colossally funny joke. First there was the man kneeling next to Daphna's mother. Eyes stretched wide, smiling broadly, he was slapping his knee. The man standing behind Daphna's mom was craning his neck, laughing so hard, it was difficult to see his face. The man in back had jet black hair while the one next to Daphna's mother was fairer. But both men had sharp, handsome features.

"They could be brothers," the teacher said. "Or maybe they were just friends? The one in the back does look somewhat familiar, but . . . no, no, maybe not. Maybe not."

Daphna's mind was already racing. Her mother had to have planted it there on purpose. What did it mean? Was she holding a clue to her mother's disappearance? Who were the two men? A moment later, she felt tears— again. It was a feeling she had grown accustomed to over the past two months. Tears and more tears.

Blinking the water back from her eyes, she heard Mrs. Zoentrope's voice come into focus.

"Strange," the teacher said. "What are those names?"

"What?" Daphna said.

She hadn't noticed at first, but there on the other side, written in loopy green ink—her mother's signature color—were three names. The first was smudged and only partly legible:

"W. Zoo . . . Ferd?" Daphna read. "Who's that?"

Mrs. Zoentrope shrugged. "No one I've ever met."

Daphna went on to the next two names.

"Cassandra P. McFuzz and Billy B. Brilliant."

Daphna's skin went cold. Cassandra P. McFuzz meant nothing to her. But wasn't *Billy* the name the antelope man had mentioned? She flipped the picture over to the other side.

Was one of these men Billy?

8

The Coming of Gum-Top

Daphna burst out of Mrs. Zoentrope's office, desperate to share the unexpected picture with Harkin and Cynthia, but she knew she would have to wait if she wanted her friends' undivided attention. Harkin was in his own office, frantically working on Gum-Top. And Daphna knew there was nothing she'd be able to do to take Cynthia's mind from her one-woman *Macbeth*.

Besides, Daphna had work of her own to do. She spent the rest of the afternoon putting the finishing touches on her rhapsody, but every few measures she couldn't resist sneaking peeks at the mysterious picture. She knew that her mother had attended the College for the Extraordinarily Talented, where she had majored in meteorology. Aside from those two facts, Daphna knew very little of her actual day-to-day life. The mother she had known was warm and kind but focused solely on her daughter and her work. The younger woman in the picture clearly had time for good friends. *Billy B. Brilliant? W. Zoo Ferd?*

At three o'clock the Blatt gong reverberated through the hallways. Daphna quickly packed her book bag and took off at a flat-out run down the many flights of stairs all the way to the lobby, where she sprinted past the statue of Ignatious Peabody Blatt to another staircase by the back entrance that led down to the science labs.

Down, down, down, she went, the telltale hisses and burbling of scientific experiments growing in intensity. Daphna glanced down one hall to see a student soldering an arm onto a robot. The distinct aroma of cinnamon wafted from another of the labs. Perhaps some student was making the world's largest apple pie? Or was the cinnamon being used as a surprise ingredient in a new face cream?

Who knew?

With a deep breath, Daphna took in the rich scent

and kept running. Now wasn't the time to think about what her fellow classmates were creating. Daphna needed someone to bounce ideas off of right now.

On the fourth floor beneath the lobby, she cut onto a white corridor that rapidly slanted downward toward a row of student offices. Through a small window, she saw Wilmer Griffith frantically writing equations on a blackboard. A room down, a young girl—no older than first grade—was knitting fur onto a mechanical dog. A room after that, Jean-Claude Broquet was busy translating the American Constitution into Medieval French. Then there was Wanda Twiddles. In her office, she was hanging upside down from a bar on the ceiling, studying the underside of a giant model suspension bridge.

Daphna hurried past one final door with an ominous sign over its window:

BEWARE: VERY LARGE GRASSHOPPER!

Then she was there: Harkin's office.

"Hey, Daph!"

Running toward her down the hall came Cynthia, dressed in her usual torn jeans, boots, and cardigan sweater.

"My one-woman *Macbeth* is finished," she cried. "I decided to have Banquo's ghost do a rumba with

Macbeth—which might be hard, since I'll be playing both parts, but I'll pull it off. If I don't get this thing on Broadway soon, I think my head will explode."

Daphna laughed. "That'd be dramatic."

"I know, right?" Cynthia said. "What's the deal with Gum-Top? Is Harkin ready for us?"

Before Daphna could answer, another voice called out—this time from inside the office.

"Who goes there?"

"It's us, Harkin," Cynthia called. "Open up!"

The door swung open, and Daphna peeked inside. Pieces of machinery—insides of cars and motors—lay strewn on the floor. On the opposite wall stood a shelf overflowing with books, mostly on engineering. To the left of the front door lay a simply enormous tome entitled *One Million and One Ways to Change a Spark Plug*.

The vast array of books and stray engine parts was nothing compared to what stood against the far wall. Daphna thought it resembled the Thunkmobile without the wheels. A series of interconnected pipes rose out of a large metal box, then twisted almost all the way to the ceiling in a series of increasingly small figure eights. Every few seconds, a puff of purple smoke whooshed out of the pipe closest to the door with a loud *clang* while a steady, thin stream of green smoke hissed out of the pipe farthest away.

Harkin was hunkered over his desk. Wearing a one-piece jumpsuit and a thick pair of metal glasses—his work attire—he was inspecting what appeared to be a small, rectangular piece of cardboard with a pair of tweezers. At first he was so engrossed by his work that Daphna thought he had forgotten about them. But then he suddenly looked up.

"I really should keep this secret for Monday," he said. "Even from you. But I just can't resist." He held up the cardboard. "I did it. Meet Gum-Top! The computer that you chew."

Daphna was stunned. Had Harkin really done it? Turned an idea first floated as a joke in first or second grade into a reality?

"My cocreators are skeptical," Harkin said, scolding them with a waved finger. "You doubt the work of the Thunk."

Daphna shook herself. "No, no. I don't—it's just that . . ."

Cynthia finished the thought for her. "Does it really work?"

Harkin slipped off the thick metal glasses and wagged his head. "It does. I chewed a piece and read the *New York Times* online. The front page appeared right before my eyes. I focused on the link to the sports section, and voilà! It took me right there. I read an article on the connection between high batting averages and eating fried jellyfish. Here. Chew!"

As he wagged the stick under Daphna's nose, she wrested it from him and held it up to the light. It certainly looked like an ordinary piece of gum. She took a deep whiff.

"What's it smell like?" Cynthia asked, leaning close.

"That's peppermint!" Harkin shouted, unable to contain himself.

"With a hint of orange," Daphna said.

"Exactly," the boy said. "The orange helps the chewable software run more smoothly."

"How about a piece for me?" Cynthia said.

Daphna looked at Harkin. "Should I break this one in two?"

Harkin shook his head. "I don't know if half a piece will emit a strong enough signal to get online. Don't chew yet, Daphna. Give me a second."

Harkin ran across the room and turned a purple knob on the side of the machine. It began to clang loudly—so loudly, in fact, that Daphna had to cover her ears.

"Sorry!" Harkin shouted. "I'm still refining it. It'll only last a second."

The machine clanged ten more times, each time louder than the one before, then stopped. As soon as Daphna took her hands from her ears, it began to shake like a washing machine in a spin cycle. An array of colored lights on its side began to flash.

"That's the computer," Harkin announced. "It's putting the chewable software into the gum."

No sooner were the words out of the boy's mouth then the machine hissed out a stream of orange smoke.

"That's the flavoring!" Harkin cried. "Now hold on."

Daphna's heart jumped. "Hold on?"

The machine began hopping up and down, thumping against the floor with a series of loud whacks. Without even realizing, Daphna and Cynthia held each other to keep from falling to the ground. Even so, the floor shook so violently that they sank to their knees.

"All right! Now watch!"

The machine stopped bouncing. With a series of fast, short *pfft*s, pieces of gum shot into the air, arced across the room, and landed in a bucket by the far wall.

"Works every time," Harkin said.

Harkin held up the bucket to Cynthia. She shoved a piece into her mouth and began to chew vigorously.

"Go ahead, Daph, dude," Harkin said.

Daphna held her gum in her hand another moment, looking it up and down, still half believing she was about to be the butt of some sort of colossal joke. But then she shrugged and popped it into her mouth. With a few good chews, the sharp taste began to spread.

"You're doing great," Harkin said.

"Doing great?" Cynthia said. She laughed. "A monkey could do this."

"Chew faster," Harkin said. "Now think of a website. Don't laugh. This is serious. Just do it!"

Cynthia rolled her eyes at Daphna. "Okay, I'm thinking about thedancingdoberman.com. But I don't see what that's going to—"

Cynthia stopped talking.

"What?" Daphna asked.

Cynthia's jaws began to work even faster. She appeared to be transfixed, looking straight ahead, seeing something no one else could. "This is amazing."

Harkin jumped into the air. "It's working, right?"

Cynthia shook herself and turned to Daphna. "I'm seeing the actual website in my head," she said. "Just by *thinking* about it. There's the home page. There's the page with the cast's bios. And there's a video of the opening-night party."

Daphna had barely chewed her piece, but now she chomped on her gum like it was the last piece in the world.

"Good," Harkin said. "Now think of a site."

Daphna thought of one of her favorites, composers.org, a website with information on famous musicians.

"Do you see anything?" Cynthia asked.

Daphna shook her head. "Not yet." She looked at her two friends accusingly. "Are you sure—"

But just like Cynthia, she was hit right between the eyes. Suddenly composers.org opened before her, almost like looking at the hologram of Harkin in her grandfather clock.

"Oh my gosh," she whispered, then looked at Harkin. "You really are insanely gifted."

Harkin rubbed his hands together wildly. "I can't deny it!"

"How long will I be online?" Daphna asked.

"For as long as the gum has flavor," Harkin said. "Which should be about five more minutes."

Cynthia paced the room, eyes staring into space. "There are the reviews. '*The Dancing Doberman* is no dog.' There's my picture. Man, I make an ugly golden retriever. And look! Someone started a fan group. 'Bark if you love Cynthia Trustwell.' They're giving free tickets to people who volunteer to give a rescue dog a home."

Daphna was getting into the spirit, also pacing the room, reading off the website that only she saw. "I'm scrolling through a biography of George Gershwin.

He grew up in New York, you know. His first hit song was 'Swanee.' He wrote *Rhapsody in Blue* when he was twenty-five."

"You've written your rhapsody at age eleven and three-quarters," Harkin said.

Daphna nodded. "I still need to name it. Something cool. Got any suggestions?"

Harkin didn't answer. Instead he reached to the ground, picked up a half-twisted hubcap, and hurled it at the door with all his might.

"Hey! Private!"

Daphna looked toward the door. Through the biography of George Gershwin, she caught a glimpse of a boy with his hair parted in the center before he disappeared.

"Myron?" Daphna said.

"It's him, all right," Harkin said.

"I caught him snooping around my office earlier this morning," Daphna said.

That was enough to get Cynthia to stop reading her press clippings.

"When I came out of my meeting with Ignatious, I saw him snooping around the offices on the sixth floor."

Daphna exchanged a worried glance with her friends. Harkin said what they were all thinking.

"Do you think he's trying to steal an idea to get

on *Cody Meyers?*"

"I don't know," Daphna said. "But let's find out."

She pushed through the door. Down the far hall, Daphna saw a shape disappear down the corridor.

"Myron!"

Daphna led the charge down the hall of offices, past Wanda Twiddles (who was now hanging upside down by one foot), Jean-Claude Broquet (who had the entire United States Constitution laid out on the floor of his office), and finally Wilmer Griffith (who was scribbling equations so furiously, he had written off the blackboard and onto the wall without even noticing).

"Where'd he go?" Harkin asked.

"Don't know," Cynthia said.

Daphna stopped running and chewed as hard as she could.

"What're you doing?"

"Going to blattschool.edu and finding Myron's office."

Daphna was amazed by how quickly Gum-Top responded to her thoughts.

She saw the site before her, then went to the section marked "Map," then scrolled to the name "Blatt, Myron."

"It's one floor up," she said.

Daphna and her friends sprinted up the stairs.

When they arrived at Myron's office, they found an empty room. There was a clutter-free desk in the corner and not a shred of evidence that Myron had done a bit of work all year.

"He's looking to steal an idea, all right," Cynthia said. "Look at this."

"He could be anywhere now," Harkin said.

Cynthia nodded, then took a scrap of paper from the floor and spit out her gum.

"Out of flavor already?" Harkin said.

Cynthia nodded. "Yeah, I just went offline."

"How about you?" Harkin asked Daphna.

If she struggled, Daphna could still make out the Blatt School website, but with a few more chews it vanished.

"Gone," she said, and spit the gum out onto a piece of tissue.

"I think it needs another flavor to sustain the link," Harkin said. "Something sharp. Maybe lime?"

"Could work," Cynthia said. "I guess we'll have to wait until Monday to catch up with Myron."

They returned to Harkin's office to lock up the Gum-Top machine for the weekend, then walked up four flights of stairs to the lobby. But the moment they pushed through the back door to the playground, Daphna saw her opening. She had been itching to talk about the antelope man. She now had another clue to add to the discussion. She reached inside her book bag and pulled out the picture.

"So, guys, listen up," Daphna said. "I want you to see something."

9

A Visit to the Basement

During the walk to Daphna's apartment, it didn't take long to boil the case down to its unassailable facts.

First, that when the antelope man had said, "Where'd she keep it?" he had to be referring to Daphna's mom.

Second, that one of the keys to discovering the antelope man's secret identity lay in figuring out the meaning of the term "Flex-Bed."

How or if any of it related to "Billy," and whether

the "Billy" in question was Billy B. Brilliant, no one knew. But by the end of talking everything out, Daphna knew where they had to start looking: a storage bin in the basement where her mom used to keep old papers.

Now that the plan was set, Daphna began to feel uneasy. A week earlier, she had finally found the courage to clear out her mother's closet and pack away her clothes in a giant trunk. That had been painful enough. To root through her mom's storage bin felt like the final admission that she was gone forever. Yes, the plane's wreckage had been found but not her mother's body, which meant that she might still be alive somewhere. What if she had survived the crash? Or parachuted to safety? Unlikely, but it was possible.

Still, Daphna knew she had no choice but to look for clues wherever she could find them. At her building, she put the picture of her mother and the two men in her back pocket and dumped her book bag in her apartment. Then she led Harkin and Cynthia to the basement. Stepping out of the elevator, the three friends found themselves in a dimly lit hallway. A row of low-hanging pipes and wires ran a foot overhead. Though Harkin and Daphna cleared them easily, the taller Cynthia had to duck periodically as she made her way down the hall.

"Pretty eerie down here," Harkin said.

"You're not kidding," Cynthia said. She pushed a strand of wires out of the way. "What do all these pipes and wires do, anyway?"

"Water, electricity, cable TV," Daphna said. "I'm not sure if even Ron knows."

She led her friends past the recycling room, Ron's office, and the cellar door of an adjoining restaurant. Next came the laundry room.

"I saw a mouse in there once when I was five or so," Daphna said. "Scared me half to death."

"Aha!" Harkin said. "I knew there was a reason you had me install a washer/dryer in your new kitchen."

Daphna stopped in front of a heavy red door.

"Here we go," she said.

She gave the door a firm push and reached around in the darkness for the switch. Light from two low-hanging bulbs filled a room that was lined with large black storage bins. Now that she was in the room, Daphna's heart began to beat faster, but with excitement as much as anxiety. Her mother had talked fondly of her childhood in upstate New York, especially her close relationship with her own parents. On the other hand, she had been strangely tight-lipped about Daphna's father. Beyond the cause of his untimely death at the hands of a cup of sour yak milk, Daphna knew nothing about him.

She led her friends down a narrow aisle lined with

storage bins, each belonging to a different tenant. Then she took a sharp right and stopped by a black bin with a thick "Apt. 3A" scrawled on the top in black Magic Marker. It was locked.

"Here it is," Daphna said.

"Do you remember the combination?" Harkin asked.

Daphna caught her breath.

"What's wrong?" Cynthia asked.

Daphna swallowed hard. "It's my mom's birthday."

She took the lock in her hands and lined up a nine for September, her birth month, then a two and a six for her birthdate: the twenty-sixth. When the lock clicked open, Daphna looked nervously at her friends, then pulled the bin open. She had expected it to be piled high with books and papers. Maybe even a few notebooks or a diary. Instead, the bin was filled with four wooden folding chairs, an old air mattress, three pillows, and a deflated soccer ball.

"Wow," she said.

She couldn't hide her disappointment. Daphna secretly wanted to find a private note from her mother: a deeply personal, loving last message sealed in a flowered envelope with the words "Read Only in Case of Death" written on the front.

"Sorry, Daph, dude," Harkin said. "This rots."

"Yeah," Cynthia said. "Not much here."

Daphna leaned into the bin and pushed aside the folding chairs. Still nothing. Frustrated, she picked up the deflated soccer ball and threw it hard onto one of the pillows, knocking it sideways into the air mattress. Then she saw it: a glimmer of red where the pillow had lain.

"Wait," she said. "Give me a hand with this stuff."

Daphna and her friends cleared out the bin and placed the chairs, pillows, mattress, and soccer ball out on the floor. Lying on the bottom was a red folder. Daphna leaned over as far as she could, snagged it by an edge, then plopped herself on the floor.

"Do you think there's anything inside?" she asked. "I mean anything good?"

"Don't get your hopes up," Cynthia said.

"But you never know," Harkin said.

As if to answer her question, ten or so pictures slipped out of the folder onto the floor. Daphna's spirits soared. Maybe there would be more photos of her mom? The first few pictures she looked at were of her mother, all right, but they were baby shots. The rest were of Daphna's grandparents. Inside the folder itself, there was an old electric bill, a second-place ribbon from a camp horse show, and a high-school diploma with a gold certificate reading "Valedictorian."

"Nice," Cynthia said. "Your mother was first in her class."

"She was smart, all right," Daphna said. "But I already knew that." She glanced back into the bin, disappointed again. "That's all there is."

"Nothing about the Flex-Bed," Cynthia said.

"Ditto the antelope," Harkin said. "Or the mysterious Billy."

"I wonder if he had the wrong apartment?" Cynthia asked.

"Maybe," Daphna said. She sighed. "All this time I was so worried about coming down here and finding out strange stuff about my mom. But there's nothing."

Harkin and Cynthia exchanged a glance, trying to find the right words to cheer up Daphna. Then there was a loud squeak from the far side of the room. Daphna sat up with a start.

"Is that a mouse?" Harkin asked.

Daphna nodded. "Let's get out of here."

As Daphna placed the pictures back in the red folder, she noticed something else. At first glance, the thin pencil markings on the back cover looked like nothing more than random squiggles. But with a hard look, Daphna saw that the markings were a drawing.

"Wait. What's this?"

She held the back cover closer. On either side of the page stood two tall trees, drawn with a few well-chosen lines and a couple of elegant swirls. In between the trees stood a simple bench. Slightly behind the bench to the right was a sharp X. Underneath the drawing was a name, written in curly script: Snods.

Daphna felt a chill. Not a light tingle up her spine, but a genuine shiver that ran all the way from her toes up to the back of her neck.

"What's Snods?" Cynthia asked.

"Me," Daphna whispered.

"So this is a message for you?" Harkin said.

Daphna nodded. "Must be." She pointed at the picture. "It's my mother's bench."

A year or so before her disappearance, Daphna's mother had donated a bench to Central Park in her parents' memory. It stood back from the bridle path, underneath a copse of trees just in from 101st Street. Daphna had been there only a few times, but her mother had visited the bench at least once a week—even in the middle of winter.

"Now we're getting somewhere," Cynthia said. "The X in the picture must mark where your mom left you something!"

"Something she didn't want anyone else to find," Harkin said.

Daphna ripped off the back of the folder and dropped the rest of it back into the storage bin.

"Come on, kids," she said. "Next stop, Central Park!"

10

Race to Sheep Meadow

By the time Daphna, Cynthia, and Harkin reached the entrance at 100th Street, the sun was just beginning to set, casting a bright orange glow over the park. They hurried past a lake and playground, turned down a wooded path, then cut across a small field. Just like in the drawing, the sturdy green bench stood between two majestic oaks. On the middle of the bench was a small silver plaque reading: "This bench was donated to Central Park in memory of Franklin and Joan Whispers."

Daphna knew she should get right to work digging at the spot where the X was in her mother's drawing, but she couldn't keep from leaning back and staring up through the trees before she got started.

"It's so peaceful," she said. "I almost forget I'm in New York."

Daphna watched a bird flutter between two branches, then followed its flight back toward the north of the park. To her surprise, a new melody came to her—the second phrase of her symphony.

Da, da, dum, dum, dee!

"Oh, no," Harkin said to Cynthia. "She's at it."

"What?" Daphna said.

"I know that look," he replied.

"How can you compose music at a time like this?" Cynthia asked.

Daphna shrugged. "It just came to me."

She stood and surveyed the terrain behind the bench. The ground was covered with leaves. Daphna took her mother's drawing out of her back pocket, studied it for a moment, then looked back to the ground.

"The X is right about there." She pointed to a spot to the right of the bench, close to the taller of the two trees. Harkin looked over her shoulder to check her sense of distance.

"I think you're right," he said. "Let's dig."

Cynthia was already down on her knees, ready to paw at the dirt.

"Come on, slowpokes."

A squirrel leaped down from a tree and stood on the back of the bench a few inches from Daphna's head.

"Oh, hey there," she said.

As a New Yorker, she was used to the comings and goings of squirrels and pigeons. The animal leaped back to the ground, sprinted for the woods, but then stopped on a dime, a few feet from where Cynthia was about to start digging.

"You won't find any nuts down there," she said.

By that point, the squirrel was scraping at the ground with its front paws. Harkin got down on one knee.

"Maybe the little dude sees something we don't?"

Daphna took a step toward the squirrel. When her shadow crossed its path, it looked her up and down, then sprinted up the closer of the two trees. Without wasting a moment, Daphna dropped to her hands and knees and scraped away dirt at the squirrel's spot. She quickly uncovered what appeared to be the top of some sort of box. Cynthia and Harkin joined in, tossing away handfuls of leaves, sticks, and muddy dirt. In less than a minute they had dug out a wooden box, a foot across and close to six inches deep. Wide-eyed, Daphna looked at her friends.

"It's my mother's old letter box."

"Go ahead," Cynthia said. "Open it!"

Daphna glanced up to make sure no one was snooping. In the distance, a mother was pushing a stroller toward a playground. In the other direction, through the trees, she could hear a group of boys playing soccer.

"Coast is clear," Harkin said. "Go for it."

The top pulled off more easily than Daphna expected. Lying at the bottom of the box was a single sheet of yellowed paper with neat typeset print across the page. Daphna held it up to the light.

"It's a page from a published book," she said.

But it was more than that. Across the typeset lines was a pair of musical staves—one bass, one treble clef—filled with a series of large notes, almost as if they had been written by a child.

"I didn't know your mom wrote music," Harkin said.

"She didn't," Daphna said with a laugh.

"What are you saying?" Harkin asked.

"I thought this handwriting looked familiar," Daphna said. "My mom copied my first sonata, 'The Sad Sandbox.'"

Her friends looked more closely.

"Why would she hide a copy out here?" Cynthia said.

"And why copy it over a novel?" Harkin asked. "Here, lemme see something."

He took the paper. Though Daphna's piece was printed in dark ink, the text underneath was still readable. Harkin read:

"'Kilimanjaro is a snow covered mountain 19,710 feet high, and it is said to be the highest mountain in Africa. Its western summit is called the Masai "Ngàje Ngài," the House of God.'

"Let's see what my search engine, Get Thunked, has to say."

Harkin typed the passage into his wristwatch computer.

"That's the opening passage from 'The Snows of Kilimanjaro,' by Ernest Hemingway," Harkin said.

"What do you think?" Cynthia asked, turning to Daphna. "That your mom went to Kilimanjaro?"

"Could be," she said.

She took the music back from Harkin and examined the first line.

"What are you thinking?" Cynthia asked.

Daphna pointed at the first three notes in the G clef.

"See those?" she asked Cynthia.

Her friend held the music up to her glasses. "Yeah, they're quarter notes."

"Not their length," Daphna said. "Their pitch."

Cynthia looked again. "Three Bs." She frowned. "So what?"

Harkin got it. "B. B. B," he whispered. "Billy B. Brilliant."

"Do you really think that's why she picked this piece?" Cynthia asked. "The three Bs?"

Daphna nodded. "Mom knew I'd eventually look for a clue in the notes. It has to be."

"So now we're getting somewhere," Harkin said, standing up to his full height. "If we put it all together, your mom went to Kilimanjaro to find Billy B. Brilliant."

"It's possible," Daphna said.

"Mount Kilimanjaro is a big place," Cynthia said. "Even if she and Billy Brilliant are there, how would we find them?"

It was a good question.

Just as Daphna set her mind to solving the problem, she had the strange sense that she and her friends were being watched. She looked up from the letter box and back over her shoulder.

There he was, standing by the edge of the path, no more than thirty feet away. The antelope man.

"I'll take that," he said.

Daphna rose slowly to her feet. Harkin took the yellowed paper and shoved it into his back pocket. Daphna held the letter box.

"Who are you?" she asked, voice shaking.

The man began to walk toward them. Under other circumstances, Daphna might have been amused. After all, here was a grown man dressed in a costume that would have drawn stares at Halloween. But as the strange man—almost more ghoul than human in the trees' shadows—seemed to glide toward them, Daphna knew that she had never been more terrified in her life.

She noticed he was moving with a distinct limp.

"You hurt your leg," she said.

"You pushed me out a window," the man replied.

Shaking now, Daphna held the box behind her back.

"Give it here, and you won't get hurt," the man said.

"One hour," Harkin whispered. "Sheep Meadow."

Daphna knew it well, a large field located in the south end of the park.

"You won't get away this time," the man called out. He was no more than ten feet away now. He laughed, a raspy guffaw that filled the woods. "There aren't any refrigerators out here."

But there was a squirrel—the same one that had helped discover the letter box. With a single leap it was back on the bench. With another it was flying through the air, paws outstretched. Then it was scurrying to keep its balance on the antelope man's head.

"Run!" Harkin called.

Cynthia and Daphna didn't need to be told twice. They broke for the cluster of trees behind them, then sprinted back up toward the park exit. Though the animal was still on his head, the man took a few steps in their direction but stopped when the squirrel jumped down and dug its claws firmly into his shoulder.

"Arrrgghhh!"

The man doubled over, grabbing wildly for his shoulder. By that time, the squirrel had leaped to the ground and was barreling for the woods.

A safe distance up the path, Daphna stopped.

"What are you doing?" Cynthia said.

"Making sure Harkin gets away," Daphna said.

Daphna turned to see Harkin take the yellowed sheet of paper out of his pocket and hold it up to the masked man.

"Looking for this?" he said.

"You're dead!" the antelope man called, and rushed toward him, arms outstretched. For a split second, Harkin remained perfectly still. He then calmly rolled up his sleeve and pressed a purple button on his wristwatch control pad. Bright orange flames shot out of his sneakers. With a giant *whoosh*, he shot straight up into the air, his ponytail flapping in the late-afternoon breeze.

"Say hello to my jet-propelled high-tops!" Harkin called.

The man dove for the boy's rising feet, missed, and did a somersault into one of the oak trees. Another burst of flames shot from Harkin's sneakers, rocketing him across the copse of trees toward the playground.

"Yes!" Daphna said. "Let's cruise!"

Daphna and Cynthia sprinted for the 100th Street exit, arriving just as Harkin touched down.

"Can I have the paper?" Daphna asked.

Harkin nodded. "Yep! Here. Take it."

Daphna shoved it into her mother's letter box and looked over her shoulder. In the far distance, the antelope man was already back on his feet, hurrying their way.

"Where to now?" Harkin asked.

"Keep to the plan," Daphna said. "Split up so we're harder to track. Meet at Sheep Meadow in an hour."

"Got it," Cynthia said. She was off, headed uptown. Harkin fired up his sneakers and took to the sky.

"Later, Daph, dude!"

Satisfied that her friends were safe, Daphna ran across Central Park West. But she stopped smack in the middle of the street. Were there really two *more* men in antelope masks? *Running right at her?* And two others crossing the street, hightailing it after Cynthia?

A cabbie screeched to a halt and leaned on his horn.

"Move it, girl!" he yelled.

He honked again, a blast that shocked Daphna back into action. Two masked men really *were* after her—and they were closing fast. Tucking the letter box under her arm, she ran for her life.

11

Return of the Thunkmobile

While running for her life down Central Park West, Daphna found herself smiling, amazed at her mother's cleverness. Along with the three Bs, her first piece of music contained another clue. "The Sad Sandbox" was named in honor of a sandbox at the 97th Street playground where she had played as a little girl. Next to the sandbox was a tree—a place where she and her mother used to bury treasures, such as dried leaves and Popsicle sticks. That's where the final missing directions had to be.

As exciting as it was to figure out where the next clue was likely hidden, Daphna still had to get away. With the antelope men gaining, she cut into Jimmy's Bar, a pub with an old upright piano in the corner where she had an open invitation to play show tunes for the patrons whenever she wanted. After playing a quick medley of songs from her favorite musical, *13*, she slipped into the bathroom, then climbed out the window to a back alley. Finally free, Daphna doubled back to the tree by the sandbox. It didn't take much digging to uncover an empty glass bottle. Inside was a sheet of lavender construction paper. On it, in light green ink, almost impossible to read, was a drawing of the globe.

"Got it," she said out loud.

What was that? A movement in the underbrush? Had the antelope men tracked her down?

Daphna shoved the lavender map into her mother's letter box, then leaped over the playground fence and hit the ground running.

Forty-five minutes later, Daphna hurried into Sheep Meadow from the west side of the park. Clutching her mother's letter box under her right arm, she stopped by the chain-link fence that surrounded the giant field and looked over her shoulder, heart pounding. Though it was hard to tell for sure in the rapidly fading light, she didn't see anyone following her. In the far distance, a group of school kids was finishing up a game of touch football. On the other side of the field was a vigorous soccer game. Daphna knew that in a matter of minutes the players would finally succumb to the darkness and head home to dinner, homework, and bedtime.

Daphna sighed. Exhausted from all the running, she plopped down on a bench. For a moment, she longed to be one of the kids playing sports—a kid with a normal family, who went to a normal school and had a perfectly unexciting normal set of talents. As a light wind blew, she wrapped her arms around herself and looked more closely at the lavender map. Two lines intersected the middle, over what appeared to be an African mountain range. Instantly, Daphna thought of the clue from the letter box. The short story by Ernest Hemingway.

"Kilimanjaro," she said out loud.

Then Daphna scanned down to two numbers listed in the corner: −3.065274, 37.359076—longitude and latitude markings.

Daphna allowed the good news to sink in. After two long months of mystery, she finally had a link to her mother.

"Hey, Daphna!"

She turned around with a start as Cynthia appeared out of the half-light. The two girls fell into each other's arms.

"Oh my gosh," Daphna said. "Did two guys follow you, too?"

Cynthia nodded. "Yep."

"How'd you get free?"

It wasn't until Cynthia pulled away that Daphna realized that her friend was wearing a completely different outfit. Gone were her ripped jeans, cardigan sweater, and pink-rimmed glasses. In their place, Cynthia wore a green peasant dress and sandals. On her head was a black wig.

"What's with the getup?" Daphna asked.

"I could only keep ahead of those weirdos for a few blocks," Cynthia replied. "Just when I was about to collapse, I remembered the thrift store on Columbus. Well, if being on Broadway has taught me anything, it's how to change costumes in seconds. So I ducked in there, grabbed some stuff from the rack, and threw it on."

With that, Cynthia took off the black wig, allowing her blond hair to spill out onto her shoulders. She reached into her pocket and put on her glasses.

"There," she said. "Now I can really see you."

"What happened next?" Daphna asked.

Cynthia shrugged. "The rest was easy. There was no

back door, so I just strolled out the front, pretended I was lost, and asked them directions to Lincoln Center in a Russian accent." She laughed. "They thought I was some sort of whacked-out tourist!"

Maybe being insanely gifted really was better than being sanely normal.

"What did you do?" Cynthia said.

Daphna glanced around the field. No sign of any masked men in black. With the coast still clear, she allowed herself a moment to tell the story. Cynthia nodded, clearly impressed.

"The old show tune, bathroom slip. You go, kiddo!"

After another hug, Daphna and Cynthia sat on the bench and Daphna took out the map she had found in the sandbox.

"Your mom must've really wanted to make sure this map didn't fall into the wrong hands," Cynthia said.

Daphna nodded. Now that the escape was over, momentous decisions were at hand.

"What next?" Cynthia asked. "Follow your mom's path?"

Daphna swallowed. "You think she'll be there?"

Her friend shrugged. "Who knows? You've got to look, don't you think?"

Daphna agreed.

How did a girl who wasn't even quite twelve just up and go to Mount Kilimanjaro?

"Let's see," Cynthia said. "I could use my salary from the show to pay for our plane tickets."

Daphna blinked. "*Our* plane tickets? You mean you'll go too?"

"Go? Of course I'm going!"

"What about the show? You just got a rave review in the *Times*."

Cynthia waved a hand. "That's what understudies are for. If you think I'm going to miss a trip to Africa, you're crazy."

Daphna stood up and paced the turf in front of the bench. "Even if we manage to get on a plane, where will we stay once we're there?"

"We'll figure it out as we go," Cynthia said. "We're pretty good at that, right?"

"What about the Insanity Cup? I know how much you want to enter with your one-woman *Macbeth*."

"I do," Cynthia said. "Really, really badly. But if we leave tonight, we can be back by Monday morning. Maybe I can round up some producers in Africa."

Daphna smiled. "Well, okay. I just hope Harkin wants to come, too."

"He won't want to miss this," Cynthia said. "If he ever shows up, that is."

Daphna took another look around the field.

The touch footballers were wandering as a group to a far exit, and the soccer teams were gathering up the cones they used to mark off their field. Nearby a maintenance man was packing up his tools. Aside from an occasional jogger, the park was emptying out. The air took on a chill. Daphna shivered.

"Where is he?" she said. "He seemed certain to get away. I mean, with those jet-propelled high-tops."

"Maybe he had to go home and check in with his parents?" Cynthia said.

Daphna could tell that her friend was trying to keep it light but was just as nervous as she was.

"Let's just give him a ring," Daphna said. She took out her cell phone.

She scrolled quickly to his number. Just as she pressed send, Daphna heard the distant pop of an engine backfiring.

"What was that?" Cynthia asked.

Before Daphna could answer, Harkin picked up.

"Thunk here."

"Where are you?" Daphna said.

"About twenty seconds away," he replied. "Get ready to jump."

"*What?*" Daphna said.

The line went dead.

"What's going on?" Cynthia asked.

Daphna heard it again, this time two bangs in

rapid succession, followed by the whir of a slightly off-kilter engine. Harkin's Thunkmobile barreled out of the darkness. Though Daphna hadn't been aware that the car was a convertible, the top was down. Harkin was wearing goggles. His ponytail blew behind him as though it were a scarf.

"Here he comes!" Daphna called.

Daphna and Cynthia scrambled onto the bench. Then they saw them. Out of the dim light, hot on Harkin's rear bumper and closing fast, came the masked men, now on five motorcycles. The girls exchanged a horrified glance.

Harkin slammed on the brakes and cut the steering wheel. Daphna gasped as his contraption skidded on the grass, turned in the opposite direction, and stopped on a dime by the bench. Caught unprepared, the five motorcycles slid by, frantically trying to stop and turn.

"Get in!" Harkin cried.

Daphna and Cynthia were already in the air. They landed in the front seat in a tangle of arms and legs.

"Hold on!" Harkin said.

He put the car in gear. It took off like a shot. Three of the motorcyclists—the original antelope man and two of his cronies—were right behind. The two others had crashed into the fence. Cynthia untangled her long legs and sat facing forward.

"Where were you?" she asked.

"Right after you guys took off, my jet sneaks failed," Harkin replied.

"So how did you get away?" Daphna said.

She, too, had righted herself in her seat.

Harkin smiled. "I'm wearing my electromagnetic undershirt. The minute the antelope man grabbed me, he got a shock he'll never forget." He flicked a switch. "Watch your heads!"

With a loud grunt, the roof of the car came down. By that time, the car had reached the end of the field. With the motorcycles once again hugging his rear bumper, Harkin careened onto a pedestrian path, rumbled down a hill, and took a sharp left onto the park drive. One of the cycles pulled even and bumped hard into the side of the car.

"Watch it!" Daphna called.

Harkin laughed. "It's all good."

He pressed an orange button on the dashboard. A mechanical arm shot out of the side of the car, slamming the motorcycle off the road, down a hill, and into the lake at 72nd Street.

"Nice work!" Cynthia said, looking out the window. "But where are we going?"

"Going?" Harkin said. "To find Billy B. Brilliant, of course!" He turned to Daphna. "You've found a map by now, right?"

Daphna was dumbstruck. "How did you know that?"

Harkin shrugged. "I just assumed you'd put something together."

"Watch it!" Cynthia cried.

Harkin swerved around a parked taxi. The two remaining motorcycles went around the other side and kept up the chase.

"So what next?" Daphna called. "To the airport?"

Harkin looked genuinely surprised.

"Don't you know me better than that?" he said. "Hold on!"

He pressed a yellow button. Daphna heard a light hum and glanced out the window just in time to see a blue wing pop out of the right side of the car. Next she saw Harkin grab a green lever high on the dashboard—one Daphna hadn't seen before—and pull it steadily toward him. Daphna felt herself being pushed back in her seat. Before she had time to register what was happening, the crazy contraption lifted off the ground. Daphna and Cynthia exchanged a glance, too stunned to speak. Harkin slapped the dashboard.

"Fly, Thunkmobile! Fly!"

With a loud *whoosh*, the car rocketed up over the trees and soared above the park. On the ground, an antelope man gasped, barely managed to avoid a tree, then skidded to a safe halt. His final companion wasn't so lucky. At the sight of the flying car, he lost control of his motorcycle, crashed into a hot-dog cart, and came up covered in mustard and onions.

"I didn't know this was also a plane," Daphna said.

Harkin was busy with the controls. "It wasn't. Once I got free of Monsieur Antelope, I realized that we'd probably be going on some sort of a trip and would need a quicker mode of transportation. So I stopped the car to make a few minor adjustments. I even had time to pick up some dinner on the way. Chinese good?"

Cynthia gulped. "Chinese food? Sure."

Harkin reached behind him and produced a bag, then spun the wheel. Daphna knew she should be nervous—terrified even. But for the first time in two months, she felt strangely calm. Maybe now she'd finally get some answers about her mother.

As the car soared over the Statue of Liberty, Daphna pulled out her cell phone and dialed quickly. Luckily, she got his machine.

"Ron?" she said. "I'm really sorry I forgot to tell you, but I'm off on a school trip for the weekend. I'll call when I can. Don't worry."

By the time Daphna clicked off, Harkin and Cynthia were already on their phones, making excuses to their parents.

"No, seriously, Mom, dude," Harkin was saying. "It's an electrical engineering conference. In Madrid. And yes, when I get back, I'll study Dad's housefly. Promise."

"And don't forget to call the theater," Cynthia told her father. "My understudy needs to go on in an hour."

"Sorry," Daphna said, when her friends had hung up. "I don't want to get you in trouble."

"Trouble?" Cynthia said. "This is the most fun I've had in years!"

"Ditto that!" Harkin said. "Now come on!" With one hand on the wheel, he used the other to rip open a container of lo mein. "Who's hungry?"

12

Off to a Village in the Valley

Night fell. The Thunkmobile rocketed over the Atlantic, twisting and turning high above the clouds. After takeoff, the ride was so smooth that the three children almost forgot that the plane was made of discarded taxicabs and a bus.

The farther the flying car traveled over the Atlantic, the more Daphna thought about another flight—the one her mother had taken two short months earlier. The one that had ended in tragedy.

Or had it? Until she had hard-and-fast proof,

Daphna couldn't be sure.

About an hour out of the city, Harkin flipped open a panel in the dashboard, revealing what looked like a minicomputer.

"What's that?" Daphna asked.

"My GPS," Harkin said.

He punched in some numbers, and a voice filled the cockpit.

"Message to the Thunk. Reduce speed to one hundred miles per hour. Descend to five hundred feet!"

"We aren't there yet, are we?" Daphna said.

"Nope," Harkin said.

"Then where are we going?"

Harkin and Cynthia said nothing. The boy maneuvered the car over a lonely spot in the ocean and shone the headlights across the water.

"I thought you'd want to see it," he said.

Daphna felt a sinking in her chest. She knew. Below was nothing but unbroken sea.

"I'm so sorry," Cynthia said.

Daphna swallowed hard. "Are you sure we're in the right place?"

Harkin nodded grimly toward his GPS.

"I took the longitude and latitude from the Coast Guard reports of where your mom's plane was discovered," he said. "But maybe I made a mistake."

Daphna forced a smile. "The Thunk doesn't make mistakes." She paused. "Oh, whatever. It's not like my mom was going to be waiting for me on a life raft for two months. I mean, she could've parachuted out and been saved, right?"

There was an awkward pause during which Daphna hoped that one of her friends would say something like "I bet you're right" or "The map's going to lead us straight to her." Instead they looked awkwardly at the ocean. Daphna knew they both thought her mom was dead but didn't have the heart to say it. Daphna's eyes welled up with tears.

"Well," she stammered. "Might as well keep going."

As Daphna wiped her eyes on her sleeve, Cynthia patted her back. "If we've followed the clues correctly, maybe Billy B. Brilliant has some answers about her."

Daphna nodded. Harkin flipped a row of switches on the dashboard, then pulled back on the green lever. With a loud purr and an abrupt lurch, the car picked up speed, gained altitude, and was soon flying over the clouds. Though she was high in the air, Daphna hadn't been so low in months. Luckily, she was with the two people in the world who knew best how to cheer her up.

First, Cynthia got Daphna's mind off her mother by telling stories about *The Dancing Doberman*. She even sang the opening number, complete with pants and barks. When she was finished, Daphna applauded.

"Brava!"

Harkin cleared his throat.

"What?" Cynthia asked.

"The Thunk will now recite a poem!"

"You're kidding!" Daphna said.

"What?" Harkin said. "You think all I know about is engine parts? I have a sensitive side too."

With no further ado, he began to recite:

"Fly me high, O Thunkmobile,
And I'm king of all I see!
Only a skunk in a lifelong funk
Could resist this car named Thunk.
That's how it seems to me.

"You be good to me, O car,
And I will be true blue.
If some punk were to call you junk,
I'd tell that punk he's full of bunk,
Then make him scrub your wheels and trunk
(That punk would scrub the trunk of Thunk),
That's what I'd make him do.
Sweet Thunkmobile, I love you!"

"Not bad," Cynthia said. "But stick to mechanics."

"Thanks a lot," Harkin said.

"Anytime."

"Okay, Daph, dude," Harkin said. "You next! Let's hear this famous rhapsody."

"I'm not going to hum a piece that's meant to be played," Daphna said.

"I wasn't expecting you to hum it," Harkin said. He flipped an orange switch, and a small keyboard emerged from underneath the dashboard.

"It's not full-length," Harkin said, "but you can give us an idea."

Daphna would have preferred to wait for better conditions. The keyboard was only four octaves. The Thunkmobile shook as it cut through the air. But Daphna knew when she was backed into a corner. With no excuses, she played her rhapsody for all it was worth, filling the small compartment with music. Competing with the whir of the Thunkmobile's mighty engine, Daphna played more loudly than usual. Once, when they dipped suddenly in the air, she missed the keyboard altogether. But fully committed to her performance, Daphna played all the way to the end, when she saw that it had happened again.

Both of her friends were staring straight ahead in a trance.

Cynthia's blue eyes were fixated straight ahead, unmoving. And Harkin was under so deeply that he had let go of the steering wheel and the Thunkmobile had begun to veer down.

"Harkin!" Daphna called.

No response.

"Yo, *Thunk!*"

He shook himself awake. Like her mother and Mrs. Zoentrope before him, he seemed completely at peace.

"Whoa, Daph! That was some piece of music."

"I put you in a trance."

"What?" Cynthia said, stirring awake too.

"A trance?" Harkin said. "Tell us about it."

"Take the wheel first, okay?"

Harkin righted the Thunkmobile, and Daphna filled in her friends on what had happened in Mrs. Zoentrope's office. Harkin and Cynthia took the news in stride, almost as if they had expected Daphna's musical gifts to possess magical properties.

"The power to heal the mind, huh?" Harkin said.

Daphna nodded. "Yeah, that's what Mrs. Zoentrope said."

"I buy that," Harkin said.

"Me too," Cynthia said.

"Oh, come on," Daphna said.

"No," Harkin said. "After your little trance, I feel like the best version of myself."

"Wow," Daphna said. "I mean, I'm flattered, but it's just music."

"Just *music?*" Cynthia said. "Don't forget the famous old saying: 'Music has charms to soothe the savage beast.'"

"And yours has an extra-special quality," Harkin said. "Always has, always will."

"Yep," Cynthia said. "You're the most insanely gifted of all." She then gave Daphna a punch on the shoulder that was a little bit too hard to be considered purely friendly. "Of course, if you think you're going to beat me out of the Insanity Cup, guess again, girlfriend. My one-woman *Macbeth* will rule the day."

Daphna had learned to take Cynthia's competitive nature with a grain of salt. It was part of who she was.

"One-woman *Macbeth?*" Harkin said. "Better than Gum-Top? You're out of your mind!"

"Hey," Daphna said. "We're all winners here, right? I'd be lost without you guys."

Cynthia patted her hand. "Me too," she said. Then she smiled. "But I'm still going to win."

Harkin flipped a switch on the dashboard and a back panel slid open, revealing a small portal with an air mattress laid out on the floor.

"Who gets the first nap?" he asked.

They slept in shifts: Cynthia, then Daphna, then Harkin (who left specific instructions to wake him up if the going got tough). By the time he woke, the little flying car was approaching Europe.

"What do you say to breakfast?" Harkin asked, stretching as best he could in the small front seat.

"Breakfast?" Daphna said. "You brought that too?"

"Nope. But doesn't Paris have the best bakeries? I'd kill for a croissant."

Harkin maneuvered his strange flying machine down around the Eiffel Tower and landed on Paris's widest street, the Champs-Élysées. Making the transition from pilot to driver easily, Harkin pulled to a halt by a corner *boulangerie*.

After such a long flight, Daphna burst out of the car and happily stretched her legs. Inside the shop Cynthia ordered an array of croissants—chocolate, almond, cheese, blueberry, and honey—in perfect French. Though Daphna didn't generally drink coffee, she joined her friends for a morning cup.

Watching the day come to life—the early-morning vendors, dog walkers, and taxicabs—Daphna wished that she could stay in Paris a week or more. Billy B. Brilliant, strange antelope men, and maps seemed a lifetime away. Why not stick around for a while and see the sights? With any luck, by the time she returned, the problems of her life in New York would have disappeared.

Of course, Daphna knew full well that no amount of good food and art museums could set right what was wrong in her life. No, this strange trip was her only hope of finding out what had happened to her mother. While Harkin and Cynthia seemed perfectly willing to linger over a second croissant, Daphna stood up.

"It's time."

Soon they were soaring up over the city.

"Next stop, Africa," Harkin said.

Africa. Daphna's spirits soared, reveling in the thrill of flying to such an exotic, exciting place. Maybe they would see some wild animals. Maybe lots.

As the minutes turned to hours, bad thoughts began to replace good. What if the drawing in the storage bin and the map had been planted by the antelope man as a way to get her far, far out of town? What if he was back in her apartment at that very moment, looking for what he really wanted?

Daphna peered out the window and allowed herself to be slowly soothed by the beauty of the white clouds below. Soon Harkin punched the longitude and latitude coordinates from the map into the computer keypad on his dashboard. On cue, the GPS began to direct the flying car.

"The Thunk must lower altitude to twenty thousand feet," it said.

"Are we almost there?" Daphna asked.

"Getting closer," Harkin said.

When the flying car poked its nose underneath

a layer of cloud at nineteen thousand feet, Daphna was surprised to see the snow-covered peaks of Kilimanjaro beneath them.

It was hard to imagine anyone living on that snowy mountain. Harkin carefully followed the instructions on the GPS, dropping altitude until the car was only two hundred feet over the snowy terrain, flying head-on into a snowstorm. As the engine strained against the harsh wind, Daphna and Cynthia clutched their seats.

"You sure we're in the right place?" Daphna called.

A massive gust of wind shook the car so hard, Daphna ended up in Cynthia's lap. Regaining her composure, Daphna looked out the window onto miles and miles of snow. Another gust ripped through the air. The car lurched sideways and began to angle sharply down. Daphna went white.

"Harkin?" Cynthia asked.

The boy pulled the green directional lever with all his might. Instead of the car righting itself, its nose dropped even further. As the contraption careened toward the hard ice below, Daphna and Cynthia scrambled to the pilot's seat and each grabbed a piece of the lever. Together, the three threw all their collective weight into pulling it back.

"Harder!" Daphna called.

"It's not working!" Cynthia cried.

The snowy ground rushed up to meet them. The wind was deafening.

Fifty feet.

Forty feet!

Thirty!

Was this the end?

Twenty!

Ten!

Daphna held her breath.

When suddenly . . . the ground opened up! The wind abated. The sun came out. The next thing Daphna knew, the car had righted itself and was soaring over a lush green valley, about a mile across and a half mile wide. The blizzard raged on either side, but down below, oak and pine trees stretched majestically toward the sky in fields dotted with zebras, gazelles, giraffes, and elephants.

Daphna was the first to regain her poise. She took another glance at the map. "This must be some sort of secret land that my mom discovered. Land this thing, Thunk. We've got some exploring to do."

13

A Man and His Monkeys

Harkin maneuvered the Thunkmobile farther down into the valley, circling over a small herd of zebras. Nearby, a family of elephants was out for a morning stroll.

"In case anyone had any doubt," Cynthia said, "we're most definitely in Africa."

They certainly were. Two hundred feet over the ground, the car coasted over three hippos taking a swim in a small pond. Two giraffes, chewing leaves off a tree, glanced up as the Thunkmobile cruised by.

"This is like a game preserve," Daphna said.

As if to prove her point, a group of monkeys swung onto the ground from a tree and began to wrestle in the dirt.

"Very cute," Harkin said. "But we've got a problem, dudes. Lots of animals. No people."

Harkin was right. The small car had already reached the far edge of the valley. A few hundred feet ahead stood the jagged side of the cliff. Up above was the raging snowstorm.

Daphna sighed. But then she noticed something out of the corner of her eye. At the far edge of the valley, a thin line of smoke was circling up from a copse of trees.

"Last I heard, zebras don't make fires," she said.

The car skimmed the top of a grove of pine and palm trees so thick that Daphna couldn't see all the way to the ground. Then the forest stopped. One hundred feet down stood a small log home. The line of smoke was coming from its chimney.

"Bull's-eye!" Cynthia said.

"Hold on," Harkin called. "I'm taking this sucker down."

With some fancy maneuvering, he soon had the Thunkmobile safely on ground. Daphna was so eager to get out that she climbed over Cynthia and all but rolled out the door. Soon her friends had joined her on the fresh grass. Though they were surrounded on all sides by a raging snowstorm, the valley air was warm.

"Check out this air," Cynthia said.

Daphna breathed deep.

"Sure beats mouthfuls of bus exhaust," Harkin said.

A firm lump in the pit of Daphna's stomach grew bigger by the second. Yes, her mother's map had brought her to this strange place. And yes, there appeared to be a cabin. But how did they know the inhabitant was going to be friendly? Clearly, whoever resided there had chosen to live apart from known civilization. Would he or she appreciate sudden visitors? Probably not.

On the other hand, if a beautiful valley like this could exist on the side of a mountain that was nearly twenty thousand feet tall, who could say that her mother wasn't waiting for her inside? In fact, maybe that was why she hadn't come home? Perhaps she hadn't been able to scale the sharp cliffs, then hike through the snow to get back to civilization?

"Well." Daphna tried to keep the eager hope out of her voice. "Should we go in?"

"We've come a bit too far to turn around without saying hello," Cynthia said.

Daphna stood on the front step, facing the solid wood door.

"It's your party," Harkin told Daphna. "Go for it."

He stepped back, leaving Daphna alone with the door and a bad case of nerves. There were so many things that could go wrong and so few that could go right. Besides, what were the odds that her mother or Billy B. Brilliant actually lived there? Just as her nerve was deserting her altogether, Daphna felt Cynthia's hand on her shoulder. She drew in a deep, steadying breath. Before she could stop herself, she knocked. For a moment, she was silent, listening for the sound of approaching footsteps. But all she heard was the distant chatter of monkeys on the other side of the trees.

"How can no one be home?" Daphna said.

It seemed cruel to travel all that way and have the one human occupant of the valley be out.

"Wait a second," Harkin said. "The door's gotta be open, right? Why not walk in and get comfortable?"

Before Daphna could answer, Cynthia was staring toward the woods, mouth agape.

"What the . . . ?"

Daphna and Harkin turned and peered into the thick pines and palms. About one hundred feet away a shape of some sort was moving toward them. At first, Daphna believed it might be a herd of elephants—a frightening thought. When she looked more carefully, she didn't know whether to laugh or be even more scared. Bounding their way through the forest was a swarm of monkeys—a good forty of them.

"They eat bananas, not people, right?" Daphna asked.

"Last I heard," Harkin said.

The monkeys burst into the yard. Pounding their chests and yelping, they moved in on the children, pinning them against the front door of the house.

"Sing them part of your one-woman *Macbeth*," Harkin yelled to Cynthia. "Maybe they'll run away."

"Funny," she replied. "I was thinking you should recite your poem."

They were trying to keep it light, but Daphna could hear the fear in their voices. What did these monkeys want? To play? Or were they dangerous?

Once she and her friends were pinned against the door with no escape in sight, the largest monkey of them all clapped twice. The others cackled wildly and stomped the ground with their feet. The large monkey clapped again. To Daphna's horror, the monkeys broke into three groups, one of which rushed forward arms outstretched, and lifted her over their heads. She was thrown into the air, only to be caught a second later by another group of monkeys that immediately tossed her to a third group. Out of the corner of her eye, she saw that Harkin and Cynthia were receiving the same treatment. They were being used as giant human balls in some sort of game. As Daphna and her friends kicked, clawed, and screamed, the monkeys merely passed them around more quickly.

Until a loud *crack*—almost like a gunshot—filled the air. A voice boomed:

"Enough funny business! Give them some room!"

Daphna fell to the earth on her stomach. Looking toward the voice through a maze of monkey legs and paws, she saw a man standing by the edge of the yard. He was medium height with a long reddish beard. His eyes were so intense, she could make out their color, hazel, from a distance. Along with a dirty flannel shirt and jeans, he wore boots that laced all the way up to his thighs. Most striking was what he held in his right hand: a giant whip.

"Go!" the man called to the monkeys.

The animals hesitated, looking longingly at the kids.

"I said, 'Go!'" the man commanded.

When his whip thwacked the ground an inch from the leader, the monkeys scampered as one to the edge of the trees, leaving Daphna and her friends lying on the ground by the front door, frozen with fear. Thankfully, it seemed the man's wrath was saved for his monkeys. As soon as they were gone, his face softened.

"You'll have to excuse my friends," the man said. "We're not used to visitors around here."

Daphna looked at Harkin and Cynthia and nodded. They rose slowly to their feet, a little banged up and a bit embarrassed, but otherwise none the worse for wear.

"Sorry to drop in like this . . . ," Daphna said. Her voice trailed off. What should she say? How could she explain everything that had led them to this moment? After a full day of travel, she couldn't come up with a single coherent sentence out of the million in her head.

What happened next didn't help. The man jerked up his powerful arm. The whip went *thwack!* against a low-hanging branch, and a single coconut dropped into his hands. He cracked it open on his knee and took a giant drink. Though Daphna found the sound of the whip terrifying, it dawned on her that if the man had wanted to harm them, he probably wouldn't have stopped for a snack first. Instead of ordering the monkeys to let them alone, he could've commanded them to hoist the children into the trees. He might have done anything.

As the man took a second drink from the coconut,

she decided it was time to be brave.

"I'm Daphna," she said. "These are my friends Cynthia and Harkin. You can call him Thunk if you want."

She reached into her back pocket and pulled out the picture.

"This is my mom," she said. "And we think you might be one of the men with her."

As soon as the words were out of her mouth, Daphna felt ridiculous. She took another look at the burly, slightly overweight, messy, bearded man in front of her. How could he be one of the thin, handsome guys with her mother?

Daphna looked to her friends for support. She could tell that they were as skeptical as she was and turned back to the man to apologize. The man tossed the coconut into the woods and reached for the photo. When he looked back up, his eyes had taken on a misty glow. Daphna could have sworn that he was choked up.

"Heather Whispers is your mother?" he said.

"Yes. She is."

He took a step closer. "How is she?"

Over the past two months, Daphna had been struck by how quickly her mood could shift. In a matter of seconds, the thrill of the man knowing her mother was replaced by the sadness of her disappearance.

"What's wrong?" the man asked. "She's not well?"

Daphna spilled the entire story, starting with her mother's crash and going through the appearance of the antelope man to the discovery of the map. By the time she finished, she was trying her best to choke back sobs but losing the battle. The man stepped closer, as if unsure whether to comfort her or not. Daphna looked at the ground, realizing that she had bared her soul to a complete stranger. It was humiliating. She swallowed back her tears.

"She's not here, is she?" Her voice trailed off.

The man shook his head. "I'm afraid not."

Daphna's chest tightened. Just because she had been expecting the news didn't make it any easier to hear. She felt Cynthia's arm on her shoulder. Daphna took a moment to control her emotions.

"And the picture? Neither of these guys is you, are they?"

Daphna fully expected the answer to be another letdown in a string of disappointments. Instead, the man smiled, revealing a full set of surprisingly small but white teeth. "In younger, thinner, less hairy days, yes. That's me, sitting next to your mom."

"You're Billy B. Brilliant?" Harkin asked.

At the mention of the name, the man's eyes registered the slightest trace of surprise. Then he pulled at his right sideburn and smiled again, this

128

time as if he was bemused by an old memory. "Billy B. Brilliant!" he whispered. He shook his head in astonishment. "Nobody's called me that for years!" When he met Daphna's eyes again, he was smiling. "Forgive me, but I've been rude. You've had quite a trip. Come in! Come in!"

14

Laptops in the Lab

"My real name is Marcus Bean," the man said, moving toward the cabin. "But you can call me Billy, if you'd like. Billy B. Brilliant was a silly name your mother came up with for me one night in college. I called her Cassandra P. McFuzz, just like it says on the picture." Billy laughed—a warm, mellow chuckle—and pushed open the front door. "Sorry I haven't had time to straighten up. As I said, I don't get many visitors. And don't worry about my monkeys. I have a strict 'no chimp' policy inside."

Billy disappeared inside his house, leaving the door wide-open. Daphna expected the inside to resemble the outside, a charmingly old-fashioned cabin, where a fireplace was used for heat and to cook. In short, the perfect home for a messy guy with a beard and a whip. When Daphna stepped into the foyer, she couldn't believe her eyes. Before her was an enormous room. There was a quaint fireplace off in the corner, but the rest of the space resembled a modern laboratory. The room was filled with rows of computers—hundreds of them, laptops and desktops of all shapes and sizes and colors—blinking, whizzing, and whirring. Four giant monitors hung down from the ceiling in the center of the room. Wires, bolts, duct tape, discarded keyboards, and computer chips littered the floor. While the outside belonged to a quaint past, the inside belonged squarely to the future.

"Door!" Billy growled. "Shut, if you please!"

The door moved by itself and closed with a gentle click.

"Lights!" he barked.

Though Daphna didn't see any bulbs, the room grew instantly brighter.

"Whip!" he commanded.

A hook descended from the ceiling, grabbed his whip, and placed it in a sheath on the wall.

"Unreal," Daphna said. Any remaining embarrassment for the way she had bared her soul outside vanished in the wake of the new wonders around her.

"Not bad," Harkin said.

"I'll say," Cynthia said. "You could make a killing doing special effects for Broadway shows."

"Could be," Billy said with a nod. "Now who's hungry? You all look half starved!" He wheeled around to face the far side of the room, where a giant computer monitor was now hissing out a plume of pink smoke. "Harrison! Lunch all around!"

A panel in the wall slid open, and a man in dress pants, white shirt, and bow tie walked gracefully into the room.

"Very good, sir," Harrison said to Billy. "What would you like?"

"Oh, just whip us up something good," Billy said. "For four people."

The man bowed. "Very good. Lunch for four. Right away."

It wasn't until Harrison was walking out of the room that Daphna noticed the neat row of staples on his neck and the bolt by his ear.

"Wait a second," she began. "Is he . . . ?"

Harkin completed the thought.

"A *robot?*" he said.

"You built him?" Cynthia asked.

Billy shrugged. "Harrison is nothing. Only took me a few months to design."

A laptop computer walked into the kitchen area on a pair of stilts. With a sharp *brrring!* its top opened and hands sprang out of its sides. With another *brrring!* a side panel opened from the wall, revealing a small kitchen complete with stove, oven, and refrigerator. Quick as lightning, the laptop began to prepare lunch.

"Meet my Cook-Top computer," Billy said. Gone was the frightening man with the whip. Now that he was showing off his inventions, Billy's whole being took on a glow. He bounced from foot to foot like a little kid in a toy store. "I programmed him with every recipe known to man, from the ancient Greeks onward. He can make macaroni that tastes like mint-chip ice cream. His steak is so good, you'll think you're eating the world's most delicious peanut butter and jelly sandwich. He's the best chef in the world, and he cooks for me every night. Get a load of this!"

Billy took a remote out of his pocket and pressed a button. From a host of unseen speakers, lively music filled the room.

"What?" Harkin asked. "A new sound system?"

"Much more than that, my dear Thunk," Billy said.

He pressed another button on his remote. A corner door burst open and two laptops, also on stilts, barreled inside and ran to the center of the room. There they stopped, and arms shot out from their sides. The laptops exchanged a bow and proceeded to waltz around the room.

"Say hello to my Dance-Tops," Billy said. "The world's first computer that can help you type a document, then teach you how to rumba." He turned to the two computers, whirling around the room in perfect time to the music. "That's right," Billy called to them. "One, two, three! One, two, three! Next week I'll program you to fox-trot."

"Do they sing too?" Cynthia asked.

"Not these," Billy said. "Let me show you my Opera-Tops."

With the click of another button, two more laptops—these were larger—strutted into the room. At the count of three, their monitors began to blink and they launched into a stirring duet from *La Traviata*.

"Beautiful, no?" Billy asked. "But that's not all."

It seemed that Billy had invented computers that could do anything. There was the Verse-Top, a computer programmed to turn any thought into an epic work of poetry worthy of Shakespeare or Keats. There was the Roller-Top, a laptop computer that could execute perfect triple-axel spins on roller skates. The list went on and on.

"Here's my Doc-Top," Billy said. "It'll give you a complete physical, take out your tonsils, then serve you your favorite flavor ice cream."

In the corner was an ordinary-looking laptop computer with a small balloon attached to the top.

"What's that?" Daphna asked.

"Balloon-Top," Billy said. "The world's first laptop that converts into a giant hot-air balloon. Actually, the first time we tried it, the whole thing caught on fire and exploded. This is the second model."

"Have you tested it yet?" Harkin asked.

"Haven't had time. But I'll get it up and running soon. Now look at Picasso-Top! This computer can paint you a masterpiece worthy of hanging at the Metropolitan Museum every time."

As Billy reached to power up Picasso-Top, Harrison announced that the Cook-Top had finished preparing their meal. Lunch was served.

What a meal: salads, pastas, cheeses, sandwiches, and five kinds of cake for dessert. When they were done, Daphna and her friends were too stuffed to do anything but lean back in their chairs and bask in the glow of a truly extraordinary day. Only after her third dessert (a piece of seven-layer cake), did Daphna remember all the reasons she had made the journey. She pulled the picture back out of her pocket.

"See the other guy in this picture, Billy? Do you remember who he is?"

At that moment, Billy was admiring Harkin's wristwatch computer.

"No fooling?" Billy was saying to Harkin. "It's really capable of intercepting information from weather satellites?"

Harkin nodded. "And see this screen? A few nights ago I hacked into the Hubble Telescope. Look!"

Harkin pressed a button, and a small screen appeared on the wristwatch with a stunning picture of a distant star system. As Billy admired it, Daphna cleared her throat and held up the picture to Billy.

"Does this ring a bell?"

Billy remained focused on Harkin's wristwatch.

"That looks like a black hole, doesn't it?"

"I think so," Harkin said. "A big one."

Daphna looked at Cynthia, who stood to her full height and let fly with a piercing high C. Billy gasped, then tugged nervously on his beard.

"Boy, oh boy," he said to Cynthia. "You have some pair of lungs."

Cynthia shrugged. "It's a gift."

"Sorry to interrupt," Daphna said. "But I need to know." She held out the picture and pointed at the man behind her mother. "Do you know this man?"

"Let's see here," Billy said, gathering himself. He held the picture up to his face and took a quick look. "Him?" He tossed the photo gently to the table. "That's Old Iggy."

"Old *who*?" Harkin asked.

"Iggy Blatt," Billy said. "Ignatious Peabody Blatt is his full name."

Daphna took back the picture. There was no dyed goatee or sideburns. His eyetooth was not yet colored silver. But the resemblance was still striking. The man in the back was a younger, more relaxed version of the famous Blatt.

"My gosh," Daphna said. "You and my mom went to college with Ignatious?"

Billy popped a piece of cheese in his mouth. "Sure. We were good friends once upon a time. Old Iggy. Always making himself crazy trying to invent new, wacky things. Why? Do you know him?"

It was an astounding question. Had Billy B. Brilliant *really* lived in this valley so long that he didn't know of the great Ignatious Peabody Blatt?

"Know him?" Daphna said. "He's the head of our school!"

"He's world famous!" Cynthia said.

"He's invented Peabody-Pitch," Harkin said.

"The Hat-Top!"

"And Blatt-Global!"

"Wait a second," Billy said, standing up. He paused, as if trying to work out the idea in his head. "Iggy Blatt is *famous*?"

Daphna nodded. "For about ten years." She wrinkled her brow. "Don't you keep in contact at all with the outside world?"

Billy shook his head. "The mountain is so high, and the weather up above is so terrible, that internet or TV signals are difficult to pick up. I only hike out once or twice a year for supplies, and I never go to big cities. I'm pretty out-of-date—which is how I like it."

"So you *really* know nothing about Ignatious Peabody Blatt?" Cynthia asked.

"Right," Billy said. "Nothing. But something you said caught my ear. What's this Peabody-Pitch you mentioned?"

"It's this cool device that reads your mind and changes the music on your iPod as you think it," Harkin said.

Billy nodded. "And this Hat-Top? Tell me about that."

"It's a laptop computer that attaches to a hat," Cynthia said. "The screen slides down in front of your face."

"So you can be online while you walk down the street," Daphna said.

"And you operate the mouse with your tongue," Harkin said.

Billy chuckled softly to himself.

"What's so funny?" Daphna asked.

"That old devil," Billy said.

"What?" Cynthia asked. "You know about these things?"

"Sure I do," Billy said. He pounded the table with his fist. "I invented them."

Daphna was stunned. Was it possible? Yes, Ignatious was a flamboyant man who hadn't come out with a new product in four years. But no one the world over denied his genius.

"Wait a second," Harkin said. "You mean you invented the Hat-Top computer?"

"Back in college," Billy said. "Freshman year. It was all in my notebooks."

"And Peabody-Pitch?" Cynthia said.

Billy nodded. "Yep. Along with a global computer for looking into anyone's room."

"That's Blatt-Global!" Daphna said. "So you're saying he stole them *all* from you?"

"Guess so," Billy said.

"But how?" Cynthia asked.

"I imagine it was easy," Billy said. He sat back down and began peeling an orange. "I dropped out of college senior year. I didn't want to face the ordinary job market where some big computer company would take my best ideas and use them just to make money. I wanted to be by myself and create. I also wanted to start from scratch. So I left my notebooks and all my sketches behind. I guess old Iggy found them."

Billy seemed to find the whole thing amusing. By now he was leaning back in his chair, chuckling. But Daphna didn't know what to think or believe. If what Billy said was true, then Ignatious was a complete fraud. But how was that possible? Ignatious Peabody Blatt *was* the premier number-one computer genius in the world.

"If what you say is true," Daphna said, "how can you let someone else take credit for your ideas?"

"Right," Harkin said. "If you're telling the truth, you've got to come back to New York with us. Then we break the news to the press."

Billy waved a hand and popped an orange slice into his mouth.

"You're nice to worry about me, but really, let Iggy keep the credit. Doesn't bother me a bit."

"How can that not bother you?" Cynthia asked.

Billy shrugged. "I've never cared much for public attention or money. I just want to do what I do for my own enjoyment. That's why I searched for a place where I could create in peace. Took me a full year to find it too. I hiked, then I biked, then I hiked some more, and I haven't regretted a single minute." He shook his head. "Iggy was always such a funny kid. Always wanting to be great. To be noticed. A waste of time, if you ask me. Life's too short."

Daphna was stunned. She had never met anyone remotely like Billy B. Brilliant—a man who claimed not to care that a former classmate of his was making a fortune off his ideas. Could such a man really exist? Or was Billy B. Brilliant the one who was lying? Maybe he had his own reasons for discrediting Ignatious? Maybe that's why he dropped out of college and disappeared?

If Billy was telling the truth—if he really had invented all of Ignatious's products—maybe he could solve the clue left by the antelope man?

"This might sound weird." She faced Billy. "Do you know anything about a Flex-Bed?"

If Daphna hoped that Billy would jump up and explain everything, she was soon disappointed.

"A Flex-Bed?" Billy said. "Never heard of it."

He yawned so widely that with his shaggy beard he resembled a roaring lion.

"Excuse me," he said. "I don't know about you, but a big meal always makes me sleepy. I'm good to snooze here, but Harrison'll show you to rooms where you can catch some shut-eye too. We'll meet back here in an hour or so, and I'll show you around the valley."

Daphna didn't know what to think. Who really was the great genius? Ignatious or Billy? Or both? But questions would have to wait.

Their large host closed his eyes. In seconds, he was quietly snoring.

15

Conversation by the Pond

Though it remained hard to accept that Ignatious Peabody Blatt had stolen his product ideas from Billy, the more time Daphna spent with Billy, the more convinced she became that he was telling the truth.

The evidence spoke for itself. Why hadn't anyone—not even once—ever been invited into Ignatious's labs? Why hadn't anyone ever—again, *not even once*—seen him create anything?

Then there was Billy. His brilliance was on full

display. There was Harrison the robot, Cook-Top, Opera-Top, Picasso-Top, and hundreds of other inventions. With talent to burn, Billy B. Brilliant could probably have created Blatt-Global and the Hat-Top computer in his sleep. On top of it all, with every passing hour, Daphna came to see that Billy had truly meant what he said after lunch. Billy didn't care if Ignatious Peabody Blatt used his ideas to get rich. To his way of thinking, he was the winner, living life on his own terms, spending his days immersed in his own projects, free from the stresses of the modern world. Indeed, Billy was a man who could spend an entire day—perhaps even a week—trying to figure out how to make his Opera-Top sing a high C with more feeling and not feel as though he had wasted a second. "Never underestimate the power of great art," he told Daphna. "It's the beauty of creating that makes the work worthwhile."

Daphna knew that her time with Billy would have to be brief. Along with Monday's competition for the Insanity Cup, there was the matter of explaining her whereabouts to Ron and Jazmine. Fortunately, Harkin, by carefully manipulating his wristwatch computer, had been able to get online for a few moments before dinner to send reassuring messages home.

With time in the valley limited, Daphna, Harkin,

and Cynthia were determined to make good use of every second. That first night, Harkin studied with Billy in his workshop until long past midnight. The following morning, Cynthia rose early, rode on elephant-back to a small grove of coconut trees, and got to work rehearsing her one-woman *Macbeth*. Daphna discovered a small pond used as a watering hole by zebras and gazelles. There, she opened her book of special music manuscript paper and let the sounds of her symphony fill her head. Totally alone with her thoughts, she sketched out the bare bones of the entire first movement in less than two hours.

The minute she finished, as if to mark the event, Billy stepped out of the underbrush. He wore a pair of purple baggy shorts, a yellow shirt, and black boots. His thick red beard appeared to be freshly washed and combed. A lone monkey was perched on his shoulder, crouched there like a cat.

"Hope I'm not disturbing you," he said.

Daphna shook her head. "No, no. I'm good."

Billy nodded and sat down on an adjacent rock. "What're you working on?"

Daphna's cheeks flushed. "My first symphony."

"Very impressive," he said. "When can I hear some of your music?"

Daphna paused. In truth, she knew the perfect time.

"There's an assembly back in New York tomorrow. I'm sure I could get you in."

Billy looked over the pond and sighed. "Wouldn't that be nice?"

Daphna was tempted to ask him to come, but she held her tongue. She knew what the answer would be. Billy would never leave his paradise in the African mountain.

In any case, there was another subject Daphna was eager to get to. Since the moment she had arrived in Billy's valley, questions about her mother had run through her mind incessantly. What was she like in college? Were she and Billy good friends? Were they good friends with Ignatious? Now that Daphna had private time with Billy, she couldn't get the words right.

"You look like a girl with something on her mind," Billy said.

Daphna gazed across the pond. On the other side, a baby zebra was reaching down for a drink next to its mother. Daphna took it as a sign. If she wanted more info, it was now or never.

"Tell me about my mom."

Billy nodded as if he had been waiting for the question since her arrival. "What kinds of things do you want to hear?"

"Anything," Daphna said. "You decide."

Two other little zebras had joined the mom across the pond. One slipped forward and got its nose wet. As it righted itself back on the shore, Billy turned to Daphna.

"How's this?" Billy said. "Did you know that she would do all her homework in light green pen?"

Daphna smiled, remembering the names on the mysterious picture, as well as the hidden map, all drawn in light green. "She wrote all our grocery lists like that too."

"I'm not surprised," Billy said. "I suppose that you know about her bracelets."

Another nod. "She had a different colored one for each day of the week."

Billy laughed. "Heather didn't change as she got older, did she? Right, a different color so she always knew what day it was. That's the kind of mind she had, very organized."

"What else?" Daphna said.

"Seems that you know everything I've got to say."

"No," Daphna said. "Keep going."

Billy stood and stretched. The monkey on his shoulder hopped to the ground. "Well, let's see. . . . She once wrote a paper for an environmental studies class on the prospects of using old bicycle seats and handlebars as an alternative fuel."

That was the mom Daphna knew. She remembered

the day her mom had come home and announced that she was reconstructing a World War I B-2 biplane. She had once lobbied Ron to put a giant windmill on the roof to supply the building with electricity.

"Did it work?" Daphna asked.

Billy shook his head. "Afraid not. I believe that the teacher pointed out that bike seats best preserve energy by staying on the bikes they came with so that people can ride them." Billy laughed. "That might have been the only bad grade your mom ever got."

"What else?" Daphna said.

Billy scratched his beard. "There was the time she used herself as a subject in a nutrition class by living only on chicken for a full week."

"For a full week?"

"Just the dark meat."

Daphna nodded. That made sense. She and her mom always fought over the legs and thighs.

"And oh, oh!" Billy said. He wagged his head, remembering. "Here's something you may not know. Your mother played the saxophone."

That news had Daphna up on her feet. Her mother had never mentioned that she played an instrument—not even once.

"The sax? No!"

"She took it up our sophomore year. I was in a jazz band, and your mom thought it'd be fun to join. So she took up the sax. Got pretty good, too, in a short time."

"Did she ever play in public?"

Billy nodded. "Once." He looked at Daphna. "It was quite something."

"Tell me."

He sat back down on a nearby log. "It was the tail end of finals, junior year. Everyone was burned out. The College for the Extraordinarily Talented was a tough place. There was a local coffee bar where we all hung out. That week no one was smiling. Everyone's mind was on their work. Your mom decided enough was enough. She went to the coffee bar and took out her sax and started to improvise the most amazing tune. She wasn't a great player—she hadn't been playing long enough—but she sounded good and had an innate feel for music. At first, people seemed annoyed. But before long, everyone was mesmerized. And then the strangest thing happened."

Daphna had a funny feeling that she knew what was coming next.

"Everyone went into a trance?"

Billy looked at Daphna, eyes wide. "You've heard the story?"

Daphna shook her head. "No, but tell me."

"There's not much to tell. As you said, everyone went into this brief but deep trance. When your mother stopped playing . . ." Billy paused. "It was strange. Everyone came back to their senses feeling wonderful—like they hadn't a care in the world."

What news! The glimmer of Daphna's musical gift had clearly come from her mom.

"Your mother wasn't a talented, trained musician like you, but she had feeling. Her music snapped everyone out of the funk." He paused. "She was quite a woman."

Daphna blinked. A tear rolled down the top of Billy's cheek. His monkey wiped it away with a deft flick of its paw just before it soaked into his beard.

Daphna's next question surprised even her. It hadn't been on her mind at that moment, but something about the obvious fondness Billy felt for her mother made it simply pop out of her mouth.

"Billy, are you my father?"

The shaggy man seemed stunned, then embarrassed. He looked at Daphna with great affection. For a split second, she thought the answer was going to be yes. It made a certain kind of sense, after all. Daphna had to have gotten her coloring from someone. While Daphna's mother was a blonde with brown eyes, she and Billy both had auburn hair and hazel eyes. Why shouldn't Billy take her in his arms and say, "As a matter of fact, I am your dad"?

Instead he shook his head a little bit sadly.

"Your father?" he said. "I'm afraid I'm not that lucky."

"Yeah," she said, trying not to let the hurt show. "Oh, well."

Daphna closed her manuscript. She and Billy exchanged an awkward glance. There was more she wanted to know—about her mother and Ignatious, too—but those questions would have to wait for another time. The news that Billy wasn't her father had made her lose her taste for more conversation.

"I guess we should walk back to the house?" Billy asked.

Daphna nodded. "Yeah."

There was a rustling in the undergrowth. Harrison and Cook-Top burst into the clearing. Daphna immediately sensed something was wrong—something serious. Harrison looked worried, and Cook-Top was waving a giant spatula.

"What is it?" Billy asked.

"Sorry to interrupt you, sir," the robot said. "But two scout monkeys detected a group of intruders."

Billy's eyes narrowed. "Intruders?"

"Yes, sir. Now preparing to parachute into the valley."

Daphna shuddered. She had thought that she had gotten away too easily.

"The antelope men," she said.

Billy nodded gravely, then turned to Harrison.

"Summon the troops," he called.

The robot bowed. "Very good, sir," and disappeared with Cook-Top back through the underbrush with the monkey hot on their heels.

"Grab your music," Billy told Daphna. "It looks like we're in for a fight."

16

Calling All Tops!

y the time Daphna and Billy reached the cabin, Harkin and Cynthia were waiting on the front steps.

"It's the antelope men, all right," Harkin said. "We saw them on Billy's video monitors, gathering on the outer edge of the valley."

"How'd they find us?" Billy asked.

Harkin shook his head in disgust. "Had to be my fault," he said. "I let them get too close when they were chasing us on their motorcycles. That's probably when they slapped a tracking device on the side of the Thunkmobile."

He opened his hand. In the middle of his palm was a tiny magnet.

"That's it?" Daphna asked.

Harkin nodded. "I just found it on the left back door."

"Don't be so hard on yourself," Cynthia said. "There were five of them, and they were really fast."

Billy rubbed an open palm through Harkin's thick hair. "Cynthia's right, Thunk. Let it go."

Cynthia looked up. In the distance a troop of antelope men lined the edge of the upper cliff, about to descend into the valley. "We know how they got here, but how are we going to fight them off?"

The door to Billy's cabin swung open. Harrison stepped out and handed Billy his whip.

"Your weapon, sir," the robot said, then got busy tying back Billy's shaggy hair with a blue bandanna.

Billy's monkeys fanned out and formed a semi-circle on the outer perimeter of the yard. Whip in hand, Billy winked at Daphna, then turned to the door and roared as loudly as he could. "Tops! Battle stations!"

After a full day in the valley, Daphna had thought she had seen it all. But what happened next made her see that Billy was even *more* brilliant than she had imagined. Nine laptop computers, all on legs, marched triumphantly in the yard and stood at attention in a sharp line.

"Meet my special defense Tops," Billy said. He strutted up and down the line like a proud general. "Okay, Tops, sound off!"

One by one, each specially designed laptop stepped forward and called out its name in a mechanized but clear voice.

"Javelin-Top! Here!"

"Itch-Top! Present!"

"Octopus-Top! Here! All eight legs!"

"Tickle-Top! Accounted for!"

"Joke-Top! Ha-ha here!"

"Flood-Top! Full!"

"Soap-Top! Slippery and ready for action!"

"Pterodactyl-Top! Wings in working order!"

"Frog-Top! *Ribbit!*"

Stunned, Daphna looked at Harkin and Cynthia. It wasn't hard to imagine the feats each of the computers had been programmed to perform.

"Good work, Tops," Billy said. "Now power up!"

One of the larger of Billy's monkeys moved down the line of laptops, typing a rapid-fire series of commands on each of their keyboards. Within moments, all nine computers were whirring and humming and beginning to exhibit their unique characteristics. Tickle-Top and Joke-Top doubled over with laughter. A burst of bubbles flew out of Soap-Top's screen. Octopus-Top sprang six arms to go with his two legs while Pterodactyl-Top sprouted ten-foot-long wings and took to the sky to check on the invaders' progress. Then Javelin-Top's arms swelled, Itch-Top began to scratch its monitor, and Flood-Top started leaking. Finally, Frog-Top bounded around the yard on a giant set of frog legs, its tongue flicking out of its screen.

"Dig the lap-dudes," Harkin said.

There was one more Top that wanted in on the action. As Billy looked around the yard, inspecting his troops, Cook-Top burst out of the cabin, squeaking wildly, waving a spatula in one hand and a bread knife in the other.

"No, no, no," Billy said. "Your place is in the kitchen."

Cook-Top hissed and released a plume of stale black smoke, then shot a burned piece of toast Billy's way.

"I said no!" Billy said, swatting aside the toast. "Do you know how many hours it took to make you? You're too valuable at home."

With a string of loud squeaks and grunts, the computer hurled the knife into a nearby tree, turned on its heel, and stormed back into the house.

"He's always been temperamental," Billy said with a sigh, then turned to Harrison. "What's the latest report?"

The robot stepped forward. "The intruders are on the edge of the cliff, sir, about to parachute in."

"Thank you, Harrison," Billy said. He looked at the children. "Don't worry. My monkeys and Tops will protect us just fine."

Daphna knew what was coming next. Harkin stepped forward, chest out, fists clenched.

"If you think we're going to sit this out, you're out of your mind."

Billy took his own step forward, casting a giant shadow over the boy. Harkin came up only to his belly button.

"No fancy ideas, Thunk. In my valley, I'm your legal guardian. I say you stay safe!"

Billy snapped his whip hard against a tree branch. A sea of coconuts rained down onto the yard. One hit Harkin on the shoulder and split open at his feet.

Billy smiled. "This battle'll be over by the time you finish your coconut milk."

Harkin kicked the broken coconut across the yard. Daphna understood his frustration. She wanted to join the fight as well. But she also had another even more pressing concern. Why in the world were the antelope men so insistent? Why did they keep coming after her? What in the world did they want? A *Flex-Bed*?

Pterodactyl-Top flew back into the yard and settled in front of Billy, lightly flapping its long brown wings.

"Intruders landing in main field!" the flying laptop announced. "Thirty of them."

Craning his neck, Harkin shook his long blond hair out of his ponytail holder and let loose with what could only be termed a thunderous battle cry. He then leaped onto Pterodactyl-Top's back, shrieking, "Fly, laptop! Fly!" With a loud squawk, the computer bird rose into the air and soared up and over the tall trees that surrounded Billy's cabin, headed toward the battlefield.

"Wait!" Billy called.

Not to be outdone, Cynthia sang out with one of her vintage, ear-piercing high Cs. As Billy, Daphna, the monkeys—even Harrison—held their ears, a giant elephant lumbered into the yard, lifted Cynthia onto its back with its trunk, and rumbled back through the woods.

What could Billy do but give in?

"Okay," he said to Daphna. "Stick close to me." He then turned to Cook-Top, who had meandered back outside. "You come too—and bring your spatula."

Cook-Top bounced up and down, squeaking wildly.

Daphna felt herself being lifted into the air by five monkeys. Suddenly she was moving very quickly through the woods. Billy was at her side, also traveling on monkey-back, while Cook-Top brought up the rear. Branches hit Daphna hard in the face. It was difficult to believe that a few days ago she had been a mild-mannered student, finishing her first rhapsody. Now she was halfway around the world, charging into an epic battle.

The brave warriors burst out the other side into wide-open grassland. Looking up, Daphna saw thirty men floating downward, antelope masked and dressed in black, each with a spear strapped to his back. Moments later, the men touched down.

"On my command!" Billy called.

Obeying orders, the children and the Tops stayed still while the lead antelope—the largest of the crew, a giant man who stood a good six and a half feet— stepped forward.

Frightened, Daphna looked to Billy. If he was worried, he didn't show it. The large man stood still, taking in the antelopes, almost as if they were interesting specimens to be studied rather than fierce warriors to be fought and defeated.

"Hey, Billy?" Harkin called from the back of

Pterodactyl-Top. "Are we going to fight or what?"

Billy shot Harkin a sharp glance, then let loose a thundering call to arms:

"Flood-Top!" he cried. "Fire when ready!"

17

It's All in the Name

Daphna would remember the battle as a mix of scrambled images. Antelope men. Monkeys. The Tops. Her friends. And orchestrating the forces, flicking his powerful whip, was Billy.

The antelope men fought hard—they hadn't tracked the Thunkmobile all the way from New York to give up without a fight—but in the end, they were no match for Billy and his bizarre array of defenders.

It began with Flood-Top. Upon hearing its name, the laptop took four quick steps forward, then stopped with a bright *brrring*. Its monitor grew to four times its original size. With a loud *pfft!* a giant spigot appeared in its middle, then *whoosh!* Water shot out of Flood-Top with the force of ten mighty fire hydrants, knocking the leader and the other antelopes off their feet and soaking them to their skins.

And that was just the beginning.

"Soap-Top!" Billy called.

A second laptop stepped forward and sprayed a stream of bubbly soap over the wet field. As the soggy antelope men stood up, they slipped back down, struggling to keep their footing. Only then did Billy shout the final command: "Charge!"

The battle soon turned into a rout. Javelin-Top picked off the wet, soapy antelopes with homemade spears while Itch-Top sent up plumes of powder that had the antelope men scratching wildly and running for the pond. Others found themselves tangled in the arms and legs of Octopus-Top or brought to tears of laughter at the hands of Joke-Top and Tickle-Top.

Cook-Top proved its mettle on the battlefield as well. Zigzagging among the fighters, it used its giant spatula to swat antelope men to the ground before flipping them into the air like pancakes.

Harkin and Pterodactyl-Top had a field day, swooping out of the sky and lifting surprised antelope men high into the air before depositing them in the trees or pond. Meanwhile, Cynthia tromped around the field on elephantback, commanding her mount to use its trunk to knock over the intruders as they struggled to make their way toward Billy's home.

Daphna might have had the most fun of all. Seconds into the battle, she found herself on Frog-Top, hopping wildly around the battlefield, directing the laptop's tongue to lick antelope men to the ground until they begged for mercy.

The fight was over in less than ten minutes. The monkeys led the captured antelope men to a field on the far side of the valley, where a squadron of elephants and giraffes stood guard. Only one intruder was left, one of the smaller antelope men, being used by two gangs of monkeys for a game of catch.

Billy decided it was time to get some answers.

"Enough!" he shouted. "Bring him here!"

The monkeys deposited their "ball" by Billy's feet. Daphna, Harkin, and Cynthia jumped off their respective mounts and gathered close as one of the monkeys reached for the antelope mask. Daphna averted her eyes, half expecting the man to look like an actual antelope or worse. When the monkey peeled the mask back, Daphna was surprised to find that, with short brown hair and pale eyes, this particular antelope was almost shockingly ordinary. And young—the type of guy who would have looked more in place on a college campus than on a battlefield in the African mountains.

Billy wasn't swayed by the antelope's good looks. The minute the mask was off, he held his whip high.

"What are you looking for? Tell me, or the monkeys will use you for a game of baseball—all nine innings!"

Crack! The whip hit the ground a foot from the man's face, sending up a flurry of dirt. The demasked antelope let out a sound that was somewhere between a squeak and a moan. From the way he was trembling, Daphna sensed that he was too frightened to speak.

Leaning close, Harkin let his long hair flop in the man's face.

"Start yapping, antelope, dude," he snapped. "Or you see that laptop over there? That's Tickle-Top! It'll have you laughing so hard, you might never speak again!"

Even Cynthia stepped up. "Or maybe you'd prefer Frog-Top? It can lick you like you were a fly."

"Wait." The word was out of Daphna's mouth before she could stop it. All eyes were on her. "Give him a break, okay?"

Harkin wrinkled his brow. "What?"

"Look at him," Daphna said. "He's scared."

Billy nodded. He leaned close to the man and

spoke more softly. "Okay, sir. Tell us then. Who sent you?"

Under the more gentle questioning, the man was finally able to find his voice.

"Wallace," he whispered.

"Wallace?" Daphna asked. "Who's that?"

A funny look passed over Billy's face.

"Do you know who it is?" she asked.

"Maybe," Billy said. He looked at the prisoner. "Did Wallace give a full name?"

The young man nodded. "Wallace Zoo-Zoo McFerd."

Billy's response was instantaneous. The moment he heard the name, he broke into a broad grin that exploded into a wild, gut-clenching, no-holds-barred guffaw. His belly shook. Tears dripped into his thick beard.

"What's going on?" Harkin asked.

"Yeah," Daphna said. "Who's Wallace?"

Billy dropped his whip and doubled over, gasping for breath. Harrison exchanged a worried glance with Cook-Top, then wiped Billy's brow with a handkerchief.

"Oh, that Iggy!" Billy said.

"Ignatious!" Daphna said.

Billy nodded and held up a finger, signaling that he would tell them the full tale once he had gathered his breath enough to speak. The minute he got control of his breathing, another wave of laughter tore through him. Daphna worried he would pass out. A monkey jumped on his shoulder and slapped his back, and Billy caught his breath again—this time, when the laughter welled up inside, he managed to push it back down. Finally, he turned to Daphna.

"Remember what I told you about the silly names your mother and I used in college?"

"Wait a second," Daphna said. She remembered the smudged name—*W. Zoo Ferd*—on the back of the picture that had fallen from her manuscript. "Ignatious is . . . Wallace Zoo-Zoo McFerd."

"Yep!"

"You're joking," Cynthia said.

"Nope."

"Ignatious," Harkin said. "He's the one who sent the antelope men."

Billy nodded. "Old Iggy liked to take credit for things. I guess he couldn't resist sending me a little message—just to be sure I'd know who was behind all this."

Daphna found it all too much to take in. She knew Billy had been telling the truth—that Ignatious had stolen the blueprints for his most famous products from Billy's college notebook. Even so, it was hard to comprehend just how far Ignatious was willing to go to get his hands on another of Billy's creations.

"We still don't know what Ignatious is looking for," Harkin said.

Cynthia stood directly over the demasked antelope. "Out with it. What does Ignatious want?"

Daphna knelt down beside him.

"No one's going to hurt you," she said. "Does Ignatious want a Flex-Bed?"

With Daphna's more gentle approach, the man managed to sit up. "Not a Flex-Bed," he said. "An *X-Head*."

"X-Head," Harkin said. "So that's what it is."

Daphna turned to Billy.

"Does that mean anything to you?"

Billy shrugged. "The X-Head? Can't say that it . . ."

His eyes went wide, leaving the rest of the sentence unspoken. He stared across the wide open field.

"What?" Daphna asked.

"X-Head," he murmured. "I should have thought of it when you first mentioned the Flex-Bed. How stupid!"

Daphna, Harkin, and Cynthia gathered close to Billy. He rubbed a hand through his beard and smiled down at them.

"What is it?" Cynthia asked.

"Put our guest with the others," Billy called to his

head monkey. He glanced at Daphna. "And treat him gently."

Billy turned toward his home.

"Come with me," he said. "I have something to show you."

18

Everything You've Ever Wanted to Know About Everything

Daphna was bursting with questions. What was the X-Head? Why did Ignatious want it? Was it the key to his next product? Did it have anything to do with her mom? She forced herself to be patient—a difficult task—until they were back in Billy's house.

"Congratulations on your glorious victory, sir!" Harrison said as Billy held up his whip to be taken by its hook.

"Thank you, Harrison. But I didn't do much. It was all my Tops and these kids."

Daphna knew it was a lie. Sure, everyone had done their part, but Billy was the true hero.

"We're going to be in the library for a while, Harrison," Billy went on. He untied his bandanna and shook out his shaggy auburn hair. "No interruptions, please."

The robot bowed. "Very good, sir."

With a brisk nod to his three young guests, Billy walked to the back of the enormous front chamber of his cabin. There stood a light blue door—Daphna realized that in their time in the valley she hadn't seen anyone use it. With a loud creak, Billy pushed it open and led them into a musty room, dimly lit by three tiny bulbs perched side by side on the far side of the ceiling. The walls were all wood, as were the two chairs and desk in the center of the room. Against all four walls stood rows of uneven, homemade bookcases. When Daphna had heard the word *library*, she had expected that Billy would have a private chamber filled with books on a wide range of subjects. But in the dim light she saw that three of the four bookcases were empty. On the other, standing on the middle shelf, was a single book, an oversize hardcover that resembled a textbook.

"I've already told you that I left behind all my

notes at college," Billy said. "But I did take along this."

He crossed the room and pulled the lone book off the shelf.

"What is it?" Harkin asked.

Billy blew dust off the cover and looked it over affectionately. "It's Henry P. Johnson's masterwork."

"Henry P. Johnson?" Cynthia said.

Billy nodded. "My favorite professor at the College for the Extraordinarily Talented."

Billy held up the front cover. The title was written in elegant gold lettering. Daphna read it out loud:

"Everything You've Ever Wanted to Know About Everything."

"Wow," Harkin said. "Must've been one smart dude."

"Johnson was a genius, Thunk," Billy said, tapping the book. "He conducted the very first brain swap between a chimp and a lemur. He was the first to experiment with a computer chip that the user could wear up his nose. He taught me most of what I know."

Daphna wrinkled her brow, more confused than ever. "That's all really neat," she said. "But what does it have to do with the X-Head?"

Billy placed the book on the desk and turned to the page just before the back cover.

"Look here."

Daphna and her friends gathered close. In the left upper corner was a detailed sketch of an eyeball looking across the page. Facing the eyeball on the right-hand side was a drawing of some sort of oval. Three arrows pointed from the oval to the eye.

"What is it?" Cynthia asked.

"I know," Harkin said, before Billy could respond. "The oval represents a new computer chip."

"Or a satellite dish?" Cynthia asked.

"Even a hat," Harkin said. "Who knows?"

Daphna leaned closer.

"What about this writing?"

Below the drawing was row upon row of nearly microscopic handwriting. Squinting, she slowly deciphered the first lines. "'The B head of the yellow wire must be retrofitted with the R cathode, by taking the Y cathode to the X quadrant of the superstructure, in order to achieve an ideal negative absolute overflow.'"

Daphna looked to Harkin, who shrugged.

"Please," Cynthia said to Billy. "Say something!"

Billy merely nodded toward the door. "It's musty in here. Let's see if Cook-Top has come down from his battlefield heroics enough to whip us up a snack. Then we'll talk this out."

Billy, Daphna, Harkin, and Cynthia sat at the kitchen table before a plate of cookies and cups of cold juice.

Billy carefully ripped out the page with the drawing and the strange microscopic text and laid it flat in the middle of the table, directly under the light. Cynthia leaned close, studying the picture and mouthing the strange words.

"What are you doing?" Harkin asked. "Memorizing it?"

Cynthia chuckled. "Sorry. A bad acting habit. Whenever I see writing, I automatically pretend it's a line I'm going to have to say onstage."

"These lines wouldn't be very interesting," Billy said. "Just a bunch of complicated math formulas written years ago one night by a young college student."

"Tell us," Daphna said.

Billy stroked his beard. "This story starts one night in my senior year. Iggy and I were studying for exams in my dorm when I got an idea. While we were on a break, I jotted this down."

"The formula for the X-Head, you mean?" Harkin asked.

Billy laughed. "That is what Iggy called it. He only mentioned it once. Unfortunately, the words *Flex-Bed* did nothing to jog my memory."

"That's understandable," Cynthia said. "It was twelve years ago, right?"

"What's it do?" Daphna asked.

Billy leaned over the drawing. His beard was so long, it brushed over the pages like a bristly sponge. "It's quite simple." He swatted away his beard and draped it back over his shoulder. "This is an eyeball, and that's a contact lens."

Harkin blinked. "Ignatious Blatt has been chasing down a new *contact lens?*"

"Not just any contacts. These work a bit like your Gum-Top. The wearers of these lenses would be online and be able to scan websites—all through their eyes."

"Really?" Daphna said. "A computer *on your eyes?*"

Billy nodded.

"How does it work?" Cynthia asked.

"Easy." Billy had the glow Daphna had seen when she'd first arrived—the glow of a little boy proudly explaining one of his inventions. "The user thinks of the site he or she wants to visit, and voilà! It appears right before his or her eyes."

"And it works?" Harkin asked.

Billy shrugged. "I never tried it. But I don't see why not. In any case, there's more."

"What?" Daphna asked.

Billy took a long look around the table. He appeared to be deadly serious.

"Mind control," he said finally.

Daphna felt a chill. "Mind control?"

Billy nodded gravely. "If my calculations are correct, the X-Head can be calibrated so that one person can control all the users' thoughts."

"You mean like get the other users to do whatever he wants when he wants it?" Harkin asked.

"Precisely."

Daphna and her friends were quiet, taking in what they had heard. Then Cynthia took off her glasses and rose to her feet. "Well, no wonder Ignatious has been trying to get his hands on it. He wants the X-Head to be his next big product. And he wants to use it to control the mind of everyone who wears it."

"Right," Harkin said. He, too, rose to his feet and began pacing the length of the table. "And now we know why the first antelope man broke into Daphna's apartment. He worked for Ignatious and was trying to find clues about the X-Head."

"He probably thought Daphna's mom had some of Billy's old notes," Cynthia said. "Or maybe even this book."

"I bet she was searching for Billy when she disappeared," Harkin said. "What do you think, Daph, dude?"

Daphna took a bite of cookie, then washed it down with some cold juice. Everything her friends said made sense, but she needed to work some things out for herself. She looked at Billy.

"I guess my mom wanted to warn you that Ignatious was looking for the X-Head." She paused. "Maybe that's why she met with Ignatious just before she left?"

"I bet Ignatious threatened her," Harkin said.

"Asked her about the X-Head," Cynthia added.

Billy stroked his beard. "Which would explain why she decided she had to come warn me." He looked at Daphna. "I always knew your mother would be smart enough to figure out how to find me if she really wanted."

Daphna sighed. It seemed her mother had sacrificed herself for a worthy cause. Still, it was all so sad.

Billy knelt beside Daphna and put a hand on her shoulder. "Your mother was a lady who always did what she thought was right. I'd bet that she'd make the same decision today."

Daphna swallowed back her tears. "Yeah."

"The least we can do," Billy went on, "is to make sure that old Iggy never gets his hands on this." He took the drawing from the table where Cynthia was, once again, looking over the small print of the formula.

"Still memorizing?" Billy asked.

Cynthia shrugged. "Like I said: bad habit. It's all Swahili to me anyway."

Billy nodded and grabbed the paper.

"Cook-Top!" he called.

The laptop chef was still outside, now having a sword fight with Joke-Top. When Harrison was finally able to retrieve the computerized chef, Billy told it what he wanted. Cook-Top whirred. An image of a stove lit up on his monitor. Then Cook-Top took the paper and held it over the lit flame. With a quick *pfft!* it was all over.

"Wow," Cynthia said. "Pretty anticlimactic."

"Maybe," Billy said. "But now we can see if Iggy Blatt can come up with a new product all on his own."

"Not a chance," Harkin said, grinning. "The dude couldn't invent ice if he was given a pitcher of water and a tray."

Despite her glum mood, Daphna smiled. "He couldn't invent mud if he was given a pile of dirt in a rainstorm."

Billy laughed, a low chuckle that seemed to rumble out of him and invited everyone to join in. And soon they were all laughing—even Daphna, finally letting all the tensions of the past few days wash away. When they had finally laughed themselves dry, Daphna and her friends retired to their rooms to straighten up and pack.

"Hey, Harkin," Cynthia asked, "do you think you can get online? I need to send an email to my folks. Tell them that I'm coming home."

"Nice idea."

With only a few minutes of fiddling, Harkin was able to get a signal. Then he tossed his wristwatch to Cynthia.

"While you're at it, write a short note to my dad."

"And to Ron," Daphna said.

"Will do," Cynthia said.

Cynthia sent off the emails while Daphna and Harkin took a moment to relax after the day's drama. Billy put up his feet and took his afternoon nap. As for Cook-Top—it began preparing a farewell banquet.

19

Time for Good-bye

Early the next morning, Daphna, Harkin, and Cynthia stood in Billy's front yard by the Thunkmobile. All their new friends—the monkeys, Cook-Top, Harrison, the special defense Tops, and, of course, Billy—had gathered to see them off.

The previous night, Daphna had taken a brief stab at convincing Billy to come along but had quickly given it up as a lost cause. It was obvious that Billy was comfortable with the choices he had made and was happy in his chosen home.

That didn't mean he wasn't open to having visitors. As the morning sun beat brightly onto his front yard, Billy smiled.

"Come back this summer," he said. "Stay for a while." He winked at Harkin. "Maybe you and I can collaborate on something."

"It's a date," the boy said.

"And you," Billy said, turning to Cynthia. "Your elephant will be waiting."

Before the girl could reply, the animal came trotting into the yard and nuzzled Cynthia with its trunk.

"Deal," she said.

Finally, Billy turned to Daphna. The time had gone so quickly. Though she cherished their conversation by the pond, hearing Billy's stories of her mother had made her hunger to know more. There was something she wanted to tell him too—something silly. With their departure only minutes away, it was now or never.

"Remember the funny names you and my mom gave each other in college?"

"Of course I do," Billy said.

"Well, my mom had a funny name for me too."

"Why doesn't that surprise me? What was it?"

Daphna laughed, even more embarrassed than

she thought she'd be. "It's pretty stupid."

"Stupider than Billy B. Brilliant?"

"Okay, if you put it like that." Daphna laughed. "My mom used to call me Miss Sadie P. Snodgrass sometimes. Or just Snods. Isn't that crazy?"

Daphna had expected Billy to laugh—or at least *pretend* to laugh. Instead he was momentarily expressionless.

"What?" she asked. "Not funny?"

Billy snapped back to life, wagging his head and pulling at his long beard. "Oh, no. No! It's great. Sadie P. Snodgrass, huh? Very like your mom. I like it. I like it very much!"

There was an awkward silence. Daphna wondered if she had done something wrong. Then Billy leaned down and kissed her cheek, scratching her face with his thick beard.

"Good-bye, Daphna."

"Bye, Billy."

Harkin and Cynthia climbed into the flying car. As Daphna turned toward the door, she threw herself into Billy's arms. The large man held her tight, then kissed the top of her head.

"See you this summer," he said.

"Yeah. This summer."

Daphna climbed into the Thunkmobile choking back tears. Cynthia squeezed her hand. Harkin flipped a switch, and the roof closed over them. He turned on the ignition, and the car came to life with a cough, a bang, and a puff of blue smoke.

"By the way," Cynthia called out the window to Billy over the sound of thc motor, "what are you going to do with the antelope men?"

At that, Billy's gang of monkeys chattered wildly among themselves. Some of them simulated a game of catch.

Billy laughed. "We'll probably make them clear some fields and haul some rocks for a while. When I think they're ready, I'll let them go. Then again, maybe I won't."

Daphna waved out the window a final time.

"Safe travels!" Billy called.

There was still so much that Daphna wanted to say and so much she wanted to know. Before she had time for another good-bye, she was slammed back into her seat. The car screamed past the group of monkeys and the cabin. Twenty feet from the edge of the clearing, Harkin pulled hard on the green lever. The car climbed quickly, narrowly clearing the wall of trees that surrounded Billy's cabin. As Daphna and Cynthia tightened their seat belts, Harkin stepped on the accelerator. The car burst out of the quiet valley air directly into the raging snowstorm of the mountain above. It was a minute of howling wind and wild bumps. But with Harkin steady at the controls, the car climbed past the majestic peak of Kilimanjaro.

Daphna looked out the window and took a final look into Billy's valley. They had defeated the antelope men and destroyed the plans for the X-Head, but Daphna knew that this didn't mean Ignatious wouldn't try something else. There were final chapters to be played out in the story. As the Thunkmobile hurtled home, she only hoped that the ending would be happy.

20

A Rude Return

A short hour into their trip home, Daphna gave voice to something that had bothered her since the previous night. Given what they now knew about Ignatious, should she and her friends even compete for the Insanity Cup?

"We should concentrate on proving to the world that Ignatious is a crook instead of trying to win a prize," she said.

"No way," Cynthia said. "If we withdraw from the

competition, Ignatious will suspect that we know something."

"He will?"

"Absolutely," Cynthia said. "But if we stay in it, we can keep our cover and work behind the scenes to expose him."

"Makes sense to me," Harkin said.

With a plan in place, Daphna and her friends took turns napping. After a light lunch, Cynthia went into the back compartment to put the finishing touches on her one-woman *Macbeth* while Daphna tweaked the end of her rhapsody and Harkin pondered the best way to introduce Gum-Top. When the Thunkmobile finally approached New York Harbor, the sun was rising over the city, casting an orange glow on the water.

"Is it really only morning here?" Daphna asked.

"Don't forget about the time difference," Harkin said. "It's much earlier in New York than in Africa. As we've flown home, we've kept even with the rising sun. It's Monday morning."

Cynthia smiled. "The competition is in a few hours."

Daphna felt a shiver. Did her rhapsody stand a chance? Who knew? But there was no turning back now. In the distance stood the Statue of Liberty.

"That lady's a sight for sore eyes," Daphna said.

Harkin directed the flying car over the last stretch of water. In moments, they were gliding easily over the city streets, headed uptown.

"A lot different from the valley, huh?" Cynthia said.

"One thing you can say about New York," Daphna said. "It never really changes. Buildings, people, taxis, and buses."

The New York they left was the New York they returned to—at least at first glance. Rush-hour traffic filled the morning streets. Busy people, bustling to work, crowded the sidewalks. But with another look or two, Daphna noticed something strange. Though it was only eight in the morning, a long line of people wended its way out the front door of a store and halfway down the block.

"I wonder why they're open so early," Daphna said.

"Or what they're selling," Cynthia added.

Harkin shrugged. "Maybe some hot new book has been released?"

"Or a shoe store is having a big sale?" Daphna said.

"It could be a church giving out free breakfast?" Cynthia said.

Under normal circumstances, any of those ideas might have been correct. But Daphna soon learned that things were anything but normal. Two short blocks later, a similar line of people wound out of another store. And that still wasn't all. A block after that, there was another—this line ran all the way down the street.

"I think we need to take a closer look," Daphna said.

Harkin pulled a series of levers and brought the Thunkmobile closer to the ground. Down below, a fourth line of people wound out of yet another store—this line meandering down the street to a bus stop.

"They aren't waiting for the bus, are they?" Cynthia said.

"Don't think so," Daphna said. Then she saw something. Her skin went cold. "Look!"

"What?"

"The sign!" Daphna said.

By that point, it had come into sharp focus. It read: MEET GUM-TOP!

Daphna was stunned. For once in his life, Harkin was speechless, trying to comprehend what had happened.

"Gum-Top?" he sputtered. "Do you mean . . . ?"

"He stole it!" Daphna said.

If there had been any doubt about Billy's version of past events, they were swept aside now. It was official: Ignatious was a fraud.

"I know who did his dirty work," Cynthia said. "Myron!"

Harkin hit his steering wheel with his open palm. "It had to be!"

It made sense. Ignatious had put his under-achieving son to work snooping around the school, looking for the best student work to steal as his own.

"We'll turn him in," Daphna said. "Tell the press about Billy."

"But Ignatious is world famous," Harkin wailed. "And who's Billy B. Brilliant? A nobody who no one has ever heard of. Who would believe us?"

"But—" Daphna began.

"But what?" Harkin went on. "I don't even have proof that I developed Gum-Top. Don't forget, I kept it so secret, no one else even knew it existed."

For the next few moments, Daphna and her friends rode in stunned silence. Harkin glided the car over store after store, with line after line of people waiting to buy their very own packs of Gum-Top. Some of the lines weren't even stretching out of computer stores. One line was coming down the block outside a candy shop; another was outside a pet store; another wound out of a bank. Every proprietor, no matter what they sold, was getting in on the action.

What was even more unusual than the hordes of

people standing in line was their behavior when they exited the stores. Directly beneath the Thunkmobile, a young woman walked right into a lamppost. A man barely missed being run down by a grocery truck.

"They're totally out of it," Daphna said.

Fortunately, the people of New York were too focused on the websites taking form before their eyes to notice the strange car flying overhead. Harkin dropped even closer to the ground.

"It's a new era," Cynthia said.

"Generation Gum-Top," Daphna said.

If she was amazed by what was happening on the average New York street, she was flabbergasted by what had become of Times Square. As Harkin guided the Thunkmobile up Seventh Avenue, Daphna's jaw dropped. In the past two days, Ignatious had bought up every single piece of advertising space in the square. Gone were the billboards promoting movies, musicals, and plays. Gone were the signs advertising cars, computers, and shaving cream. Now every single one of them was a tribute to the glories of Gum-Top.

"I've seen actors with smaller egos," Cynthia said.

The signs were as much a testament to Ignatious himself as to the product he purported to have developed. At 42nd Street was a giant billboard that featured a photo of Ignatious holding out a piece of chewing gum. The words below read:

Up a street, a billboard showed Ignatious placing a piece of gum in his mouth with a caption saying:

YOU CAN CHEW CLEARLY NOW!

Gone was the giant billboard of Ignatious that Daphna had admired the night she had seen *The Dancing Doberman*. In its place was an even bigger billboard, an absolutely enormous picture of Ignatious's face, his mouth open wide in hysterical laughter. The text read:

IT'S FINALLY HERE!

"I can't believe that a week ago I would've been cheering that bum on," Harkin said. "Now he makes me so mad, I want to make him a special pair of rocket-engine sneakers and blast him to the Andromeda galaxy." He turned to the window and screamed down, *"I made the Gum-Top! It's my idea! Mine!"*

"Watch it!" Daphna cried.

Harkin was so furious, he had come inches from crashing his car into yet another billboard of the not-so-great Blatt.

"Let's get over to school," Cynthia said. "Maybe there's a way to expose Ignatious yet. Like they say about opera, it ain't over until the fat lady sings."

Harkin pulled on the green lever. The little car gained altitude for the short trip uptown. Straight ahead was a blimp. On one side was a giant picture of Ignatious's face. On the other it read in gold lettering:

GUM-TOP!

Harkin shook his head. "The next day or two is going to be really tough around here."

21

Showdown Outside the School

Three blocks down the street from school, Daphna could see that life at her beloved school had been drastically changed. The police had set up a barricade to control the enormous crowd that had swarmed to the old Brackerton grounds. Reporters strolled the sidewalk peppering passersby with questions, hoping all the while for the grand prize: a shot at an interview with Ignatious himself.

"All this for a lousy crook," Harkin muttered.

He slammed on the brakes by a narrow parking spot between two SUVs. Once Daphna and Cynthia were out, Harkin flipped a switch on his wristwatch computer. The car collapsed and with its telltale *scrinch!* rolled into the space. As the three friends headed the final blocks toward the main school gate, Daphna saw that the mob was even bigger than she had first thought. Along with the police and the press, vendors had set up carts, selling anything they could.

"Get your Gum-Top dental floss!" one man called. "Cleaner teeth mean clearer websites!"

"Special sunglasses here!" another yelled. "See your Gum-Top websites in three D!"

"I'll paint your eyetooth silver, then dye your sideburns red!" an enterprising artist cried, waving a paintbrush. "Look like the Great Blatt in fifteen seconds!"

A few steps closer to the school, a man was selling life-size posters of Ignatious along with a limited supply of Ignatious masks. A woman was offering to tutor nursery school students for the yearly Blatt admissions tests.

"You think your child is only extremely gifted?" a sign outside her booth read. "In three sessions Joanna C. Jasper will turn *extremely* into *insanely*!"

"What a scene," Harkin said.

"People'll think of anything," Cynthia said.

"Look on the bright side," Daphna said. "All these people might make it easier for us to sneak in unnoticed."

A sensible enough thought, but Daphna had forgotten a critical fact. Yes, Ignatious was famous, but in her own smaller way so was Cynthia. Her disappearance from *The Dancing Doberman* had been well reported on theater websites and papers. All it took was one reporter to recognize her for the floodgates to open.

"There she is! Cynthia Trustwell!"

A wave of information-starved reporters sprinted toward the children.

"Remind anyone of Billy's monkeys?" Cynthia asked.

"Tell me, Cynthia," a reporter cried, "are you back to do *The Dancing Doberman*?"

Cynthia adjusted her glasses. "Absolutely. I'll go on tomorrow night."

"Was your disappearance linked to Gum-Top?" another asked.

"Not at all. We were at a conference in Madrid."

One reporter nodded toward Harkin.

"What about your tiny friend? Isn't that Barkin Ruckenheiser, inventor of the exploding sneakers?"

"The name is Harkin Thunkenreiser!" the boy

thundered. "And while I may seem short to you, I am in the low-to-normal height range for my age group."

"All right! All right!" the reporter said, scribbling notes. "Not born too short."

"Furthermore, my sneakers don't explode. They fly!"

"Got it," another reporter said. "It's your car that explodes, am I right?"

That was all Harkin could stand. He puffed out his chest and stood to his full height. "The Thunkmobile does not explode. In fact, we just flew it all the way back from Africa!"

"You heard it here, folks!" a reporter shouted into his mic. "The kids flew in from Africa to try out Ignatious Blatt's Gum-Top!"

At the mention of his beloved Gum-Top, Harkin's face turned bright red. His upper lip twitched.

"*Ignatious's* Gum-Top?" the boy shouted.

"Careful," Daphna whispered. "Remember—we need proof before we say anything."

"Not now," Cynthia said.

But it was a lost cause.

"Ignatious Peabody Blatt is a fraud!" Harkin exploded. "A *fraud*! He didn't develop *any* of his ideas! Not Blatt-Global! Not Peabody-Pitch! Not the Hat-Top computer!"

The ridicule was everything Daphna had feared.

Just like that, she found herself staring into a sea of befuddled faces. Then came the rapid-fire reactions.

"Ignatious didn't create his products?" a man cried. "The boy is crazy."

"It's like saying George Washington was a British spy!"

"Or Abraham Lincoln didn't free the slaves!"

"Every knows that Ignatious is a genius. The greatest of all time!"

"And a humanitarian too. He just gave twenty million dollars to build refreshment stands in the Sahara Desert!"

"And another fifteen to fight gorilla dandruff!"

Everyone was shouting at once, individual voices blending together to create a huge, frightening din. Then the fervent cries turned on a dime to laughter— wild guffaws, hearty chuckles, and delighted giggles echoed up and down the street.

To Daphna's dismay, it got worse. Once the crowd had laughed itself dry, it turned on Harkin.

"Hey, kid. Take your sneakers and fly to the moon!"

"Cut your ponytail, little man. It's corroding your brain!"

It was all too much for Daphna to take.

"Harkin's telling the truth!" she shouted. "He is. I promise."

"All right then, girlie," a reporter said. "Give it to

us. If Ignatious Peabody Blatt didn't create the Hat-Top computer, who did?"

"Who created the Hat-Top computer?" Harkin said. "Billy B. Brilliant, that's who!"

All was still. Even the pigeons perched on the Indian restaurant took a momentary break from their pecking and cooing and cocked their ears toward the street. Vendors stopped hawking their wares and leaned close as twenty or more microphones were shoved toward Harkin.

"What?" a reporter asked.

"You heard him," Daphna said. "Billy B. Brilliant!"

"Billy B. Brilliant?" someone shouted.

"Who's that?" a vendor called to Daphna. "The name of your pet rock?"

"No, it's a new cartoon character!" someone else yelled. "I saw him on the Disney Channel."

The street exploded once more in a cacophony of shouts and laughter. Daphna had suspected that Ignatious's reputation would hold him safely above any accusations, but she hadn't thought the reaction would be so utterly dismissive. Most people in the area were laughing so hard, they were having trouble standing up.

Daphna felt Harkin tense beside her. She wouldn't have been surprised if she had seen steam come out of his ears.

"You don't believe me?" he called. "Billy B. Brilliant is the real genius behind Ignatious's inventions. We saw all his inventions in Africa. He's made Cook-Top! Frog-Top! Joke-Top!"

"Joke-Top?" a reporter cried.

"The kid is cracking," a vendor called out. "Get him a nurse!"

"No, take him into custody!"

No sooner were the words spoken than two policemen grabbed Harkin under the armpits and began to drag him toward the school.

It was then that a voice echoed across the school grounds. A familiar voice.

"A moment, if you please!"

The crowd's attention turned to the door. Could it be? Was it . . . ?

It was!

Standing at the main entryway to the school was none other than the famous founder himself, Ignatious Peabody Blatt. His suit was yellow, his tie emerald green, and his shoes a bright plum. The officers let Harkin shake himself free as reporters pushed and shoved up to the school fence, holding out their microphones.

"We can all question the grace of Mr. Thunkenreiser's delivery," Ignatious said, moving to the top step of the school entranceway. "But our esteemed student brings up a fair point." He paused. "You see, once upon a time there was a Billy B. Brilliant!"

What? Daphna looked at Harkin. Could it be? Was Ignatious coming to their defense? About to admit his crimes? In *public*? Though he appeared outwardly calm, Daphna noticed that Ignatious's right eyebrow was arched at a slightly steeper angle than usual. Everyone pushed closer.

"It's time to set the record straight, dear friends," Ignatious said above the whir of television cameras. "This is not a story for the faint of heart. How sad it is! Years ago, Mr. Brilliant and I were classmates together at the College for the Extraordinarily Talented. Such good friends we were. But one night I discovered him riffling through my prized notebooks. Imagine my horror when I discovered that Mr. Brilliant was no more than a common criminal, attempting to steal my greatest ideas."

A collective gasp filled the school grounds. Daphna noticed Myron standing beside his father. As always, his hair was perfectly parted down the middle. On his feet, he wore his trademark yellow loafers.

"Steal from you?" he called. "I'll kill him!"

Ignatious smiled at his son, who was now clenching his fists. "Such a good boy, but murder is hardly necessary. Here's the truly sad part, my friends. Even though I forgave him—that's right, I told Billy that I wouldn't report him to the school authorities—he felt so terrible about what he had done that the poor fellow disappeared. Last I heard, he was living in a hut in western Peru, making ends meet by hosing down giraffes for a local circus. So tragic!"

Ignatious pulled a sky blue handkerchief from his coat pocket and dabbed his eyes. When he continued, his voice trembled with feeling.

"Let us all take a moment to remember the Blatt School creed. 'Be insanely gifted! Work insanely hard!' But most important of all: 'Be insanely good!' Poor Billy B. Brilliant had the first two qualities in spades, but he didn't have the last. That's why this tale has such relevance today. I implore my students—all students at all schools the world over—not to let the same thing happen to you. Be gifted, yes, but above all, be honest."

The crowd broke into a wave of spontaneous applause. Ignatious bowed deeply, blew a kiss, then disappeared inside his school. As for Harkin, he continued to press his case.

"He's lying," he called. "Billy B. Brilliant isn't in western Peru. He's in Africa. Furthermore, I developed Gum-Top. Me! Right here in my lab. Myron stole it!"

Daphna watched in shock; her heart sank like a stone. It was one thing to be laughed at but almost worse to be ignored. Harkin was shouting at the top of his lungs, but now no one was listening.

"Cool it," Cynthia said.

"She's right," Daphna said. "We have to plan our next move."

"Gum-Top is mine!" Harkin said. "It's mine! It's—"

Daphna did something she'd never even considered in six years of friendship. She yanked Harkin's ponytail.

Doubled over, the boy grabbed the back of his hair.

"You touched my hair!" he cried.

"Quiet," Daphna hissed. "Here's what we have to do. First we find Myron and grill him about how he stole Gum-Top. Then we check your office, Thunk. Ignatious probably cleaned it out, but you never know. Maybe Blatt left a clue when he stole your idea."

"I can help too," Cynthia said. "When I visited Ignatious before we left on our trip, he asked me to drop by his office today to confirm the night he's going to see *The Dancing Doberman.* I'll go now and see what I can find out."

"We'll meet back at the theater just before the assembly," Daphna said. "Sound good?"

Harkin nodded. "Yeah," he said. "Good."

Plan in place, Daphna led Harkin and Cynthia through the maze of reporters, onlookers, and vendors and slipped through the front gate into their school.

22

The Charcoal Grill Toaster

On most mornings, students jammed the Blatt School playground, grabbing a final few minutes of playtime before the day's studies. With the Insanity Cup only an hour away, few children occupied the playground, and they were working. Wanda Twiddles was perched on the bottom of the slide, practicing a short speech about the inner workings of her latest suspension bridge. Wilmer Griffith was on a swing, nose buried in a thick black binder full of charts of the Andromeda galaxy. Atop the jungle gym like a rare bird was Jean-Claude Broquet. He was holding a scroll, emoting dramatically in what Daphna could only assume was Medieval French. Only Thelma Trimm was using the playground as it was intended and was playing a vigorous game of hopscotch, grunting loudly with each leap, "Insanity Cup is mine! Insanity Cup is mine!"

Daphna and her friends slipped into the back entrance of the school without meeting a single eye. Though the lobby was a little bit busier, what students were present were also lost in their own thoughts. Ignatious's statue lorded over its domain with a grin that Daphna now found wicked.

"'Be insanely gifted,'" Harkin read from his plaque. "'Work insanely hard. Be insanely good.'" He shuddered. "Make me sick."

"You said it," Daphna said.

"I'll drop by the crook's office to see what I can find out," Cynthia said. "Wish me luck."

The actress hurried toward the stairwell. A step past the statue, she glanced to her right and left to make sure no one was looking, then took a piece of gum out of her mouth and stuck it on Ignatious's foot. With a grin to her friends, she hit the stairway at a run.

"Our turn now," Daphna said. "Where do we look

for Myron? He could be anywhere."

Harkin reached into his pocket and pulled out two thin sticks of gum.

"Gum-Top," Daphna said.

Harkin nodded. "I figured out a way to get online and hack into the school's security camera system. Chew with me. Hopefully, we'll be able to see where he is."

Daphna popped the gum into her mouth. She purposely didn't think about composers.org but focused all her thoughts on the Blatt School website.

"Did you see that?" Harkin cried.

The image became clear. Smack in the middle of the school's home page was a picture of Ignatious holding out a piece of Gum-Top. The banner atop the page read: "The Great Blatt Does It Again!"

"Stay calm," Daphna said.

"Yeah, yeah," Harkin muttered. "I'm calm, all right. Go to the school's security page. See the small camera icon on the lower left-hand corner? Now let's start scanning the rooms from the bottom up."

"I'm already at Wilmer's office," Daphna said.

The large boy had put a blackboard on each wall, as well as another one on the ceiling, and covered every inch with diagrams and figures.

"I can't understand a thing," Harkin said.

"Me neither," Daphna said. "Check out Wanda's

room. The model of her latest bridge has four levels!"

"Do you remember that sign across from my office that reads 'BEWARE: VERY LARGE GRASSHOPPER!'?" Harkin asked.

Daphna was already peering inside the room.

"The bug is a foot long."

"Two feet!"

"Its eyes are two giant Frisbees."

"Its antennae are two giant windshield wipers."

"Let's get out of here."

"I'm already gone," Harkin said. He drew in a deep breath and followed the security camera down the hall. "The moment of truth. My office next."

Daphna didn't expect to find any remaining traces of Gum-Top. But what met her eyes next was almost more than she could bear. Where Harkin's fantastic machine had once stood was now a blank wall with a lone wire sticking out of a plug. Also gone were Harkin's binders with his notes. All that remained was a single overstocked bookshelf, Harkin's small desk, and a smattering of engine parts on the floor.

"They stole it," Harkin said. It was as if he hadn't actually believed it before. "Ignatious really stole Gum-Top!"

"Wait," Daphna said. "If the school's surveillance cameras were on this weekend, we can find the footage."

Harkin shook his head. "Ignatious may be evil, but he's not stupid. If there was footage, he's erased it by now. But who cares? We know who the thief is anyway: Myron."

"Probably," Daphna said. "We just have to find him."

"We'd better hurry," Harkin said. "My Gum-Top is losing flavor, and I only have one more piece."

Luckily, the two friends didn't have to search much longer. Scanning up to the next level, Daphna saw a boy in a purple shirt and yellow loafers sprinting down the hallway.

"Got him!" Daphna said.

As Myron disappeared into his office, Daphna and Harkin spit out their Gum-Tops and bolted to the back stairwell. With the hour of the assembly approaching, some students were getting a start on hauling their presentations up to the school theater. Half a flight down, Daphna found herself face-to-face with the mouth of an absolutely immense tuba.

"Make way for the world's first Blugle-horn!" a small boy with red hair announced.

As Daphna and Harkin flattened their bodies against the wall to let him pass, the boy pushed the instrument up the stairs on a small set of wheels. He stopped to talk, blocking the stairwell.

"You're a musician," the boy said to Daphna. "I'll

bet you think my horn plays really low, right? Bet you think it sounds sort of like a tuba, right? Well, that's not true."

"Hey," Harkin said. "If you could move it along, we've got to get go—"

The boy lifted his lips to the mouthpiece and filled the hallway with a giant *BLAAAATTT!* Daphna had never heard a musical note quite so loud or ugly.

"See?" the boy said.

"Nice," Daphna stammered. Her ears were ringing.

"Want to hear the opening phrase of my concerto?"

"Uh, why don't we wait to hear it at the assembly?" Harkin said.

"Good enough," the boy said, and pushed the horn past them up the stairwell.

"How was he ever accepted here?" Harkin whispered.

Daphna shrugged. "Who knows? Maybe his insane gift is playing loudly."

Two girls appeared carrying a giant cage covered by a blue sheet.

"Meet Hugo!" the first girl said. "The world's most talented rat."

"That's all right," Daphna began. "But we really . . ."

The first girl pulled off the sheet, revealing a two-foot rat wearing a custom-made tuxedo and top hat.

Daphna cringed. An occasional cockroach or mouse was part of city life. But a two-foot-long rat? Even one so elegantly dressed was more than her stomach could handle.

"What does he do?" Harkin asked.

The second girl grinned. "Sing and dance, of course!"

Thankfully, the girls didn't insist on a demonstration. With a cheerful good-bye, they continued up the stairs.

Harkin looked at Daphna. "Let's see if we can finally get down to Myron's office."

No sooner did they reach the third basement level—Myron's floor—than an enormous *BANG* reverberated down the hall. A steady stream of black smoke billowed out of a distant doorway, followed by an ear-piercing cry: *"Noooooooo!"*

"Myron!" Harkin said.

"Do you think he's hurt?" Daphna asked. She sprinted ahead and barged through the door. Atop Myron's small metal desk stood a machine that resembled a giant silver toaster but with two clear funnels that pointed upward on either side. Clearly, the contraption was Myron's year-end project. Just as clearly, it wasn't in working condition. Small flames shot out of the funnels. Worse, Myron was manning a fire extinguisher, spraying the foam onto the floor instead of onto his burning contraption. He slipped and fell hard on his rear end. Daphna grabbed the extinguisher and put out the fire with two well-aimed spurts as Harkin turned on the air vent high to clear out the smoke.

"Myron?" Daphna asked. "What happened?"

A moment earlier, she had wanted his blood. But now, lying in a puddle of foam in his absurd yellow loafers, he looked downright ridiculous. It was hard not to feel sorry for him.

"It caught on fire!" Myron moaned.

"We can see that," Harkin said. "But what in the world is 'it' supposed to be? A toaster?"

Myron struggled to his feet and kicked his desk. A flurry of sparks shot out of his strange machine.

"Not a toaster," he said, waving away another gust of smoke. "An instant charcoal grill. In my prototype, this puppy cooks a hamburger in thirty seconds."

Daphna noticed what appeared to be four hamburgers lying on the foamy floor, charred beyond recognition. She wouldn't have been surprised if someone had told her they were hockey pucks.

"I'm sunk," Myron said. He took one of the burgers from the ground, then stated the obvious. "See? It's burned!"

Myron still tried to take a bite, foam and all. With great effort, he was able to get his teeth to break into the destroyed burger. Unfortunately, he couldn't pull them back out.

"Mmmmmmfffppppff!" he moaned, pointing helplessly at his mouth.

Harkin rolled his eyes.

"MMMmmmmmffppff!" Myron said again. This time he pointed at a closet.

"All right," Harkin said. "Hold on."

In the closet was a small toolbox. Harkin found a wrench and screwed its jaws onto the burger.

"Hold on," Harkin said. "I'm going to have to really pull."

It took three tries, but the burger finally came loose. Then Myron ran to the trash can to pick the remaining bits out of his teeth.

"Serves you right," Harkin said.

"What?"

"Don't pretend you don't know what I'm talking about!" Harkin said.

"I don't."

"You stole Gum-Top!"

Myron finally turned from the trash. "Gum-Top? You're crazy! That's my father's invention."

"Is not," Daphna said. "It's Harkin's."

Myron laughed. "In your dreams."

"Why were you snooping around our offices on Friday?" Daphna asked.

"It doesn't take a genius to see you were trying to steal someone's idea," Harkin said. "Especially when all you could come up with on your own is this grill."

Myron's face scrunched up like he had eaten a sour lime. His look reminded Daphna of how upset he had been in the playground when he had defended his father.

"I've got half an hour to get it operational!"

"Okay, forget the stupid grill," Harkin said. "You still stole Gum-Top!"

Myron shook his head. "Think whatever you want. But I didn't say anything to anyone. And Gum-Top is my dad's idea! You really think you're going to get away with trying to steal an idea from him?"

"But you were looking in Harkin's window!" Daphna said.

"I was walking by and got curious. Don't tell me you've never looked in other people's offices?"

Daphna stopped short. She did it all the time. Everyone did.

"Well, sure," she stammered.

"See?" Myron said.

"That still doesn't answer what you were doing down in the fourth-floor basement last Friday," Harkin said.

"I thought I was on mine. I lost track of where I was."

Daphna looked at Myron skeptically. "You got lost a lot that day. First looking for Yuri's office."

Myron laughed. "If I stole Gum-Top, I wouldn't give it to my father. I'd enter it myself! But you are totally missing the point. The kids in this school aren't only insanely gifted, they're insanely competitive. Take Wilmer—he's so desperate to win, he hasn't slept all weekend. Wanda wants it so badly, she built a model suspension bridge across the East River. And your friend Cynthia—she's the nuttiest of all. She'd do anything to see that one-woman *Macbeth* of hers on Broadway. She's been talking about it all year!"

Myron's accusation shocked Daphna. "You're out of your mind! Are you saying Cynthia would cheat?"

"She's no crook," Harkin said.

"Whatever you say," Myron said. "Listen, I'd love to keep chatting, but I'm running out of time to fix my grill."

Harkin nodded at the smoking contraption. "You're still going to enter that?"

"It's better than whatever you've come up with," Myron said. "Maybe that's why you're going around saying Gum-Top is yours. You have nothing of your own."

"Nothing of my own?" Harkin cried. "Have you

forgotten about the Thunkmobile?"

"That piece of yellow junk?"

"That piece of junk flies!"

"That piece of junk looks like junk. No way Cody Meyers will want something that ugly on his show."

"And he's really gonna want a grill that looks like a toaster that makes hamburgers that could be doorstops?"

"All it needs are a few minor adjustments. Now a little privacy. The master must create."

But the master had even less time than he thought. The hollow sound of the Blatt gong filled the room.

"Is it time for the assembly?" Daphna said. *"Already?"*

Harkin smiled broadly at Myron. "Good luck with your toaster. You've got *Cody Meyers* in the bag."

Myron frowned. "Get out, shrimp."

"Don't worry. We're going."

Daphna and Harkin hurried to the hall.

"I still don't trust him," Harkin said.

"Me neither," Daphna said. "But without any proof, what are we going to do?"

The Blatt gong sounded a second time.

"What do we do?" Harkin said. "Go to the assembly and hope that Cynthia found out something from Ignatious. Come on!"

23

The Insanity Cup

ld Iggy wasn't even there."

Cynthia was with Daphna and Harkin on the fourth floor of the school, outside the Blatt School theater. A beautifully redone assembly hall, it seated one hundred people in plush velvet seats in the orchestra section, and one hundred more in the balcony.

"What a waste," Cynthia went on. "I could've spent the time rehearsing *Macbeth*."

Cynthia grew even angrier when Harkin and

Daphna filled her in about their discussion with Myron.

"That little weasel suggested that *I* might have been the one to have stolen Gum-Top? I'll shove his yellow loafers down his rotten throat."

"Let it go," Daphna said.

Harkin smiled.

"What?" Cynthia asked.

"If it makes you feel any better, you should've seen his project."

"Bad, huh?"

"The worst. A charcoal grill that makes burgers the consistency of cement."

Cynthia allowed herself a satisfied grin. "I know that shouldn't make me so happy, but I don't care. It just does."

"Let's forget about Myron for now," Daphna said. "What's next? Go to the assembly and keep our eyes and ears open for clues?"

"Sounds like about all we can do for the time being," Harkin said.

"Let's grab some seats," Cynthia said.

That would prove to be easier said than done. As Daphna stepped into the theater itself, she saw that nearly every seat in the orchestra section was already taken. Less surprising was the flurry of precontest chatter, flying fast and furious.

"I finally did it," a voice rose above the din. "Made a steam engine that runs on garbage!"

"So what? I've made a plane!"

"My robot built a rocket!"

Daphna exchanged a glance with her two friends. "I used to think Blatt students were nice."

Harkin nodded. "The Insanity Cup has unleashed everyone's inner psychopath."

"All to be on a stupid talk show," Cynthia said. "Who cares?"

"Easy for you to say, I suppose," Harkin said. "I mean, you're on stage every night. For lots of these kids, showing their stuff on TV is the be-all and end-all."

Cynthia blew a bubble and let it pop over her lips. "A waste of energy, if you ask me."

Daphna thought again of Myron and shook her head. Cynthia had known fame since she was six. She was the last person in the school who would need to steal to get on TV.

"Shall we?" Harkin said, pointing down the aisle.

Daphna looked out over the theater. "Love to, but there're no seats. Should we head up to the balcony?"

"Not so fast," Cynthia said. "Follow me."

"Where?" Harkin said.

"I see three seats up front."

Daphna followed her two friends down the aisle,

her heart racing faster with every step. The Insanity Cup. It was just a silly contest—Cynthia was right about that—but it was impossible not to get caught up in the mood of the room. It was as though everyone's competitive energy had been mixed into a big pot, shaken, stirred, heated up, and ignited. Students were positively aching to show off their projects.

"Yo, Mr. D'Angelo!" Daphna heard a boy call out to the popular teacher. "I've taught my monkey how to play the clarinet."

"I've taught my dog how to whistle 'The Star-Spangled Banner'!"

"My dog *rewrote* 'The Star-Spangled Banner'!"

A student in the back row lofted a paper airplane to the front of the hall.

"Hey!" a voice called out. "That's the blueprint to my submarine!"

To everyone's amusement, the paper airplane landed in Ms. Frank's hair. She crumpled it into a ball, then shot it back to its owner with a quick kick from her famous thigh-high boots. As the student body cheered, the three friends continued down the aisle. Outside they had briefly taken the spotlight; now they were roundly ignored. No one cared that Cynthia had missed a few performances of *The Dancing Doberman*. No one cared that Harkin had lost his mind and claimed that Ignatious had stolen all his ideas from a bozo named Billy B. Brilliant. The Blatt students were concerned with one thing and one thing only: themselves.

As they approached their seats, Daphna turned her focus to the stage. Wearing a bright red dress that perfectly matched the color of her lipstick, Elmira Ferguson was standing behind a podium while a technician set up a microphone. Behind her was a baby grand piano. On the other side of the podium stood a sturdy oak table. Hanging down from the center rafters was a movie screen for those students whose insane gifts required a demonstration with slides or video.

"Here we go," Cynthia said.

"Nice," Daphna said. "Front-row center."

"How'd you spot these anyway?" Harkin asked.

Cynthia shrugged. "I'm an actress. I'm used to looking for empty seats. Come on, let's sit."

Cynthia took the one closest to the aisle while Harkin sat down in the middle. As Daphna settled back into the plush velvet of the remaining seat, Cynthia turned to Harkin.

"Hey, lemme use your wristwatch computer?" she said. "I want to send a quick email to my parents telling them we're back."

"It's yours," the boy said, holding out his wrist. "And while you're at it, send emails for us too."

"You got it."

As Cynthia got to work, Elmira Ferguson raised her hand for silence.

"Let's get started, shall we? We have one hundred insanely gifted students here, and we want to give everyone an equal chance."

A round of applause rippled across the theater. Another paper airplane sailed through the air, this one gliding to a safe landing on the stage next to the headmistress's foot. As a row of older students began to stomp on the floor, Elmira kicked the paper airplane offstage, then raised her hand once again for silence.

"There is one introduction to make before we start. We all know him! We all love him! Let's give an insane welcome to our good friend Ignatious Peabody Blatt!"

As Blatt made his way from the wings to a raucous round of applause, flashbulbs popped. The whir of TV cameras filled the room. The entire theater balcony was filled with the press.

"Far be it from him to pass up on some publicity," Harkin whispered.

"Or a new outfit," Cynthia said. "Look at him. No wonder he couldn't meet with me. He was changing!"

In the hour since they had met outside the school, Ignatious had changed into a pink shirt, orange suit, and blue suspenders. His cowboy boots were sea green. To mark the occasion, the Great Blatt appeared to have dyed his eyetooth gold and his sideburns silver.

"Thank you, dear friends! Thank you!"

Students and faculty had risen to their feet. Daphna and her friends were the only people sitting in the entire room.

"Do we stand?" Cynthia asked. "We are in the very front row."

"I don't know about you," Harkin said, "but I'm not even clapping."

"Me neither," Daphna said.

Ignatious paced the stage, blowing kisses and crying, "Thank you, dear students! Thank you!"

The students began to stomp the theater floor once again. This time the beat was punctuated with a riotous chant: "Gum-Top! Gum-Top! Gum-Top!"

Daphna could practically feel Harkin's blood percolating in his veins.

"Easy," she whispered.

It was too late. Harkin rose to set the world straight. Cynthia pulled him back to his seat.

"*Shhh!*" she said.

"Save it for later," Daphna said.

"But . . ."

"Later!" Cynthia said.

"Yes, yes," Ignatious said, gesturing broadly. "I'm so very proud of Gum-Top!" He glanced to the front row and caught Harkin's and then Daphna's eyes. "But now, boys and girls, before we get started in the judging for the first Blatt School Insanity Cup, I wanted you, my dear, cherished students, to be the first to hear about something extra-special. *My next product!*"

Another product?

It was as though Ignatious had set off a package of firecrackers in the middle of the room. With the introduction of Gum-Top, everyone assumed that Ignatious would rest on his laurels for a while. Was he really coming out with something else so soon?

"It's Blatt-Foot!" a boy shouted. "Toenail polish that turns your big toe into an iPod!"

As conjectures flew across the room, Harkin looked at Daphna. "I don't like the sound of this."

"Me neither."

"You will see that some of your teachers are passing something out—something that comes in a container—one for each eye," Blatt continued. "For my next invention is a sort of contact lens. But not just any contact lens. This invention of mine is a computer that the user puts in his or her eyes. *A computer that I call the X-Head!*"

Harkin shot out of his seat so quickly, Daphna

feared that he would take off. "The X-Head?" he shouted. "That's Billy idea!"

Harkin's words were lost in an explosion of applause and shouts as teachers lined the aisles, passing out contact cases to the entire student body.

"The X-Head?" Daphna asked Harkin. "How in the world did he get it?"

"I don't know," he said. "But I'm putting a stop to this right now!"

Harkin got no more than a step toward the stage before Cynthia stuck out an arm and pushed him backward. The very second Harkin's rear end hit his seat, there was a loud *click*. Daphna looked to her lap. A seat belt had snapped shut around her! Another had snapped shut around Harkin.

"What's going on?" he asked.

Daphna didn't have time to answer. The chairs dropped straight through the floor. The last thing Daphna saw as she disappeared into the lower depths of the old Brackerton mansion was Cynthia's face gazing down at her with an inscrutable smile.

24
A Way Out

Daphna and Harkin came to a rough landing on a dirt floor. How far had they fallen? One hundred feet? Two hundred? It was hard to tell. But there was no doubt about where they were: in the dim light, Daphna could make out the outlines of four walls and a door made of bars.

"A cell," Daphna said.

"Try a dungeon," Harkin said.

There was one piece of good news. When Harkin tried his seat belt, it opened. So did Daphna's. Soon she and Harkin were pulling at the door. Locked.

With a sigh, Daphna felt the walls—the room was made of stone. The air was damp.

"This is seriously creepy," she said.

Harkin looked back up to where the trapdoor in the ceiling had already closed tight. Then he met Daphna's eyes.

"What I want to know is where's Cynthia?"

It didn't take long for the two friends to piece together the facts. But it took a good five minutes more for Daphna and Harkin to believe what those facts suggested. Had Myron been right? Had Cynthia been the one to betray them? As hard as it was to accept, it began to look that way. Why else had she been able to lead them to the empty front-row seats? Why hadn't her seat descended into the dungeon along with theirs? Most important, who else could have possibly gotten Ignatious the formula to the X-Head?

"It would explain how the antelope men found us at Billy's, too," Harkin said. "Cynthia might have put that tracking device on the Thunkmobile."

"Why would she do it?" Daphna asked.

"Maybe Ignatious agreed to fund her one-woman *Macbeth* in exchange for the X-Head?" Harkin said.

"She wouldn't do that," Daphna said. "Would she?"

Harkin shrugged. "I don't know. People have been going nuts at this school lately. And Cynthia has been obsessed about her show."

Daphna tried to spin alternative scenarios. Maybe Cynthia was being framed? Maybe Myron really was the thief? Maybe someone else? But every time Daphna tried to think of a reason Cynthia was innocent, she returned to the image of her friend's strange smile, seconds before she disappeared. Why had Cynthia looked so closely at the X-Head formula, as though she was committing it to memory? Why had she pushed Harkin back into his seat seconds before the chairs fell? Why had she asked to use his wristwatch computer?

Harkin paced the small cell.

"Our options are limited," he said.

Without Harkin's wristwatch computer, they had no way to send out a message for help. And even if they did, what could anyone really do? Daphna and Harkin could already see how it would play out. Once they were released (if they were released), Ignatious would simply deny everything. So would Cynthia. It would work, too. After all, there was no hard evidence to prove that either Gum-Top or the X-Head weren't Ignatious's ideas. Even if Billy B. Brilliant somehow materialized from Africa, the media would never take the word of an overweight hermit over the man they think is the greatest genius in the world.

"Maybe it's stupid," Daphna said, "but I can't help hoping that we're wrong and that Cynthia is out there, trying to break us out."

"Yeah," Harkin said, leaning back into his chair. "That'd be nice, wouldn't it?"

If Cynthia was trying to engineer their escape, she wasn't having much luck.

Half an hour had passed before a man in a black turtleneck and dark slacks emerged from the darkness of the dimly lit corridor on the other side of the door.

"I brought you lunch," the man said. "I'll be back for the trays in an hour."

He left the food by a narrow opening at the bottom of the door.

"You have to let us out!" Daphna said.

"At least tell us who won the contest?" Harkin called.

The man continued down the corridor without turning to acknowledge the questions. Daphna looked down at her plate—the spaghetti and meatballs smelled surprisingly good, and despite everything, she was hungry.

"Might as well eat," she said. "You never know. Some energy might help us figure out our next move."

"Maybe," Harkin said. "Anyway, I'm half starved."

The two friends carried their trays to their respective seats. Daphna took a long swig of milk, then a bite of pasta.

"Not bad," she said.

Harkin laughed.

"What?"

"Hard to believe, but the last thing I had in my mouth was a piece of Gum-Top."

Daphna smiled. "Yeah, me too."

She took a second bite of pasta but stopped midchew.

"What?" Harkin asked. "Got an idea?"

"Gum-Top."

"Gum-Top?" Harkin wrinkled his brow. "Ignatious stole it, remember?"

Daphna was so excited that she almost upset her tray when she stood up.

"Gum-Top, Harkin! You have another piece, right?"

"Yeah, I do. One . . ." Then Harkin got what Daphna was thinking. "I mean, *yeah!*"

"Let's see if we can chew our way online from down here and send out some emails."

Harkin riffled through his pockets for the gum. "Who should we contact? My parents won't do any good. The police?"

Daphna was pacing now. "No, they'd never believe us. Let's assume the worst: that Cynthia made a deal with Ignatious to take her on *Cody Meyers* in exchange for stealing Gum-Top and the X-Head."

"Which would mean," Harkin said, "that her *Macbeth* was picked as the winner of the Insanity Cup."

"Right!" Daphna said. She wheeled around. "What would happen if hard workers like Wilmer, Wanda, and Jean-Claude found out the whole thing was fixed?"

Harkin's eyes went wide. "They'd go nuts."

"Bonkers!"

"They'll be out for some serious blood!"

"We might be able to convince them to break us out!"

"We might at that!"

Harkin finally found the piece of gum. "You want to do the honors?"

Daphna popped the last remaining piece of Gum-Top into her mouth and got chewing.

25

A Surprise Rescuer

Daphna sat in her chair, maniacally working her jaws.

Harkin paced anxiously. "You've been chewing for two minutes already!"

"I'm doing my best! It's hard to get online from down here."

Daphna had seen a glimmer of the Blatt School website, www.insanelygifted.com, in her head, but it disappeared before she had time to scroll to the link to student email.

"Lemme try," Harkin said.

Daphna rose to her feet. "With my chewed piece of gum? I can do this."

"Chew faster!"

"I am."

"Faster!"

And then it happened.

"I'm online!"

Working quickly, Daphna navigated to student email, called up a blank letter, and addressed it to Wilmer, Wanda, and Jean-Claude. With Gum-Top's flavor beginning to fade, she thought out a quick message.

```
Trapped in basement dungeon. Suspect
the contest was rigged. Help us stop
Ignatious before he . . .
```

The connection was fritzing out. With the Blatt School website disappearing, Daphna quickly pressed Send.

"Did you send it off?" Harkin asked.

Daphna nodded. "I think so." The gum lost its flavor. When she spit it out, she realized how badly her jaw ached.

When five minutes turned to ten and ten to twenty, Daphna began to give up hope.

"You think they got the message?" Harkin asked. Unable to sit still, he was up and pacing.

"I hope so."

"And you're sure you got it off in time?"

"I think so."

Then Daphna heard it: the sound of footsteps.

She ran to the cell door and peered down the dim hallway. Daphna held her breath but then exhaled heavily: It was the guard, returning to pick up their trays. He did his job efficiently and offered no information, either about who had won the contest or how long Daphna and Harkin could expect to stay locked up. When he was gone, Daphna sank back into her seat, so downhearted that she didn't talk to Harkin for two full minutes. She didn't even look up when she heard another set of footsteps heading toward them.

"Him again," Harkin said. "The guard."

Daphna smiled ruefully. "Maybe he's bringing dessert?"

She sat up, ears pricked. These footsteps sounded different—lighter, faster. Daphna looked at Harkin. Clearly, he had heard the same thing. They ran to the cell door.

A small figure darted around the corner, then hurried toward them, in and out of the dim light. Was she seeing things?

"Thelma?" she said.

The pigtailed girl was half trotting, half skipping toward them. Then she was inserting a key into the cell door, her face scrunched into its usual frown.

"Thelma," Harkin repeated.

"Don't be so surprised," she snapped. "I intercepted your email to Wilmer."

The door clicked open.

"Why?" Harkin asked.

Thelma pursed her lips like she had just sucked on a bad piece of fruit. "Who cares?" she cried, pigtails flapping. "There are more important issues at hand. The X-Head, for instance. Everybody is already wearing it. Before long Ignatious will be able to get inside their heads, control their minds—have his way with the entire city." The girl shook herself. "I am *such* a fool. No brains at all."

"You're a fool?" Daphna asked. "I don't get it."

Thelma's filmy blue eyes widened. "Don't tell me you guys are even bigger morons than me. What do you think? That after your friend Cynthia sent Ignatious the formula, thousands of copies of the X-Head magically materialized, ready to be distributed? No, Ignatious needed someone here to oversee the operation. And that someone was me."

Harkin gasped. Daphna didn't think she had ever seen her friend look so surprised.

"You?" the boy said.

Thelma frowned and wrapped a pigtail around her finger. "That's right, Thunk. Who else in this joint do you think could do it? Wilmer? *Myron?* Don't make me laugh."

Who would have thought that Thelma had the skill to convert Billy's formula overnight into an unlimited supply of ready-to-go X-Heads?

"Didn't think I was smart enough, huh?" Thelma said.

"No," Daphna said. "I always knew you were smart. Honest. It's more that *I* feel stupid. I never suspected that Ignatious would use students to do his work."

"Me neither," Harkin said.

Thelma let loose a high-pitched burst of laughter. It might have been the first time Daphna had seen her with her mouth open in six full years as classmates. Daphna could see why. Thelma's two front upper teeth were crooked, forming an X in the center of her mouth.

"You guys don't know much, do you?" Thelma snorted.

"What do you mean?" Daphna asked.

"What do I mean?" Thelma said. She shook her head and began to pace. "Don't you see it? That's the whole point of this stupid school. Yeah, it's a great place, right? We learn a lot. But do you really think that Ignatious founded it out of the goodness of his heart? He founded it so he could *steal* his students' best ideas. So Myron could steal your Gum-Top, Thunk. So he could bribe Cynthia to steal the formula for the X-Head. So he could use someone like me to get it ready. Ignatious Peabody Blatt cares more for the color of his sideburns than his students—you can bet on it!"

Daphna's eyes were wide in amazement. Could it be true? Had Ignatious's sole purpose for founding the school been to steal ideas from his students? It was impossible to believe.

But it made perfect sense.

"For a bunch of insanely gifted kids, we're a bunch of morons," Thelma went on. "If I had known exactly what I was doing, I would've never helped Ignatious get the X-Head ready so quickly. But now we've got to stop him."

"Can he really control the minds of the users?" Daphna asked.

Thelma shook her head. "Not yet. The X-Head has to be in the eye for six hours or so before he has full control. But after that? He could command the entire city to bark like a dog or baa like a goat if he wants. Now hurry!"

The girl scurried back down the hall, leading Daphna and Harkin quickly around a corner, then down an even darker corridor, then to the left, then back to the right.

"This way!" Thelma barked, and trotted up a back stairway.

"So were we right?" Daphna asked. "Ignatious gave Cynthia the Insanity Cup?"

"Not only was your friend declared the winner, but old Ignatious only allowed five other contestants to even enter!"

"No!" Harkin said.

"It's true," Thelma said. "And no one good either. The first was this young kid with a giant tuba."

"You mean Blugle-horn," Harkin said. "We met him."

"Who else?" Daphna asked. "Was there a dancing rat?"

"Yeah, a tap-dancing rodent was there," Thelma said. "Along with some guy who wrote poetry in Finnish and a girl who said she had evidence of ice cream on Mars."

Daphna and Harkin followed Thelma out into a small storage closet filled with erasers, boxes of chalk, and other assorted school supplies. Thelma pushed open a door and slowly stuck her head into the lobby. Daphna stood behind her and held her breath.

"Coast is clear," Thelma said. "Everyone must be at the TV studio."

"Which is where we'd better get going," Harkin said.

The three children stepped into the lobby. As always, it was impossible not to be drawn to the giant statue of Ignatious Peabody Blatt or to notice the school credo in bold black lettering:

> BE INSANELY GIFTED!
> WORK INSANELY HARD!
> BE INSANELY GOOD!

"What a joke," Harkin said.

Daphna sighed. "After all these years of thinking the great Ignatious Peabody Blatt was the most amazing person on Earth, it's hard to get used to the fact that he's a cheat."

Thelma chewed a pigtail. "Tell me about it."

Despite Ignatious's shady motives, his school had been a wonderful place for many of his students.

Daphna looked at Harkin and Thelma. "Just because Ignatious doesn't live up to his own motto doesn't mean we can't, right?"

"Right," Harkin said.

Thelma turned to the door. "Let's go!"

Daphna and Harkin followed their guide through the back playground and out a side exit that led past the Indian restaurant to 97th Street.

"What are we going to do once we get to the studio?" Daphna asked. "Complain about how Cynthia won? We'll just look like a bunch of bad losers."

"That may be," Thelma said. "But we have to find a way to expose Ignatious and stop Cynthia."

Daphna shivered. It was still hard to believe that one of her best friends had betrayed her.

"What's wrong?" Harkin asked her.

"Just trying to get used to the new reality," Daphna said.

As if to put to rest any nagging doubts, Daphna got her final proof. Across Columbus Avenue stood a newsstand with a computerized news feed running across its top. The headlines were big enough to make out from a distance.

"FAMOUS CHILD ACTRESS TO APPEAR ON 'CODY MEYERS'!"

"TRUSTWELL TO PERFORM ONE-WOMAN 'MACBETH' ON TV! THEN BLATT TO PRODUCE SHOW ON BROADWAY!"

And finally: "CODY TO CYN: C YA SOON!"

As if to rub it in, a cab whizzed by with its radio blaring: "That's right, friends! Ignatious Peabody Blatt has a new product. The X-Head! Magical contact lenses! What will this man come up with next?"

"It stinks, doesn't it?" Daphna said.

Harkin could only nod.

"Come on, guys," Thelma said. "If we want to stop them, we've got to hurry!" She turned to Harkin. "Don't you have some sort of flying car we can use?"

"That's the Thunkmobile to you," Harkin said. "Now follow me!"

26

Chaos at the Studio

"Can you unscrunch it?" Daphna asked. The children stood by the side of Harkin's contraption. "I mean, Cynthia has your wristwatch."

Harkin grinned. "The Thunk plans for every contingency." He reached for a small emergency valve on the back right hubcap. With a cough and a shudder of pink smoke, the car rolled sideways into the street and unscrunched to its full size. Harkin jumped behind the wheel, Daphna took the passenger seat, and Thelma climbed over her to the middle.

"Okay," Harkin said. "Hold on till I get this puppy airborne!"

He gunned the engine, then slammed it into gear. The Thunkmobile rocketed past cabs on Columbus Avenue.

"Yee-haw!" Thelma cried. "I like the way your buggy moves."

"But watch the bus," Daphna called. "The bus!"

Indeed, Harkin was gaining rapidly on a bus. Instead of slowing down, he pressed hard on the accelerator.

"Fly, Thunkmobile!" he cried, yanking on the green lever.

The car whooshed into the sky, barely skimming the top of the bus and a delivery truck before soaring high over the buildings of Central Park West.

Thelma beamed. "Awesome takeoff. Look at those people down there. They're squirrel size!"

"Where's Cody Meyers's studio?" Daphna asked. "Downtown?"

"Yep," Thelma said. "On Fourteenth Street."

"Hold on," Harkin said. "This is gonna be a short ride."

A short ride but plenty of time for Daphna to look more closely out the window and see what had become of New York. The lines out of stores they had seen earlier that morning were now twice as long. New owners of X-Heads filled the streets, walking aimlessly down the sidewalks staring blankly before them. On 59th Street, a young woman came within inches of getting run down by a cab. On 54th, a man walked directly into an open manhole as another bumped into a hot-dog vendor. And the theater district was chaos. Cars honked and slammed on their brakes as passersby wandered in front of traffic, staring at websites only they could see.

"It's a city of zombies," Daphna said.

"No wonder Billy wanted the formula destroyed," Harkin said.

"Billy?" Thelma said.

Daphna caught Thelma up on their African adventure, from their introduction to Billy through the battle of the Tops and the discovery of the formula in Billy's old textbook.

"So he let Cook-Top burn the formula?" Thelma said.

Daphna nodded. "Yeah. But not soon enough."

"Look!" Harkin called. "That must be the studio."

Across Union Square Park, swarms of people stood behind a series of police barricades. Reporters and TV crews wandered around looking for something to report or someone—anyone—to interview. Lines of people waiting to buy their very own X-Heads came out of every single store.

As Harkin circled closer to the ground, the same blue limousine that he and Daphna had seen outside the opening for *The Dancing Doberman* pulled up to the front of the hall.

"It's the mayor again!" Daphna said.

Harkin and Thelma pressed their faces to the window.

"Look at him waddle out of the car," Harkin said.

"He's a bowling ball, and his wife is a pencil," Thelma said.

Harkin was hovering no more than a hundred feet over the crowd. Once the mayor was inside, people below finally began to look up and point.

"It seems we're making an entrance," Harkin said. "Let's find a place to land."

Daphna grabbed the door handle and looked at the street.

"That's weird."

"What?" Thelma said.

"It's not us they're looking at."

Pedestrians stared past the Thunkmobile to something else flying even higher in the sky. Daphna wheeled around to see a small dot floating above them.

"What's that?" she asked. "A plane?"

"I think it's a helicopter," Harkin said.

Daphna squinted. "Is it a blimp?"

"It's a balloon!" Thelma cried.

Daphna's heart jumped. She looked at Harkin, giddy with disbelief.

"Do you think it's him?" Daphna asked.

"I think so," he said.

Who else could it be?

"It's Balloon-Top!" Daphna said.

The balloon—for it was a balloon—was close enough for Daphna to make out a large man with a red beard, waving both arms. Next to him was a laptop computer holding a spatula and a pot.

"Is that Billy B. Brilliant?" Thelma asked.

"It is," Daphna said, laughing. "And look. He brought along Cook-Top!"

27
Two Landings

Though Daphna had left Kilimanjaro only a short time earlier, it seemed like a lifetime since she had last seen Billy. Excited, she waved wildly out the window. Billy saluted in return and made a funny face. Daphna stuck out her tongue.

"What are you doing here?" she called, even though she knew he couldn't hear her. She turned to Harkin. "I wonder what he wants."

"Isn't it obvious?" Thelma asked. "He caught wind

that Ignatious had the X-Head."

Daphna knew Thelma was probably right, but she had hoped that Billy's reason for traveling back across the world was more personal. Maybe it had something to do with her?

"We'll find out soon enough," Harkin said.

Heart pounding, Daphna gave Billy a final wave, then turned to the street. A sea of people was looking up at the two strange flying contraptions. The police tried to wave them off, but as soon as they saw that the flying car and balloon were both determined to land, they helped clear a short runway on 14th Street. Daphna saw the street rushing toward her, growing larger and larger before they hit the ground with a sharp bump. Harkin slammed on the brakes and the car skidded to a halt by the studio door. Daphna rolled down the window and took a deep breath. Reporters and onlookers pressed up to police barricades. Across the way, a group of vendors sold anything they could.

"Special X-Head contact-lens solution!" Daphna heard a man call. "Get it here! See those websites more clearly!"

The minute Daphna set her feet on the street, reporters began shouting questions from behind the barricade. Harkin winked at Daphna and Thelma.

"This'll shut 'em up."

He pressed the button on the Thunkmobile's left hubcap.

Scrinch!

The car collapsed, then rolled into a narrow space between two police cars. As the crowd whistled and cheered, Harkin took a bow. But he was about to be shown up. Daphna looked over just in time to see Billy bring Balloon-Top to the ground twenty feet down the street. Billy and Cook-Top bounded out of the balloon's basket. Grinning mischievously, Billy typed a command into Balloon-Top's keyboard. With a blinding flash, the balloon deflated, then rolled back into the basket, which then collapsed into an ordinary orange laptop.

The square was stone silent. But when Billy picked up the computer and waved to the crowd, wild applause filled the street. Even reporters and police cheered long and loud.

"I get it!" someone called. "He's a magician!"

"It's Ignatious Blatt in a fat suit!"

"No! The Wizard of Oz!"

Billy laughed, then ambled over toward Daphna.

"You came," she said.

Billy nodded. "That I did, Daphna."

Daphna's heart began to pound wildly. Billy's hazel eyes seemed to be dancing in their sockets. He shambled back and forth like a great, big, nervous bear.

"Why?" Daphna said. "Is everything all right?"

As Billy began to answer, the reporters broke through the police barricade and charged forward.

"Let's get to the bottom of this!" one cried, waving his microphone in front of Billy's beard. "Who are you? What's the story on this crazy balloon? Are you part of a circus?"

After twelve years of solitude, the microphones, questions, and people were overwhelming. But he was soon spared the spotlight.

"Who is this?" Harkin said, stepping squarely in front of the microphones. "This man is the true inventor of the Hat-Top, that's who. The true inventor of Blatt-Global and Peabody-Pitch. And the true inventor of the X-Head. Ladies and gentlemen, meet Billy B. Brilliant!"

"Inventor of the Hat-Top?" a policeman cried. "Impossible!"

"Of Peabody-Pitch? *Him?* Never!"

"The kid's insane!"

"It's absurd!"

"Ridiculous!"

"How dare he?"

Then a familiar voice rang down the street.

"It's true, my friends! It's all absolutely true!"

Daphna wheeled around, then nearly fell over. Stepping out of a black limousine was the last person on Earth she ever thought would defend Billy B. Brilliant: *Ignatious Peabody Blatt himself!*

28

The Triumph of Ignatious

Wearing a suit of light lavender, Ignatious walked calmly toward the crowd. His vest was bright red. His sideburns were dyed a pale shade of copper.

"Can you believe it?" Harkin whispered. "He changed again!"

As reporters furiously scribbled notes and photographers snapped pictures, Ignatious smiled broadly at Billy.

"There he is! My long-lost friend!"

Ignatious locked him in a quick embrace. Billy patted his back hesitantly.

"Yes, and I see you've made quite a name for yourself, Iggy."

Ignatious laughed and looked around at the teeming crowd. "Yes, I have, haven't I? By using some of your work, I'm afraid. I do hope you'll forgive me. When you left college, you left behind your notes. I couldn't resist."

Daphna was confused. Was Ignatious admitting everything he had done?

"Wait a second," a reporter said. "Is that true?"

"It is!" Daphna cried.

"And he didn't even try to share the credit," Harkin said.

"That's where you're wrong," Ignatious called, directing his words to the crowd. "I did try."

Thelma blinked. "You did?"

Reporters pushed closer. The event was being recorded on everything from TV cameras to cell phones.

"Of course I did," he said. "I tried to find Mr. Brilliant for years. But he had disappeared. Isn't that right, my friend?"

"It is, actually," Billy admitted. He tugged on his beard. "I've been out of touch for a while."

"You heard it here first, folks!" a reporter shouted.

"Blatt tried to share credit! He tried to share the credit!"

The crowd cheered. Daphna felt a twinge of panic.

"Wait a second," she said. She turned to Ignatious. "You said that Billy tried to steal from you. You said he was living in a hut making a living by hosing down giraffes."

The crowd quieted. Reporters pushed their microphones closer. Ignatious chuckled. "Oh, yes. I suppose I did. Got me on that one." He shrugged and turned again to the swarm of reporters. "You see, when I was first starting out, I wanted to share my success with him. Make him my partner. I looked for Billy far and wide."

"Over the past year, you've been looking far and wide to get his formula for the X-Head," Daphna said.

"Right," Thema said. "And once you found it, you made me make it work."

"And you had Myron steal Gum-Top!" Harkin cried. "Which was my idea!"

"Yes, yes," Ignatious said with a laugh. "Guilty as charged. On all counts!"

Reporters shouted into microphones. Onlookers murmured wildly, amazed by the news. Daphna had never been more confused. Had Ignatious been suddenly stricken by a guilty conscience? Why was he admitting everything?

"I suppose you might say that my success has gone a bit to my head over the years," he went on. "Where I once tried to include Billy, I'm a bit more greedy now. Power mad, some people say. I don't deny it. Which is why I so wanted to find the X-Head."

Billy narrowed his eyes. "I know why. For mind control."

Blatt grinned widely, then held a finger to his lips. "*Shhh*, old friend. Not so loud." He glanced at his watch, then went on at a whisper. "But since you mentioned it, in about four hours' time I should have control of the entire city."

He snapped his fingers. The back doors of his limousine opened. Out stepped a group of teachers from school. Bobby D'Angelo, Horatio Yuri, and Josie Frank walked onto the street. A moment later, Wilmer, Wanda, and Jean-Claude popped out of a back door. To Daphna's horror, the very last person out of the car was none other than Mrs. Zoentrope. Each of them carried a bag that read: BLATT SCHOOL. Daphna could see from their vacant stares that they were all wearing the X-Head.

Ignatious laughed and called out: "Thank you, students and teachers. Please distribute the product."

On cue, the students and teachers walked directly into the crowd.

"X-Heads!" Josie Frank called. "Get your free X-Heads!"

"Put the X in your eyes!" Wilmer called.

"You and the Great Blatt!" Jean-Claude announced. "Perfect together!"

Anyone in the crowd who wasn't already wearing an X-Head pushed close to get one.

"See this little scene?" Ignatious told Daphna. "Other students and teachers are doing the same throughout the city. Sure, it's expensive to give away all my X-Heads for free. But think of the benefits."

Billy turned to the crowd and yelled at the top of his lungs.

"Don't put them on! They're not safe!"

Ignatious laughed harder. "Gallant try, Brilliant. But I'm afraid your X-Head is simply too popular now."

Daphna was about to shout herself, but another limo pulled up to the front of the TV studio.

"Ah, excellent!" Ignatious said. "She's finally here!"

"She?" Daphna said. "Who?"

Ignatious grinned wildly. "You'll see soon enough!"

Daphna knew. She turned back to the limo just in

time to see her old friend step onto the street. Gone were her customary jeans and cardigan sweater. In their place, she wore a flowing red gown. Her hair was up in an elegant bun. Her fingernails were painted bright blue.

Cynthia.

29

A Rhapsody for the City

In Daphna's mind, none of Cynthia's performances lived up to the one she was giving now. At least, Daphna *hoped* that Cynthia was giving a performance. If her old friend felt at all badly about what she had done, she wasn't acting it. Cynthia strutted to the front of the limo and waved twice to the crowd.

"Ladies and gentlemen," Ignatious cried, "I give you the winner of the Insanity Cup!"

As the crowd cheered even louder, Cynthia

bowed. Daphna's legs felt like two sticks of rubber. Had her friend—the girl who had flown with her all the way to Africa—really gone over to the dark side?

"Cynthia!" Daphna shouted.

The actress finally looked her way. As the two friends locked eyes, a small ray of hope burned through Daphna. Yes, Cynthia was a superb actress. But underneath the confident and polished veneer, Daphna thought she saw a twinge of guilt. Maybe her old friend would listen to reason?

"Please," Daphna said. "Tell us it isn't true."

"It isn't as bad as it looks," Cynthia said. "Ignatious explained it all to me."

"Ignatious?" Harkin said.

"The X-Head is good for the world," Cynthia went on. "It'll allow people all over the world—poor people—to have access to computers. Billy was keeping the technology to himself. Ignatious is doing a good thing."

"Ignatious wants to control everyone's mind," Daphna said. "And he's already halfway there. Look!"

She waved at the crowd. At first glance, the onlookers appeared perfectly normal, innocently cheering Ignatious. With a closer look, Daphna saw it. The vacant stares. The incurious expressions. It was as though the populace of New York had been turned into ghosts of their real selves, partly aware of their surroundings but mostly lost in a world of websites.

When Daphna looked back at Cynthia, she saw that no amount of theatrical training could keep the alarm out of her friend's eyes.

"See?" Daphna said.

"They're already zombies!" Thelma cried.

"Not zombies," Ignatious said, waving his hands. "They're merely online, enjoying the multitudinous benefits of the X-Head." He rustled in his pockets and pulled out a small package. "In fact, Cynthia dear, isn't it time that you tried on a pair?"

"Get those away from her," Harkin said.

Cynthia took a step toward the crowd, realizing for the first time what she had done.

"Listen," Daphna said. "I know how much your one-woman *Macbeth* means to you. But I also know that you aren't a person who wants to be remembered for helping Ignatious Peabody Blatt take over the city. Just hang in there. You'll find another producer."

"You can still make this right," Harkin said.

Ignatious grabbed Cynthia's arm. "Enough of this idle chitchat. The girl has a performance to give."

"Not so fast." Cynthia pulled herself away. "I need to think."

"Think?" Ignatious cried. "There's nothing to think about. We had an agreement, Miss Trustwell.

Don't you want to see your show on Broadway? Now come! Cody Meyers is waiting!"

He pushed Cynthia toward the studio, but Harkin cut her off.

"You know what you have to do." He leaned close. "Remember what happened on the Thunkmobile?"

Cynthia wrinkled her brow. "The Thunkmobile? When?"

"On the way to Kilimanjaro."

Daphna was just as confused as Cynthia.

"When Daphna played her music," Harkin said.

Cynthia's eyes widened. "Oh," she said. "You mean . . . ?"

"Enough!" Ignatious called.

"That'll never work!" Daphna said.

"Yes, it will." Harkin gestured to the crowd. "Look at them!"

Daphna turned in a slow circle. The free X-Heads had done their work quickly. Nearly everyone in the crowd was multitasking, looking at the confrontation between Ignatious and the children but reading or scrolling through websites at the same time.

"And you think that *I* can fix this?" Daphna asked.

"Maybe not," Harkin said. "But after I woke out of the trance your music created, I had never felt better. Never."

"Me neither," Cynthia said.

"Mrs. Zoentrope is right," Harkin went on. "Your music has the power to heal."

Daphna looked helplessly to the crowd. "But heal an entire city?"

"Why not?" Harkin said.

Ignatious blinked nervously. "This is absurd! Hurry, Cynthia!"

Cynthia walked right by Ignatious and stepped directly up to a reporter's microphone.

"An announcement, if you please," she said. "Yes, I was declared the winner of the Insanity Cup. It's true. But it's also true that I didn't win it fairly. So I would hereby like to give my opportunity to perform on *Cody Meyers* to the student who really deserves it. The most insanely gifted of them all. The greatest composer in the city. Give a big round of applause to Daphna Whispers!"

"Good girl!" Billy called.

"Wait!" Ignatious cried. "No!"

"You heard it here, folks!" a reporter yelled above the noise of the crowd. "Trustwell gives away her spot!"

Daphna looked at Cynthia.

"Really?"

Her friend nodded. "Do your thing." Cynthia glanced at the crowd, then back at Daphna. "Just promise you'll try to forgive me when this is all over?"

Daphna knew that what her friend had done was unspeakable. On the other hand, her instincts told her that Cynthia was truly remorseful.

"I promise," she said.

"Good," Cynthia said. "Now go play."

Ignatious was there, blocking her path.

"Not so fast," he said. Daphna could see a thin trickle of sweat on his forehead. "You've forgotten that Cody Meyers will never let anyone perform without my permission."

"Very true," a reporter cried. "Meyers has to okay the winner!"

"Who cares?" Billy bellowed.

Daphna wheeled around. The large man was staring Ignatious straight in the eye.

"She doesn't need Cody Meyers. She can play right here!"

Ignatious blinked. "What?"

Daphna was just as confused as Ignatious.

"What will she play on?" Thelma asked. "The curb?"

"No, I got it!" a police officer cried. "She'll play a fire hydrant!"

"No," Billy announced. "She'll play on this."

With that, the great man reached into his long coat and pulled out what appeared to be a twisted piece of metal.

"You heard it here, friends!" a reporter shouted. "Daphna Whispers will play an eggbeater!"

"No," Billy said. He reached back into his pocket. "I meant this!"

He pulled out a small blue laptop.

"What is it?" Daphna asked.

"It's a Frisbee!" someone shouted. "Whispers is going to play a Frisbee!"

Billy chuckled and flicked a switch on its side. With a bright *brrrring*, the computer sprang four legs. The crowd gasped. Then with three loud *beep*s, the computer opened and the keypad began to stretch.

"Run for your life!" a reporter cried. "It's alive!"

As onlookers pushed, shoved, screamed, and pointed, Billy's contraption hissed twice. Then, with a final *brrrring*, the numbers and letters on the keypad turned into the eighty-eight keys of a keyboard.

"Meet Piano-Top," Billy called.

"I told you!" a reporter cried. "He is a magician!"

"No," Harkin said, laughing. "He's Billy B. Brilliant!"

Everyone began pushing and shoving even harder, not to get away but to get a better view. While the police held the crowd at bay, Billy turned to Daphna.

"You can do it," he said. "Free the city from the spell of the X-Head."

Daphna swallowed hard. "You really think I can?"

Billy nodded. "I know you can. Just like your mother used her sax to break us out of our little funk back in college."

Daphna sat at the piano and looked out at the crowd. What she saw took her breath away. Before her was the future, at least as Ignatious Peabody Blatt wanted it: a horde of people looking at Daphna vacantly while simultaneously distracted by websites—a city full of citizens hours away from being under Blatt's total control.

The reporters jabbered away, more concerned with being loud than getting the facts straight.

"That's right, folks! Her name is Daphne Sisters!"

"We hear her mom recently disappeared in a tragic skateboard accident!"

"She lives in a studio apartment that morphs each night into a spaceship!"

For a moment, Daphna was too amazed to move, awed by the task before her. Could her music really snap an entire population out of the X-Head's spell? Terrified, Daphna thought of the person she cared about most: her mother. Wouldn't she want Daphna to gather her courage and do her best?

As TV cameras zoomed closer, Daphna sat up as straight as she could and heard the opening strain of her music in her head.

Baa, baa, de, duh!

Then, with a final look at the seemingly endless crowd, Daphna remembered something: She had never given her piece a title.

"I call this *Rhapsody for the City*."

Daphna cleared her throat.

She looked at Billy for support.

She lifted her hands to play . . .

. . . when a shadow fell over Piano-Top and a deafening whir filled the air. With a sharp gasp, Daphna looked up. Looming overhead was the red helicopter. A rope ladder dropped to her side.

"Not so fast, Daphna Whispers!" Ignatious cried.

And then she was in his arms. With a quick jerk, up the ladder flew. Billy, Harkin, Thelma, Cynthia, the reporters—everyone in the crowd—grew very small. Ignatious threw Daphna into the backseat of the mighty helicopter.

"Fly!" Ignatious shouted to the pilot. "Fly!"

30

The Chase

Like all students at the Blatt School, Daphna had imagined being invited for a ride in Ignatious's traveling office. But she had never imagined boarding the red helicopter under these circumstances or how extravagant the interior would be. Orange velvet lined the walls. The plush seats were embroidered with fine blue silk. A red curtain separated the backseats from the front. The windows were tinted light green. The rotor—thunderously loud from outside—was entirely muted within.

"Nice, isn't it?"

As the giant machine rocketed upward, Ignatious slipped into the backseat next to her. Gone was Ignatious's customary smooth polish. His smile was chilling. His eyes narrowed menacingly.

"What are you going to do with me?" Daphna asked.

"Don't worry, dear. This will be a short flight."

A familiar voice came from the front.

"Where to, boss?"

Daphna's eyes widened. Ignatious laughed again.

"An old friend of yours."

He drew open the curtain. The antelope man without his mask turned from the pilot's seat and smiled, revealing a row of uneven, chipped teeth. Daphna drew in a deep breath, remembering the first night they had met. It seemed years ago that he had broken into her apartment looking for the X-Head.

"There she is," he said. "The girl who booted me out a window."

"You broke into my apartment!"

The antelope man didn't respond but repeated his question to Ignatious: "Where to?"

"Yeah, Dad. Where to already?"

Daphna saw the yellow loafers.

"Myron?"

The boy looked back from the front passenger seat with a self-important smirk. "I'm Dad's right-hand man now. Isn't that right, Dad?"

"Take us over the harbor," Ignatious said to the antelope man.

"Got it."

"The harbor?" Daphna asked. As hard as she tried, she couldn't keep her voice from shaking. "Why are we going there?"

When Ignatious met her eyes, the old smile was back.

"So sorry, Daphna, dear. But did you really think I'd let you ruin my fun?"

"Fun?"

"Yes, fun." Ignatious's eyes sparkled. "The X-Head! Didn't you see how everyone was wearing it? Don't forget, Daphna, I know everything that goes on in my school. I know about Mrs. Zoentrope's trance. I even know what happened to your mother when she first heard 'The Sad Sandbox.' I can't risk having your beautiful music break the spell of my X-Head. I have so many things to do!"

"Things? What things?"

Ignatious brushed a pinkie over his goatee, pushing down an errant hair. "Some little things and some bigger ones too. For instance, I thought it would be nice if everyone in the city addressed me as His

All-Powerful Insanely Gifted Blatt." He chuckled. "And besides that, well, I've always wanted to be mayor, isn't that right, Myron?"

"Right, Dad!"

Daphna could feel the blood rushing through her temples.

"Mayor?" she said. "What about Mayor Fiorello?"

Ignatious waved a hand. "A mere inconvenience, my dear. Yes, he's awfully popular, but he's also up for reelection next fall. You see, in about, oh, four or five hours, I'll have full control of the X-Head. After that, a few words into my little pinkie ring and, presto, everyone lucky enough to be wearing it—which will soon be practically everyone in the world—will obey my every command! So don't you see that becoming mayor of New York City is the least that I can do? Next election day, I'll simply command everyone to write in my name. By the way, do you know what would be really nice? I'd love to have my face carved in the side of Mount Rushmore. Don't you think my profile would look smashing next to Abraham Lincoln's and Teddy Roosevelt's?"

"You'll never get away with it."

Ignatious smiled, a giant grin that exposed his gums and teeth all the way down to the last molar.

"That's where you're wrong," he said. "Because I will. And I'm sorry to say that you're the only person standing in my way. Your music, my dear. Played by you. But worry not—once you're gone, nothing will stop me!"

"Once I'm *gone?*"

"Why, yes," Ignatious said. "Don't tell me you thought this was a joyride?"

Ignatious's copper sideburns and red goatee seemed to glint in the strange helicopter light. The founder of the Blatt School for the Insanely Gifted *looked* insane, capable of anything.

Myron turned from the front seat.

"Wait a second, Dad. . . . You aren't going to . . ." He swallowed hard and nodded at Daphna. "You know . . . ?"

Ignatious collected himself.

"It's one of life's painful lessons, dear boy: Sometimes, in order to succeed at the highest level, one has to have the courage of one's convictions." He turned to the antelope man. "To the harbor! Double time!"

The antelope man pushed the throttle. Daphna tried to draw in a deep lungful of air but couldn't catch her breath. Ignatious couldn't be about to push her out of the helicopter into the water? He was the Great Blatt. The genius of all geniuses. An educator! A humanitarian!

"Wait!" she said.

"I have waited," Ignatious replied coolly. "I've been waiting for twelve years for this chance. Waiting time is over."

And then Daphna saw them. To her right, like a gift from the heavens, the Thunkmobile appeared with Harkin at the wheel and Thelma in the passenger seat, giving a thumbs-up. Looking out from the opposite window, she saw Balloon-Top, with Billy at the controls and Cynthia and Cook-Top at his side.

"That fat, bearded fool!" Ignatious cried, looking at Billy. He leaned forward. "Faster!"

"I'm flooring it," the antelope man said.

"Wait a second, Dad," Daphna heard from the front seat. "You can't just—"

"Shut up, Myron!" Ignatious cried. "I can do whatever I want."

They were now over New York Harbor, headed directly toward the Statue of Liberty. Daphna looked out the window at the water below. Was it just that morning that they had flown back over it from Africa? Was she about to be dumped out the door to her death while her best friends watched, unable to do anything about it?

Ignatious flicked a switch. Daphna's door swung open and a strong gust of wind blew into the helicopter. Daphna gasped and grabbed onto the curtain.

It was a long way to the water. To fall would mean certain death.

"It's been a pleasure," Ignatious shouted above the sound of the screaming wind. "If it's any consolation, you were always one of my favorite students."

He moved to push her out. But when Ignatious lurched forward, Daphna ducked under his hands, grabbed hold of his thick sideburns, and pulled his face hard to the seat. Ignatious was too strong. With an angry grunt, he sat back up.

"I like your fighting spirit," he said. "But it's not enough. Say good-bye, Daphna!"

The helicopter swerved violently. Daphna looked up front. Myron had the antelope man in a headlock. No one was flying the helicopter!

"What?" Ignatious said.

Daphna didn't lose her chance. She elbowed Ignatious in the stomach, jumped to the front, and punched the antelope man hard in the nose. Though the antelope man dropped to the copter floor with a loud "Oof!" Ignatious quickly recovered from Daphna's blow and took the controls.

"No one can stop me," he cried, shoving wildly on the joystick.

Daphna gasped. They were losing altitude, headed straight toward the Statue of Liberty's torch.

"Move it, Dad!"

The boy scurried over Daphna and hip checked his father off the pilot's seat. Ignatious hit the floor with a loud bump.

"You can drive this thing?" Daphna asked.

"A little bit. Hold on!"

Daphna looked out the windows. Her friends were on either side, waiting to see what they could do. Below, the harbor was lined with police boats, giving chase over water. The noise inside the helicopter was deafening.

"Come on," Daphna said to Myron. "You can do it. Nice and easy!"

Myron Blatt had an insane gift after all: Yes, his charcoal toaster had been a disaster, but he was a natural-born pilot. With the boy at the controls, the helicopter slowed, tilted left, straightened out, then finally touched down.

"Welcome to New York's greatest tourist attraction!" Myron cried. "Lady Liberty's torch!"

Daphna shook with relief.

"We made it!" she said. "Nice!"

An arm closed tightly around her throat.

"Perfect," Ignatious cried. "I'll be your tour guide!"

31

The Truth Is Revealed

Ignatious dragged Daphna out onto the torch. The wind was blowing hard.

"Let me go!" Daphna shouted.

She was crying but now more out of anger than fear. Struggling hard, she tried to kick and claw her way out of Ignatious's arms, but he held her fast.

"No, no, no, my little lady," he said. "You're my ticket to freedom!"

"Freedom?" Daphna called. "Are you crazy?"

By that time the Thunkmobile and Balloon-Top

hovered on either side.

"You'll never get away!" Harkin yelled.

"There are police boats all over the harbor!" Thelma said.

"And police cars all over the streets," Billy said.

Ignatious laughed. "Maybe. But I don't see any police planes. Now leave! Let me get back on the helicopter with the girl."

"So you can kill her?" Billy said. "Not a chance!"

"You'll be thrown in jail for life," Harkin said.

Ignatious's body once again convulsed in giggles.

"Only if Daphna is able to play her piece! Or have you forgotten that nearly everyone else in the city is under the spell of the X-Head!"

Daphna was enraged. How dare this lunatic hold her hostage?

"You'll never get away with it," she cried over the howl of the wind. "Then you'll be in jail for not one but two murders!"

That got Ignatious's attention. "Two murders? Who are you talking about?"

Daphna finally let it out. "My mother!" she cried. "I know where she was going when she died—she figured out where Billy was and was on her way to tell him that you were on to the X-Head! She saw its potential for bad and knew she might not come back, which is why she left me the map. Her plane crashed and now she's gone forever!"

It was the first time that Daphna had said it out loud, and somehow, she finally knew that it was true. She had carried a hope on her shoulders for so long that it felt almost good to let it go, to admit that her mother really was gone. Still, with the relief came a crushing wave of sadness. The next thing Daphna knew, she was crying as hard as she ever had in her life. Then she turned and kicked Ignatious in the shins and hit him in the chest before he managed to press her tightly into his arms.

"Now, now," Ignatious said. Just like that, the old, oily, sweet-talking Ignatious had returned. "Don't fight me. Your mother was a wonderful lady. It's true that I asked her about the X-Head. But you must believe me that I never pressured her. She chose to fly her plane to find Billy. I didn't force her. Not a bit, my dear. I would never do that. Your mother's death is so sad. It still breaks my heart!"

Out of the corner of her eye, Daphna saw Billy jump from Balloon-Top to the torch. The next thing she knew, the burly man was pulling her away from Ignatious. Then—*wham!*—he cocked his right arm and punched Ignatious hard in the nose. The Great Blatt hit the green metal torch with a loud *thwack*.

"How dare you tell those lies to my daughter!" Billy cried.

No one spoke. Daphna looked at her friends in the Thunkmobile and Balloon-Top, stunned, then slowly turned to Billy.

"Did you say . . . *daughter*?"

Billy looked across the harbor, then finally nodded. "I did."

He got down on one knee and took Daphna's hands. By that time, microphones hung down from TV helicopters. Reporters stood on hastily erected fire ladders, feverishly jotting notes. Though his confession was being watched and recorded by thousands, Billy spoke from the heart.

"I hope you'll forgive me. When you asked if I was your father and I said no, I thought I was telling the truth. You see, your mother and I were involved in college. Boyfriend and girlfriend."

"More that that," Ignatious growled from floor. "Why don't you tell her, Billy? Or are you still too much of a coward?"

"Tell me what?" Daphna said.

Billy swallowed hard. "That picture you had of your mother, Iggy, and me. Well, it was taken on your mother's and my wedding day."

"Right!" Ignatious cried. "And she should have married me! She should have married me!"

Daphna gasped. It was all too much to comprehend. Had Ignatious loved her mother too?

"What? Really?"

"Yes," Billy said. "It was our wedding day." He looked at Ignatious. "And I'm sorry, Iggy, but she loved me, not you." Billy sighed and looked back at Daphna. "We married, but I'm sorry to say I wasn't quite ready for it. I always loved your mother, but then I got this wanderlust—this urge to see the world. Silly, wasn't it? To think I gave up you and your mom for that. But then you mentioned your mother's silly pet name for you."

Daphna's voice caught in her throat. "Miss Sadie P. Snodgrass?"

Billy smiled. "Yes, that's it. That's the name that your mother and I used to joke we'd name our child, if we ever had one. Believe me, Daphna, if I had known that you were on the way, I never would have left."

Daphna's eyes filled with tears, out of equal parts confusion and joy. Billy took her hands.

"This is why I came back to New York. Not to stop Ignatious and the X-Head, but to work up the nerve to tell you the truth. I know that Ron and his family already take good care of you. I don't know if you'd want someone else in your life. But when you left, I got thinking about how lucky I was. Imagine! To discover that I'm the father of a wonderful girl."

After all the years, it was hard to believe that what

she had always wanted was staring her in the face. Daphna flung herself into Billy's arms. He held her tight. Daphna had many questions—loads of them— but they could wait. Now it felt good to be held, to be in the arms of a man who, despite everything, she was proud to call her father.

In fact, Daphna was holding Billy so tightly that she didn't even notice what happened next until Ignatious was already falling off the torch into a police net.

"What . . . ?" Daphna asked.

"He was about to push you off," Harkin called from the Thunkmobile.

Cynthia smiled. She had jumped onto the torch. "So I pushed him first!"

Daphna peered over the edge. Down below, she could see Ignatious in handcuffs being led onto a police boat.

"But we aren't quite through, Daphna," Billy said.

"Oh?"

"You aren't getting off the hook that easily," Cynthia said.

"What do you mean?"

"We've been in touch with the mayor," Thelma said.

"And Cody Meyers," Harkin added.

"You're scheduled to play your rhapsody on his

show in . . ." Billy glanced at his watch. "About ten minutes."

Daphna blinked. "Ten minutes! Really?"

Billy laughed. "Yes, really. Don't forget. You still have to play. Nothing else will break the power of the X-Head. Now, no arguments!"

"Really?" Daphna blinked. "On national TV?"

Billy laughed. "Remember, I'm your dad now. Come! Play!"

And so she did.

32
Endings and New Beginnings

The next day, Daphna's picture was on the front page of every newspaper in town. Some featured her atop the Statue of Liberty. Others pictured her onstage, playing at the *Cody Meyers* studio. Still others pictured her after the performance, in Billy's arms, holding a bouquet of roses. The headlines screamed the news:

RHAPSODY FOR THE CITY
SAVES NEW YORK

ORPHAN GIRL WORKS MAGIC!

HOLY TRANCE, BATMAN!
THAT GIRL CAN PLAY!

And finally, the *New York Tribune* featured a picture of Ignatious falling from Lady Liberty's torch with a headline reading:

IGNATIOUS PEABODY GOES BLATT!

After her successful concert, Daphna, Billy, her friends, and all the students of the Blatt School were invited to the mayor's home at Gracie Mansion for a party.

"You're all insanely gifted," the mayor said in a short speech. "But more impressively, when the chips are down, you're insanely good to one another. And that makes me proud. Remember, children: It's perfectly fine to want to be the best, but it's more important to do the right thing."

"Well said!" Billy called.

The children cheered and celebrated with ice cream and cake.

Later that day, Daphna continued the celebration at home with Ron, Jazmine, Little Jack, and a surprise guest, Billy B. Brilliant. Billy charmed Little Jack by playing hide-and-seek for a full two hours. Then Mrs. Zoentrope joined them for dinner.

"Your piece was magical," she told Daphna. "Your mother would have been so proud."

After dinner, Billy came over to Daphna's small apartment and looked through the old pictures of her mother's parents that she had found in the basement.

Which was when Daphna asked the question she had wondered about since Billy had first told her that he was her father.

"How did you and Mom meet? Were you boyfriend and girlfriend all through college?"

Billy pondered how to best answer the question for a minute. "It was our first semester in Introduction to Advanced Molecular Biology." He smiled. "Your mother showed me how to dissect a gnat. Anyway, first we were friends, then we were something more than that. And then . . . well, then we got married."

Daphna knew that there was more to the story, but she could also tell that Billy wanted to keep some of it private. The two were quiet for a moment, lost in their thoughts.

"But it's strange," Daphna said. "I wonder why she felt funny telling me about you. Or let me believe that a cup of sour yak milk had killed you."

Billy mulled it over. "I imagine that she was mad

at me for disappearing—and I don't really blame her. Maybe she didn't want to get you excited about someone you were unlikely to ever meet? Who knows? But knowing your mother, she had her reasons."

Finally, Daphna asked the question that had been on her mind since the day before, atop the Statue of Liberty.

"Do you think that Ignatious turned evil because my mom chose you instead of him?"

Billy scratched his beard. "Well, I don't know about that. Iggy was always too ambitious for his own good. Then again, your mother was quite a lady."

"Yes," Daphna said with a sad smile. "She sure was."

The following day Daphna went to school. As expected, there was a group of stubborn reporters lined up outside, looking to milk the story—the powerful X-Head and the girl who set the city free—for all it was worth. After answering a few quick questions, Daphna hurried through the front gate.

After a day under the thumb of the X-Head, the children of the Blatt School were back to their usual selves. No one's eyes were glazed over; no one stared into space, mumbling the words on a website only he or she could see. Instead, Daphna walked into a thick crowd of happy children playing four square, freeze tag, and catch. Wilmer Griffith, Jean-Claude Broquet, and Wanda Twiddles were playing a vigorous game of knee hockey.

Even Myron Blatt was there, but now instead of defending his father, he was sitting atop the jungle gym, flying a make-believe helicopter, regaling other students with his exploits as a pilot. Daphna smiled. It had to be hard to have a father like Ignatious. Though it was difficult to completely forgive Myron for stealing the formula for Gum-Top, she understood how hard it must have been to tell his famous dad no. In any case, despite his father's fall from grace, Myron seemed strangely happier.

"Hey, Daph!" he called. "Look at me. Flying high!"

Daphna waved, then glanced at another student who had found popularity. Like Myron, Thelma Trimm was surrounded by other kids, all looking to join her in a game of hopscotch. Perhaps more striking, for the first time since kindergarten, her hair wasn't in pigtails but blow-dried. Her face still showed traces of the rouge she had worn to appear on three early-morning talk shows.

Finally, Daphna cut across a game of red rover and found her two closest friends. Harkin was scribbling furiously in his notebook. Cynthia was reading a script.

"Hey there," Daphna said. "What's up?"

Harkin looked up. "Did you realize that with a few

minor adjustments I could take the Thunkmobile into outer space?"

Daphna hadn't realized. But she wasn't surprised either.

"Go for it," she said. She turned to Cynthia. "How was the show last night?"

The actress shrugged. "Once a dog, always a dog." She held up the script she had been reading. "This is a new musical coming to town. They want me to play a giant talking ice-cream cone."

It was still almost impossible to believe what Cynthia had done. It was unforgivable, really, to betray her best friends. But at the same time, Daphna could almost understand it. Like many Blatt students, Cynthia was never satisfied with what she had already achieved. Six Broadway shows? How about seven? There was always another mountain to climb. Over the past year, her one-woman *Macbeth* had become an obsession. When Ignatious had offered to produce it in return for gathering information about the X-Head, Cynthia had snapped. Daphna saw a tear roll down her cheek.

"I'll still never forgive myself for what I did."

Daphna and Harkin exchanged a glance.

"That's too bad," Harkin said. "Because we do."

Cynthia took off her glasses and wiped away the tear. "Thanks. I'll make sure you don't regret it."

Elmira Ferguson stuck her head out of the back door of the school. To mark the end of the Blatt era, she wore a coat of bright orange lipstick and had finally changed her pink high heels to purple.

"Children! Please line up! We have a special announcement!"

Harkin looked up from his notes. "Wonder what's going on?"

"Got me," Daphna said.

The teachers filed out one by one and took their places in the yard. They were all there, from Mr. D'Angelo to Mrs. Zoentrope—all happily X-Head free. When everyone was in position, Elmira stood by the door. A moment later, a large man with a boyish, handsome face stepped out and waved.

"Wait a second," Harkin said. "Is that . . . no!"

"Who?" Cynthia asked.

"It can't be!" Daphna said.

Hard as it was to believe, the clean-shaven man was Billy B. Brilliant.

"He finally looks like the guy next to my mom in the picture," Daphna said.

Cynthia nodded. "You're right."

Harkin got tired of standing on ceremony.

"Hey, Billy!" he called.

The man looked their way and rubbed his cleanly shaved cheek. Mrs. Ferguson cleared her throat, and the playground quieted.

"After discussion with the board of trustees," she began. "I am very proud to introduce the Blatt School's new headmaster. Billy B. Brilliant."

Cheers filled the playground. Who better to lead the Blatt School into the future than Billy?

And so the semester at the Blatt School continued. Over the next days, the papers were filled with news of Ignatious Peabody Blatt. A week after his arrest, he stood trial for his crimes. Despite Blatt's hiring the best lawyers in town, the jury sent him to prison, where he lobbied successfully for more colorful uniforms.

Though life was hardly ideal for Ignatious, many who he had hurt during his rise to power came into their own.

After Daphna's success, Mrs. Zoentrope became the most sought-after music teacher in the country.

After his father went to prison, Myron moved in with an aunt and worked part-time giving helicopter rides to tourists around New York.

Wilmer Griffith, Wanda Twiddles, and Jean-Claude Broquet formed a club: the Insanely Supportive Society. Every month a good-citizen award was given to a different person in the school.

Then there were Daphna's closest buddies.

Though Harkin never got the Thunkmobile into orbit, he sold the basic design to a major American auto manufacturer. With any luck, a year or so down the line Americans would soon be driving—and flying—in their brand-new Thunks.

As for Cynthia, after *The Dancing Doberman*, she turned down the role of the singing ice-cream cone and moved on to *Armpit*, a new rock musical. As punishment for her unfortunate role in the saga of the X-Head, Cynthia agreed to perform one thousand hours of community service. Over the next year, she spent every afternoon at a different public school, singing her one-woman *Macbeth*, spreading the gospel of Shakespeare and musical theater throughout the city.

Then there were Billy and Daphna.

Over his first few weeks as head of school, Billy discovered that Ignatious had actually done an excellent job with the school that bore his name. The only significant change Billy introduced in the first week was the announcement of a summer program. That June, Daphna, Harkin, Cynthia, and four other lucky students spent two weeks at the valley, studying and vacationing.

As for his own inventing, Billy grudgingly took credit for all of Ignatious's work. Though Billy didn't introduce any new products to market, he kept Cook-Top on hand to prepare his every meal. As he put it to the press, "Every man must have a hidden vice. Cook-Top is mine."

After some thought, Daphna decided to stay in her studio across from Ron and his family. Though Billy took an apartment on the top floor of the school, father and daughter had dinner most every night and spent every Sunday together. As before, the rest of Daphna's time was taken up with composing. After the success of her rhapsody, the Chicago Philharmonic commissioned her to finish the symphony she had begun in Mrs. Zoentrope's office.

Daphna never forgot her mother. As she worked on her symphony, she often found herself daydreaming that her mom would dramatically reappear at its world premiere. Of course she knew her mother was gone. But was there any harm in holding out the smallest ray of hope? Hadn't the power of her *Rhapsody for the City* defeated the X-Head? Who knew what she'd accomplish with her first symphony?

For, as Billy B. Brilliant had once told her in the valley of Kilimanjaro, "Never underestimate the power of great art."

About the Author

Dan Elish is the insanely gifted author of many novels for both adults and children, including *The Attack of the Frozen Woodchucks*; *13* (based on the Broadway musical); and *The Worldwide Dessert Contest*. When he's not busy typing furiously away on his Lap-Top (not a Gum-Top or a Hat-Top or even a Balloon-Top), you can find Dan in New York City, where he lives with his wife, Andrea, and daughter, Cassie, and son, John. Visit Dan online at www.danelish.com.

